Gilbert & Gubar's

The Madwoman in the Attic

After Thirty Years

Gilbert & Gubar's The Madwoman in the Attic *After Thirty Years*

Foreword by Sandra M. Gilbert

Edited with an Introduction by
Annette R. Federico

University of Missouri Press
Columbia and London

University of Missouri Press, Columbia, Missouri 65201
Printed and bound in the United States of America

2010

Library of Congress Cataloging-in-Publication Data

Gilbert and Gubar's The madwoman in the attic after thirty years / edited with an introduction by Annette R. Federico ; foreword by Sandra M. Gilbert.
p. cm.
Includes index.
ISBN 978-0-8262-1869-8 (cloth edition : alk. paper)
ISBN 978-0-8262-1927-5 (paper edition : alk. paper)
1. Gilbert, Sandra M. Madwoman in the attic. 2. Gubar, Susan, 1944- Madwoman in the attic. 3. English literature—Women authors—History and criticism. 4. Women and literature—Great Britain—History—19th century. I. Federico, Annette, 1960-
PR115.G54 2009
820.9'9287—dc22
2009034323

∞™ This paper meets the requirements of the American National Standard for Permanence of Paper for Printed Library Materials, Z39.48, 1984.

Design and composition: Jennifer Cropp
Printer and binder: Thomson-Shore, Inc.
Typefaces: Minion, Bernhard Modern, and Trajan Pro

To Susan Federico

Contents

Foreword:
Conversions of the Mind ix
Sandra M. Gilbert

Acknowledgments xv

Introduction:
"Bursting All the Doors":
The Madwoman in the Attic after Thirty Years 1
Annette R. Federico

1. After Gilbert and Gubar:
Madwomen Inspired by *Madwoman* 27
Susan Fraiman

2. Modeling the *Madwoman*:
Feminist Movements and the Academy 34
Marlene Tromp

3. Gilbert and Gubar's Daughters:
The Madwoman in the Attic's Spectre in Milton Studies 60
Carol Blessing

4. Feminism to Ecofeminism:
The Legacy of Gilbert and Gubar's Readings of Mary Shelley's *Frankenstein* and *The Last Man* 76
Katey Castellano

5. Enclosing Fantasies:
Jane Eyre 94
Madeleine Wood

6. Jane Eyre's Doubles?
Colonial Progress and the Tradition of New Woman Writing in India 111
Narin Hassan

7. Revisiting the Attic:
Recognizing the Shared Spaces of *Jane Eyre* and *Beloved* 127
Danielle Russell

8. The Legacy of Hell:
Wuthering Heights on Film and Gilbert and Gubar's Feminist Poetics 149
Hila Shachar

9. The Veiled, the Masked, and the Civil War Woman:
Louisa May Alcott and the Madwoman Allegory 170
Keren Fite

10. Sensationalizing Women's Writing:
Madwomen in Attics, the Sensational Canon, and Generic Confinement 183
Tamara Silvia Wagner

11. Ghosts in the Attic:
Gilbert and Gubar's *The Madwoman in the Attic* and the Female Gothic 203
Carol Margaret Davison

12. Elizabeth Gaskell:
A Well-Tempered Madness 217
Thomas P. Fair

13. Mimesis and Poiesis:
Reflections on Gilbert and Gubar's Reading of Emily Dickinson 237
Lucia Aiello

Contributors 257

Index 261

Foreword

Conversions of the Mind

Sandra M. Gilbert

Note: Because Susan Gubar has been coping with a serious illness, I've drafted this foreword on my own. But I hope I've spoken for both of us in recounting the excitement, energy, and even joy with which we wrote *The Madwoman in the Attic,* and, equally important, the pleasure that the responsiveness of our readers inspires in us.

At the risk of hyperbole, we want to say that there's a kind of ecstasy for us in reading Annette Federico's collection, just as we experienced a kind of ecstasy in writing *Madwoman.* No, not ecstasy meaning a fashionable street drug, and not ecstasy in the sexual, mystical sense so famously defined by John Donne. But yes, "ecstasy" signifying, as the *American Heritage Dictionary* puts it, "intense joy or delight" and having as its root the "Greek ekstasis" meaning both "astonishment" and a kind of displacement of the ordinary. It isn't, after all, usual to read a book about a book that one wrote many years ago, and it's especially joyful, delightful, and even astonishing when the writers whose essays are included in that new book are kind, sympathetic—indeed flattering—and of course (from our point of view) exceptionally astute in their analyses of our thought. But then, as the contributors to Federico's volume seem so clearly to understand, our experience in writing *Madwoman* wasn't a quotidian scholarly experience. The book—or rather, the idea and plan for the book—seized us in a way that we felt was truly astonishing: we were taken out of ourselves, that is, transported out of our "regular" academic and personal lives by a series of epiphanies that altered our thinking, our careers, and even our *selves* with what now seems like exceptional speed. In the poem about Elizabeth Barrett Browning that begins

"I think I was enchanted / When first a sombre Girl — / I read that Foreign Lady —," Emily Dickinson wrote about her own initial encounter with a woman who, for her, incarnated the female literary tradition, explaining that she and her world had been transformed by a "Conversion of the Mind." And we too had been, for much the same reason, radically changed.

To be sure, our individual experiences were part of the remarkable mass experience of feminist "consciousness raising" that has now come to be called the second wave of the women's movement. Before we met in 1973 in an elevator at Indiana University—we were two new teachers in the English department—we'd read Simone de Beauvoir and Betty Friedan, Kate Millett and Gloria Steinem. We were subscribers to *Ms.* magazine, and as young, working wives and mothers we knew all too much about the hurdles women had to overcome—obstacles that feminists on both sides of the Atlantic had begun to protest with increasing passion. Still, when we were asked within months to plan a course on literature by women, we found ourselves confronting a subject foreign to us both. Neither of us had studied this "field" that barely existed; nor had either of us ever had undergraduate or graduate courses led by women in *any* field. Yet soon we were sitting in a pizza parlor debating the syllabus for our class, and then, a few months later, there we were in a classroom, surrounded by thirty eager students along with numerous stacks of dittoed texts (that was a pre-Xerox era) and daunting piles of books we'd never read through the lens of gender.

One of us (Susan) was an eighteenth-century scholar who'd been thinking about monstrous women in Pope and Swift; the other (Sandra) was a modernist who had written a dissertation on D. H. Lawrence but had begun rereading *Little Women* and *Jane Eyre* with her eight-year-old daughter. Having studied freakish females in male-authored texts, Susan was now preoccupied by the monsters in many *female*-authored works while Sandra was musing on the retreats of unruly heroines (Jo and Jane) to attic refuges; and as soon as we began discussing our ideas in class, both of us were fascinated by recurrent images of madness, confinement, rage, fire-and-ice, disease and dis-ease in the novels and poems we were teaching. At first our insights felt weird or even crazy. How could we have spent years as dutiful undergraduates and graduate students without learning anything about this body of work we were suddenly encountering, with its compelling motifs and extraordinarily brilliant writing? Yet we quickly understood that our reading was transforming us in unprecedented ways. We'd each been planning books on other subjects, but within weeks we were torn away from our earlier projects and transported out of what had been our usual scholarly concerns in an ekstasis—an escape from the stasis of the usual—that astonished and delighted us, despite the considerable pain and oppression we were encountering as, for the first time, we studied in detail the lives and works of women throughout history.

What's the use of recounting here the countless things we learned? If you've read *Madwoman* you know what some of them are; they're among many things that all the feminist critics of our generation learned. That Jane Austen wasn't a decorous spinster but a complex and subversive thinker. That Elizabeth Barrett Browning wasn't an opium-addicted invalid with cocker spaniel curls but rather an impassioned feminist and political revolutionary. That the Brontës weren't a trio of lovelorn sisters stranded on a moor but Byronically burning rebels. That George Eliot wasn't always the paragon of morality and maturity introduced by our professors but as conflicted as her often tormented heroines. That Emily Dickinson wasn't "a little homekeeping person," as John Crowe Ransom thought and as we'd been taught, but rather—in Adrienne Rich's words—a kind of "Vesuvius at home."

We had called our team-taught class "The Madwoman in the Attic" (after rejecting less interesting or snappy titles) and now we outlined a book of that name. A few months later, Sandra left for California, where her husband, children, and a new job were waiting in Davis. But our unexpectedly absorbing project had electrified us. We began researching and writing the book immediately, two thousand miles away from each other, exchanging drafts by tedious snail mail and accumulating huge phone bills. We wrote on typewriters in between changing diapers (Susan) and ferrying children to afterschool programs (Sandra), while our husbands pitched in at supermarkets and softball games. We traveled from the West Coast to the heart of the country, to the East Coast and back to the West Coast, seeking places to meet and edit our work. Finally we finished the book, in a fever of discovery, just a few years after we began it. And—ecstasy indeed!—we did not lack for readers.

That we quickly found readers isn't to say, of course, that academia's initial reaction to our work was glowingly positive. Even as we wound up our relatively brief class (a special eight-week course) and began outlining our project, we applied for aid from the NEH and several other granting organizations in an excess of hope and excitement, naïvely sure that ideas we ourselves found inspiring would elicit support from major foundations. But there were few models for collaborative work in the humanities: to what equivalent of the NEH or the Rockefeller Foundation might Cleanth Brooks and Robert Penn Warren have turned in the earliest days of the New Criticism? And, though they were famous for *Understanding Poetry* (1938), what other literary thinkers had collaborated on anything significant since? In any case, two obscure young women scholars proposing to write on a strange new subject (a *female* literary tradition?) could hardly be compared to the influential theorists whose writings virtually every English major had studied in college and graduate school. So, no grants were forthcoming: we resigned ourselves to annual appeals for assistance from our own campuses—both of which, to their eternal credit, did come through with clerical help, prompt sabbaticals, and summer research stipends.

But the apparently widespread story that Marlene Tromp recounts in this volume (a tale of how we "prepared a stack of envelopes addressed to the best presses, and, if [we] had an unfavorable review from one, [we] simply slid the manuscript . . . into the next envelope and sent it off again") is, as Tromp herself points out and as we're happy to affirm, apocryphal. University presses, it turned out, were far more receptive to new ideas than were hidebound academic granting organizations, perhaps because their editors (unlike some foundation officials) were always on the lookout for new ideas that might turn out to be commercially as well as intellectually viable. We sent our prospectus to five presses, all of which responded with interest. Our mutual friend Robert Scholes steered us toward Ellen Graham at Yale, who was wonderfully encouraging. Soon, as our plans for the work became ever more complex, we signed a two-book contract with her. And then, when several years later we finally delivered our humongous typescript (at least 900 pages long) in two typewriter paper boxes, we briefly tried to pretend to her that the second box contained a copy of the work in the first. No success: "This is part one of the book and this is part two, right?" she said wisely, in her kind southern accent. But despite the literal weightiness of our words, she continued to sustain us with her warmth and enthusiasm, as did the various referees she recruited.

As for other readers—readers in the "real" world, book critics for magazines and newspapers along with academics writing for professional journals—those too were so phenomenally responsive that our state of ecstasy, both delight and astonishment, continued unabated. Just as the history and the tradition that we'd discovered in our classroom struck a transformative chord in us, we had evidently struck such a chord in others. It was 1979, the second wave of the feminist movement was cresting, and an astonishing number of women (along with some men) were experiencing Dickinsonian conversions of the mind, like the one that had metamorphosed us into very different kinds of thinkers from those we'd been before we team-taught our class in 1973.

Since then we've team-taught several other classes, including a seminar that the NEH sponsored in 1981, and coauthored or coedited many books: the hypothetical "second" volume of *Madwoman* turned into the three volumes of *No Man's Land: The Place of the Woman Writer in the Twentieth Century*, and the stacks of dittoed texts that we distributed to our Indiana students in 1983 were incorporated into three successive editions of the (now) two-volume *Norton Anthology of Literature by Women: The Traditions in English.* But we've never ceased to be delighted and astonished by the energy and sympathy with which readers respond to *The Madwoman in the Attic.* To this day, we're moved to a kind of ecstasy by such responsiveness, which we encounter not only in essays like those collected here but also in the words and thoughts of students we meet in classrooms and lecture halls. By now we've encountered these eager students in institutions not just around the country but around the world. They are mostly women, and they are almost always seeking the same metamorphic insights that Emily Dickinson experienced when she read the words of Elizabeth Barrett Browning, and that inspired us to use up countless typewriter ribbons as we drafted the pages of *Madwoman.* We've learned richly from these readers and these students—learned that although some skeptics and some antifeminists might claim that we're living in a "post-feminist era" marked by indifference or even contempt for the revisionary excitement that animated so many of us three decades ago—classrooms and bookstores are still populated by people yearning for intellectual conversions that might once have felt shocking or crazy. But as Dickinson puts it in another poem, "Much madness is divinest sense."

Acknowledgments

I owe thanks to all of the contributors for their enthusiastic support for this feminist project of re-vision. It's been work I believe in, and they have sustained that faith every step of the way. Sandra M. Gilbert and Susan Gubar have been kind and encouraging advocates; they generously spoke to me about the genesis of *Madwoman*, read a draft of the book, and worked on a foreword at a time when both had other pressing responsibilities. Having them involved in this project has been a privilege.

I would also like to thank Clair Willcox at the University of Missouri Press and the anonymous readers of the manuscript; everyone involved in the process offered valuable insights, smart recommendations, and enough reassurance to keep me at it.

The idea for this book originated in a seminar on the Brontës that I taught at James Madison University in fall 2007. I'd like to acknowledge the students in that class, who convinced me that the long chapters I assigned from *The Madwoman in the Attic* are still both controversial and intoxicating. Thanks also to the JMU Department of English for practical and moral support, and especially to Chuck Dotas—the voice of reason.

Gilbert & Gubar's The Madwoman in the Attic *After Thirty Years*

Introduction

"Bursting All the Doors"

The Madwoman in the Attic after Thirty Years

Annette R. Federico

> Ladylike veils and costumes, mirrors, paintings, statues, locked cabinets, drawers, trunks, strongboxes, and other domestic furnishings appear and reappear in female novels and poems throughout the nineteenth century and on into the twentieth to signify the woman writer's sense that, as Emily Dickinson put it, her "life" has been "shaven and fitted to a frame," a confinement she can only tolerate by believing that "the soul has moments of escape / When bursting all the doors / She dances like a bomb abroad."[1]

When it was published in 1979, Sandra M. Gilbert and Susan Gubar's *The Madwoman in the Attic: The Woman Writer and the Nineteenth-Century Literary Imagination* was immediately recognized as a pathbreaking work of criticism. Their fresh, confident reexaminations of crucial nineteenth-century works by women permanently changed the way future scholars would read Jane Austen, Mary Shelley, the Brontës, George Eliot, and Emily Dickinson. For Victorianists, the book was an exciting departure. For feminists, many of whom came of age in the 1980s and 1990s, it was a revelation. Martha Vicinus, Ellen Moers, Elaine Showalter, Ann Douglass, Nina Auerbach, Patricia Meyer Spacks, and other critics represented the vanguard of feminist scholarship in the 1970s, part of a vital community of students, scholars, and teachers who were engaged in rediscovering forgotten women writers and rereading canonical authors through feminist models. Following Elaine Showalter's influential reappraisal of a neglected feminine tradition in *A Literature of Their Own* (1977), Gilbert and Gubar argued that "nineteenth-century literary women *did* have both a literature and a culture of their own—that, in other words, by the nineteenth century there was a rich and clearly defined female literary subculture, a community in which women consciously read and related to each other's works" (*Madwoman,* xii). Their astonishingly original approach to Victorian women's writing changed our understanding of the gendered nature of nineteenth-century literary culture and of contemporary critical practices. Breathing beneath dominant Victorian myths of women as domestic angels and fairy tale maidens were patterns of confinement, starvation, monstrosity, and rebellion. And pulsing beneath standards of objectivity and critical distance was the urge for experiential, even transformative, reading—the process, modeled in *Madwoman,* of "reading our own lives as well as the texts we study" (*Madwoman,* xiii).

The Madwoman in the Attic set out to uncover how a masculine literary tradition and unexamined patriarchal metaphors shaped women's experiences, their creativity, and their resistance to coercive models of literary achievement. Reinterpreting Harold Bloom's influential theory of a male "anxiety of influence," Gilbert and Gubar argued that women experience an "anxiety of authorship" that requires them to deny the power and self-assertion implicit in their art. They examined works by canonical figures with a strong sense of their interrelatedness, persuasively unveiling the shared plot concealed in their prose and poetry. Indeed, Gilbert and Gubar's book was the first sustained analysis of the political, economic, and psychological obstacles placed before women writers. In over seven hundred pages of analysis, richly allusive and sweeping in scope, they identified coded forms of protest and revealed the persistence of images and motifs with such insight and verve that Annette Kolodny, in a 1980 review, described their readings as "nothing short of breathtaking, uncovering—in even the best known of these texts—shapes and strategies we had never seen before."[2] Carolyn Heilbrun, whose own work on women's lives was helping to bring feminist critique to the forefront of the academy, claimed that *The Madwoman in the Attic* was simply "imperative reading" for both scholars of the nineteenth century and for feminists.[3] The book was nominated for the 1979 National Book Critics Circle Award in Literature, and for the 1980 Pulitzer Prize in General Nonfiction—highly unusual for a work of literary criticism. It was reviewed in over thirty publications in English and gained almost unprecedented critical and popular attention. *The Madwoman in the Attic* transformed our approach to women's writing, feminist critique, and the politics of literary canonization.

Part of the general sense-making enterprise of literary criticism involves self-reflexively analyzing the effects *of* literary criticism. This collection of essays, by both established and younger scholars, is designed to map out some of the different directions taken in both feminist literary criticism and Victorian studies after *Madwoman.* Although not a *Festschrift*—*Madwoman* was only the beginning of two long and productive academic careers—this book hopes to recognize and honor Sandra M. Gilbert and Susan Gubar's contributions to feminist criticism and to nineteenth- and twentieth-century literature. Joyce Carol Oates called *Madwoman* "one of the most important works of literary criticism of the twentieth century," and by the time the second edition appeared in 2000, it was an acknowledged classic. But not a musty, outdated one. As Gilbert and Gubar demonstrated in their own rereading (and making) of nineteenth-century classics, when we return to familiar texts with new questions and more varied experiences, the changes we track can be invigorating. If sometimes Gilbert and Gubar's readings seemed extravagant or too insistent, the "plot" of the book too thick with forced connections, there was also the undeniable excitement of seeing well-known novels and poems unlocked and presented in a completely new way. Gilbert and Gubar introduced tropes and metaphors—madness and monstrosity, domesticity and escape, starvation and burial—that became part of the vocabulary for reading nineteenth-century women's texts.[4] Thirty years later, the image of the madwoman, no longer "cabin'd, cribbed, confined" by the explicit social structures and implicit psychological demands of the patriarchal order, has taken on a cultural and critical life of her own.

Susan Gubar has remained committed to the idea that literary criticism can be connected to the critic's own story of development, what she calls "a sort of intellectual bildungsroman."[5] In *Rooms of Our Own* (2006), she writes, "Some will object that narrative exigencies obscure critical clarity, just as criticism drains narration of its subtleties." But she goes on to explain that sometimes narrative criticism can help "bridge a widening gap between intellectual matters that might sound arcane or specialized but that profoundly impinge on the everyday lives of ordinary people."[6] I want to reflect on the influence of *Madwoman* on both nineteenth-century studies and feminist criticism by first dipping into my own story of development, beginning about thirty years ago, when feminist writers and readers, following *Madwoman*'s example, started "bursting all the doors" of the Anglo-American canon.

Women's Lit, 1979

I was nineteen in 1979, a sophomore in college, an eager, obedient English major. I was fortunate to be enrolled in an honors program modeled after the tutorial systems of Oxford and Cambridge that was designed to prepare promising students for postgraduate degrees—not that I ever imagined myself in the exalted position of a college professor. (Was it a coincidence that I had had no women professors?) Academically, I wasn't exposed to women's studies,[7] but I was distantly in tune with the "women's movement" and what we now call "feminist awareness" was lurking around the corners of my private experiences. Books were an important connection. When I was an adolescent, a relative gave me *Girls Are Equal Too!* by Dale Carson (1973); my older sister introduced me to *Our Bodies, Ourselves* (1973); and I even tried to read her copy of *Sisterhood Is Powerful* (1970) when I was about fifteen—I distinctly remember my intellectual confusion at the essay titled "The Politics of Orgasm" (what was *that*?). For a couple of years in college, I didn't bother to shave my legs, was a loyal subscriber to *Ms.*, and I was training as a phone counselor for a university crisis center called Careline that focused on women's issues, including sexual assault. Still, there was an unquestionable intellectual disconnection between my inchoate feminist consciousness and my formal education in literary study. In the tutorial college, we were given a long reading list for the year and the assignments for our weekly three-hour meetings, and we always used the authoritative *Norton Anthology*. Sophomore year we were making our way through eighteenth-century British literature; the title of my final paper was "Warm Kisses and Cold Cash: The Maternal Theme in *Moll Flanders*." The papers our students are writing on *Moll Flanders* in 2009 could have the same title as mine did in 1979, but my bet is that they are writing quite different kinds of papers, informed by courses on gender and performativity in the eighteenth century, feminism and economics, and critical analysis of motherhood, sexuality, and mass culture. I had no such courses, and no meaningful theoretical, or even historical, context for what struck me about Moll's situation, her attitude toward motherhood, and the different power structures she has to negotiate. I was just trying (I thought) to make sense of a literary character.

For it was *literature* that we were studying, not another thing. And it was very good training. I learned how to read closely, execute research assignments responsibly, ask objective literary questions, construct an argument. Was I aware that something was happening in the academy that had to do with liberation politics? That new ways of reading and writing about literature were being explored? That the canon was about to undergo a thorough bulldozing? Vaguely. The jacket of the Norton *Major Authors* in 1979 showed a grid of portraits and photographs of some of the "Majors" with approximately sixty faces, ten down, six across, in black and white. One afternoon when I was loitering around the English building, I got interested in these miniature portraits of the great writers and tried to identify them. Some were tricky: George Herbert and John Donne had pointy beards; Dickens, Arnold, and all the other Victorians had bushy beards. The women major authors (it would not be correct to say "major women authors" if the category "women authors," whether major or minor, was just being formed) were easy because there were only two of them: Elizabeth Barrett Browning and Virginia Woolf. If you have seen portraits of these women, you know they look nothing alike.[8]

Meanwhile, in 1974, in Bloomington, Indiana, five years before I looked at the faces on the cover of the *Major Authors* and wrote my paper on *Moll Flanders,* two assistant professors of English decided to team-teach a class on a new academic subject called literature by women (they describe their department head as "enlightened").[9] Inspired by their mutual fascination with *Jane Eyre,* they called the course "The Madwoman in the Attic" and focused on the amiable girls' books they loved as young adults by Jane Austen, the Brontës, Louisa May Alcott. In that eight-week class, with no standard editions available, no textbooks, and no anthologies, they relied on notes, shared memos, mimeographed handouts, and the passion and receptivity of their undergraduate students.[10] In their introduction to the second edition of *Madwoman* (2000), Gilbert and Gubar movingly describe the class as a "journey of conversion.... We were in a mutual state of what can only be described as revisionary transport, the same condition in which so many of the early second-wave feminists of the now too easily dismissed seventies found themselves. The personal was political, the literary was the personal, the sexual was the textual, the feminist was the redemptive, and on and on!"[11]

There was little distinction at that time, they have said, between marching in a protest and being a college teacher. "It was not easy to stand up to a class of undergraduates and say I was a feminist critic," says Sandra Gilbert. What they were doing was "disreputable, problematic, and rooted in a world struggle." Reading these nineteenth-century women writers at that moment in American political history went straight to the emotional truths of their students' lives. There *was* something at stake in meeting regularly a few times a week and talking about *Jane Eyre* or "I'm Nobody! who are you?" Perhaps the Victorian novel was compelling to women readers in particular, they argued, because it was the scene of "people beginning to gain power," a reflection of a changing world. They read Emily Dickinson's poetry "in hysteria" to their students, "astonished at how ferocious she was!" Within the context of the Victorian gender ideology of separate spheres and the very real limitations placed on women's education and social and political agency, both teachers and students in "The Madwoman in the Attic" were amazed by what these writers had achieved, and their readings were exuberant, celebratory, and reciprocal.

It ultimately became clear to Gilbert and Gubar that there was a complex, cross-historical conversation among nineteenth-century women writers.

Like explorers or pioneers, they set themselves the task of tracing the dynamics of its formation. With no fellowships or funding, no release time, no external grants (the NEH turned them down), writing collaboratively when that practice was unheard of in the humanities (and when Sandra was at UC-Davis and Susan at Indiana), they wrote *The Madwoman in the Attic* in three and a half years and sent it to five publishers (all of them were interested). *Madwoman*'s intelligence and boldness, the energy of its prose, and the personal and political commitment its authors confessed in every chapter made it a threshold work in interpretive analysis and in the development of feminist literary history and theory. As one of the contributors to this book wrote to me, *Madwoman* was "a flag on the mountaintop for young women scholars,"[12] not only as a model of feminist criticism but as a revolutionary act within the academy, where sexism was still sometimes buried in New Critical rhetoric about intellectual rigor—and sometimes not buried at all but alive and well in the mailroom and at the tenure meeting. Susan Gubar recounts a story from her first year at Indiana that shows how much has changed in thirty years: she was standing in the mailroom in the English offices when a senior male professor who was in a hurry handed her a stencil to type. "He had assumed that any woman in this space was there to serve him as a secretary."[13]

If this story seems incredible even to me, I wonder how it must seem to third-wavers. Still, once in a while the feminist generation gap is narrowed by current events. During the 2008 presidential primaries, Kate Zernike wrote an op-ed piece in the *New York Times* under the headline, "Postfeminism and Other Fairy Tales," about the "perfect storm" of the Eliot Spitzer scandal and the media's treatment of Hillary Clinton. The article looked at the reactions of younger and older feminists, suggesting that the feelings expressed by many women, of all ages, about both Spitzer's conduct and Clinton's candidacy, points to continuity rather than division among American feminists.

> The bridge from [Katha] Pollitt's generation to its successors was apparent . . . in an e-mail message a friend of Chelsea Clinton's sent around. Attached was an article by the early and unreconstructed feminist Robin Morgan that detailed in full-throated outrage the bias against [Hillary] Clinton, and women. Chelsea herself apparently appended a note saying that while she did not agree entirely with Morgan's point, she was starting to understand *what older women were complaining about.* "I confess that I did not entirely 'get it' until not only guys stood up and shouted, 'iron my shirt' but the media reacted with amusement, not outrage."[14]

Similarly, Hanna Rosin, writing for *Slate,* described her "Ashley Dupré" moment (a reference to the name Spitzer's prostitute used): "I read her story and *the old '70s feminist* in me (admittedly a tiny presence) rears up."[15]

Neither Chelsea Clinton nor Hanna Rosin are veterans of that era, but it's significant that both define the "older feminist" lurking inside in terms of their frustration with the way their culture dismisses serious questions and normalizes sexist assumptions—and especially in terms of their *anger.* It was the Victorian woman writer's rebellious, smoldering anger that became the central trope of Gilbert and Gubar's readings in *The Madwoman in the Attic,* the figure who "arises like a bad dream, bloody, envious, enraged, as if the very process of writing had itself liberated a madwoman, a crazy and angry woman, from a silence in which neither she nor her author can continue to acquiesce" (*Madwoman,* 77). "Dramatizations of imprisonment and escape are so all-pervasive in nineteenth-century literature by women," they wrote, "that we believe they represent a uniquely female tradition in this period" (*Madwoman,* 85). A crucial insight was the double bind of the Victorian woman writer and the damage her impermissible anger caused the psyche. "It is through the violence of the double that the female author enacts her own raging desire to escape male houses and male texts, while at the same time it is through the double's violence that this anxious author articulates for herself the costly destructiveness of anger repressed until it can no longer be contained" (*Madwoman,* 85). Gilbert and Gubar argued that from the female point of view, the madwoman, the monster, the witch, the evil Queen are not simply antagonistic images used as a foil to the "pure" heroine, but images of the woman author herself who "seeks the power of articulation" (*Madwoman,* 79). The madwoman in women's literature, they claimed,

> is usually in some sense the author's double, an image of her own anxiety and rage. Indeed, much of the poetry and fiction written by women conjures up this mad creature so that female authors can come to terms with their own uniquely female feelings of fragmentation, their own keen sense of the discrepancies between what they are and what they are supposed to be. (*Madwoman,* 78)

The connections were suddenly everywhere—when Mary Shelley creates a monster whose anxiety, speechlessness, and confusion turn into uncontrollable rage; when little Jane Eyre thinks "Unjust! Unjust!" and Bertha Mason sets the bed on fire; when Marmee in *Little Women* says, "I am angry nearly every day of my life," or when Dorothea's marriage becomes "a perpetual struggle of energy and fear," her inner world dominated by "a reaction of rebellious anger" close to hatred; when Emily Dickinson uses surprising imagery of loaded guns and exploding bombs—these were the readings in Gilbert and Gubar that gave many women readers a shock of recognition. They also changed the way scholars would look at nineteenth-century literature. "With a stroke of the pen," writes Rita Felski, "Victorian literature was cast in a new light. A literary tradition often associated with antimacassars and overstuffed sofas, stifling decorum and fusty gentility, was suddenly awash with subversive energies, seething desires, and feminist rage."[16] *The Madwoman in the Attic* gave feminist criticism and Victorian studies a new vocabulary and a new way of reading; the book made undervalued texts newly visible, reversed assumptions about literary history and tradition, legitimized feminist literary theory in the academy—and initiated an important and continuing conversation about women, reading, and difference.

"Passionate Innocence"

In 1988, Jane Marcus wrote in *Art and Anger* that her interest in Virginia Woolf "clearly grew out of my own anger and the anger of my generation of feminist critics who were trying to change the subject without yet having developed a sophisticated methodology."[17] "Feminist anger" is a very '70s concept, but if you do an Internet search for those two words you will find that it hasn't entirely disappeared from either the social sciences or the blogosphere.[18] What has been added is the "sophisticated methodology" Marcus refers to. If *The Madwoman in the Attic* seems intellectually primitive to some feminists, maybe that's because it is: primitive in the way the primitive part of our brains, the basal ganglia, drives high-level cognition.[19] The primitive thing, the fundamental experience, those "click" moments women used to send to *Ms.* magazine when they realized that sexism was not merely a personal problem—those instinctive, vestigial responses are often the things that get the complex theoretical reactions started.[20]

In fact, the controversy surrounding *Madwoman* when it appeared in 1979, both in academic journals and in the mainstream media, might be traced to disagreements about its analytical complexity. Did Gilbert and Gubar go straight to the truth about women's art, or did they apply a distorting master narrative, "a repetitious sexist drama"?[21] Did they bridge differences among women writers by identifying a common struggle against "patriarchal poetry," or did they limit women's achievements by reducing them to a symptom? For a book of literary criticism, the initial responses to *Madwoman* were surprisingly passionate. Frances Taliaferro, for example, writing in *Harper's,* thought it transforming: "For the amateur who encounters it all at once, for the first time, this book is a plunge into a new and bracing element. . . . I read it in a state of sustained excitement because it offered a new way of seeing."[22] Nina Auerbach called it "a jubilant achievement," and Katherine Frank recognized that the "150 pages devoted to [Charlotte] Brontë . . . are so important that they might be extracted and stand on their own as a whole book." *Madwoman* was "extraordinarily exciting," wrote Helene Moglen, "deeply insightful, broadly imaginative, breathtakingly risky. Its failure as well as its success spark further formulations. It is the work to which most feminist criticism and theory of these next years will have to refer, in support and disagreement."[23]

On the other hand, Rosemary Dinnage, writing in the *New York Review of Books,* said "Gilbert and Gubar belittle their women subjects by ignoring their generosity and detachment, by representing them—as they particularly wished not to be—as women before writers."[24] Mary Jacobus's review in *Signs* made a similar point, claiming that Victorian women have always sought "the freedom of being read as more than exceptionally articulate victims of a patriarchally engendered plot."[25] Phoebe Pettingell thought it "a pity that so much intelligence and insight should give way to questionable theorizing and simplistic jargon."[26] Even critics who admired much of the book and recognized its importance often expressed serious reservations about Gilbert and Gubar's implicit claims for a universal "ur-Woman"[27] and their chosen focus on Anglo-American authors. Postmodern feminists have pointed to the limitations of Gilbert and Gubar's naïve liberalism and their unwillingness to interrogate assumptions about a grounded female subject. *Madwoman* has also been criticized by postcolonial theorists and African American feminists for its failure to recognize the unequal relationship between white, Western feminists and societies inhabited by the "Other."[28] Clare Hemmings and Josephine Brain have described the progressive narrative of second-wave feminism as "moving inexorably from exclusion to inclusion, sameness to difference, unity to fragmentation."[29] Because *Madwoman*'s imperatives seem to meet the first half of these binaries, some feminists have understandably distanced themselves from the apparent simplicity of Gilbert and Gubar's approach to women's writing, which "essentializes" women's creativity through associations with maternity, madness, and the female body. If "the dominant and most familiar attribution to the feminist seventies is of course essentialism, an accusation so frequently repeated, that it stands as justification for not reading texts from the feminist seventies at all (any more)," *Madwoman* should be entirely outdated by 2009.[30] Susan Gubar has readily admitted "it was a book of that time period," when there was a palpable desire to recover a lost unity, a shared female experience.[31] But if that essentialist impulse is reflexively repudiated as retrograde, biologically reductive, and exclusionary, younger scholars and students are in peril of missing out on exactly what was seen as enabling about *Madwoman.* From the book's famous first sentence ("Is a pen a metaphorical penis?"), *The Madwoman in the Attic* showed how fundamental and how connected *metaphors* of sexuality, power, and embodiment have been to the ways women in Western culture have imagined their own art and creativity—that experience generates metaphors just as metaphors create experience (*Madwoman,* xiii).

If Gilbert and Gubar rejected 1950s New Criticism—the idea that a work of literature was a transcendent or well-wrought object beyond the reaches of historical contingencies and power structures—their approach also implicitly challenged poststructuralist theories of the text as a closed space of signification. In the 1980s and 1990s, poststructuralism's emphasis on difference, language, and textuality made Gilbert and Gubar's style of analysis (despite their highly sophisticated theoretical arguments and their immersion in textuality) look too easy, as if their success in reaching a broader audience of women readers and getting reviewed in *Harper's* was evidence of a kind of theoretical dumbing down. (Or, as if feminist efforts to change the subject to women made the academy looked dumbed down, that is, feminized.) The rise of poststructuralism and cultural studies and the influence of Derrida, Foucault, and Lacan made it "difficult to do feminist work in a literary historical context."[32] In "What Ails Feminist Criticism?" Gubar wrote that the influence of French theorists, combined with the formidable task of trying to change critical practices and assumptions, led to the

> recondite abstractions [that] characterize postmodern feminist theory. The consequence for criticism of a linguistic model deriving from philosophy has been to divorce feminist speculations from literary texts or to subordinate those texts to the epistemological, ideological, economic, and political issues that supplanted literary history and aesthetic evaluation as the topics of writing *about women.*[33]

I take "literary history" to mean taking a hard look at what constitutes a tradition and asking how particular writers engage with that tradition, and I read "aesthetic evaluation" to mean both close reading and the recovery of good writing by forgotten women. These were precisely the projects of 1970s feminist scholarship, which was, make no mistake about it, also "about women." And while deconstruction seemed to be grabbing all the headlines in the late 1980s, interrogating the canon (and politicizing it) has been what has most changed academic study in the last thirty years. Writers that most students and scholars had never read were trotted out in *Madwoman* almost casually as proof of the pervasiveness of the patterns and tropes Gilbert and Gubar identified with the woman writer's rebelliousness. In chapter 5, "Jane Austen's Cover Story (and Its Secret Agents)," Gilbert and Gubar remind the reader that Austen was a precursor for "the literary ladies who would emerge so successfully and plentifully in the mid-nineteenth century, popular lady novelists like Rhoda Broughton, Charlotte Mary Yonge, Home Lee, and Mrs. Craik who strenuously suppressed awareness of how their own professional work called into question traditional female roles" (*Madwoman,* 169). In their discussion of associations of veiled women with spirituality, they reference Elizabeth Cady Stanton, Margaret Fuller, Lucy Stone, Harriet Martineau, Victoria Woodhull, Louisa May Alcott, and Mary Elizabeth Braddon's *Lady Audley's Secret*—a novel no one had heard of in 1979 but is now considered a crucial work of Victorian sensation fiction, right beside Wilkie Collins. They bring Mary Elizabeth Coleridge into the conversation about Victorian women's poetry next to little-known works, in 1979, by Christina Rossetti (including a semi-autobiographical novella, *Maude*) and Elizabeth Barrett Browning. Their informed and compressed (three-page) reading of Charlotte Perkins Gilman's "The Yellow Wallpaper" reintroduced a virtually unknown story by a prodigiously intelligent woman into the history of the literary woman's struggles, disabilities, and self-liberation.[34]

Gilbert and Gubar influenced the direction of nineteenth-century studies because of the sheer scope of their reading but also because of the framework for their analyses of Romantic and Victorian novels that would be familiar to every nineteenth-century scholar—and to many common readers. Contrary to assumptions about the book's universalizing tendencies and accusations that it "naturalizes" social, historical, and economic realities, *Madwoman* keeps its focus on the contexts of Victorian women's history, the subjectivities that history produced, and the paradoxes, counterhistories, secrets, illnesses, and self-divisions that it engendered.[35] Gilbert and Gubar did not just argue from an esoteric theory; they insisted on the *literary* implications of this condition, and they showed, in richly detailed readings, how it becomes manifest.

If *Madwoman* was a product of the "naïve dawn" of feminist criticism, it was perhaps that irrepressible belief in what they uncovered about women's writing that made the book so radical and affirming. When I asked why they thought *Madwoman* has held up so well, given all the changes that have happened in feminist criticism over thirty years, Susan said, "For the clarity of a universalizing vision." For Sandra, it was "because of our wonder and amazement at what we didn't learn. Because of our passionate innocence. . . . We were seized by this book, it was like writing poetry. It came from a powerful source of inspiration." Gender, they agree, must *always* be combined with other factors when we talk about identity, the imagination, culture, writing, reading—and feminist criticism's move toward inclusion, plurality, and multiculturalism was legitimate and needed. But the momentum behind *Madwoman* in 1979 was self-justifying. "We don't repudiate anything," Gilbert and Gubar told me firmly. "Not at all. It had to be done."[36]

The Queen's Looking Glass

I didn't read *Madwoman* until 1983, when I was a master's student. A few days after I bought it at the university bookstore, I wrapped this 719-page, 6 x 9–inch book in a pressure-sensitive plastic cover to protect it from damage (I still have my copy intact). Who had dared to write like this about literature—so largely and poetically, and with such audacity and wit? Here, at length, is a paragraph from chapter 3, "The Parables of the Cave":

> There is a sense in which, for us, this book is a dream of the rising of Christina Rossetti's "mother country." And there is a sense in which it is an attempt at reconstructing the Sibyl's leaves, leaves which haunt us with the possibility that if we can piece together their fragments the parts will form a whole that tells the story of the career of the single woman artist, a "mother of us all," as Gertrude Stein would put it, a woman whom patriarchal poetics dismembered and whom we have tried to remember. Detached from herself, silent, subdued, this woman artist tried in the beginning, as we shall see, to write like an angel in the house of fiction: with Jane Austen and Maria Edgeworth, she concealed her own truth behind a decorous and ladylike façade, scattering her real wishes to the winds or translating them into incomprehensible hieroglyphics. But as time passed and her cave-prison became more constricted, more claustrophobic, she "fell" into the gothic/Satanic mode and, with the Brontës and Mary Shelley, she planned monstrous escapes, then dizzily withdrew—with George Eliot and Emily Dickinson—from those open spaces where the scorching presence of the patriarchal sun, whom Dickinson called "the man of noon," emphasized her vulnerabilities. Since "Creation seemed a mighty Crack" to make her "visible," she took refuge again in the safety of the "dim hypaethric cavern" where she could be alone with herself, with a truth that was hers even in its fragmentation. (*Madwoman,* 101-2)

The utopian commitment to resurrect the Victorian woman writer and to redress her wrongs made *Madwoman* an unexpectedly moving work of literary criticism. For some readers (certainly not all), much of its power had to do with Gilbert and Gubar's style.[37] In this paragraph, for example, they begin with their "dream" for the book and what "haunts" them about that dream's elusiveness; the metaphor of "reconstructing" is carried through to the end of the paragraph and informs the strategy of the paragraph itself, which is threaded meaningfully with the names of eight different women; the evocation of silent, lost mothers is repeated and the motif of reconnection is implicit in the allusion to Stein; the spatial metaphors that echo throughout *Madwoman* are here, as is the reversed mythology of the "fall" into monstrosity; the chain of phrases, the long sentences (only five in the whole paragraph) are charged with a seriousness that works as much emotionally as it does polemically; finally, there is the skillful interweaving of imagery from Dickinson's verse. In fact, the whole paragraph is saturated in evocative concrete images; there are few purely theoretical abstractions (if any). In their analysis of a metaphor—in this example, "piecing together" lost stories, reading the fragmented hieroglyphics in the Sibyl's leaves—Gilbert and Gubar's prose becomes itself vitally metaphoric. And indeed, in their relentless dissection of the metaphors that have contributed to the construction of "literary paternity"—the pervasive idea that "the text's author is a father, a progenitor, a procreator, an aesthetic patriarch whose pen is an instrument of generative power like his penis"—Gilbert and Gubar exposed the misogynist assumptions about creativity in a way that seemed, to some readers, simply unanswerable (*Madwoman,* 6). Their examples of masculine assumptions and attitudes about women and writing—from seemingly everywhere in Western culture—initiated an original theory of women's underground efforts to redefine themselves and their art against male metaphors and male-ordered social and political regimes.

In chapter 1, "The Queen's Looking Glass: Female Creativity, Male Images of Women, and the Metaphor of Literary Paternity," Gilbert and Gubar range from fairy tales to classical and biblical mythology, Freud and Woolf, Elizabeth Barrett Browning and *The Faerie Queene* to explain the pervasiveness of the female angel/monster image in Western culture and the ubiquity of the "mythic masks male artists have fastened over [a woman's] human face" (*Madwoman,* 17). In their analysis of the Grimms' story of "Little Snow White" as a paradigmatic feminine plot, Gilbert and Gubar argue that the only significant action in the tale arises from the relationship between the wicked Queen—older, fiercer, "a plotter, a plot-maker, a schemer, a witch, an artist, an impersonator, a woman of almost infinite creative energy, witty, wily, and self-absorbed as all artists traditionally are" (*Madwoman,* 38-39)—and Snow White, "sweet, ignorant, passive," obedient, domestic, angelic (36). If the impure Queen is punished for her creative assertiveness, they ask, what about pure Snow White's future? How happy is this happy ending? For has she not "exchanged one glass coffin for another, delivered from the prison where the Queen put her only to be imprisoned in the looking glass from which the King's voice speaks daily" (*Madwoman,* 42)? In the following chapter, Gilbert and Gubar creatively extend this paradigmatic tale to ask the big questions for the future of feminist literary theory:

> If the pen is a metaphorical penis, with what organ can females generate texts? . . . What does it mean to be a woman writer in a culture whose

> fundamental definitions of literary authority are, as we have seen, both overtly and covertly patriarchal? If the vexed and vexing polarities of angel and monster . . . are major images literary tradition offers women, how does such imagery influence the ways in which women attempt the pen? If the Queen's looking glass speaks with the King's voice, how do its perpetual kingly admonitions affect the Queen's own voice? Since his is the chief voice she hears, does the Queen try to sound like the King, imitating his tone, his inflections, his phrasing, his point of view? Or does she "talk back" to him in her own vocabulary, her own timbre, insisting on her own viewpoint? We believe these are the basic questions feminist literary criticism—both theoretical and practical—must answer. (*Madwoman,* 46)

These still remain the fundamental—primitive—questions for feminist analysis, questions about agency, voice, authority, self-knowledge, autonomy; about the hidden injuries of false choices, circumscribed choices, the "vexing polarities" feminists have identified and fought against; these are the issues that still come up in classes on women's literature or feminist theory, in women's studies, in feminist cultural studies, in women's book clubs, and probably sometimes still in the private lives of many women, young and old.[38] For when Gilbert and Gubar wrote that the basic questions put by feminist literary criticism must also be answered "practically" as well as theoretically, they were suggesting that what we wrote in our dissertations and our criticism and how we presented literature to undergraduates was connected to a psychological condition and to a complex process of socialization that had something to do with gender politics in the real world. They were not just doing things with texts. Gilbert and Gubar have said in conversation that the academic institutionalization of feminist criticism "took the edge off" the movement; incorporation—which was the goal—made teaching and research less a form of activism, more a matter of professional advancement. When they were writing *Madwoman* in the mid-1970s, the personal really *was* political, and, as Marlene Tromp says in her essay in this volume, that famous feminist slogan "did not mean that individual acts were the best way to effect political change, but rather that we can often trace the disabling patterns we experience in our personal lives to larger political and social causes, particularly when we can match those patterns to many women's lives." "All along it felt personal," said Sandra about writing *Madwoman,* and, indeed, the "plots" that Gilbert and Gubar uncovered in Victorian women's writing had surprising echoes in the lives of modern women. Second-wave feminist literary critics identified the "phenomena of evasion and concealment in women's writings" that reflected many women's own experiences in navigating patriarchy (*Madwoman,* 75).

Gilbert and Gubar cite Elaine Showalter's crucial observation, in 1975, that feminist criticism saw meaning "in what has previously been empty space. The orthodox plot recedes, and another plot, hitherto submerged in the anonymity of the background," they wrote, "stands out in bold relief like a thumbprint" (*Madwoman,* 75). Consciousness of gender shifts the focus, exposing hidden details and designs.

> But what is this other plot? Is there any one other plot? What is the secret message of literature by women, if there is a single secret message? What, in other words, have women got to hide? Most obviously . . . what literary women have hidden or disguised is what each writer knows is in some sense her own story. Because, as Simone de Beauvoir puts it, women "still dream through the dreams of men," internalizing the strictures that the Queen's looking glass utters in its kingly voice, the message or story that has been hidden is "merely," in Carolyn Kizer's bitter words, "the private lives of one half of humanity." More specifically, however, the one plot that seems to be concealed in most of the nineteenth-century literature by women which will concern us here is in some sense a story of the woman writer's quest for her own story; it is the story, in other words, of the woman's quest for self-definition. (*Madwoman,* 75-76)

It is understandable why this "everywoman" subplot might be liable to accusations of universalism. Can there be "the woman's quest" for any one kind of deliverance? Maybe what made some readers uncomfortable was that Gilbert and Gubar were not afraid to invite women readers to see a connection between books by George Eliot, Mary Shelley, or Charlotte Brontë and their own realities. As Janet Gezari explains, *Madwoman*

> represented women writers as historical beings engaged in a search for identity, equality, and authority that mirrored, and was intended to mirror, that of many women, not just writers. Gilbert and Gubar were committed to the idea that women were substantial selves capable of exercising some control over their choices, and that experience or "life" had some presence prior to its articulation in language.[39]

Rita Felski has observed that Gilbert and Gubar's "description of Victorian women struggling against a repressive society to find their true selves often made these women sound remarkably like American feminists of the 1970s."[40] But one of the strengths of *Madwoman* was "its intensification of the reader's urgency to break free and tell her own story."[41] In an overview of the recent "ethical turn" in literary theory, Lawrence Buell writes about the liability for any kind of criticism that seems invested in identificatory reading:

> The image of textual encounter as personal encounter is not without its perils, three of them being the temptation to reify the metaphor, the implication that reader resistance is unethical (a symptom of obtuseness, of insensitivity, of ethical underdevelopment), and an astringency toward aesthetics as such . . . Yet the model of reading experience as a scene of *virtual interpersonality* that *enacts, activates, or otherwise illuminates* ethical responsibility may nonetheless prove one of the most significant innovations of the literature-and-ethics movement.[42]

I want to suggest that it is something of a false rivalry to pit humdrum feminist ethics against subversive feminist political critique.[43] *The Madwoman in the Attic* may be said to offer a model of the reading experience as *both* an ethical "scene of virtual interpersonality" and a politically imperative practice of seeing past those obvious interpersonal connections in order to apprehend characters and scenes where the impermissible or marginalized people live—Bertha Mason in the attic, for example. *Madwoman*'s concept of reading literature as palimpsestic, as "works whose surface designs conceal or obscure deeper, less accessible (and less socially acceptable) levels of meaning" (*Madwoman,* 73), has not only been a central model for feminist analysis, but an influential one for Marxist critics who try to make visible working-class characters and coded forms of unease in the bourgeois novel, and even for New Historicism's interest in the "trace," the "leftover," and the anecdote.[44] *Madwoman* first taught us to read beyond the "masculine pattern"—the rise of the middle-class hero in the novel, the overreacher in tragedy, the rake, the rogue, the detective, the pioneer. These male models "occupy powerful public roles from which women have almost always been excluded" (*Madwoman,* 68). There are other spaces—usually domestic spaces—in the Anglo-American literary tradition, they argued, where quiet rebellions are fomenting. The academic subject of the book was the Victorian woman artist's revolutionary struggle to be articulate, truthful, and self-determining. But the subtext of *The Madwoman in the Attic,* as almost everyone could see, was *Viva la revolution.*[45]

Madwoman in the Academy

The contributors to this collection represent both the diversity of feminist criticism now and the tremendous expansion of the nineteenth-century canon. They have taken as their subjects specific nineteenth- and twentieth-century women writers, the state of feminist theory and pedagogy, Milton studies, genre studies, film, race, and postcolonialism. Their approaches range from ecofeminism to psychoanalysis, and although each essay opens *Madwoman* to a different page, all provocatively circle back—with admiration and respect, objections and challenges, questions and arguments—to Gilbert and Gubar's groundbreaking work.

Although virtually all the contributors make reference to various critical contexts, the first four essays specifically explore the legacy and influence of *Madwoman* for literary criticism and theory. Susan Fraiman gives a concise overview of *Madwoman*'s strategies and its importance for feminism, and goes on to offer provocative ideas about how the book can be brought into the classroom. It is, she argues, "a gateway not only to feminist criticism but also to the methods and concerns of contemporary theory more generally." Fraiman reminds us of the explanatory power of 1970s feminist criticism and shows that today's students respond eagerly to the book's psychoanalytic framework, as well as its insistence on the way social conditions affected women writers. Marlene Tromp's essay is connected to Fraiman's in that both ask questions about *Madwoman*'s relevance for feminism today. Tromp contacted 400 scholars in Anglo-American nineteenth-century studies, Romanticism, and Milton studies who might have encountered *Madwoman* as part of their academic training. The testimonials she cites sketch out the book's personal importance to many scholars who were coming of age in the 1980s (I was not the only one, apparently, to protect my edition in plastic). An interesting feature of Tromp's essay is her assessment of reviews and criticism of Gilbert and Gubar from the 1980s and 1990s. Critics who raise objections about *Madwoman,* she argues, ignore the book's stature as a model of feminist *practices.* Gilbert and Gubar's "intellectual and professional courage, their sense of community, their commitment to their lives both inside and outside the academy" have much to bring to the next phases of feminism.

Two essays in this section explore the influence of *Madwoman* for different literary fields: Milton studies and Romanticism. One of the most daring and influential assertions about literary history and influence is formulated in chapter 6 of *Madwoman,* "Milton's Bogey: Patriarchal Poetry and Women Readers." Gilbert and Gubar take Virginia Woolf's enigmatic phrase in *A Room of One's Own* and ask what it might mean for women writers, concluding that Milton's misogyny in *Paradise Lost*—the myth of woman's sinfulness and her secondness—required later women writers to "devise their own myths and metaphors" (*Madwoman,* 189). Carol Blessing provides a thorough and fascinating overview of Milton studies post-*Madwoman,* showing convincingly that, indeed, the gloves were off as Milton scholars sought to reclaim their beloved author from condemnation. "Milton's bogey" was "a monumental step in the critical journey of both feminist theory and Milton studies," writes Blessing, and if Gilbert and Gubar are less central for the new generation of scholars, their reading of *Paradise Lost* has made a permanent contribution not only to a central work of the literary canon but to the issue of canonicity and women's reading overall.

That issue is still very much a part of feminist theory, but there have been new developments: ecofeminism has evolved into one of the most ethically invested forms of feminist criticism from the 1970s. As Katey Castellano argues, even though the "granddaughters" of Gilbert and Gubar's feminist criticism lost interest in activism in preference to theory, their "great-granddaughters"—ecofeminists—"aspire to direct the message of feminist criticism back to a wider public audience." In her analysis of Mary Shelley and "green Romanticism," Castellano looks at how an ecofeminist rereading of two books Gilbert and Gubar made central to the Romantic canon, *Frankenstein* and *The Last Man,* can open conversations about the role of public intellectuals. Castellano also applies Gilbert and Gubar's angel/monster image to Romantic images of nature as benevolent earth/mother or as avenging madwoman, claiming that *Frankenstein* and *The Last Man* envision "a proto-ecofeminist embrace of nature's ferocious agency."

Gilbert and Gubar's readings of *Wuthering Heights* and *Jane Eyre* are confident, controversial, and virtually unavoidable when we talk about these novels in our classes. Their interpretations have stood up to thirty years of Brontë studies with amazing stamina. Gilbert and Gubar's persuasive and original reading of feminine repression and rage in *Jane Eyre,* especially, seems as if it has always been there. (Of *course,* Bertha Mason does what Jane wants to do—tears the wedding veil, sets the bed on fire, destroys Thornfield!) Even contemporary revisions of *Jane Eyre,* such as the 1997 play by Polly Teale, seem to engage Gilbert and Gubar's foregrounding of the Bertha/Jane double as much as they do Brontë's novel. Three essays in this book return to the attic, framed by trauma theory, postcolonialism, and race. Madeleine Wood builds on *Madwoman*'s reading of the red room as the paradigmatic scene of Jane's story of growth, but she rejects a reading of the novel as a pilgrimage toward maturity and equality. Instead, Wood identifies in that childhood experience the source of an adult trauma that is endlessly repeated, as Jane seeks an absent father who will undo the psychic damage inflected by a violent and dysfunctional *maternal* family. Her psychoanalytic reading concludes skeptically: the spiritual equality Jane sought in her relationship with Rochester is compromised by their enclosure and retreat from the world at Ferndean.

Central to the essays by Narin Hassan and Danielle Russell are critiques of *Madwoman*'s essentialism or universalism. Asking how Gilbert and Gubar's reading of *Jane Eyre* can engage questions of race and empire, each finds echoes and incarnations of Brontë's novel in works by two uniquely placed writers, women from different centuries and distinct historical locations: the Indian novelist Krupabai Satthianadhan and the American Toni Morrison. Hassan traces the ways Gilbert and Gubar's feminist reading of *Jane Eyre* intersects with important questions of identity and native subjectivity that concern postcolonial studies. "If representations of native women support Jane's feminist progression," Hassan asks, "how can we read the work of native women who produced their own narratives of individual and cultural progress?" Hassan thinks especially about how a doubling figure such as Bertha Mason works in Satthianadhan's 1887 autobiographical novel, *Saguna.* There were complex negotiations between native women and their British counterparts. Reading Jane as a figure for English nationhood and Bertha as a figure of colonial oppression, she writes, is just one way of examining how the English novel engaged with the imperial project.

Gilbert and Gubar claimed that *Jane Eyre*'s story could belong to Everywoman, that her quest provides a "pattern for countless others" and that her problems are "symptomatic of difficulties every woman in a patriarchal society must meet and overcome" (*Madwoman,* 339). Their position has been attacked for dismissing forms of oppression experienced by women of color, but Danielle Russell argues that despite its disregard of race and ethnicity, *Madwoman* made an important contribution to feminist criticism: the pattern of Jane Eyre's struggle—oppression, starvation, madness, coldness, and an encounter with an enraged double—can be traced even in a contemporary novel that foregrounds the horror of slavery. *Jane Eyre* and *Beloved* were written 140 years apart, but Russell shows that these important works of fiction contain surprising parallels in their settings, characterization, and plot. Russell sets up the conversation about feminism and race through a discussion of Morrison's *Playing in the Dark* and then performs a careful reading of *Beloved* against the female plot Gilbert and Gubar identified in *Jane Eyre.* She concludes that the paradigm Gilbert and Gubar established for Victorian women's writing can be accommodated to analyses of race and ethnicity, as well.

Gilbert and Gubar's chapter on *Wuthering Heights,* "Looking Oppositely: Emily Brontë's Bible of Hell" is a startling feminist reading of a classic that, before 1975 or so, most critics were interested in for its technical, narrative puzzles and its relation to Romanticism.[46] In Gilbert and Gubar's interpretation, *Wuthering Heights* is not a love story about two soulmates but rather a myth of lost female origins within Victorian patriarchy, a rebellious revision of *Paradise Lost* where hell and heaven are reversed: marriage, culture, womanhood, and gentility make up the prison that destroys Catherine's spirit. Hila Shacher's essay examines the influence of Gilbert and Gubar's Miltonic reading in popular culture, focusing on three film adaptations of Brontë's novel. She argues that postfeminist (and post-*Madwoman*) culture has invited or demanded a more woman-centered story: the novel is now played on screen less as one of modern Western culture's most enduring love stories and more as a psychosexual drama inescapably bound up with issues of gender. Even the popular MTV version seems to fold in a story of lost mothers and feminine hauntings, though its conservative conclusion demands a restoration of the traditional family unit.

If there are two metaphors or images that stand out in Gilbert and Gubar's analyses of Victorian women writers, they are those of the title of the book: madwomen and attics, feminine rage and confinement. Several of these essays look at the undeniable legacy of those powerful images for feminist criticism, reading very different texts through Gilbert and Gubar's construct of the woman writer's "mad" alter ego and her escape from confinement. Carol Davison, Tamara Wagner, Keren Fite, and Thomas Fair each focus on genre. Thirty years after *Madwoman,* nineteenth-century studies has radically reevaluated women's interventions in sensation fiction, domestic realism, and the female gothic. Keren Fite studies the influence of *Madwoman* on feminist critics' handling of generic categories. Critics' treatment of Louisa May Alcott illustrate how the madwoman allegory has turned into a "hard-and-fast-assertion": Alcott's literary experiments are twisted to fit into a feminist construct, following Gilbert and Gubar, of the woman writer "secretly exercising strategies of duplicity to ensure her anguished survival." Similary, Tamara Wagner's focus on the "generic confinement" of Charlotte Yonge and other noncanonical realists takes up Gilbert and Gubar's evocation of madness and domestic imprisonment and applies those tropes to a set of writers who deliberately tried to distance themselves from the sensation novelists of the 1860s. Wagner argues that sensation fiction's underpinning interest in gothic tropes has marked it out as "subversive," thereby leaving a group of domestic women writers (Margaret Oliphant, Eliza Lynn Linton, and Yonge) underexplored. By paralleling realist and sensational women writers, Wagner broadens the application of *Madwoman*'s analysis of the strategies available to Victorian women novelists. Carol Davison argues that the madwoman as identified and theorized by Gilbert and Gubar is actually "Ann Radcliffe's long-lost daughter." Although *Madwoman* recognizes that the tropes of imprisonment and escape originated in the gothic novel, the book problematically denies the female Gothic its rightful and consequential place in literary and novelistic history. By reading *Jane Eyre* as a gothic novel and linking it to Radcliffe, Davison seeks to restore the connections between the scene of the madwoman's rebellion and an earlier genre. All three essays show how feminist fantasies of escape can be re-imagined (or distorted), put to quite different ideological uses in different fictional genres. Finally, in his essay on

Elizabeth Gaskell and the industrial novel, Thomas Fair also revises Gilbert and Gubar's reading of the Victorian woman writer's "mad double," arguing that Gaskell's portrayals of women's psychology and social position must be considered "as an imperative alternative to the oppressed and enraged madwoman." Gaskell, he argues, often sees value in a father's or husband's protective role, and many of her novels emphasizes the heroine's freedom to act even within the confines of their socially and economically designated "sphere," rather than to remain immobilized (in metaphorical attics) by their disadvantages. Rejecting gothic tropes altogether and often focused on the economic injustices caused by industrialism, Gaskell's novels determinedly dramatize the connections between women's psychology (not necessarily disabled) and their economic, political, and social situations.

Madwoman's final chapter, "A Woman—White: Emily Dickinson's Yarn of Pearl," argues that Dickinson deliberately adopted poses and self-dramatizations as strategies to resolve the anxiety of feminine creation. Her poetry, alternating between coyness and lyric outbursts, constitutes "the 'dialogue' in an extended fiction whose subject is the life of that supposed person who was called Emily Dickinson but who also christened herself, variously, Emilie, Daisy, Brother Emily, Uncle Emily, and simply Dickinson" (*Madwoman*, 583). Lucia Aiello takes issue with Gilbert and Gubar's analysis of Emily Dickinson as the quintessential madwoman/artist, for such a reading relies excessively on the "mimetic over the poietic" in characterizing women's relationship to their art. Gilbert and Gubar reduce Emily Dickinson's literary innovations to her psychic disposition—art is a coping mechanism. Aiello appreciates the importance of Gilbert and Gubar's theory for feminist criticism and the recovery of forgotten women poets, but she is interested in "recovering" Dickinson's verse from Gilbert and Gubar's influence by testing their readings against other interpretations and untangling, to some extent, a binary version of literary history.

I hope the essays presented here do some justice to *Madwoman*'s influence—its capaciousness, its daring, and its limitations. There is always, of course, more to say (especially after thirty years). Gilbert and Gubar's treatment of Jane Austen (such as the brilliant reading of *Northanger Abbey*) and of George Eliot's complex authorial self-division and impersonation certainly deserve reassessment. Their influential analysis of burial, hunger, and impotence in *Villette* and *Shirley* revealed Charlotte Brontë as one of the truly great writers of feminine subjectivity, the Victorian novelist who dramatizes most disturbingly and convincingly the emotional reality of the powerless or marginalized person, her frustration, depression, and anger. Gilbert and Gubar also opened the door to the Victorian women poets, virtually an undiscovered country at the time of *Madwoman*'s publication.

Works by Elizabeth Barrett Browning, Emily Brontë, and Christina Rossetti were hard to locate outside of university libraries, much less adapt for use in a college course—even a reliable edition of *Goblin Market* or *Aurora Leigh* was unavailable in 1974. Twenty years later, Blackwell published an anthology of *Victorian Women Poets* (1995) that included 51 writers; Oxford's *Nineteenth-Century Women Poets* (1997) included 102; and Broadview has expanded the canon even further in *Victorian Working-Class Women Poets: An Anthology* (2008), edited by Florence Boos.

I suspect that a great deal of criticism on Victorian literature post-*Madwoman* has quietly absorbed its historical focus, its critical questions, and certain of its feminist observations. *The Madwoman in the Attic* introduced a generation of students and scholars to an idea of Victorian women's literary history that was linked to a symbolic underground: starvation and sin, whiteness and wounds, attics and drawing rooms, sewing, poison, mirrors, veils, masks. Their wide-ranging and remarkably inclusive study made visible writers and texts most scholars hadn't experienced, and cracked open the door to other stories (other attics) for feminist inquiry. In a 2008 article in *Dissent*, Judith Walzer reflects on the influence of four books of feminist criticism published in the 1970s, by Patricia Spacks, Ellen Moers, Elaine Showalter, and Gilbert and Gubar. Although these books unquestionably "started something" in the academy, Walzer wonders about their continued relevance:

> What these four critics did was not simply to "start something"—create a new field—but to take a crucial step forward in the practice of criticism. In their work they reestablished the idea that the social environment surrounds us all—writers, too—and that it is different for genders, groups, and individuals. . . .
>
> Remembering these books should help to rescue the entire critical enterprise from the persistent distractions that threaten to make it irrelevant. These critics know that the realities of life and literature are too engaging, too important, to get stuck out there where there is no subject—except a theory and one's own self-conscious use of it. This body of work always has a subject outside of itself, a subject that is as relevant today as it was when the books were written. It is worth reading (or re-reading) to see how criticism ought to be practiced.[47]

It is important to remember that Gilbert and Gubar taught that eight-week course in 1974 because they knew deeply from their own experiences that something was missing in academic study and that they had an opportunity, even a responsibility, to offer students another, and remote, point of view—let's say, that of the Victorian woman writer (and neither were trained as Victorianists: Sandra's field was twentieth-century poetry, Susan's was the eighteenth century). Thirty years after *Madwoman,* most college and university English departments have established courses not only on women's literature but on a multiplicity of literatures and viewpoints; American students are eager to learn about literature from the Middle East, South America, Africa, and the Caribbean; about African American, Asian American, gay and lesbian writers. The effort to carve out a legitimized space for these stories and histories has taken vision, what Florence Howe called "courage and tools, . . . not unreasonable goals of literary study."[48] *The Madwoman in the Attic* contributed both courage and tools to that visionary project and helped to dismantle sexist assumptions about women writers, women readers, and women in the profession. Gilbert and Gubar's perceptive readings in nineteenth-century fiction and poetry—they are models of close textual analysis—and their claims for the ingenuity and daring of Victorian women writers—working within their own tradition and seeking the authority of their own voices—can continue to inspire differently situated scholars and teachers who still believe that literature has the power to change lives. The essays in this book engage provocatively the range of issues Gilbert and Gubar introduced to feminism and to nineteenth-century studies as we continue to work out negotiations and compromises within the profession between Emily Dickinson's "bursting all the doors"—going out into a new critical frontier—and finding "a room of one's own" where feminist commitment can thrive. As a feminist symbol, the raging madwoman is not without controversy. But the power of this image—to cross generic boundaries, inspire resistant readings, and disrupt conventional ideas about sexuality, creativity, myth, history, and narrative—persists not only in the comparatively small house of literary scholarship, but also in many private corners and attics in our so-called postfeminist world.

Notes

1. Sandra M. Gilbert and Susan Gubar, *The Madwoman in the Attic: The Woman Writer and the Nineteenth-Century Literary Imagination* (New Haven: Yale University Press, 1979), 85. Further references will be given parenthetically.
2. Annette Kolodny, review of *The Madwoman in the Attic* by Sandra M. Gilbert and Susan Gubar, *American Literature* 52, no. 1 (March 1980): 129.
3. Carolyn Heilbrun, review of *The Madwoman in the Attic* by Sandra M. Gilbert and Susan Gubar, *Washington Post Book World,* November 25, 1979.
4. Since *Madwoman,* these metaphors have been reimagined and challenged by writers in very different disciplines. For example, Deborah Keahey and Deborah Schnitzer's *The Madwoman in the Academy* (2003); Marta Caminero-Santangelo's *The Madwoman*

Can't Speak: Or Why Insanity Is Not Subversive (1998); Nancy Holland's *The Madwoman's Reason: The Concept of the Appropriate in Ethical Thought* (1998); and Linda Schierse Leonard's *Meeting the Madwoman: Empowering the Feminine Spirit* (1994). Recent and current artistic and media projects likewise show the influence of Gilbert and Gubar's discussion of madness and female creativity, such as Amherst's Madwoman Productions, dozens of madwoman studios and blogs, and the marketing of "I Am the Madwoman in the Attic" mugs, T-shirts, aprons, notebooks, mousepads, etc., at http://www.cafepress.com/opheliasart.

5. Susan Gubar, *Rooms of Our Own* (Urbana: University of Illinois Press, 2006), 218.

6. Ibid.

7. The first women's studies program in the United States was put into place in 1970 at San Diego State University. By 2000, there were approximately 615 programs. "Between 1978, when 'women's studies' first appeared as an indexing category in Dissertation Abstracts International, and 1985, the total number of dissertations recorded under the heading was more than thirteen thousand." Mari Jo Buhle, introduction to *The Politics of Women's Studies: Testimony from the Founding Mothers,* ed. Florence Howe (New York: Feminist Press, 2001), xv.

8. The eighth edition of the Norton *Major Authors* includes about 93 writers, 27 of them women, or about one-fourth. I had no formal exposure to most of these writers, especially the earlier ones, as an undergraduate and read many of them for the first time in 1992 as an assistant professor when I taught my first class on women's literature using another Norton anthology: Gilbert and Gubar's *Norton Anthology of Women's Literature: The Tradition in English,* first published in 1985. The book went into its third edition in 2007, with 220 writers, 56 of them new additions.

9. Sandra M. Gilbert and Susan Gubar, introduction to *The Madwoman in the Attic,* 2nd ed. (1979; New Haven: Yale University Press, 2000), xix–xx.

10. Sandra M. Gilbert and Susan Gubar, personal communication, May 1, 2008. Further references to or quotations from this conversation should be apparent in the text.

11. Gilbert and Gubar, introduction to *Madwoman,* 2nd ed., xx.

12. Marlene Tromp, personal communication, December 21, 2007.

13. Gubar, *Rooms,* 180.

14. Kate Zernike, "Post-feminism and Other Fairy Tales," *New York Times,* March 16, 2008; my italics.

15. Ibid.; my italics.

16. Rita Felski, *Literature after Feminism* (Chicago: University of Chicago Press, 2003), 66.

17. Jane Marcus, *Art and Anger: Reading Like a Woman* (Columbus: Ohio State University Press, 1988), xxi.

18. See, for example, Sarah Cheverton, "'No Longer Reasonable': Exploring Feminist Anger," in *The Feminist Seventies,* ed. Helen Graham, Ann Kaloski, Ali Neilson, Emma Robertson (York, U.K.: Raw Nerve Books, 2003), 105–8.

19. "Primitive brain is 'smarter' than we think, MIT study shows," February 23, 2005, http://web.mit.edu/newsoffice/2005/basalganglia.html. I am indebted to Marshall Gregory for introducing this idea to me.

20. "Remember the old feminist device of the mental 'click' that you experience when you find yourself confronting what used to be sexism? By the time I ran into Susan in the elevator, I'd encountered a tap-dance worth of potential clicks, without paying attention to them." Sandra M. Gilbert, introduction to *Madwoman,* 2nd ed., xvii.

21. Frank Lentricchia, "Patriarchy against Itself: The Young Manhood of Wallace Stevens," *Critical Inquiry* 13, no. 4 (Summer 1987): 773.

22. Frances Taliaferro, review of *The Madwoman in the Attic* by Sandra M. Gilbert and Susan Gubar, *Harper's*, December 1979.

23. Nina Auerbach, review of *The Madwoman in the Attic* by Sandra M. Gilbert and Susan Gubar, *Victorian Studies* 23, no. 4 (Summer 1980): 507; Katherine Frank, review of *The Madwoman in the Attic* by Sandra M. Gilbert and Susan Gubar, *Philological Quarterly* 59, no. 3 (Summer 1980): 383.

24. Rosemary Dinnage, "Re-creating Eve," review of *The Madwoman in the Attic* by Sandra M. Gilbert and Susan Gubar, *New York Review of Books* 26, no. 20 (December 20, 1979). Sandra Zagarel and Nina Auerbach replied to Dinnage in defense of *Madwoman:* "Dinnage seems to want to cling to an image of the nineteenth-century female as a model of one-dimensional compliance, but actual nineteenth-century texts make it impossible to preserve that image; Gilbert and Gubar have not invented their madwoman, but have explained her ubiquity." "Men, Women, and Lit," *New York Review of Books* 27, no. 3 (March 6, 1980).

25. Mary Jacobus, review of *The Madwoman in the Attic* by Sandra M. Gilbert and Susan Gubar, *Signs* 6, no. 3 (Spring 1981): 522.

26. Phoebe Pettingell, "A Prey to Madness," review of *The Madwoman in the Attic* by Sandra M. Gilbert and Susan Gubar, *The New Leader,* February 25, 1980.

27. Toril Moi, *Sexual/Textual Politics* (London: Routledge, 1985), 67.

28. See especially Gayatri Chakravorty Spivak, "Three Women's Texts and a Critique of Imperialism," *Critical Inquiry* 12, no. 1 (Autumn 1985): 243–61; Toril Moi, *Sexual/Textual Politics;* Frank Lentricchia, "Patriarchy against Itself"; Mary Jacobus, review of *The Madwoman in the Attic;* Dean Flower, review of *The Madwoman in the Attic, Hudson Review* 33, no. 3 (Autumn 1980): 421–30. Susan Gubar takes up the changes in two decades of feminist criticism in "What Ails Feminist Criticism?" *Critical Inquiry* 24 (Summer 1998): 878–902.

29. Clare Hemmings and Josephine Brain, "Imagining the Feminist Seventies," in *The Feminist Seventies,* 12–13.

30. Ibid., 13.

31. "It's convenient in an era of sound-bites and laser politics to call what happens to a woman's body essentialism and to think that the label has produced a reasoned and persuasive critique." Nancy K. Miller, "Madwoman Revisited," in *Making Feminist History: The Literary Criticism of Sandra M. Gilbert and Susan Gubar,* ed. William E. Cain (New York: Garland, 1998), 99.

32. Gilbert and Gubar, introduction to *Madwoman,* 2nd ed., xxxviii.

33. Susan Gubar, "What Ails Feminist Criticism?" 896; my italics.

34. The MLA International Bibliography cites only two short articles on "The Yellow Wallpaper" published before 1979 (both in *American Literary Realism 1870–1910* 8 [1975]). In framing this obscure short story as part of their narrative of the Victorian woman writer's metaphorical confinement and escape through madness, Gilbert and Gubar helped to open Gilman's whole body of work to feminist analysis. Today there are dozens of editions of "The Yellow Wallpaper," including a Bedford Critical Edition, Oxford Classics, Modern Library Classics, casebooks, study guides, a dual-textbook edition, and teaching guides, including an MLA *Approaches to Teaching* imprint. Almost every anthology of American literature now includes "The Yellow Wallpaper."

35. Frank Lentricchia claimed, "They like to start with a psychosexual proposition, mention the social in lip service, and then leap to the literary, which is supposedly both mirror and epiphenomenon of the psychosexual" ("Patriarchy against Itself," 781). Gilbert and Gubar replied, "Though we argued in the first page of *The Madwoman* that in order to explore the female literary tradition we had to confront 'first, the social position

in which nineteenth-century women writers found themselves, and second the reading that they themselves did,' he insists that we see 'biology' as 'the ground of a unique psychic difference.'" Sandra M. Gilbert and Susan Gubar, "The Man on the Dump," *Critical Inquiry* 14, no. 2 (Winter 1988): 397. When I asked about the supposedly underhistoricized readings in *Madwoman,* Sandra Gilbert told me, "We had no women teachers, no one to teach us these things. I read everything I could about the social, metaphysical status of governesses" (personal communication, May 1, 2008).

36. Compare the longevity of another important book on Victorian women's writing, Terry Eagleton's *Myths of Power: A Marxist Study of the Brontës* (London: Palgrave Macmillan, 2005), first published in 1975. In his "Introduction to the Anniversary Edition" (2005), Eagleton writes, "This is a pre-feminist study in what nowadays is for the most part a post-feminist world, and it bears the marks of it almost everywhere. Today, I would prefer to argue that gender is the place where all the other contradictions by which the [Brontë] sisters are besieged, and which this book tries to sketch, are most poignantly focused." *Myths of Power,* xiv.

37. Style is revealing, and not only in terms of accessibility. Gubar notes that Judith Butler's style has a "preponderance of subject-verb disagreements," speculating that this reflects an intellectual difficulty in reconciling poststructuralism and feminism. "What Ails Feminist Criticism?" 896–98.

38. Susan Gubar has described a group of Cornell undergraduates who were in her women's literature course in 2008 as being "every bit as excited as my students in the seventies." Personal communication, May 1, 2008.

39. Janet Gezari, "Sandra M. Gilbert and Susan Gubar's *The Madwoman in the Attic,*" *Essays in Criticism* 56, no. 3 (2006): 266.

40. Rita Felski, *Literature after Feminism,* 67.

41. Nina Auerbach, review of *The Madwoman in the Attic,* 506.

42. Lawrence Buell, "In Pursuit of Ethics," *PMLA* 114, no. 1 (January 1999): 13; my italics.

43. Katey Castellano's essay on Mary Shelley in this collection, for example, explicitly links environmental ethics with women's historic struggles against oppression. Unlike some social justice movements that have kept their focus on one subject position, feminist politics and feminist philosophy has developed the concept of "intersectionality." Feminism's original focus on women has broadened to embrace not only issues of sexuality, violence, and the family but also the environment, globalization, the peace movement, etc.

44. See Catherine Gallagher and Stephen Greenblatt, *Practicing New Historicism* (Chicago: University of Chicago Press, 2000).

45. "*The Madwoman in the Attic* is less a revolutionary manifesto than a bible of revolution, giving definitive form to the collective work of a decade." Nina Auerbach, review of *The Madwoman in the Attic,* 505.

46. An important exception is Carol Ohmann, "Emily Brontë in the Hands of Male Critics," *College English* 32, no. 8 (May 1971): 906–13.

47. Judith B. Walzer, "The Breakthrough: Feminism and Literary Criticism," *Dissent* (Spring 2008), http://www.dissentmagazine.org/article/?article=1170.

48. From Florence Howe's address as MLA president, December 1973. Quoted in Joanne Glasgow and Angela Ingram, introduction to *Courage and Tools: The Florence Howe Award for Feminist Scholarship 1974–1989,* ed. Joanne Glasgow and Angela Ingram (New York: Modern Language Association, 1990), xxvii.

1

After Gilbert and Gubar

Madwomen Inspired by *Madwoman*

Susan Fraiman

"Is a pen a metaphorical penis?" Thus begins Sandra M. Gilbert and Susan Gubar's *The Madwoman in the Attic,* with a first sentence only slightly less famous than that of *Pride and Prejudice.* This was, of course, back in the dark ages—long before it had become routine for literary critics to rehearse their childhoods or parse their eroticism in public. Thirty years ago, to say "penis" in print was rather daring. Gilbert and Gubar might well have called upon the dandified, Continental "phallus." Many would do so in the decade to come. But no—for them, only the plain-spoken, tell-it-like-it-is word "penis" would do. I begin here because I want to recall and to celebrate how audacious, original, and even profane *Madwoman* was at the time of its publication. This essay will reflect on the intervention *Madwoman* made in the late 1970s, on the influence it had on me and those of my generation throughout the '80s, on the ways it has been usefully critiqued and elaborated in subsequent years, and on its continuing pedagogical value in the training of graduate students today.

Early in their preface, Gilbert and Gubar refer to Charlotte Brontë as an "often under-appreciated nineteenth-century novelist."[1] If this description takes us by surprise in 2009, when few novels are taught so frequently as *Jane Eyre,* it is in part thanks to *Madwoman,* whose focus on Brontë has helped to gain her a central place in accounts not only of women's writing but also of the British novel and the Victorian period. Without question, one of *Madwoman*'s most lasting contributions has been to the sweaty project of tearing down and rebuilding the canon. By rereading works such as *Jane Eyre* and *Frankenstein,* Gilbert and Gubar made the familiar strange; by resurrecting works such as Brontë's *The Professor* and Shelley's *The Last Man,* they made the strange familiar. The result of their labors has been to heighten if not wholly redefine our appreciation for the likes of Charlotte Brontë and Mary Shelley, who can no longer be seen as secondary figures with an alarming tendency to stray from the path of realism. Beyond this, while overhauling the reputations of known women, *Madwoman* ranged widely and ever so casually over many more candidates for recovery, calling our attention to neglected nineteenth-century writers from Louisa May Alcott to Charlotte Mary Yonge. Indeed, six years before Gilbert and Gubar actually edited *The Norton Anthology of Literature by Women,* the very Norton-esque heft of their first coauthored volume argued implicitly for the massiveness of women's contribution to the Anglo-American literary tradition.

This was hardly an argument with canonicity per se nor was it an attempt to look beyond the strictly literary at various popular women's genres. It was, on the other hand, far more than a polite effort simply to include great works by women according to existing criteria. Rather, at a time when a similar project was being undertaken by African Americanists, Gilbert and Gubar joined other American feminist critics in denaturalizing the canon—historicizing its formation, questioning its terms of inclusion, and starting a process that would quickly encourage a broader study of cultural forms. If D. A. Miller and Ann Cvetkovich would go on, for example, to raise our awareness of Victorian sensation novels, they were surely enabled to do so by *Madwoman*'s prescient recuperation of a nineteenth-century thematics of secrets, insanity, and cruelty—pivoting on female figures.[2] Gilbert and Gubar's revision began by contesting Harold Bloom's patrilineal theory of literary influence; from there they proceeded to a study of books by women, with the goal of saying how these are marked as well as linked by ideologies and strategies involving gender. In helping to formulate a woman-centered criticism, Gilbert and Gubar made several closely related assertions that would be fundamental to American gynocritics for the next ten years. These assertions are familiar to those of us whose training coincided with the emergence of feminist scholarship. Our students, however, do not take them for granted, and these days we ourselves may feel defensive and old teaching courses that even reference "women" in the title. So before I consider ways of updating such courses, I want to reiterate and affirm a few of the assumptions that made them possible.

First, that literary production is inextricable from social conditions and that these are structured in part by gender. Texts by women, constrained by and contributing to notions of the feminine in a particular context, share certain features and differ in some though not all ways from texts by men. It is the job of a feminist poetics to collate and affiliate works by women in order to make visible and to value this difference. Along with Elaine Showalter, Deborah McDowell, Nancy Miller, and a great many others, Gilbert and Gubar endeavored, in short, to explore the culturally constructed *gender specificity* of works of literature.[3] In *Madwoman*'s account of nineteenth-century women's writing, this specificity lay primarily in the troping of female anxiety and confinement as well as in covert expressions of feminist rage. This brings me to a second cluster of assertions. Like other oppositional critics emergent in the late 1970s, Gilbert and Gubar looked to books by outsiders for subtexts, alter egos, and counterplots—for elements, that is, posing a challenge to dominant ideologies and generic conventions. By shattering the surface, decoding the ostensible, they reinvented genteel novels by Austen and sweet poems by Dickinson in terms of their ability to subvert and explode. Examining texts they described as multilayered or "palimpsestic," they focused on that which, most deeply buried, was also most furiously insurgent. Their criticism was, in short, *political;* it grew out of the twentieth-century movement for women's rights, and it chose purposefully to identify modes and sites of rebellion in women's writing.

There is, finally, a third set of assertions exemplified by *Madwoman* and typical of American feminist criticism generally. Gilbert and Gubar's big book offered not only a genealogy of ties between female writers but also a narratology downplaying heterosexual romance in favor of ties between female characters: Fanny Price and Mary Crawford, Catherine Earnshaw and Isabella Linton, Dorothea Brooke and Rosamond Lydgate, Jane Eyre and Bertha Mason. Its madwoman paradigm transformed rivals into doubles, reconciled wife and mistress, showed us Bertha acting on Jane's behalf. By intertwining women, this work gave us stunning new readings and, equally important, struck a blow to the traditions of fairy tale and cat fight. Along these lines, one thing only remains to be said. Their names composited like partners in a law firm, their fates knotted like members of a rock band, Gilbert and Gubar have demonstrated the power of sisterhood not least in their own remarkable collaboration. Gender specificity, political agenda, ties between women defying compulsory heterosexuality: these premises were taken for granted during the period we now identify with "difference" or "cultural" feminism (falling roughly between 1975 and 1985), when an emphasis on women and sexual difference was revamping scholarship across the disciplines. Though complicated in important ways by subsequent work in such areas as postcolonial studies and queer theory, they are premises that were crucial to my own training as a critic, that continue to inform my writing and my pedagogy, and that influenced other strains of late-twentieth-century theory to a greater extent than is often acknowledged.

Here begins the pedagogical section of this essay. Radical theologian Mary Daly was long known for her controversial practice, harkening back to 1980s separatism, of limiting her feminist ethics course to female students. While I myself can see the advantages of an all-female classroom, I also value the thoughtful male students who seek out my courses in order to interrogate conventions of gender and sexuality. In another sense, however, I remain true to the separatist ethos of the 1980s by continuing, not a little self-consciously, to teach feminist theory from an all-female syllabus. In my graduate-level course, for example, I use primary texts by British and American women writers—a fluid roster including Harriet Jacobs's *Incidents in the Life of a Slave Girl,* Radclyffe Hall's *The Well of Loneliness,* Karen Yamashita's *Through the Arc of the Rainforest,* Jennie Livingston's film *Paris Is Burning,* Octavia Butler's *Parable of the Sower,* among numerous others—to introduce theoretical readings and debates centered on each. In keeping with *Madwoman*'s readings of women writers, we are typically attuned to elements of subversion and happy to explore figurations of sisterhood. The course has been completely transformed over the years and is slightly reinvented each time I teach it, but no matter how many changes I make, it always seems to open with Charlotte Brontë, or perhaps Jane Austen, and thus, more often than not, with a chapter by Sandra Gilbert and Susan Gubar.

As I have suggested, however, our class not only takes up *Madwoman* as a compelling model, illustrating the premises and procedures outlined above, but also attempts to gauge its limitations and juxtapose it with more recent scholarship. Indeed, the lineup of female writers now serves to challenge as much as to assert their use of a common language; the very gender of figures in Hall and Livingston (if not that of the authors themselves) is up for grabs; and the assignment of foundational texts such as Gilbert and Gubar's means coming to terms with those aspects of early feminist work that have not worn well. From a vantage point three decades after its original publication, I see the weaknesses of this magisterial study as arising by and large from its historical moment as well as from the psychoanalytic leanings of its framework.

The questions I would raise about *Madwoman,* represented here by its chapter on *Jane Eyre,* fall into three categories. First, while this is by no means another psychosexual reading of Brontë, its psychoanalytic approach to the text's doubleness does implicitly view the "repressed" level of Brontë's novel as more original and real than the manifest level, which is regarded as mere cover story. Though I have said I agree with the *political* priority given to the angry subtext, I would not give it the *epistemological* weight that Gilbert and Gubar's model, based on the individual psyche, would seem to suggest. Rather, I prefer to see both docility and defiance regarding gender as social structures of feeling available to Brontë in her time and place.

Second, while the mad double theory works well to claim for Jane the violence projected onto Bertha Mason, it also has the effect of reducing Bertha to little more than a facet of Jane's mind. As Gayatri Spivak has famously remarked, for critics to celebrate the Anglo woman's subjectivity without noticing the price paid by Bertha is to repeat Brontë's own staging of pale Jane's success at the darker woman's expense. As we all now realize, the readiness of early feminist criticism to generalize about women too often glossed over distinctions and inequities among them, and it would take additional readings of *Jane Eyre*—of which there have now been many—to bring out the meanings of race, nation, and class as they interact with gender in Brontë's novel.

The third and final issue is related to the first two. *Madwoman,* let us be clear, is contextual in its assumptions. As I have noted, it insists that women's historical subordination to men has an effect, albeit highly mediated, upon literary production. In addition, though many forget this, its purview is not *all* women's writing, but writing by British and American women in the course of a carefully specified century. Nevertheless, I think it's fair to say that, having framed their argument in loosely historical terms, Gilbert and Gubar are more interested in psychological than social conditions, and are therefore usefully supplemented by critics who do more to explain in specific historical detail why, for example, an English governess in the 1840s might be having bad dreams.

In the graduate classroom, then, following on Gilbert and Gubar, I might teach Suvendrini Perera and Susan Meyer on the racial and colonial thematics of Brontë's novel; Mary Poovey on the vexed figure of the governess midcentury; and Anne McClintock on the fascination of genteel Victorians with women of the laboring classes, their hands swollen and faces darkened by the dirtiness of their work.[4] The result of these critical juxtapositions, I hasten to add, is not simply to tout the later texts but also to show their degree of indebtedness to *Madwoman.* After all, it was Gilbert and Gubar who first cast a sympathetic eye on Bertha and made her available for further recuperation, and it was likewise Gilbert and Gubar who first identified Jane's "ambiguous status as a governess" (349). I would also note that discussions of native and working women cannot grapple with race and/or class apart from some concept of the "feminine"; and needless to say, we remain indebted to Gilbert and Gubar for launching our inquiry into the discursive production of gender. As I see it, therefore, feminist critics of the past three decades have enlarged rather than displaced *Madwoman*'s view of Brontë's text. These days when I teach *Jane Eyre* we still go straight to the attic, but what we find is not one but at least three madwomen shaking the rafters of Thornfield. There is Bertha Mason, Jane's angry psychological double; Bertha Mason, dehumanized, self-immolating subaltern; and finally, my personal favorite and addition, Grace Poole, the laboring woman half-awake to the distant sounds of Chartism.[5]

Clearly *Madwoman* works well in the graduate classroom to demonstrate the continuing explanatory power of Anglo-American feminist criticism since the late 1970s; as the first in a series, it sets in motion a train of feminist thought that can then be followed up to our present day. Teaching Austen as well as Brontë, I invariably begin with Gilbert and Gubar, whose claiming of bad girls Catherine De Bourgh and Mary Crawford helps to bring out the darkness I see in Aunt Jane, countering the still pervasive myth of her harmlessness. Let us not forget, too, that Gilbert and Gubar are superb close readers. I may call on Claudia Johnson to historicize Regency-era notions of personal happiness, placing *Pride and Prejudice* in dialogue with the political debates of Austen's time, but nothing works better than *Madwoman* to foster an intimate, nuanced engagement with the linguistic texture, narrative details, and shifting tones of Austen's novels and juvenilia.[6]

I want to close with the somewhat less obvious suggestion that *Madwoman* works equally well to point students in the direction of other postmodern approaches to literature and culture. I have already mentioned its use of psychoanalysis to explore the splittings, doublings, repressions, and rebellions in books by Brontë and her peers. I have also noted the tension between this and more materialist methodologies implied if not elaborated by the opening section. Beyond this, I would say that *Madwoman,* published by Yale University Press in the heyday of American deconstruction, gives a taste of those poststructuralist critical practices underwritten by the likes of Lacan and Derrida. There is, for example, Gilbert and Gubar's sense of women's writing as self-referential—staging the anxieties of female authorship even while authorizing female narrators like Jane Eyre and Lucy Snowe. And certainly their study teaches students to read from the margins, to pull a stray thread and watch the rest unravel, to dwell on the unintended and unsaid. After *Madwoman,* readers can no longer assume that primary characters are more important than secondary ones, or that the end of a narrative necessarily trumps the middle. There is, in addition, this volume's investment in disobedience, discipline, madness, and incarceration, making *Madwoman* a good segue to the Foucauldian thematics so central to contemporary queer theory.

In the training of graduate students, then, *Madwoman* provides a gateway not only to feminist criticism but also to the methods and concerns of contemporary theory more generally. Its method of skeptical close reading runs parallel to that of deconstruction, while its interest in the "deviant" and abject looks ahead to queer theory. *Madwoman*'s feminist approach can nevertheless be distinguished from these in at least one important way. Whereas much queer theory recruits poststructuralism in the service of an anti-identitarian politics, the project represented by *Madwoman* assumes the provisional stability and strategic uses of identity categories like "woman" and "lesbian." And much as I appreciate the pressure exerted on these categories by those who note their exclusivity and normativity, I also see them as necessary if not sufficient to thinking about gender and sexuality, and to a politics stemming from these. Since 1979, we have learned to emphasize that gender is neither fixed, undifferentiated, nor necessarily paramount as an axis of identity and framework for analysis. Yet if gender is not *always* salient (and never uniformly so), it may bear reiteration that *sometimes* it is. At a moment when feminism and identity politics of any kind are regarded warily—too incipiently essentialist for many within the academy, too alarmingly polemical for those outside it—*Madwoman*'s greatest value may just lie in its second-wave willingness to give *women*, with all their motley madnesses, priority.

Notes

1. Sandra M. Gilbert and Susan Gubar, *The Madwoman in the Attic: The Woman Writer and the Nineteenth-Century Literary Imagination* (New Haven: Yale University Press, 1979), xii. Subsequent references will be given parenthetically in the text.
2. D. A. Miller, *The Novel and the Police* (Berkeley: University of California Press, 1988), 146–91; Ann Cvetkovich, *Mixed Feelings: Feminism, Mass Culture, and Victorian Sensationalism* (New Brunswick, N.J.: Rutgers University Press, 1992).
3. Elaine Showalter, *A Literature of Their Own: British Women Novelists from Brontë to Lessing* (Princeton: Princeton University Press, 1977); Deborah E. McDowell, "New Directions for Black Feminist Criticism," *Black American Literature Forum* 14, no. 4 (1980): 153–59; Nancy K. Miller, "Emphasis Added: Plots and Plausibilities in Women's Fiction," *PMLA* 96, no. 1 (1981): 36–48.
4. Suvendrini Perera, *Reaches of Empire: The English Novel from Edgeworth to Dickens* (New York: Columbia University Press, 1991); Susan Meyer, *Imperialism at Home: Race and Victorian Women's Fiction* (Ithaca: Cornell University Press, 1996); Mary Poovey, *Uneven Developments: The Ideological Work of Gender in Mid-Victorian England* (Chicago: University of Chicago Press, 1988); Anne McClintock, *Imperial Leather: Race, Gender, and Sexuality in the Colonial Contest* (New York: Routledge, 1995).
5. On the madwoman as subaltern, see Gayatri Chakravorty Spivak, "Three Women's Texts and a Critique of Imperialism," *Critical Inquiry* 12, no. 1 (1985): 243–61; on the madwoman as domestic servant, see Susan Fraiman, *Unbecoming Women: British Women Writers and the Novel of Development* (New York: Columbia University Press, 1993), 88–120.
6. Claudia L. Johnson, *Jane Austen: Women, Politics, and the Novel* (Chicago: University of Chicago Press, 1988).

2

Modeling the *Madwoman*

Feminist Movements and the Academy

Marlene Tromp

The most significant collaborative books in my library are *The Madwoman in the Attic; Feminist Revolution,* an analysis of the methods and practices of second-wave feminism; and *Manifesta: Young Women, Feminism, and the Future,* an articulation of the significance and work of third-wave feminism.[1] While the coincidence of scholarly and feminist collaboration might not seem a particularly remarkable fact, it is striking given the role that these books have played in speaking to and stimulating the second and third waves of the feminist movement. In this essay, I want to explore the relationship between not just the *content* of Gilbert and Gubar's work, but their *practices* and *strategies,* which I will examine in their historical feminist context in the United States. I will argue that, in spite of the critiques launched against Gilbert and Gubar for what their book did not do, the work was revolutionary for the academy and beyond. Moreover, I will suggest that the utopian vision of feminist practice—clearly part of what prompted the book—mirrored and was mirrored by feminists working throughout the culture. This vision, as I see it, continues to be vital for women and academics and can inspire us to continue the work feminists before us have done.

To explore the central themes of this essay, I examine the academic and popular reception of Gilbert and Gubar's work as the dialogue appears in the 1970s and 1980s, when feminist literary criticism, and the place of Gilbert and Gubar's work in a new field, was being defined. Further, I situate

Madwoman in its context in the early feminist movement and the arguments being made about feminist activism and strategies. I especially attend to the evaluation of Gilbert and Gubar's practices and the feminist model provided by the book, a model that, I argue, reflected the feminist activism "in the streets" in the 1970s. I have culled this information from published scholarly reaction as well as the writings of feminist activists of the 1960s and 1970s.[2] To my knowledge, in spite of all that has been written on *Madwoman,* no one has yet ventured into the archives of feminist activism when studying this influential work. Additionally, in order to explore more reflective feminist evaluations of Gilbert and Gubar's project (as second and third "wavers" from the 1990s and 2000s have sought to position and understand the impact of *Madwoman*), I look to those assessments presented in both published arguments and responses when I contacted 400 academics from public and private institutions and in each state in the United States.[3] Finally, I ask what the practices of *Madwoman in the Attic* and Sandra Gilbert and Susan Gubar—their intellectual and professional courage, their sense of community, their commitment to their lives both inside and outside the academy—can teach us for the next phases of feminism.

Life Study

Gilbert and Gubar indicate in the preface to *Madwoman* that they "inevitably ended up reading our own lives as well as the texts we study" (*Madwoman,* xiii). Sandra Gilbert offered a term for this practice in an essay she published on feminist criticism in 1979: "For most scholars of literature by women . . . research into heretofore forgotten or rejected materials seems to have become a kind of re-search for their own lives—that is, a crucial species of Life Study, and thus an essential rereading of history in the interest of what Rich has called 'survival.'" The body of work of Gilbert and Gubar and *Madwoman* in particular call for a consciousness of the relationship between "Life Study" and activism on the streets. As Gilbert articulated it, "I believe that the work of feminist critics in academic departments is an essential component of work in the 'real' world, because English departments are workplaces and mind-shaping structures as powerful and 'real' as, for example, factories, farms, or prisons."[4] My essay is, in many ways, about "experience" and what it means—politically, socially, practically—to be a woman and a feminist in the United States, as well as the relationship of those social locations to the academy. For all of these reasons, I will open, as so many feminist arguments do, by indicating what experiences brought me to this project.

This article really began when I presented the proposal for my dissertation on marital violence in Victorian fiction and was discouraged by some members of my committee because I was "too close" to the material I wished to study. Because I was a feminist activist who had worked for six years in battered women's shelters, some felt that I could not offer an "objective" study. My dissertation director, Elizabeth Langland, did not discourage me; instead, she explained how Gilbert and Gubar had fought to have their voices heard in a climate that was not always welcoming of their ideas or that denigrated the activist element of their work. As I heard the story, Gilbert and Gubar prepared a stack of envelopes addressed to the best publishers; if they had an unfavorable review from one, they simply slid the manuscript into the next envelope and sent it off again. Although they had confidence in their work, they developed this system because they expected resistance to a critical feminist practice. I know now that the story is apocryphal—Gilbert and Gubar did not, in fact, have to circulate the manuscript but had quick success. Still, this narrative about feminist work in the academy was like a life raft to me. I can remember precisely where my director and I were standing on campus when she told me this story, the quality of the air, the sunlight, the time of day. It made an extraordinary impression because it was a professional and personal turning point in my life.[5]

I suddenly felt that I had a practical model for feminist survival in the academy. Within a year, I had successfully defended my dissertation on the topic I had proposed, and when the first article I sent out came back with a reader's report that praised the elegant writing, the thoughtful argument, the new insights, but indicated that the reader could not accept the feminist critique I was making of the novel, I pressed on. Remembering the spirit of that story about Gilbert and Gubar (and sharing it with others many times in my career) became a significant force in my intellectual and personal resolve. The article was ultimately published by a fine journal, and I am now a full professor and endowed chair, cracking away at my fifth and sixth books. Not only was the work of Gilbert and Gubar crucial in my success, but it has been clear to me for many years that I was not alone in gleaning inspiration from it to persevere in spite of ideological resistance. It was also evident, from the content of the book and their responses to the critiques of it, that providing this kind of inspiration was a part of Sandra Gilbert's and Susan Gubar's mission. One colleague who wrote in response to my query, Lucy Morrison (Salisbury College), noted that she not only found *Madwoman* "intensely liberating" but that when she encountered Gilbert and Gubar in person, "They were warm and collegial—and funny. . . . And they were so encouraging of us, urging us to pursue our particular interests and not to become discouraged if others turned away from our work or tried to invalidate us."[6]

The most striking aspect of this echo of my own experience is the fact that it is *still* happening; now *Madwoman* and Gilbert and Gubar are inspiring third-wave feminists, three decades after the publication of their first coauthored book. This gives us, perhaps, the most profound sense of the book's import. The content of *Madwoman* was radical, to be sure, but so were the feminist practices that it called for and nurtured. As I will argue, the personal and political aspects of their work—and feminists' work, more generally—are often profoundly related, and readings of Gilbert and Gubar's work were always political and structural as well as intellectual. These elements maintain the book's importance for feminist scholars today.

So why did *Madwoman in the Attic* make waves? Why was it such a revelation in 1979 when it appeared? There had, after all, been other book-length feminist studies—even ones that focused on women's literature (Elaine Showalter's *A Literature of Their Own*, Ellen Moers's *Literary Women*, and Nina Auerbach's *Communities of Women*, for example)—but no other was a finalist for the Pulitzer Prize in nonfiction and the National Book Critics Circle Award in Literature. Nor did *Madwoman*'s splash come from the fact that it introduced feminism to America—it was published nearly a decade after the New York Radical Feminists staged their high-profile protest at the Miss America pageant, and this was only one of many actions, slogans, and news events surrounding radical feminism in the 1960s and 1970s. Instead, the book was entering into, and became a significant part of, widespread feminist debate about practice and content in both the academy and in popular culture (though it was still possible, when *Madwoman* was published, to consider gender an insignificant element of reading). I would argue that part of what gave *Madwoman* its power was that Gilbert and Gubar, through both their content and their practices, elegantly embodied many of the central second-wave feminist concerns of the day, and became, in this way, a clarion call for the feminist revolution.

Radical Feminism

Madwoman was a radical act, one that spoke to people inside the academy and out. Perhaps one of the most important things *Madwoman* did was to acknowledge (and argue critically for) one of second-wave feminists' central theses: the personal is political. In their preface, Gilbert and Gubar express their gratitude to "Mrs. Virginia French for devoted childcare without which even the act of composition would have been impossible." They also "acknowledge what has been profoundly important to both of us: the revisionary advice and consent of our husbands, Elliot Gilbert and Edward Gubar, and our children, Roger, Kathy, and Susanna Gilbert, and Molly and Simone Gubar, all of whom, together, have given us lives that are a joy to read" (*Madwoman,* xiv). Even while *Madwoman* argues for the special challenges faced by women writers of the nineteenth century, Gilbert and Gubar identify the special challenges of twentieth-century women academics and the absolutely requisite support of family, spouses, and responsible child-care providers. Their argument identifies the challenges of women's personal lives as fit subjects for discussion in their work, and they spoke openly in interviews and articles about the compelling role of their family responsibilities in their professional lives. As Janet Gezari notes about the time of *Madwoman*'s publication, "a new interpretative community of readers, as well as a new community of writers, was coming into being [in 1979]. Women were establishing a considerably larger presence in the academy, and they were doing this without having to give up the prospect of children."[7]

To simply acknowledge these challenges, however, would not have been enough for *Madwoman* to merit the application of the feminist phrase "the personal is political." The work must also make the connection between person and politics in an overarching social analysis, and, indeed, *Madwoman* pointed to the way that these early writers were compelled to resist literary and cultural history and their own oppressive cultural context: "What [the woman writer of the nineteenth century] suggests is that in patriarchal culture, female speech and female 'presumption'—that is, angry revolt against male domination—are inextricably linked" (*Madwoman,* 35). To write, then, against the expectation and models for women, whether in 1879 or 1979, was an act of literary and cultural resistance to patriarchy. In *Madwoman,* Gilbert and Gubar rejected New Critical analysis that had held sway for so long in the academy and that focused on the text in isolation from social, political, and personal context. Instead, Gilbert and Gubar sought to understand how particular women were struggling to find a voice in spite of patriarchy. Their turn to psychoanalytically influenced analysis of individuals within a larger social context allowed them to ask questions about particular women's experiences and then to bring those examples together to ask what they suggested about women's lives in patriarchy.

The themes in this project were strikingly similar in content and practice to the work of the New York Radical Women, Redstockings, and Women's Liberation Front—all radical feminist organizations. The Redstockings' Carol Hanisch first argued in the 1960s and 1970s that "the personal is political," by which she did not mean that individual acts were the best way to effect political change but rather that we can often trace the disabling patterns we experience in our personal lives to larger political and social causes, particularly when we can match those patterns to many women's lives. These second-wave feminists believed that through consciousness-raising, which focused on surfacing concerns and identifying patterns of oppression that appeared in many individual women's lives (through "bitch sessions" and with the skills of a trained organizer), they would have the power to develop political goals and strategies for action. In this way, they felt many political ills could be remedied.[8] The women of Redstockings were determined to bring their ideas to fruition in a mass movement, and thus was born *Feminist Revolution,* a book detailing the history, theory, and practice of radical feminist activism. After a five-thousand-copy private print run in 1975 that left an extraordinary demand for the book, Random House made a bid to pick it up as a mass-market paperback. The authors of *Feminist Revolution* welcomed the opportunity to "burst through the dogma surrounding the question of women [and] assert our commitment to . . . the liberation of women" by detailing those practices that defined the movement (*Revolution,* 10-11). *Feminist Revolution* hit the popular press in 1978, just as Gilbert and Gubar were enacting in *Madwoman* many of the very practices Redstockings described—for nineteenth-century women and, implicitly, for women in their own moment.

Simply to say that *Madwoman* was revolutionary, however, does not capture the energy of the book's impact on women. The relationship between the personal and political elements of their argument—the kind of connection for which radical feminist organizations were striving—was amply apparent to *Madwoman*'s readers. Karen Waters (Marymount University) writes:

> I became acquainted with *Madwoman* when I went back to school to get my Ph.D. I was juggling a family, a job, my classes, and a sick father, and wondering if putting myself through the agony of keeping all the balls in the air was going to be worth it. Then I took a course in feminist literary theory and found *Madwoman.* I read it from cover to cover (I still have my underlined, dogeared copy that I treasure), and I decided that if this was the future of scholarship on women writers, then I wanted to be a part of it! The innovation and thoroughness of Gilbert and Gubar's scholarship was, to me, astounding and ground-breaking; I had never encountered anything like it. The text helped generate in me a new-found excitement for literature that carried me through my program, sustained me as a junior faculty member, and still exists today. Whenever I want to refer to sound scholarship on nineteenth-century women writers, this is still the text that I go to, and that I send my students to as well.

Emily Orlando (Fairfield University) says, "It's hard to imagine a book that's more profoundly influenced readers of women's literature—such clarity and continuity and one of the most memorable opening lines in all literary scholarship. Gilbert and Gubar's book [was] wholly transformative."[9]

Understanding the book's impact means, in part, understanding the academic climate it entered. While new feminist scholarship was already beginning to make its mark on the academy, Carol Martin (Boise State University) recalls that *Madwoman* "provided new ways of looking at literature at a time when women scholars needed sisterly support. While the academic climate at my institution was generally positive for women, it was still possible for a colleague to ask, with very little irony, in referring to my new special topics course on Women Writers: 'When are we going to get a course on "Male Writers"?' . . . Gilbert and Gubar gave us both intellectual support and a sense of being part of a community of women scholars who were challenging and changing the curriculum and the scholarly conversation." Gezari notes, "When they came together to teach and write, Gilbert and Gubar formed the core of a support group which would include other feminist critics similarly committed."[10]

Gilbert and Gubar were often *the* feminist scholarship to which the new generation of graduate students was being introduced. As Marion Rust (University of Kentucky) remembers, Gilbert and Gubar were "virtually the only feminist critics I was introduced to at Harvard." After reading them, Rust notes, she had the very sort of experience that Kathie Sarachild describes as one of the central goals of the women's liberation movement: "I began to realize that most of what I read not only neglected my experiences as a woman but actually denied my personhood in the very methods of its address, whether by ridiculing persons in my condition or implicitly conveying the assumption that such creatures were unfit to comprehend the pages before them." Not everyone who read *Madwoman,* of course, agreed with the argument, but it often still produced inspiration. Margaret Dean (Eastern Kentucky University) recalls that while the book had a "major impact" on her work, it was largely due to her desire to critique and revise its arguments about Milton. Her first publication responded to the stir created in her field of study by Gilbert and Gubar's book. For Redstockings, grappling with a new understanding would ideally encourage conversation and debate, but would also "prompt people to organize and to act on a mass scale."[11] Cloistered, individual responses couldn't shape a movement.

The response to *Madwoman,* however, was itself a movement. Encountering *Madwoman* was both a personal and a political experience for many academic women who were beginning to act on a mass scale to change the academy: women who were attending graduate programs in much greater numbers but who were still being primarily taught by men,[12] women who were still facing a wage gap of almost 50 percent in spite of the passage of the Equal Pay Act nearly ten years prior, women who were responsible for caring for their children, regardless of their employment status outside the home. *Madwoman*'s attention to the relationship between the personal and political drew the attention of women outside the academy, as well. Because it offered a means of understanding the resistance to women's voices as well as the possibility of looking to one another for models that could inspire a response, the book sold tens of thousands of copies and was not only reviewed in the *New York Times* but was named by the paper as recommended summer reading in the year following its publication. Gilbert and Gubar managed to break through to both academics and the cultural mainstream. The first *New York Times* review, while making some criticisms of *Madwoman*'s reach, noted that it was a "bold new interpretation" and suggested that a reader would be "tempted to become a critical collaborator by going back to the texts themselves in search of further evidence"—the very invitation most feminists hope to generate.[13]

Ellen Bayuk Rosenman (University of Kentucky) notes an experience with the text similar to that of the *Times* reviewer. "What I felt most was a tremendous gulf between my profession and my personal and political commitments, in which feminism played a major role. . . . Feminist criticism was the cure. . . . Published by Yale, thick as a doorstop, with 797 footnotes (I counted) and an index as long as a small-town phonebook, [*Madwoman*] had an intellectual as well as physical heft that went a long way toward establishing feminist criticism as a respectable field." In response to reading the book and engaging its lessons, Rosenman "dumped Shakespeare [her original dissertation topic] to consort with Virginia Woolf—probably the scariest and smartest thing I've ever done. . . . We all became feminist critics—an identity that was not only a theoretical orientation or a set of critical assumptions but a psychological affirmation. It is easy to forget that it had not existed a few years before."[14]

Rosenman opens her comments with the remark, "It might be an exaggeration to say that *The Madwoman in the Attic* changed my professional life. Then again, it might not." For many people, *Madwoman* modeled not only professional courage but also personal courage and a desire for large-scale social change. Gilbert and Gubar and the feminists who were inspired by their book were practicing what Redstockings preached (and what the feminists in radical feminist groups all across the country were doing). *Madwoman* not only linked the personal and the political for the authors the book examined but for women themselves—in and outside the academy. In her "Foreword" to *Making Feminist History*, a study of Gilbert and Gubar's impact on the academy, Carolyn Heilbrun underscored this seminal critical theme in their work: "Perhaps the greatest danger to feminism in the academy today is its failure to reach outside academic walls. . . . Gilbert and Gubar can be read by anyone who reads attentively; they speak outside as well as within their literary stronghold."[15] *Madwoman* challenged readers to see nineteenth-century women positioned within a particular social and political context, a context that affected them personally and psychologically, but it also challenged readers to see themselves as sisters of these nineteenth-century women, to identify with them in consciousness-raising and with one another.

The Pro-Woman Line

In order to analyze the experiences of women, Gilbert and Gubar, like other critics before them, focused on the works and experiences of women. While this may not seem a radical strategy today, focusing on women—and not simply to pathologize them—was still a new phenomenon. This meant recognizing that women were "messed over, not messed up" by patriarchy. It sought to condemn the oppressiveness of social structures rather than the women themselves. Moreover, the pro-woman line, as articulated by early feminists, "took the focus off individual struggle and put it on group or class struggle."[16] *Madwoman* sought to discover the conditions of patriarchy and its impact on women and to uncover a female poetics, one that considered women and women writers as a class. "Separate to Integrate" by Barbara Leon and "Consciousness Raising: A Radical Weapon" by Kathie Sarachild argued that women must be able to study women and to do so apart from men because of the "political conflict of interest with men at that point in social and political history."[17] Like Elaine Showalter, these feminists believed that such separatist groups ideally existed "for the purpose of making themselves unnecessary," by learning what they needed to learn about women and activist responses during periods of oppression and then integrating with equality when that oppression was eliminated.[18] Sarachild predicted that women who organized in such a way would face personal attacks and a minimizing of the value of exploring women's issues—all ways of "keep[ing] the issues and ideas we were discussing out of the realm of subjects of genuine study and debate." Moreover, "when we said that men oppressed women, or that all men were among the beneficiaries in the oppression of women, [people would respond] 'Men are oppressed too!'"[19] Indeed, this characterized many of the criticisms of Gilbert and Gubar's work when it was first published.

In the academy as in the culture at large, a separate focus on women met with some resistance. William E. Cain, reflecting on their scholarly reception, notes that Gilbert and Gubar received the treatment Sarachild described: they "have been roughly indicted in tones of voice that are seldom employed for male scholars of comparable importance." Critics complained, for example, that *Madwoman* "documents *ad nauseum* male fear and resentment"; another called their work "bogus," and a third dismissed it as "twaddle."[20] While every work of literary analysis is subject to criticism, the tone of these remarks is striking. Dean Flower grumbled in the *Hudson Review* that Gilbert and Gubar's "effort to construe [the] experiences [of women authors] as 'uniquely female' meets insuperable difficulties," describing some of their arguments as "patently desperate." His argument came complete with a list of men whose suffering matched that of the women Gilbert and Gubar described ("Men are oppressed too!"). In a letter to the *New York Times,* responding to a review of *Madwoman* and the thesis that women had an "anxiety of authorship," Zelda Austen jibed, "So what else is new? The same is true of almost every English-speaking male writer of the period as well."[21] Gilbert and Gubar's book set out to demonstrate that while men experienced "anxiety of influence" (as described by Harold Bloom), what women experienced was a more damaging fear, structured by sexist oppression culturally, personally, and developmentally (*Madwoman,* 48-49).

As late as the 1990s, in a study of feminist criticism—a book in which Gilbert and Gubar's work takes a significant place—the authors argue that "unsympathetic academics continue to characterize feminist criticism as discontented women carping about the negative representations of themselves that they face when reading texts." They also note the "unreservedly *political* purpose of all feminist writing." Indeed, in 2007, *Modern Age* (a publication dedicated to conservative ideas) published an essay that lamented, "What began as a tiny movement in the 1970s has become a grave danger to the young, especially to young women. And since college students are the leaders of the future, what is at stake now is the very foundation of Western society and civilization." "Ideological feminism," the author warns, "is not a harmless eccentricity, but wields great power in the universities of the West."[22]

Annette Kolodny, in a discussion of feminist literary criticism in the wake of *Madwoman* (in 1980), argued that objections to feminist work like those I have described to Gilbert and Gubar were usually structured to obscure the underlying sexism of the one objecting. Moreover, women's "reticence at taking full responsibility for" the central goal of feminist work (what Kolodny described as "an overriding commitment to a radical alteration—and improvement, we hope—in the nature of [women's] experience") plays a role in the ongoing resistance to feminism. Elaine Showalter agreed with this point. Though calling feminist criticism "extraordinarily influential and effective" in the academy, she asked if the "feminist enterprise . . . still frightens us by its audacity."[23] While it is not difficult to imagine why women who were just breaking into the profession and were mostly confined to the ranks of junior faculty might be frightened about triggering a backlash in their field or among their peers, Gilbert and Gubar clearly did not express the reticence Kolodny describes.

With their provocative opening question, "Is a pen a metaphorical penis?" and their insistence on the repressive quality of the cultural myths generated by sexism, Gilbert and Gubar tackled directly the burden of patriarchy for women as a class—the kind of articulation and action for which feminists in the women's liberation movement were calling. This argument resonated powerfully for women academics and writers. As Olga Abella (Eastern Illinois University) put it, with *Madwoman* she began to see "how much of me was male identified and how much of me was usurped by patriarchy. It was amazing how much I began to grow emotionally and intellectually after that discovery. . . . Their arguments almost felt forbidden, like rhetoric from an underground revolutionary network."[24] Abella's language here is astute: Gilbert and Gubar's rhetoric certainly echoed that of the underground revolutionary networks. Many of the ideas emerging in New York Radical Women, Redstockings, the Women's Liberation Front, and others in the women's liberation movement percolated in *Madwoman in the Attic.*

This is not to say that there were not academic feminist positions other than the one Gilbert and Gubar took up. In fact, there was a lively debate going on in the field, and the publication of *Madwoman* turned up the torque on that debate. Feminist critics clashed over the best strategies for intervention in the academy. These debates often circulated around different readings of the character of patriarchy, the dangers or uses of essentialism, and the qualities of an effective feminism, and, of course, such disputes affected the reception of *Madwoman.* Nina Auerbach, while offering earnest praise for the project, was wary of granting "patriarchal structures . . . a power they do not seem to have earned." Nina Baym made a sweeping condemnation of *Madwoman* and charged it with essentialism, a position shared by Frank Lentricchia. Mary Jacobus, while noting the book's strengths, made a similar criticism, arguing that the authors came "dangerously close to suggesting a schematized and essentialist view of the relations between women and writing."[25]

Myra Jehlen and Rachel Blau DuPlessis's review of *Madwoman* praised the project for demonstrating "the way women's writing is generated as a reaction to patriarchal culture[, a] contribution . . . to which all future feminist criticism will be indebted," but critiqued what they saw as a failure to take history and historical specificity into account in their argument—the creation of what amounted to, in their analysis, a "universal woman." In a single-authored argument that appeared a few months later in *Signs,* Jehlen suggested that such a focus on women as a separate group, rather than in comparison to men, would reduce the "feminist impact on the universe of male discourse." This essay, like *Madwoman,* brought a storm of retorts—

sixteen full pages of essay-like "letters" in *Signs*—that argued for the efficacy of speaking from a "strong sense of solidarity with women writers, with their lives, their works, their presence," as well as for reformulations of her call for comparative work. Toril Moi, in *Sexual/Textual Politics,* summed up the tenor of these feminist debates from the mid-1970s to the early 1980s by placing *Madwoman* at center stage and offering an extended argument against Gilbert and Gubar's desire to "write the narrative of a mighty 'Ur-woman'" that speaks for women too broadly. She condemned this figure for embodying "precisely what the ventriloquism of patriarchy has always done."[26]

Gilbert and Gubar have responded to these critiques across the decades, both in their scholarship and in direct responses to their critics. Their rejoinder to Moi's and others' critiques regarding essentialism is perhaps most succinctly laid out in an interview with Sandra Gilbert in 2002. Marysa Demoor and Katrien Heene suggest that Gilbert and Gubar "seem to opt (with Gayatri Spivak) for a 'strategic essentialism'—a provisional assumption that there are men, women and meanings in history" in response "to the criticism leveled at [Gilbert and Gubar's] writings by those postmodernist theorists who posit a 'polyvocality' inevitably leading to the disappearance of woman in a phallocentric discourse."[27] Radical feminist organizers had to respond to a similar charge of ignoring the differences between women, particularly with regard to race, class, and sexuality—a charge from which the feminist movement surely grew—but Sarachild still argued that without the ability to make generalizations based on the personal experience of women and the lessons of history, activists could not generate an effective means of resisting oppressive structures. They would be limited, she argued, to changing the situations of particular individuals only (if even that was possible). Elsewhere she said, all "exploited [people of every group] must unite in order to break out of prisons [built by privilege]."[28] One might articulate this position in both Gilbert and Gubar's work and in Redstockings as one of the central aims of feminism: a call for community.

Sisterhood Is Powerful

The early second-wave feminists complained that the phrase "sisterhood is powerful" was often deeply misunderstood and misrepresented in the media. It did not mean erasing difference or disagreement. Indeed difference and disagreement were vital to building stronger feminist arguments according to the Redstockings. What it meant to those feminists was what was expressed in "the opening words to the Helen Reddy song, 'I Am Woman,' ('I am woman, hear me roar in numbers too big to ignore')."[29] They reasoned that if women could form community, cross the boundaries that separated them, and collaborate, they could change the world.

Gilbert and Gubar consistently expressed a longing for community—thematically in *Madwoman* but also from women scholars generally and for the benefit of women. They sought to achieve this at the most fundamental textual level of their work. In one early review, Suzanne Juhasz indicated that "feminist literary critics have been at work for the past decade on various aspects of Gilbert and Gubar's materials, [and that] the authors are the first to acknowledge in their generous notes and references." This effort to honor the feminist community and previous work was deeply valued by radical feminists, who argued that "not realizing you need those who go before you in order to do something new yourself" was a move that made "coordination and unity [and, thus, a meaningful women's movement] impossible."[30] It continues to be deeply important to third-wave feminists today. As Baumgardner and Richards put it, we must "tap into and raise awareness of our revolutionary history . . . to have access to our intellectual feminist legacy and women's history" (*Manifesta,* 279). Many literary critics, particularly women of color, had argued that a failure to acknowledge the work of other feminists harmed both the women themselves and the richness of feminist ideas. Farah Jasmine Griffin, for example, argued that, while studying black women's writing was becoming more popular, the "black women scholars who [had] pioneered [that work] were becoming less and less visible—not only as members of university faculties but also in the footnotes of a voluminous scholarship devoted to black women's writing." Echoing an analysis William Cain made of Gilbert and Gubar's critics, Griffin added that "it is quite likely that the . . . critique of essentialism was made possible by the very terms and successes of black feminist literary critics who were among the first to call attention to the constructed nature of racial and gender identity."[31]

Carolyn Heilbrun underscored this problem, expressing the "tendency of [some] women, in a movement of our own, to seek to destroy others in the name of some kind of purity of motive," but she set the authors of *Madwoman* apart: "Gilbert and Gubar have never done that, and their reach outward to other critics has been both wide and generous." In speaking of Nina Auerbach and Gilbert and Gubar, Jane Marcus argued in 1988, "feminist critics have built a community in the margins and together have pushed back the borders of the academy" and provided context for so much work that came later. Marcus shared the view of some radical feminists that critique, while painful, could bring growth in the movement. "I am sure that Sandra Gilbert and Susan Gubar would be the first to insist that . . . sisterly criticism of their work be offered, for they continue to write, to grow, and to change. If feminist criticism has taught us anything, it has taught us to question authority, each other's as well as our oppressors." As Hanisch argued for the Redstockings, "The only way that we are ever going to achieve real sisterhood so that we *can* roar in numbers too big to ignore is to challenge other women's ideas by putting forth our own and pointing out where we think others are wrong and having them point out where we are wrong politically. . . . It's not easy and it's not pleasant, but it is necessary."[32] Similarly, Baumgardner and Richards argue in *Manifesta* that "autokeonony" (a term they draw from Sarah Lucia Hoagland's work), or "self in community," must be on the "Third Wave's agenda." As they explain it, "We have to make it clear to our mothers, our foremothers, and ourselves that our actions are not a rebellion but a necessity of speaking our truths; they are not *against,* but *for*" (*Manifesta,* 219).

In his study of Gilbert and Gubar's work, William Cain argued, "It is not too melodramatic to say that Gilbert and Gubar fell prey to the rich range of women's voices they did so much to liberate. By authenticating feminist theory and criticism as an academic enterprise, as a serious and theoretically complex endeavor, they empowered many of their own staunchest critics. Gilbert and Gubar created a space for theory in feminism that rival theories . . . confidently entered." Indeed, Susan Gubar expressed concern in her 1998 piece, "What Ails Feminist Criticism?" that some critics have "framed their arguments in such a way as to divide feminists, casting suspicion upon a common undertaking that remains in dispute at the turn of the twentieth century" and worried that there was "an atmosphere of censorship that silences or polices our feminist debates." I would argue that conditions in the academy that compel the continued work of feminists do more to create this situation for both women and men than feminist critics themselves. In 1994, Gilbert and Gubar offered the more sanguine assessment that opposed feminist positions "need [not] annihilate [each] other," but can participate in a "shared revisionary project." In her 2006 introduction to the *Cambridge Companion to Feminist Literary Theory,* Ellen Rooney agreed and took up Gilbert and Gubar's concerns about feminist infighting. She argued that fragmentation, rather than undermining feminism, led to a "dissemination of feminism," "a diaspora of feminist discourses," because "when feminism divides, it multiplies."[33]

Still, concerns about the possibility of a unified feminist movement in spite of differences between women and an out-and-out resistance to feminism remains. A recent article in *Bitch* magazine, a third-wave periodical, expresses concern about the fact that "you'd be hard-pressed to find much sisterhood in the pages of the Grey Lady [*New York Times*]" when it comes to reviews of feminist works. The author protests that newspapers hire women who describe themselves as "postfeminists" to write reviews of such books and that, in general, "books that take women's issues in hand are rarely taken seriously. It's not just that they are criticized, which they are, but rather that the books, their authors—and heck, the whole feminist movement—are routinely treated with a mixture of giggly naïveté and barbed antifeminist prejudices," examples of which she offers in some detail.[34]

In spite of these ongoing internecine tensions and external obstacles, Gilbert and Gubar always sought to support interconnectedness, to underscore the value of relationships in their work at many levels. Their scholarship echoed the concerns of Nancy Chodorow, who argued that an understanding of gender depended upon understanding the relationships between individuals and groups of people. It also echoed the work of feminists who saw danger in isolating individual women rather than seeing them in relation to others—both in terms of their oppression and in terms of activism. In *Madwoman,* the fates of individual authors (including their own) are always linked to the relationships they have with one another and with their culture; indeed, the word "relationship" appears more than once in every ten pages of *Madwoman.* Annette Kolodny saw this impulse in Gilbert and Gubar's work and described it as a "complex relational quality" that they had retained from Bloom's work as they revised it.[35] Fostering relationships was clearly a practice to which they were committed practically, and not just in theory. Gwen Curry (Georgetown College) speaks to the value of her relationship with the authors. Curry writes that she chose to study at Indiana University because of Gubar and notes that "the contrast between the cooperative (rather than competitive) attitudes of Susan and [Sandra and their] female colleagues who taught collaboratively, compared to the good old boys" who intimidated her and undermined her sense of herself "gave me lasting confidence." "I think I owe my success in my career to Susan," she said.[36]

Perhaps one of the most moving things I read during my interviews was a description of the experience of working with Gubar when she was pregnant. Whereas most female academics have described a sense of having to conceal or at least downplay pregnancy and motherhood during the 1980s lest it undermine their "professionalism," Gilbert and Gubar celebrated such human relationships in the academy as well as in their work. Curry explains that when she arrived at graduate school, Gubar "was eight and a half months pregnant with Simone. (We were reading Simone de Beauvoir in [Gubar's] class when the baby arrived.) Our class of 30 toasted Simone with one shared bottle of wine poured out into tiny little toothbrushing paper cups. Susan was writing *Madwoman* during that time and so all the classes I took with her incorporated her ideas for the book in some manner. She autographed my copy of her book at my defense: 'From one madwoman to another.'"[37] While the gulf between women, because of their differences, may be difficult to cross practically and theoretically, Gilbert and Gubar clearly set out to do this work, and it was a commitment shared by activists, who sought to connect with international organizers and those who engaged in other activist groups, like black feminists; this kind of work required bold (and sometimes uncomfortable) boundary crossing.

Crossing Boundaries

Achieving the broad-ranging sisterhood Gilbert and Gubar sought required transgressing many time-honored boundaries. To make an argument that spoke to the anxiety of authorship for women *generally,* they had to cover vast ground. Responding to Harold Bloom's thesis about literary patricide required that their project lay out an equally sweeping discussion. For this reason, Gilbert and Gubar's analysis of women crossed literary periods—from the Romantics to the Victorians to the moderns. It crossed both the ocean and departmental hiring territories, exploring American and British literature alike. "Instead of situating a woman writer in her period, they argued for a distinct women's literary tradition," and in this way their argument "[took] on the century," Juhasz explained in an early review. While Kolodny faulted "the book's . . . sometimes indiscriminate yoking together of American and British materials," she called it "an indispensable addition to every Americanist's bookshelf." Even their harshest critics noted that this practice achieved a "remarkable and valuable examination of the significance and modulations of gender as an ideological determination of women's writing" and noted that they "brilliantly uncover[ed] the modern feminist meaning of women's writing."[38]

Another professional boundary they crossed was that between scholarship and pedagogy. While interest in the classroom and classroom practices has often been perceived as a de-professionalizing move for academics, Gilbert and Gubar acknowledged the intimate link between teaching and scholarship that had, indeed, helped produce the book; they noted in their preface, "This book began with a course in literature by women we taught together at Indiana University in the fall of 1974" (*Madwoman,* xi). Other feminist critics, too, when reviewing developments in the burgeoning field of feminist studies in 1976 were asking, "What do we put at 'center stage' . . . for our students?" Scholars I interviewed noted the way *Madwoman* helped speak to the gulf between scholarship and the classroom and served as an antidote for the painful experience of being "adrift in composition administration, for which [she] had absolutely no training since elite doctoral institutions cultivated a patrician disregard for the realities of the employment scene" and the pragmatics of teaching. Moreover, the new critical models offered in *Madwoman* made fresh the experience of teaching classical (and newly valued) texts. As David Collings (Bowdoin College) noted, "The resulting explosion of feminist scholarship on [*Frankenstein*] helped transform the book into a key text for feminist teachers of romanticism, and certainly influenced my teaching. . . . I also found their discussions of the monster in the mirror . . . very instructive and have built on that notion, and complicated it in much of my teaching and research." Several colleagues, among them David Miller (Mississippi College), noted that they were first introduced to the book by a feminist professor and that they have, over the years, found themselves "back in the attic" again and again. Ken Egan (Drury University) remarked, "My teaching also became so much richer because these scholars/theorists showed me how archetypal images of women in classic literary texts could both affirm and subvert popular images captured in fairytales and films. Second, my students tell me they find *Madwoman* readable, accessible, useful (a welcome departure from theorists such as Cixous and Derrida!). . . . for teaching purposes, *Madwoman* remains vital and useful." Some explained that teaching actually became the pivot in relating to *Madwoman:* "It wasn't until I started teaching Milton that the seed planted by Gilbert and Gubar started to sprout in me, when I was far away from the male professors who had turned Milton into someone who inspired awe in me." One colleague noted that she tried to "pay it forward" by "follow[ing] Susan's example of helping and encouraging young women I have taught."[39]

The crossing of boundaries, of course, was often met with resistance (and dismissal), but a resistance that could be overcome and could form the basis for professional success. As Elizabeth Winston (University of Tampa) noted, "When I mentioned my excitement about the book—especially its metaphorical style—to a senior professor of literature, he said, 'That's not literary criticism. That's only wordplay.' But his dismissal didn't stop the stream of ideas flowing from Gilbert and Gubar's text. *Madwoman* gave me the confidence to try my own hand at crossing genres." In her own writing project, she "combined conceptual analysis with a fictional narrative about creative inspiration that featured an autobiographical subtext. Without Gilbert and Gubar's exemplary scholarship, I wouldn't have thought to explain [another author's] notion of dialectic through a scene in a Giant Supermarket checkout line, where a woman 'buys' ideas from Dickinson and Dewey, Blake and I. A. Richards. The piece, 'Food for Thought: A Parable for Writers,' was published in 1984 in *English Journal*."[40] Winston's narrative points to a multiplicity of ways in which the transgression of boundaries (professionally, intellectually, generically) can have a synergistic power and can generate other transgressions that apply pressure to the edges of the profession, our intellectual practice, and the way we understand our fields.

Early radical feminists advocated crossing boundaries in their theorizing and practice between the workplace and home, between the internal politics of male-female relationships (like sex and housework) to the public arena, and between groups of women with different concerns, because they believed in attending to concerns that had been "dismissed as 'petty.'" "Whole areas of women's lives were declared off-limits" even though they "were the key areas in terms of how women are oppressed as a particular group."[41] Third-wave feminists, too, recognize the vital nature of such work, arguing that we must value "(monetarily) stay-at-home parents, aiding employees who want to spend more time with family and continue to work, equalizing pay for jobs of comparable worth, enacting a minimum wage that would bring a full-time worker with two children over the poverty line, and providing employee benefits for freelance and part-time workers" (*Manifesta,* 280). Turning to the connection between work and the home and between theory and practice made an innovative assessment of oppression and avenues for liberation possible—in reading, writing, and activism.

Collaboration

Gilbert and Gubar also violated the virtual demand for single-authored manuscripts in the humanities. While the call for collective action and collaborative history writing permeated the women's liberation movement, tenure requirements often pressured women to work independently. To this day, feminists are discouraged from collaborative scholarship (in the name of their careers), but they continue to engage in such work nonetheless. In the introduction to *Manifesta,* Jennifer Baumgardner, one of the coauthors, notes that a friend of hers remarked when she and Amy Richards got their book contract, "Important books aren't co-written, you know." Still, Baumgardner challenges women to write books "with a friend whose brain and politics [you] admire . . . as an act of sisterhood with a girl (or a boy) who's fierce like you, but in different ways" (*Manifesta,* xxi). Mills, Pearce, Spaull, and Millard, feminist critics who chose to collaborate in Gilbert and Gubar's wake, noted that "collective work is more time-consuming and more difficult than individualistic writing, [but] it has been a valuable experience for us all, and, for us, is an important part of feminist practice. Our discussions and criticism have been enabling rather than competitive, and in this way we have differed radically from the conventional receptions of texts . . . essentially negative academic notions of research, criticism and publication."[42] Gilbert and Gubar themselves later noted that "much of the exhilaration of writing [came] from working together. . . . We have continually exchanged and discussed our drafts . . . so that we feel our book represents not just a dialogue but a consensus" (*Madwoman,* xiii).

In the early reception of Gilbert and Gubar's work, Kolodny made note of this feature of the project more than once. "Every page," one essay noted, "attest[ed] to the 'exhilaration' of a successful collaboration," and it is perhaps no coincidence that she went on to say that the work was "essential for anyone wanting to grasp the key questions motivating feminist literary criticism." Later, as Heller and Gezari note, Gilbert and Gubar delivered their remarks at a Victorian studies conference at the University of California–Santa Cruz and an MLA session "as a dialogue, which is [also] how they frame the introduction to the anniversary edition of *Madwoman*." Gezari remarks, "I had never before seen, and haven't seen since, a performance like it: each of them read parts of the paper, not one after the other, but in successive, mutually enabling exchanges." One review joined their names with a slash and said, "Gilbert/Gubar (who for the purpose of this review exist as one corporate giant form) . . . is a sibylline persona." It is no wonder that Scott Heller, in his meditation twenty years after the publication of *Madwoman* noted that "Gilbert-and-Gubar, pronounced as if one word, became shorthand for one kind of feminist scholarship." As David Collings notes, "For me their collaboration was important . . . for the image it provided of the emergence of a new feminist community of critics." *Madwoman* became for many, in its content and practices, "an important feminist document in its own right. Indeed," as Margaret Stetz (University of Delaware) writes, "I found myself returning to it again and again." I was struck by the number of colleagues who indicated in my interviews that they, like myself, "still [had their] original paperback copy."[43]

"The Power of History," the Future of Feminism, and the *Madwoman*

There is no question that now and then, feminist work in the academy has made an impact. In spite of what she saw as indiscriminate identification of doubles and too broad an application of their thesis, Helene Moglen argued in her review of *Madwoman* that Gilbert and Gubar "ushered feminist criticism into a new age of maturity. For that most readers will know enough to be supremely grateful." In spite of the fact that Bloom himself "suffer[ed from] an inability to express useful judgment upon . . . the 'literature of Women's Liberation,'" we can discern the progressive effect of feminist criticism on the scholarly community and even on powerful, mainstream, white male critics.

Elizabeth Langland has elegantly charted such a feminist bildungsroman in her discussion of Wayne Booth. She noted that, while certainly not a feminist before the advent of books like *Madwoman,* Booth acknowledged the "sudden, transformative impact of feminist criticism on his own beliefs and critical practices": through feminism, he "changed his orientation to the text through the world and to the world through the text." Indeed, it would have been hard to avoid or ignore feminist criticism in the 1970s and 1980s. The number of essays with "feminist literary criticism" in the title during that period are dizzying, some worrying that feminist literary criticism did not have a "unified" set of goals or bear the mark of a "coherent" school of thought, and others arguing that such divergence might be "the only critical stance consistent with the current status of the larger women's movement," identifying it as a "playful pluralism."[44]

There continues to be debate about how to "do" feminism. *Manifesta* argues that, for third wavers, feminism is "like fluoride. We scarcely notice that we have it—it's simply in the water" (*Manifesta,* 17). Yet there is little political action to organize them. And there are still worries about feminism's central goals and practices. Martha Nussbaum, for example, advocates identifying a universal set of capabilities so that feminists who have social power, including those in capitalist, white-dominant nations, can exercise their power globally to demand conditions that give women access to those capabilities, while Chandra Talpade Mohanty argue that positions like Nussbaum's are another form of western imperialism; she advocates for feminist solidarity that attends to social location.[45] While these disagreements are significant, feminism has not lost its driving force, its mission. Echoing Hanisch's words on mutual critique, Mills, Pearce, Spaull, and Millard describe the range of feminist critical reading practices available to the critical community as "flexible positions" that can be engaged and practiced "as they stand, or revised, adapted or combined with others." Sarachild would have agreed because "new knowledge is the source of consciousness-raising's strength and power. Methods are simply to serve this purpose, to be changed if they aren't working." This is not a sign of the movement's failure. Nancy LaGreca concurs, noting in her discussion of feminist studies of Latin American women writers' work that current theory does not always address the crucial issues, particularly as far as race, ethnicity, and global issues are concerned (a concern raised about *Madwoman*), but "the critical act of *showing how existing theory falls short* allows feminist literary theory to remain inclusive and continue to make positive change." Susan Gubar noted recently in a *PMLA* special issue considering feminism in the academy, "the great divide between the success of feminist criticism inside the academy and the backlash against feminism at large remains striking and disturbing," adding, "Feminist critics today realize that we have never been cocooned within institutions of learning, that our job is not yet done, and that we must continue to use our interpretive skills to turn inside out the signs of our times."[46]

For me, as a feminist critic, this charge is a call to remember the significance of *Madwoman* and the historical context in which it emerged and with which it engaged, so it can still speak to us today. As Sarachild argues in "The Power of History" and Connie Brown and Jane Seitz claim in "You've Come a Long Way, Baby" in *Sisterhood Is Powerful,* knowing our history is crucial to "the strength and power of the movement and the durability of the movement's gains." Going back to "the roots, going back into history . . . [is] really about moving forward. It's about creating the new, not opposing it. It's about building on the shoulders" of what's been done and written already. Jane Elliott agrees in a recent article for *PMLA* on feminist theory, cautioning that "we tend to assume that theory that is no longer novel is no longer useful—that what is uninteresting is also unimportant."[47] While I would quibble with Elliott's use of "interesting," suggesting that it no longer excites us only because it is fully integrated into our practice, I think that her point about the value of looking back to our critical history and using the strategies we learned in those early decades is still apt.

Speaking particularly about *Madwoman,* Rosenman agrees: "While the label 'second wave' and our contemporary emphasis on gender rather than women might seem to relegate *Madwoman* to a position of purely historical interest—'this is how they did it in the old days'—it set ideas in motion that resonate today. . . . Above all, we assume the salience of 'difference' as an analytical category. . . . *Madwoman* set the feminist agenda for the rest of my career, but even more important than its argument was the way it freed and forced me to assess the value of my scholarship: does it really matter to me?" Modeling the *Madwoman* does not mean remaining in old practices or repeating choices that we don't think will push our understanding any farther. There is still a wage gap, women are still largely responsible for child care, even when they're full professors, and we understand in whole new ways today how race, ethnicity, sexuality, class, ableness, health, and global position figure women. While we must incorporate the insights of a whole new range of fields, we must also recognize that we still have a deep need for feminism and for the *Madwoman.* Redstockings defined its principles as follows: "We ask not if something is 'reformist,' 'radical,' 'revolutionary,' or 'moral.' We ask: is it good for women or bad for women. . . . We define the best interests of women as the best interests of the poorest, most insulted, most despised, most abused woman on earth. . . . Until Everywoman is free, no woman will be free. When her beauty and knowledge is revealed and seen, the new day will be at hand."[48]

Recently, articles appearing in *Israeli Studies* and *Critical Middle Eastern Studies* citing *Madwoman* have employed Gilbert and Gubar's models in new ways. Critics in emerging fields, like disability studies, have hearkened back to "The Corpus of the Madwoman: Towards a Feminist Disability Studies Theory of Embodiment and Mental Illness." Indeed, Lina Wilder (Connecticut College) noted that one doesn't even have to have read the book, but simply been exposed to its groundbreaking ideas, to experience the "eureka" moment it still offers. Marion Rust noted that she would "never lose hold of the goal of addressing and, yes, correcting, the fundamental sense of alienation from discourses I was told spoke to the human condition, but which quietly rendered me inhuman. For the question of what a book makes of its reader remains; and for this question, I believe we have Gilbert and Gubar to thank." Ann Kibbie (Bowdoin College) says, "To say that [*Madwoman*] opened new doors for me (doors that I never even knew existed) is an understatement. . . . And, however many 'waves' of feminist criticism may have washed over it by now, I still find [*Madwoman*] indispensable."[49]

I am aware that this essay is a "rave"—my reading here has worked to suggest that the practices offered in *Madwoman* and by Gilbert and Gubar made an enormous impact in the academy and that they continue to be instructive to contemporary feminists today. I was, throughout, conscious of Sarachild's caveat that it is destructive to a feminist movement to deny "the value of the pioneering work. . . . Or [in] competing with it, [to claim] to be doing a better (smoother) job. Of course something can actually be better . . . than the first efforts[, but] if it is actually better it does not deny its roots, but appreciates them."[50] This does not mean that we should not benefit from the work other scholars have done to carefully and insightfully assess the valuable ways in which we might revise or build upon *Madwoman*'s literary scholarship. I looked, however, for valuable ways to build the women's movement in the academy and beyond. Today, you can buy T-shirts, buttons, and calendars emblazoned with the logo, "I Am the Madwoman in the Attic." The Web site on which they are featured includes other provocative third-wave-ish logos like "This T-Shirt Is My Prom Dress," "Guess Who's Getting a Divorce? Break Out the Cosmos!" and "Alpha Female."[51] Contemporary artists like Eiko Grimberg have produced works of art bearing the name "Madwoman in the Attic," as has the British detective series *Cracker* and an artist's studio in Rhode Island. Gilbert and Gubar's work has clearly entered the cultural parlance and continues to make an impact on young women even today. What could be a better model, even as we grow to new understandings, for future feminist criticism?

Notes

1. Sandra M. Gilbert and Susan Gubar, *The Madwoman in the Attic: The Woman Writer and the Nineteenth-Century Literary Imagination* (New Haven: Yale University Press, 1979); Kathie Sarachild, Carol Hanisch, Faye Levin, Barbara Leon, and Colette Price, eds., *Feminist Revolution* (1975; repr. New York: Random House, 1979); Jennifer Baumgardner and Amy Richards, eds., *Manifesta: Young Women, Feminism, and the Future* (New York: Farrar, Straus and Giroux, 2000). Further references will be given parenthetically.

2. I have had the benefit of living and working with feminist activists from Redstockings in Gainesville, Florida, and of taking a history class on the women's liberation movement conducted by Kathie Sarachild, where I gained access to documents on the movement's history produced by Gainesville Women's Liberation as well as many locally published documents.

3. I contacted four hundred scholars in four fields (nineteenth-century American, Victorian, Romanticism, and Milton studies) who were most likely to have encountered *Madwoman* as a part of their academic training. I selected teachers at private and public colleges/universities from every state to avoid a possible bias; the list of schools was developed using computer-generated random numbers, which had been assigned to state and public institutions alphabetically. When I could not locate information on a college's Web site about scholars' areas of study, I elected the next school on the list, but this happened in only three cases. I allowed "snowballing," which means that I was willing to have the message passed on if someone knew a colleague who might (positively or negatively) comment on Gilbert and Gubar's work. I had an approximately 15 percent response rate, which—given modern "spam" filters and the fact that (particularly for colleagues outside of my own field) many people would not have known my name—seems quite high. Some of the people who responded asked not to be quoted for the article but wished to share their insights for my information. Six percent of the respondents (1 percent of those contacted) indicated that they did not know *The Madwoman in the Attic.*

4. Sandra M. Gilbert, "Life Studies, or Speech after Long Silence: Feminist Critics Today," *College English* 40, no. 8 (April 1979): 854, 858.

5. Elizabeth Langland had a vital role in inspiring me and supporting my work. Without her encouragement—it is a perfect example of her intellectual and personal generosity that she and I were engaged in a conversation like this in the first place—I would have found the dissertation process very defeating. I have continued to call upon her wisdom and guidance throughout my career. Indeed, my praise for the work of Gilbert and Gubar applies to my work with Elizabeth Langland, as well.

6. Lucy Morrison, personal communication, April 19, 2008.

7. Janet Gezari, "Sandra M. Gilbert and Susan Gubar's *The Madwoman in the Attic,*" *Essays in Criticism* 56, no. 3 (July 2006): 265.

8. Carol Hanisch developed this concept and articulated it in many forms. See especially Shulamith Firestone and Anne Koedt, eds., *Notes from the Second Year: Women's Liberation. Major Writings of the Radical Feminists* (New York: Radical Feminism, 1970), and Kathie Sarachild, "Consciousness-Raising: A Radical Weapon," in *Feminist Revolution,* 144–50.

9. Karen Waters, personal communication, May 5, 2008; Emily Orlando, personal communication, April 15, 2008.

10. Carol Martin, personal communication, April 16, 2008; Gezari, "Sandra M. Gilbert and Susan Gubar," 269.

11. Sarachild, "Consciousness-Raising," 145.

12. By 1987, English departments had a roughly 50/50 split of men and women. See

Elizabeth Kolbert, "Literary Feminism Comes of Age," *New York Times,* December 6, 1987.

13. LeAnne Schreiber, "I'm Nobody. Who Are You?" *New York Times,* December 9, 1979.

14. Ellen Bayuk Rosenman, personal communication, May 9, 2008.

15. Carolyn Heilbrun, foreword to *Making Feminist History: The Literary Scholarship of Sandra M. Gilbert and Susan Gubar,* ed. William E. Cain (New York: Garland, 1994), xv.

16. Carol Hanisch, introduction to "The Personal Is Political," http://scholar.alexanderstreet.com/pages/viewpage.action?pageld=2259 (January 2006): 1–5, 2.

17. Leon, "Separate to Integrate," in Sarachild et al., eds., *Feminist Revolution,* 153; Sarachild, "Consciousness-Raising."

18. Leon, "Separate to Integrate," 157. Elaine Showalter revised her sensibility of this goal in the early 1980s: "I began by recalling that a few years ago feminist critics thought we were on a pilgrimage to the promised land in which gender would lose its power, in which all texts would be sexless and equal, like angels. But the more precisely we understand the specificity of women's writing not as a transient by-product of sexism but as a fundamental and continually determining reality, the more clearly we realize that we have misperceived our destination. We may never reach the promised land at all; for when feminist critics see our task as the study of women's writing, we realize that the land promised to us is not the serenely undifferentiated universality of texts but the tumultuous and intriguing wilderness of difference itself." "Feminist Criticism in the Wilderness," *Critical Inquiry* 8, no. 2 (Winter 1981): 205.

19. Sarachild, "Consciousness-Raising," 146. See also Sarachild, "Psychological Terrorism," in *Feminist Revolution,* 57–61.

20. William Cain, introduction to *Making Feminist History,* xix.

21. Dean Flower, "Jane Eyre's Heirs," *Hudson Review* 33, no. 3 (Autumn 1980): 421–30; Zelda Austen, "Madwoman," *New York Times,* February 3, 1980.

22. Sara Mills, Lynne Pearce, Sue Spaull, and Elaine Millard, introduction to *Feminist Readings/Feminists Reading* (Charlottesville: University Press of Virginia, 1989), 1, 3; Anne Barbeau Gardiner, "Feminist Literary Criticism: From Anti-Patriarchy to Decadence," *Modern Age* (Fall 2007): 399, 395.

23. Annette Kolodny, "Dancing through the Minefield: Some Observations on the Theory, Practice, and Politics of a Feminist Literary Criticism," *Feminist Studies* 6, no. 1 (Spring 1980): 16–17; Elaine Showalter, "Comments on Jehlen's 'Archimedes and the Paradox of Feminist Criticism,'" *Signs* 8, no. 1 (Autumn 1982): 161.

24. Olga Abella, personal communication, April 20, 2008.

25. Nina Auerbach, review of *The Madwoman in the Attic* by Sandra M. Gilbert and Susan Gubar, *Victorian Studies* 23, no. 4 (Summer 1980): 506; Nina Baym, letter to the editor, *Tulsa Studies in Women's Literature* 4, no. 1 (Spring 1985): 159; Mary Jacobus, review of *The Madwoman in the Attic* by Sandra M. Gilbert and Susan Gubar, *Signs* 6, no. 3 (Spring 1981): 521.

26. Myra Jehlen and Rachel Blau DuPlessis, "The Tongue of Power," *Feminist Studies* 7, no. 3 (Fall 1981): 542; Jehlen, "Archimedes and the Paradox of Feminist Criticism," *Signs* 6, no. 4 (Summer 1981): 576; Showalter, "Comments on Jehlen," 161; Toril Moi, *Sexual/Textual Politics* (New York: Methuen, 1985): 66–67.

27. Marysa Demoor and Katrien Heene, "Of Influences and Anxieties: Sandra Gilbert's Feminist Commitment," *European Journal of Women's Studies* 9, no. 2 (May 2002): 181. Interestingly, Spivak compares the misuse of this phrase to the misuse of "the personal is political" that I described earlier: "When, in the United States, the statement 'the personal is political' came into being, given the socio-intellectual formation, it really

became quite quickly 'only the personal is political.' In the same way, my notion just simply became the union ticket for essentialism. As to what is meant by strategy, no one wondered about that." See Sara Danius, Stefan Jonsson, Gayatri Chakravorty Spivak, "An Interview with Gayatri Chakravorty Spivak," *boundary 2* 20, no. 2 (Summer 1993): 35.

28. Sarachild, quoted in Leon, "Separate to Integrate," 154; Sarachild, "Consciousness-Raising," 148, 150.

29. Hanisch, "The Liberal Takeover of Women's Liberation," *Feminist Revolution,* 166.

30. Sarachild, "The Power of History," in *Feminist Revolution,* 33; Juhasz, review of *The Madwoman in the Attic* by Sandra M. Gilbert and Susan Gubar, *English Language Notes* 17, no. 4 (June 1980): 308.

31. Farah Jasmine Griffin, "That the Mothers May Soar and the Daughters May Know Their Names: A Retrospective of Black Feminist Literary Criticism," *Signs* 32, no. 2 (2007): 484.

32. Carolyn Heilbrun, foreword, ix–xv, xii; Jane Marcus, *Art and Anger: Reading like a Woman* (Columbus: Ohio State University Press, 1988), xxi, 227; Hanisch, "The Liberal Takeover," 166.

33. Cain, introduction to *Making Feminist History*, xxxii; Susan Gubar, "What Ails Feminist Criticism," *Critical Inquiry* 24 (Summer 1998): 880, 900; Sandra M. Gilbert and Susan Gubar, "The Mirror and the Vamp," in *Making Feminist History,* 20; Ellen Rooney, introduction to *The Cambridge Companion to Feminist Literary Theory* (Cambridge: Cambridge University Press, 2006), 14–15.

34. Sarah Seltzer, "Hard Times," *Bitch* 39 (Spring 2008): 28.

35. Nancy Chodorow, *The Reproduction of Mothering* (Berkeley: University of California Press, 1978); Annette Kolodny, "A Map of Rereading; or, Gender and the Interpretation of Literary Texts," *New Literary History* 11, no. 3 (Spring 1980): 451.

36. Gwen Curry, personal communication, April 23, 2008.

37. Lyn Robertson, personal communication, April 25, 2008; Curry, personal communication.

38. Scott Heller, "The Book That Created a Canon: 'Madwoman in the Attic' Turns Twenty," *Chronicle of Higher Education* 46, no. 17 (December 17, 1999): A20; Juhasz, review of *The Madwoman in the Attic,* 308–10; Kolodny, review of *The Madwoman in the Attic* by Sandra M. Gilbert and Susan Gubar, *American Literature* 52, no. 1 (March 1980): 129, 132; Penny Boumelha, review of *The Madwoman in the Attic* by Sandra M. Gilbert and Susan Gubar, *Review of English Studies,* n.s., 33, no. 131 (August 1982): 346; Jehlen and DuPlessis, 544.

39. Rosenman, May 9, 2008; David Collings, personal communication, April 18, 2008; David Miller, personal communication, April 18, 2008; anonymous personal communication, April 15, 2008; Ken Egan, personal communication, May 30, 2008; Olga Abella, April 20, 2008; Curry, personal communication.

40. Elizabeth Winston, personal communication, June 11, 2008.

41. Sarachild, "Consciousness-Raising," 145.

42. Mills et al., *Feminist Reading,* 12.

43. Kolodny, review of *The Madwoman in the Attic,* 132; Gezari, "Sandra M. Gilbert and Susan Gubar," 269; Nina Auerbach, review of *The Madwoman in the Attic* by Sandra M. Gilbert and Susan Gubar, *Victorian Studies* 23, no. 4 (Summer 1980): 505; Heller, "The Book That Created a Canon," A20; Collings, April 18, 2008; Margaret Stetz, personal communication, April 16, 2008; Miller, April 18, 2008; anonymous personal communication, April 15, 2008.

44. Moglen, review of *The Madwoman in the Attic* by Sandra M. Gilbert and Susan Gubar, *Nineteenth-Century Literature* 35, no. 2 (September 1980): 229; Kolodny, "Map of

Rereading," 465; Langland, "Wayne Booth, the Feminists, and Feminist Criticism," *Pedagogy* 7, no. 1 (2007): 81; Showalter, "Feminist Criticism," *Critical Inquiry* 8, no. 2 (Winter 1981): 205; Kolodny, "Literary Criticism," *Signs* 2, no. 2 (Winter 1976): 404; Kolodny, "Dancing through the Minefield: Some Observations on the Theory, Practice, and Politics of a Feminist Literary Criticism," *Feminist Studies* 6 (Spring 1980): 20, 19.

45. See especially Martha Nussbaum, *Sex and Social Justice* (New York: Oxford, 1999) and Chandra Talpade Mohanty, *Feminism without Borders: Decolonizing Theory, Practicing Solidarity* (Durham, N.C.: Duke University Press, 2003). The call for community among feminists/women continues to plague us. I would advocate for a position that honors the charge Mohanty makes to avoid white, western imperialism in our feminism, but would be less reticent than she in calling for western women to engage with women and women activists globally to achieve specific ends in particular communities. We cannot, I think, leave women who are fighting for justice at the mercy of insufficient resources or without the opportunity to collaborate with others with whom they have political affinity.

46. Mills et al., *Feminist Reading,* 4; Sarachild, "Consciousness-Raising," 148; Nancy LaGreca, "Feminist Literary Criticism of Latin American Women's Writing: Context, Approaches, and Analysis of the 1990s and Early 2000s," *Revista de Estudios Hispánicos* 40 (2006): 399, italics in the original; Gubar, "Feminism Inside Out," *PMLA* 121, no. 5 (October 2006): 1713, 1716.

47. Sarachild, "Power of History," 40, 42; Elliott, "The Currency of Feminist Theory," *PMLA* 121, no. 5 (October 2006): 1701.

48. Rosenman, May 2008; "Redstocking's Principles," *Feminist Revolution,* 205.

49. Yael S. Feldman, "From *The Madwoman in the Attic* to *The Women's Room:* The American Roots of Israeli Feminism," *Israeli Studies* (Spring 2000): 266–86; Hasna Lebbady, "Redefining the Margins: Embodied Knowledge in 'Ali and a Spinner Too?'" *Critique: Critical Middle Eastern Studies* 12, no. 2 (Fall 2003): 131–40; Elizabeth J. Donaldson, "The Corpus of the Madwoman: Towards a Feminist Disability Studies Theory of Embodiment and Mental Illness," *NWSA Journal* 14, no. 3 (Fall 2002): 99–119; Lina Wilder, personal communication, May 1, 2008; Marion Rust, personal communication, April 16, 2008; Ann Kibbie, personal communication, April 28, 2008.

50. Sarachild, "The Power of History," 33.

51. See http://www.cafepress.com/opheliasart (accessed May 29, 2008).

3

Gilbert and Gubar's Daughters

The Madwoman in the Attic's Spectre in Milton Studies

Carol Blessing

When I was a graduate student in the later 1980s, some of my female classmates had sworn off studying John Milton's works, particularly *Paradise Lost,* because of the author's sexism. My (male) Milton course professor summarily announced early in the semester that we would not be discussing the purported misogynistic constructions of Eve, as apparently his previous classes had become derailed by the presence of *The Madwoman in the Attic*'s discussion of "Milton's bogey," the condemnation of the great poet. Interestingly, Milton's sexism is still the primary topic my undergraduates wish to discuss, without my provocation and without reading *Madwoman;* when I send them forth to research the issue's scholarship, they inevitably encounter responses to Gilbert's and Gubar's volume.

While *The Madwoman in the Attic* began as a book aimed at rereading women writers in the light of patriarchal influences and their encounters with, and rebellion against, the long male-centered literary tradition, the book has reverberated beyond its primary focus. Section 6, "Milton's Bogey: Patriarchal Poetry and Women Readers,"[1] arguably the best-known portion of the work, revolutionized Milton studies. Basing their argument upon the words of the first feminist literary critic, Virginia Woolf, Sandra M. Gilbert and Susan Gubar cast Milton as the archetypal misogynist whose work exacerbated negative views of women and burgeoning women writers. Neither Gilbert nor Gubar would claim to be Milton scholars, but their work appropriated a provocative selection from Virginia Woolf's journal, some of which was also incorporated into *A Room of One's Own,* combining it with their laudable rhetorical skills and ability to make fascinating connections. Read through Romantic and feminist lenses, the premier British epic became an object of condemnation but also potential freedom for literary women. Mary Shelley's *Frankenstein* and Emily Brontë's *Wuthering Heights* become subversions of *Paradise Lost,* God, creation myths, and heaven and hell. *Madwoman* did not merely relegate Eve's evil nature to negative female stereotypes but re-created her as a Romantic antihero, willing to rebel both against the primordial male authority of the Creator and her husband. Thus, Eve was metamorphosed into an exemplar for female writers who could overcome Harold Bloom's literary anxiety of influence by looking to themselves as models; Eve became the ultimate archetype of the female writer in her alienation. What Milton scholars fixated upon, though, was not the potentially liberatory aspect of *Madwoman*'s analysis but the ways in which Milton had been brought to task, tried, and executed as the overbearing patriarch of English letters. Shortly after *Madwoman*'s publication, critics began addressing its critiques, some agreeing, but most firing back in defense of Milton.

Although Virginia Woolf was by 1918 "an experienced, widely published literary critic" according to Gilbert and Gubar, her discussion of John Milton was not widely influential in readings of *Paradise Lost* prior to 1979 (*Madwoman,* 190). Woolf had termed Milton "the first of the masculinists," whose influence Gilbert and Gubar expanded to cast a shadow over not only female writers who came after but all females by implication, as the daughters of Eve: "The story that Milton, 'the first of the masculinists,' most notably tells to women is of course the story of woman's secondness, her otherness, and how that otherness leads inexorably to her demonic anger, her sin, her fall, and her exclusion from that garden of the gods which is also, for her, the garden of poetry" (*Madwoman,* 191). In Gilbert's and Gubar's reading, Milton's Eve exceeded her Genesis misdeeds to become a creature aligned with Satan, Sin, and Death even before her fall, made not in God's image but Adam's, irredeemably lost.

The authors expanded Woolf's comments on Milton, then, into not only an apologia for women readers and writers but also a new way of reading Milton's work. For a volume ostensibly focusing on Romantic and Victorian literature, *Madwoman* made deep inroads into seventeenth-century scholarship by bringing gendered readings of *Paradise Lost* to the forefront, realigning Milton studies so thoroughly that any contemporary reading of *Paradise Lost* must now address issues of cultural, biblical, and literary patriarchy and Milton's misogyny. Eve became the central figure of the epic, with the gender-divisive summation of Adam and Eve's relation to the Divine, "He for God only, she for God in him," its most quoted line.[2] In the 1980s and 1990s, it became commonplace to open a scholarly essay on *Paradise Lost* with a quotation from "Milton's Bogey" and then either support or refute Gilbert and Gubar's reading of Eve. Indeed, some important book-length studies worked to overturn the negative reputation Milton had gained, including the most blatant rebuttal, *Feminist Milton* by Joseph Wittreich, who sought to resuscitate Milton through appropriating feminist terminology. The gloves were off as Milton scholars sought to reclaim their beloved author from condemnation and worse, the threat of losing his position as the highest-regarded British poet. Indeed, pronouncing Milton misogynist caused some feminists to reject study of Milton altogether, echoing both Woolf's assertions and Gilbert and Gubar's explication and expansion of her reading. In fact, feminist and antifeminist readings became a, if not the, primary critical focus on *Paradise Lost* from most of the 1980s through early 1990s. Both Milton scholars and feminists in literary studies (and those who claimed to be both) took on *Madwoman*'s challenge to Milton.

One strongly feminist critique of Milton actually predated that of *Madwoman in the Attic,* Marcia Landy's 1972 essay "Kinship and the Role of Women in *Paradise Lost,*" published in *Milton Studies.* Landy claims that "rather than being a misogynist, Milton was a representative seventeenth-century poet who was committed to the centrality of marriage, to the designated roles of man as creator and provider and of woman as procreator, submissive to her husband's natural authority."[3] Focusing on the domestic role of Eve, however, Landy criticized Milton's presentation of gendered hierarchy and Eve's primary identification as mother as a way to subject her status to Adam's. Her essay prompted a rebuttal from über Miltonist Barbara Lewalski, who blithely reasserted that Milton's universal appeal transcends gender concerns: "Happily, though, great poets have a way of rising like phoenixes from whatever ashes are left in the wake of social and intellectual revolutions, so no doubt it will not be long before we can all again read Milton for what is of enduring importance rather than what is historically conditioned in his conception of man and woman."[4] Lewalski's essay unintentionally set up the prime argument of Sandra Gilbert's 1978 article, "Patriarchal Poetry and Women Readers: Reflections on Milton's Bogey" in *PMLA* (the first version of the *Madwoman*'s section on Milton). While Gilbert may or may not have read Lewalski's essay, she and other feminist critics would refute its thesis with their full energies: the depiction of women in literature was not something to ignore, excuse, or transcend but was the major focus for literary studies.

The earliest print reply to Gilbert came in *PMLA*'s Forum. Philip Gallagher skewered Gilbert for her "specious readings" of *Paradise Lost,* terming her work a "litany of misreadings" and unraveling her arguments with his own readings of the epic.[5] His arguments include the following: it is the character of Adam who is misogynistic, not Milton, who shows him as such; Satan is tyrannical, not egalitarian, as Gilbert had claimed; Adam does not lose his love for Eve, it is only Eve who thinks so; and Gilbert misinterprets Eve's status as a "'divine afterthought,'" as "in *Paradise Lost,* Eve was always part of God's design," surpassing her portrayal in Genesis and the mind of Milton's fallen Adam (Gallagher, 320). In her reply to the letter, Gilbert countered that Gallagher had engaged in "'misreading' both me and Milton" (Gallagher, 321). Using Gallagher's response to typify gendered differences in reading, she asserted that the argument of her essay, rather than being focused on Milton studies, is "'the implications of Milton's ideas for women'" (Gallagher, 321). That distinction was lost on many Milton scholars, for their project became to defend Milton and *Paradise Lost* against charges of misogyny rather than examine Gilbert's project of discussing nineteenth-century women writers who had reread and, from necessity, rewritten the work.

Joan Malory Webber's posthumous 1980 *Milton Studies* article, "The Politics of Poetry: Feminism and *Paradise Lost,*" similarly attacked Gilbert's work as typifying "the naïve intensity of many readers' involvement in the poem" and demonstrating lack of both historical contextualization and consideration of genre in her analysis.[6] Webber faults Gilbert for not reading Milton's other works, especially his prose and *Paradise Regained* along with Foxe's *Book of Martyrs,* for doing so would provide needed background in Milton's revolutionary stance, his reading of the Bible, and his featuring of everyday people in the epic. Further, as Gallagher claimed and others would argue, Gilbert misreads Milton by assuming statements in his works necessarily contain his points of view, as "Western epic traditionally undermines itself, providing criticism of the culture it is supposedly designed to admire. . . . *Paradise Lost* takes every advantage of its complex tradition's capacity to appear to be doing one thing while actually achieving something else" (Webber, 7). Webber agrees with Northrop Frye that Milton's use of opposites influences his characters of Adam and Eve, whom Frye says embody Jungian differences as a typical characteristic of the epic. Writes Webber, "Part of Milton's task in justifying the ways of God to men is to explain why these differences exist. . . . Eve reflects every female potentiality that could enter the mind of a Renaissance epic writer and Christian humanist. . . . she combines the opposite epic functions of witch and inspiration, being both Adam's downfall and his means of recovery," arguing that *Paradise Lost* is not mired in misogyny or a straightforward condemnation of women, but a multifaceted, complex work that makes understanding Milton's view of women quite slippery (Webber, 11). The female representation of Sin is countered by Eve's connection to Mary in *Paradise Lost* and the climactically positive depiction of Mary in *Paradise Regained.* Webber similarly counters Gilbert's condemnation of Milton's patriarchal stance with the context of his radicalism: "No doubt revolutionary fathers are as hard to accept as any other kind, but at least their inclination is to force rejection of patriarchy and conservative patriarchal systems, not to espouse them" (Webber, 6). Interestingly, Webber's pleas for situating the epic firmly in its milieu presaged contemporary studies that concentrate their efforts on Milton's political/religious contexts and constructs.

One of the most important journal articles to use a feminist and cultural studies approach to *Paradise Lost* and engage with Virginia Woolf's discussion of Milton, the university, and the literary canon was the 1983 essay by Christine Froula, "When Eve Reads Milton: Undoing the Canonical Economy," which appeared in *Critical Inquiry.* Her essay provoked a vigorous debate within the journal and has been reprinted in several collections, including the *Longman Critical Reader* and the five-volume *John Milton: Twentieth Century Perspectives* published by Routledge. Froula traces the idea of the canon from the Old Testament through the male-dominated literature epitomized for Woolf by *Paradise Lost.* Grounding her thesis in Elaine Pagels' *The Gnostic Gospels,* Froula parallels the masculinization of prophetic power and spiritual authority by the Roman Catholic Church to the masculinization of the social power mediated by literature and the exclusion of women writers from the literary canon. As the Church fathers suppressed Gnostic writings in forming the biblical canon, so Milton's elaboration of Genesis dramatizes its subordination of Eve's knowledge, or gnosis, to the "higher" authority and law of Adam and God as a masculinist psychic and cultural feat that compensates for Eve's procreative power.[7] Although Froula cites Gubar's "'The Blank Page' and the Issues of Female Creativity," she does not refer directly to *The Madwoman in the Attic.* In an e-mail interview, however, Froula describes *Madwoman*'s influence on her own teaching and study of Milton, recalling that it

> was empowering in two ways. First, along with the work of Mary Ellmann, Kate Millett, Elaine Showalter, and others, it exemplified the intellectual power of feminist criticism and its impact on the discipline of literary studies. Second, because Gilbert and Gubar's reading differs from mine, it took me only so far when it came to teaching the poem. For me, its great value lay both in what it says and in what it leaves unsaid and thus impelled me to try to say.[8]

Diane Kelsey McColley's popular book-length study *Milton's Eve,* also published in 1983, labors to present a positive perspective of Eve and Milton's works in general. While again not directly quoting *The Madwoman in the Attic*'s discussion of Milton's bogey, she does reference Gilbert's earlier work on Milton through footnotes. The entire focus of her work is to rescue Milton from feminist readings that criticize him and his creation of Eve, readings that do not go deeply enough into historical, religious, and artistic contexts and subtleties. McColley's work contrasts prevailing early modern literary and visual representations of the Fall and Eve with those in *Paradise Lost,* seeing the latter as more progressive in his view of women. The work hypothesizes:

> This study is an effort to extricate Eve from a reductive critical tradition, as Milton sought to redeem her from a reductive literary and iconographic tradition, and to establish a regenerative reading of her roles: that is, to show that Milton has fashioned an Eve who in all the prelapsarian scenes is not only sufficient to stand and able to grow, but who while standing and growing, however vulnerably, is a pattern and composition of active goodness and a speaking picture of the recreative power of poetry itself.[9]

The ambitious thesis stakes out the territory common to the humanist enterprise of many Milton scholars, who view *Paradise Lost* as a regenerative work, contrary to the repressive tome criticized by Woolf and in *Madwoman. Milton's Eve* admirably covers a wealth of art and writing, including classical antecedents for Renaissance works, laboring to present Milton in one perspective, as clearly superior to his sources in his own lack of misogyny. McColley's footnoted reference to Gilbert's 1978 *PMLA* article (*Madwoman* is not directly cited) and other feminist criticism of *Paradise Lost* faults them for being "partial in both senses of the word"; as she asserts, "Gilbert's use of evidence ignores the dramatic decorum of the bits she chooses, taking speeches clearly meant to be parodic, impercipient, or fallen as if they were Milton's own opinions and omitting his radical emendations of dualistic and misogynistic assumptions."[10] This criticism echoes that of Gallagher and other formalist critics, who charge Gilbert with flattening Milton's language and overlooking subtleties of tone, poetic devices, irony, and the pre- or post-fallen status of the speakers. McColley joins with Shullenberger (whose article follows) and others more focused on the historicity of the text to criticize Gilbert and *Madwoman* for ignoring seventeenth-century religious contexts that either shape Milton or against which he rebels. McColley, for example, reads Milton against himself, using *Areopagitica, De Doctrina Christiana,* and the marriage tracts to situate his epics, and concluding that pre-fallen Eve is a symbol of the Church and her pre-lapsarian relationship with Adam a representation of allegorical readings of the *Song of Solomon.*

William Shullenberger's "Wrestling with the Angel: *Paradise Lost* and Feminist Criticism," from the 1986 *Milton Quarterly,* references Gilbert's work within its first page, taking *Madwoman* to task for being a "polemic which develops within, and never questions, its very first offhand remark about Milton's 'undeniable misogyny.'"[11] His essay becomes a full-scale refutation of section 6 of *Madwoman,* the founding argument against Milton's bogey that would continue in Milton studies for some time. Concerned that women would be kept from Milton's works because of *Madwoman*'s argument, Shullenberger feels there is much to be gained by women studying Milton, provided that they are willing to accept Milton within his cultural contexts or read Milton's works as Shullenberger does. The essay critiques the strain of feminist literary theory virtually founded by Gilbert and Gubar and lauds other female critics who rescue Milton from charges of misogyny (presumably the nonfeminist women). Citing Joan Webber's 1980 "The Politics of Poetry," Shullenberger exceeds Webber's thesis that Milton "prepares the way for feminist thinking" to assert, "The subtext of *Paradise Lost* encourages and supports feminist reading" (Shullenberger, 71).

His essay continues to counter Gilbert's analysis, along with other feminist readings by Froula, Jackie DiSalvo, Marcia Landy, and Maureen Quilligan, whose analyses of *Paradise Lost* focus on the patriarchy of Milton's God, the patriarchal family structure, the subjugation of Eve, and the identification of Eve with Satan. Shullenberger instead argues, again through references to Webber, that Milton's God might begin as patriarchal but He eventually cedes power to the Son, "who embodies the more 'feminine' qualities of love and mercy associated with the New Testament God," going on to view the Son in maternal terms (Shullenberger, 72). Shullenberger argues extensively that Adam and Eve are different (or separate) but equal, and that the domesticity of Eve's gendered role is not demeaning. Finally, he vehemently counters the assertion of Satan's role as hero with whom Eve and women can identify in their fight against patriarchy. The conclusive tour de force of the essay comes as Shullenberger essentially brands feminism as neurotic:

> The dynamics of identity in the poem are considerably more complicated than feminist criticism has yet acknowledged: so complicated, indeed, as to challenge feminist critics to re-examine their own psychological premises. For the model of an ego-centric self, whose horizons of knowledge are contained by the authority of the self's experience, is at best naïve and narcissistic, and at worst the destructive parody of identity which Milton presents us in Satan. (Shullenberger, 80)

Shullenberger's responses to Gilbert and others take on a decidedly campaigning tone. Feminists must "'see beyond Milton's bogey'—the bogey, that is, invented by feminist criticism" to view Milton's works as Shullenberger does as "a possible source of life, health, and strength" (Shullenberger, 80, 81). The quote illustrates the hyperbole *Madwoman* provokes among Milton scholars feeling under attack.

The most complete rebuttal to *The Madwoman in the Attic*'s section on Milton's bogey came in Joseph Wittreich's *Feminist Milton,* published in 1987, which praises Shullenberger's "fine essay."[12] It is clear the direction Wittreich's argument will take. The book actually engages directly only a few of the arguments of Gilbert and Gubar, except to note the "bifurcation of the critical enterprise which Sandra Gilbert and Susan Gubar define and which their followers have deepened," that is, the separation between "how to read Milton" and "how Milton came to be read" (Wittreich, 7-8). What Wittreich does, rather than proving his hyperbolized title, is cover how women have read *Paradise Lost.* His reader-response approach, which focuses primarily on the horizon of expectations from the early eighteenth to early nineteenth centuries, aims at countering the *Madwoman*'s examples of female readership by showing positive responses to Milton from other women. Sprinkled with anecdotes from women's journals and letters that praise Milton, the volume hypothesizes that although "*Paradise Lost* is no longer thought to be a poem in which Milton curries favor with women," that is a problem of the later readers and critics, not the work itself. He argues, without a great deal of support, that *Paradise Lost* was "a particularly important part of the educational system for women" and that "women, no less than men, were engaged by Milton, especially in times of fierce strife when freedom was being crushed beneath the despot's sway and when a tempest of evil days was seen blackening the English nation" (Wittreich, 1, 4). Thus, there had been a time when women had recognized its progressiveness, "a forging ground for their own ideal of educated and responsible womanhood, an ideal then founded upon sexual equality rather than, as today, upon sexual difference" (Wittreich, 4).

Contradictions abound in *Feminist Milton.* Wittreich sets up an interesting opposition by repeatedly distinguishing between Miltonists and feminists; the two camps apparently cannot coexist—a feminist cannot be a Miltonist, or vice versa. This seems to prove *Madwoman*'s argument, rather than refute it, and puzzlingly undermines his project's title. Early on, he seems to side with Barbara Lewalski's "Milton on Women—Yet Once More" and her "inference that the so-called feminist issues now being focused on by literary criticism are anachronistic, superimposed on a poem to which they are not germane." Yet later, without apparent irony, he refers to "Milton's feminist consciousness" (Wittreich, 7, 119).

The strongest sections of the book delineate the various speakers' viewpoints from Milton's, as "Milton's female readership" was "always quick to distinguish between Milton's views and those of his characters" such as Satan and Adam, echoing the decrees of other Miltonists that Milton frequently presents arguments only to refute them. Complexities and "shifting perspectives" in *Paradise Lost* allow for easy misreadings, but the careful reader knows better than to label Milton a mouthpiece of the patriarchy. While misogynistic religious phrases appear, they are more often than not undermined, says Wittreich: "In speech after speech the clichés of Christianity are embedded so that they may be challenged" (Wittreich, 87, 91, 85). Similarly, masculinist epic conventions are necessarily used, but often become questioned or inverted. "Given the epic pretensions of *Paradise Lost,* it is no surprise to find patriarchal or misogynistic attitudes. They are staples of the militantly masculine world of epic poetry; part of the epic formula, they are Milton's bogie, as much as a bugbear to him as to his later female readership." Wittreich ends his reading of *Paradise Lost* with a focus on Eve's final speech, one that disproves I Timothy's censure of women and links Eve's prophetic gifts with seventeenth-century Quaker women (Wittreich, 101, 107).

Feminist critic Mary Nyquist published four essays (including one in her coedited book, *Re-Membering Milton*) on theoretical approaches to Milton's works in 1987 and 1988; the two relating most closely to Gilbert's and Gubar's work will be discussed here. Her "Fallen Differences, Phallogocentric Discourses: Losing *Paradise Lost* to History" opens with a reference to Woolf but does not engage *Madwoman*'s use of her, as Nyquist provocatively opines, "Milton may be what Virginia Woolf said he was, the first of the masculinists, but he is certainly not the last. . . . Milton's misogyny would seem actually to be exceeded by that of his ostensibly more enlightened twentieth-century commentators."[13] Her work centers on the connections other critics have made between Eve and Dalila, from *Samson Agonistes,* as well as between Milton's own disastrous first marriage and the marriages of Adam and Samson, arguing that reception history has intensified Milton's alleged sexism.

In "The Genesis of Gendered Subjectivity in the Divorce Tracts and in *Paradise Lost,*" Nyquist analyzes strains of feminist approaches to Milton, noting that the more recent movements of "third-wave feminism" and "postfeminist feminism" are engaged in "attacks mounted against Western bourgeois or liberal feminism."[14] Referencing such humanist critics as Barbara Lewalski, Joan Webber, and Diane McColley, she insightfully observes, "Because much academic criticism on *Paradise Lost,* especially that produced in North America, has been written within a liberal-humanist tradition that wants Milton to be, among other things, the patron saint of the companionate marriage, it has frequently made use of a notion of equality that is both mystified and mystifying" (99). This desire, "intent on neutralizing oppositions" has carried over into "feminist biblical commentaries on Genesis," particularly regarding the two creation accounts of male and female that Milton uses in *Paradise Lost* and the divorce tracts (100). Nyquist then considers Eve's account of her creation as a product of the late seventeenth century as she interrogates the critical inclination towards universalism, saying, "Eve's speech plays a pivotal role, historically and culturally, in the construction of the kind of female subjectivity required by a new economy's progressive sentimentalization of the private sphere" (120). Eve's story essentially paves the way for female novelists, including those Romantic and Victorian writers featured in *The Madwoman in the Attic.*

Several of the essays in *Milton and the Idea of Women,* a 1988 collection edited by Julia M. Walker, take a mixed or negative view of Milton's progressive course for women. Susanne Woods's "How Free Are Milton's Women?" argues that Milton is not misogynistic but is "locked into his culture's assumptions of woman's inferior position."[15] This would contradict the many who saw Milton as a social progressive, for to ignore or restrain one-half of the population hardly seems revolutionary. Woods, however, does see growth in Milton's consciousness; while in his earlier poetry he demonstrates an "indifference to matters of gender," in *Paradise Lost* he shows an "effort to give woman full dignity, freedom, and agency in a male supremacist environment."[16]

Janet E. Halley's "Female Autonomy in Milton's Sexual Poetics" takes on the now-familiar debate encompassed by early feminist analyses of Milton and females critics who counter in defense of him. Representing the two sides are Marcia Landy and Sandra Gilbert, as feminists, and important Milton scholars Barbara Keifer Lewalski, Joan Malory Webber, and Diane Kelsey McColley as their opponents. Halley locates the debate in the latter group's attribution of autonomy to Eve. While they "charge that the application of contemporary feminist thinking to Milton is ahistorical,"[17] their work to create Eve's subjectivity often uses "a means of transcending history altogether" (231). Indeed, the debate between feminists and those whom Halley terms "antifeminist and liberal feminist" hinges upon a crucial question: "Is autonomous female subjectivity possible?" (232). At its essence, this debate in Milton studies incorporates the debate over feminist theories and their opponents:

> If the first wave of feminist criticism of Milton, regarding Eve as an object of male imagination and desire, neglected the problematics of her subjectivity, its opponents—not only in their scholarly polemics but also in propria persona—have made that question inescapable. Their reading of Eve reminds us that real women actively participate, with widely varying degrees of consciousness and irony, in forms of subjectivity and

> desire prepared for us by a history dominated by patriarchal power. Their challenge calls for a reformulation of the feminist project in Milton studies. (Halley, "Female Autonomy," 232)

With that pronouncement, Halley's essay focuses largely on the heterosexual enterprise of *Paradise Lost* as a social construction limiting willing females to domestic and/or secondary roles. Seventeenth-century Puritan marriage conventions portrayed women as choosing this bond, rather than having marriage partners forced upon them. Halley says that Lewalski "offers heterosexual interdependence as a strategy for reading *Paradise Lost*," thus participating in, rather than analyzing, the system Milton uses, and in turn "offers a model for Webber and McColley" (Halley, "Female Autonomy," 232). Writes Halley, "It is no accident that Lewalski, Webber, and McColley are able to build convincing arguments about Eve's subjectivity—its creation was one of the major ideological projects of the seventeenth century in England, and of Milton himself after his own disastrous first marriage" (233).

Making Feminist History: The Literary Scholarship of Sandra M. Gilbert and Susan Gubar, edited by William E. Cain and published in 1994, provided another reassessment. Jodi Mikalachki's chapter, "Responding to the Bogey: Sympathy and Feminist Milton Criticism," covered the influence of Gilbert's *PMLA* article and *Madwoman*'s work on Milton studies from 1979 to 1992. It is the chapter's thesis that *Madwoman* burdens Milton with sole responsibility for male dominance in religion and literature. Mikalachki terms him "the overdetermined father of patriarchal literary tradition."[18] By placing Milton in this key position, Gilbert's analysis essentially sets his works up for prominent critical debate, as Mikalachki rightfully asserts—"One thing is clear: since the early 1980s women's issues and women themselves have come to dominate Milton criticism"—but she goes on to ask, why has "Milton criticism not emerged as a powerful focus of feminist and gender criticism?" (114). The chapter proceeds to critique the liberal framework of both *Madwoman*'s use of Milton and the bulk of feminist criticism written in reaction to the work, as the concept of gender remains untheorized. Like Halley, Mikalachki sees Lewalski, Colley, et al. as bound by the shortcomings of liberal humanist thinking and/or liberal feminism. All are caught in a hermetic circle, unable to say something truly new about Milton or to argue an oppositional point. "Whatever differences in interpretation they might evince, then, both Gilbert and Gubar and their detractors consider Milton in the context of the same cultural paradigm of liberalism, and all emphasize his commanding importance as a man and a poet in English literary history" (115). As Milton cannot be any longer seen as the center of either the literary canon or of early modern studies, feminist criticism of Milton suffers from marginality, says Mikalachki, and has "nothing to offer feminist or gender criticism in other fields" because of its generally untheorized nature (116). Mikalachki, however, sees *Madwoman* as significant "to the extent that gender has become virtually the only issue in Milton studies. . . . By placing Milton at the center of their feminist revision of literary history Gilbert and Gubar accomplished a feminization of Milton criticism that has effectively killed the king" (116).

Mikalachki's essay overstates several points. Did Gilbert and Gubar really set out to prove that Milton was the canon's center, or is he the most obvious example of patriarchal writing and religion, used to demonstrate how female readers and authors re-visioned his works? The idea that Gilbert and Gubar dethroned Milton is the most hyperbolized statement. His works are in decline, as any undergraduate literature professor can tell you, because of their difficulty, as students do not often study either classical languages or translations of the classical works Milton employs. *Paradise Lost* becomes more and more an insurmountable read. Surprisingly, though, the gap between Milton's religious world and ours is closing, with more attention to conservative religious groups and clashes over church/state connections. A recent volume of *Milton Studies* focused on the continued importance of Milton, working to quell rumors to the contrary and defend his significance, albeit through preaching to the choir. I would argue that feminist readings have actually infused Milton studies with more vigor, although Mikalachki's important admonition to theorize gender should be vital to a newer wave of Milton studies. With the current focus on historical contextualization, critiques of gendered constructions have become and will continue to become more prevalent.

Richard Bradford's ambitiously titled *The Complete Critical Guide to John Milton* (2001) rightly features Sandra Gilbert's "Milton's Bogey" at the start of his feminist criticism section. Bradford summarizes Gilbert's argument this way: "women both as literary subjects and readers of literature were continually shadowed by the presence of Eve, the archetype of naiveté, gullibility, vulnerability and dangerously unsophisticated instinct."[19] The section reviews works by Landy, Froula, McColley, Webber, Wittreich, and Nyquist, as well as by David Aers, Bob Hodge, and Edward Le Comte. Bradford's own biases shine through in his account of feminist approaches to Milton; he applauds McColley's *Milton's Eve* because "it represents a sub-tradition of critical writing where the largely late-twentieth century interpretive strategies evolved by feminism are balanced against more impartial, historicist readings," and he includes with McColley both Lewalski and Webber for showing "how the ideology of feminism as a broader movement can cloud, sometimes deliberately obscure, the objective detail of literary scholarship."[20] That such a statement could be made in 2001 is astonishing, but nevertheless it was published in a survey discussion of literary theories.

With the new millennium, much of feminist studies metamorphosed into gender studies, prompting *Milton and Gender,* a collection edited by Catherine Gimelli Martin in 2004. Several of the essays reference Sandra Gilbert's appropriation of Woolf as departure points for their own arguments. James Grantham Turner finds Gilbert engaged in misreading Woolf, whose comments upon Milton reflected more specifically Woolf's own Modernist predispositions and echoed Samuel Johnson's condemnation of Milton's misogyny rather than showing her own careful analysis of *Paradise Lost,* as Woolf admits to reading only sections of the epic. More importantly, Woolf primarily focuses not on Milton as "the first of the masculinists" but on her appreciation of his aesthetics: "The transition from ideology to art—'But what poetry!'—is not (as Sandra Gilbert argued in her influential 'Reflections on Milton's Bogey') an intensification of the complaint against masculinism, a darkening of the page, but the glowing of an awakened judgment."[21] *Madwoman*'s use of Woolf, however, fueled the critical fire: "Since Gilbert's powerful intervention, several generations of scholars, of both sexes and many ideological persuasions, have launched rescue missions on Milton's behalf." Often, these defenses have quoted passages from the divorce tracts, claiming Milton's progressive view of the sexes shines through there. Reading the divorce tracts alongside *Paradise Lost,* Turner asks, "What *is* the relationship between poetics, biblical hermeneutics, and the ideology of masculine power?" arguing that Milton is actually more egalitarian and less masculinist in *Paradise Lost* than in his famous tract *Tetrachordon.* The latter often becomes a forum for Milton's venting over his own failed and humiliating marriage, a period Woolf underestimated in her comments on his "domestic quarrels."[22]

By contrast, Martin argues against "charges of blatant masculinism" in both the divorce tracts and Milton's work as a whole, targeting Gilbert and Gubar's work as a particularly harmful critical lens.[23] She opens her essay on *Samson Agonistes* with a quotation from *The Madwoman in the Attic,* taking to task the authors' condemnation of the drama and overall reading of Milton as a misogynist. "Yet while their advice is specifically aimed at a female readership, Gilbert and Gubar are hardly unique in carrying on Samuel Johnson's old campaign against Milton's reputed misogyny, masculinism, paternalism, and elitism" (53). The problem, according to Martin, is that most readers, influenced by their view, "ignore the strikingly egalitarian spousal debate" in *Samson Agonistes.* Later, she censures Gilbert and Gubar for their feminist position that causes them to "reject the 'liberal' or egalitarian case for equality in favor of late twentieth-century 'identity' politics and its separatist ideal of female 'embodiment.'" Milton's *Colasterion,* claims Martin, espouses "rational conversation" of both sexes, a view more progressive than that of Michel de Montaigne and Sir Thomas Browne. According to Martin, Milton's humanism allied him with gender equality before modern feminism, whose project actually works against that equality (Martin, "Dalila," 53, 56-58).

In a third essay in *Milton and Gender,* Dayton Haskin castigates *Madwoman*'s assessment of George Eliot's Miltonic readings, which has colored modern critical views:

> In more recent times the project of exploring the intertextual relations between Eliot and Milton has been inhibited by other entanglements; for instance, by the assumption that in *Middlemarch* Edward Casaubon represents Milton and provides an apt illustration of what Virginia Woolf denominated "Milton's bogey"; by the claim that the interest in Milton shown in the novel is an aspect of Eliot's self-loathing and accounts for an "authorial vengeance" that she takes on Dorothea Brooke "In the service of female submission"; and by the idea (which Eliot pointedly rejected) that the arguments Milton advanced in favor of divorce are deeply flawed by their patriarchal assumptions about marriage and were in any event a cover for his own self-interest.[24]

Haskin, then, criticizes Gilbert and Gubar not for their assessment of Milton but for their application in terms of how Victorian women writers reread, appropriated, and rewrote his works. Haskin finds the connection *Madwoman* makes between Casaubon and Milton particularly problematic, as Eliot admired Milton's radical stance, particularly in the divorce tracts. Instead, both Lydgate and Dorothea are closer to Milton ideologically. Thus Milton did not serve to suppress or oppress either Eliot or Dorothea, as Haskin conjectures: "While other Victorian readers may have been made marble by thinking of Milton as a massy twin pillar of English literature, the author of *Middlemarch* had long since been drawing strength from his independent spirit."[25]

This last comment brings full circle many of the contradictory qualities of "Milton's Bogey." The work is written by non-Miltonists, focusing more on Romantic and Victorian women writers rather than on a rigorous study of *Paradise Lost.* Its publication in both *PMLA* and in *The Madwoman in the Attic* attracted a wider audience than typical Miltonists; the timing spoke well to a field of literary critics engaged with such interrelated issues as feminism, gendered writings and readings, and canon formation and maintenance. Eliciting critical response from a full spectrum of ideological views, from most conservative to Marxist to postmodernist, Gilbert and Gubar's declamation of Milton not only revitalized readings of *Paradise Lost* but also acted as reagent for the evolution of feminist scholarship. Literary studies could no longer be "done" in the same supposedly neutral manner that assumed universals or that presumed, à la Bloom, that an "anxiety of influence" would be passed exclusively from father to son. Women writers were now recognized as having to grapple with patriarchy in religion, literature, and their intersections. While critics of *The Madwoman in the Attic* rightly find the volume falls short in contextualizing Milton's seventeenth-century writings and in theorizing and questioning categories of masculine and feminine, "Milton's Bogey" was a monumental step in the critical journey of both feminist theory and Milton studies. As a new generation of scholars enters Milton studies, perhaps Gilbert and Gubar's work will become less central in evaluating Milton, *Paradise Lost,* and Eve. But they have made a lasting contribution to rereading a central work of the traditional literary canon and to reconsidering the issue of canonicity and women's writings and reading.

Notes

1. Sandra M. Gilbert and Susan Gubar, *The Madwoman in the Attic: The Woman Writer and the Nineteenth-Century Literary Imagination* (New Haven: Yale University Press, 1979). Subsequent references will be given parenthetically in the text.
2. John Milton, *Paradise Lost* (Oxford: Oxford University Press, 1991), book 4, line 299, 428.
3. Marcia Landy, "Kinship and the Role of Women in 'Paradise Lost,'" *Milton Studies* 4 (1972): 5.
4. Barbara Lewalski, "Milton on Women—Yet Once More," *Milton Studies* 6 (1974): 19.
5. Philip J. Gallagher and Sandra M. Gilbert, "Milton's Bogey," *PMLA* 94, no. 2 (1979): 320. Subsequent references will be given parenthetically in the text.
6. Joan Malory Webber, "The Politics of Poetry: Feminism and 'Paradise Lost,'" *Milton Studies* 14 (1980): 4. Subsequent references will be given parenthetically in the text.
7. Christine Froula, "When Eve Reads Milton: Undoing the Critical Economy," *Critical Inquiry* 10, no. 2 (1983): 321–47.
8. Christine Froula, personal communication, January 12, 2008.
9. Diane Kelsey McColley, *Milton's Eve* (Urbana: University of Illinois Press, 1983), 4.
10. Ibid., 19 n. 6.
11. William Shullenberger, "Wrestling with the Angel: 'Paradise Lost' and Feminist Criticism," *Milton Quarterly* 20, no. 3 (1986): 70. Subsequent references will be given parenthetically in the text.
12. Joseph Wittreich, *Feminist Milton* (Ithaca, N.Y.: Cornell University Press, 1987), 13 n. 32. Subsequent references will be given parenthetically in the text.
13. Mary Nyquist, "Fallen Differences, Phallogocentric Discourses: Losing *Paradise Lost* to History," in *Post-structuralism and the Question of History,* ed. Derek Attridge, Geoff Bennington, and Robert Young (Cambridge: Cambridge University Press, 1987), 212.
14. Mary Nyquist, "The Genesis of Gendered Subjectivity in the Divorce Tracts and in *Paradise Lost,*" in *Re-membering Milton,* ed. Mary Nyquist and Margaret W. Ferguson

(New York: Metheun, 1987), 99. Subsequent references will be given parenthetically in the text.

15. Susanne Woods, "How Free Are Milton's Women?" in *Milton and the Idea of a Woman,* ed. Julia M. Walker (Urbana: University of Illinois Press, 1988), 16.

16. Ibid., 30, 27.

17. Janet E. Halley, "Female Autonomy in Milton's Sexual Poetics," in *Milton and the Idea of a Woman,* ed. Julia M. Walker (Urbana: University of Illinois Press, 1988), 230. Subsequent references will be given parenthetically in the text.

18. Jodi Mikalachki, "Responding to the Bogey: Sympathy and Feminist Milton Criticism," in *Making Feminist History,* ed. William E. Cain, 105–22 (New York: Garland, 1994), 106. Subsequent references will be given parenthetically in the text.

19. Richard Bradford, *The Complete Critical Guide to John Milton* (London: Routledge, 2001), 167.

20. Ibid., 169.

21. James Grantham Turner, "The Aesthetics of Divorce: 'Masculinism,' Idolatry, and Poetic Authority in *Tetrachordon* and *Paradise Lost,*" in *Milton and Gender,* ed. Catherine Gimelli Martin (Cambridge: Cambridge University Press, 2004), 35.

22. Ibid., 36, 41.

23. Catherine Gimelli Martin, "Dalila, Misogyny, and Milton's Christian Liberty of Divorce," in *Milton and Gender,* ed. Catherine Gimelli Martin (Cambridge: Cambridge University Press, 2004), 61. Subsequent references will be given parenthetically in the text.

24. Dayton Haskin, "George Eliot as a 'Miltonist': Marriage and Milton in *Middlemarch,*" in *Milton and Gender,* 208.

25. Ibid., 220.

4

Feminism to Ecofeminism

The Legacy of Gilbert and Gubar's Readings of Mary Shelley's *Frankenstein* and *The Last Man*

Katey Castellano

The Madwoman in the Attic redefined nineteenth-century women's literature as a struggle for female self-definition against the literary heritage of Western patriarchal culture. In the process, Gilbert and Gubar transformed *Frankenstein* from being read as Mary Shelley's almost accidental articulation of her husband's intellectual discussions to a novel about Shelley's personal, yet learned, re-vision of "the male culture myth of *Paradise Lost.*"[1] *Frankenstein* stages the tension between representations of women as "Angels of the House," such as the patient Elizabeth, and women as "Eve/Sin/Monster," represented by the semiautobiographical creature whose affect alternates between self-loathing and murderous rage. By further suggesting that the creature's self-loathing reflects "the literal monstrosity many women are taught to see as characteristic of their own bodies," *The Madwoman in the Attic* aspired not only to transform the way we read women's literature but also to change the way women view themselves (240). As they more generally excavated the "roots of authority" in fairy tales and literary culture, arguing that "as a creation 'penned' by man, moreover, woman has been 'penned up' or 'penned in,'" Gilbert and Gubar established their own freedom to be critical feminists in a predominantly male academy (13). At the same time they wanted their readers—women who grew up reading and internalizing the misogynist messages in literature—to find critical freedom as well.

This politicized model of literary criticism led to the status of Gilbert and Gubar as public intellectuals, for unlike most books of literary criticism, *The Madwoman in the Attic* was read both by academics and by nonacademics with an interest in feminism. Within the academy, *Madwoman* inspired a plethora of new feminist readings of Mary Shelley's *Frankenstein.* At the same time, the volume was attacked by literary critics because, through the interpretive lens provided by the burgeoning fields of deconstruction and postcolonial theory, it seemed to espouse an essentialist view of women and to neglect women outside of white, middle-class experience.[2] Responding to these criticisms in the *Madwoman's* second edition, Sandra Gilbert states, "As an early venture it just couldn't be as theoretically sophisticated and specialized as some of its granddaughters, [yet] it seems to have communicated its political aspirations to a number of readers outside our field."[3] Thirty years later, Gilbert and Gubar continue to assert that feminist literary critics should have "political aspirations," which implies an audience outside of academia, even as critical theory and new historicism seem to have repositioned literary criticism permanently in a sphere outside of the public's interest and understanding.

Even though the "granddaughters" of Gilbert and Gubar's feminist literary criticism shunned public intellectualism in favor of greater, yet more arcane, theoretical sophistication, the great-granddaughters of feminist literary critics—ecofeminists—aspire to direct the message of feminist criticism back to a wider audience. As a political position, ecofeminism arose with the same feminist movement that inspired Gilbert and Gubar in the 1970s, yet it was not until the 1990s that ecofeminism emerged, along with ecocriticism more generally, as a viable, acknowledged method of literary criticism.[4] Ecofeminists have, like Gilbert and Gubar, called for a need to return to "the dream of a common language" in their rereading of literature, myth, and history. Greta Gaard and Patrick D. Murphy's groundbreaking volume, *Ecofeminist Literary Criticism,* for example, argues that ecofeminist literary criticism "emphasizes the urgency of political action aimed at dismantling institutions of oppression and building egalitarian and ecocentric networks in their place."[5] Although current ecofeminist readings tend to focus on contemporary women's literature about the environment, since nineteenth-century literature was written during the emergence of our industrial-capitalist society (which created our global environmental degradation), ecofeminist literary criticism can be productively extended to investigate nineteenth-century literature.

Public discourse, moreover, continues to evoke the figure of Frankenstein's creature when expressing a pessimistic or cautionary view of technological and industrial change. Anne Mellor points out that "condemners of genetically modified meats and vegetables now refer to them as 'Frankenfoods' . . . critics of nuclear, chemical, and biological weapons alike often make use of this monitory figure."[6] The tale of *Frankenstein,* then, continues to resonate with the anxiety aroused by the speed of our society's unrelenting technological alteration of the natural world; similarly the fear of a worldwide pandemic, like the one in *The Last Man,* continues to haunt contemporary culture. In addition to the many futuristic books and films that deal with worldwide epidemics, such as *Outbreak, Twenty-Eight Days Later, Twelve Monkeys,* and the many adaptations of Richard Matheson's novel *I Am Legend,* Shelley's *The Last Man* anticipates the public health issues that arise within a globalizing economy. Even a cursory glance at the news media reveals that our global economy is under the threat of pandemics such as AIDS, SARS, ebola hemorrhagic fever, the Avian flu, or multi-drug-resistant TB (and this list is by no means stable or exhaustive). Shelley's *The Last Man* initiates the genre that Priscilla Wald calls an "outbreak narrative," which tells "a contradictory but compelling story of the perils of human interdependence" and recognizes that the global scope of that interdependence is intimately connected to our concerns about "ecological balance and impending disaster."[7] Both *Frankenstein* and *The Last Man* grapple with profoundly modern ecological issues—scientific experimentation, infectious disease, and fertility and population—and an *ecofeminist* rereading of these texts reveals the way patriarchal power contributes to these problems.

Jettisoning the tradition of the Wordsworthian "green" pastoral,[8] Mary Shelley's proto–science fiction novels harness the rhetorical tradition of the prophetic mode to warn that the androcentric pursuit of scientific and imperialist "progress" may yield unintended and irreversible ecological and social consequences. At the beginning of *Frankenstein,* Victor tells his captain, Walton, "If you are inclined, listen to my tale. I believe that the strange incident connected with it will afford a view of nature, which may enlarge your faculties and understanding."[9] The prophetic mode of *Frankenstein* interrogates Victor's *view of nature,* focusing on the ecological ethics of human interaction with the nonhuman, yet they do so from a uniquely feminist perspective that explores the way gender roles contribute to social and environmental ethics.[10] In the first section of this essay, I suggest that by adapting and molding together these two modes—prophecy and feminist critique—Shelley turns Romantic prophecy into what we would today recognize as feminist ecocritique. The second section analyzes more specifically how Shelley exposes the social and environmental consequences of the masculine logic of domination. Finally, I return to Gilbert and Gubar's paradigm of the nineteenth-century woman vacillating between angel and madwoman to explore how the earth-angel-mother turns into a monster-madwoman seeking revenge. In this way *Frankenstein* and *The Last Man* envision a proto-ecofeminist embrace of nature's ferocious agency.

"Deciphering these sacred remains": Feminist Spirituality and Environmentalist Prophecy

In response to the misogynistic representations of women in *Paradise Lost,* Mary Shelley's *Frankenstein,* according to Gilbert and Gubar, embarks on "the alternative of *rewriting* Paradise Lost *so as to make it a more accurate mirror of female experience*" (220). More recently, Anne Mellor has argued that Shelley's *Frankenstein* engages in a "feminist critique of science" based "upon an extensive understanding of the most recent scientific developments of her day."[11] Both of these feminist critics argue that Mary Shelley's *Frankenstein* reworks or re-visions some aspect of patriarchal culture. Taking these feminist readings together, an ecofeminist reading reveals that Shelley excavates and identifies inextricable connections between social and environmental ethics by appropriating and revising the Miltonic prophetic message and mode; the dire consequences of Frankenstein's scientific ambition serve as a dual warning against male Romantic solitude (social ethics) and scientific alterations of the natural world (environmental ethics).

As discussed earlier, *Frankenstein's* prophetic intervention during the emergence of industrial pollution and technological advancement has retained its relevance into our postmodern age. As a champion of secular humanism who believes that humanity defines itself through being "antinatural," Luc Ferry decries the potency of the "old science fiction myth" of *Frankenstein* because of its potential to mobilize antihumanist, illegitimate fears (in Ferry's mind) that "technology is getting away from us, so that *we are no longer masters of our own mastery.*"[12] *Frankenstein's* prophetic, pessimistic, and antihumanist tone, however, anticipates some of the "deep green" responses to technology. Hans Jonas, for example, proposes that environmental ethics should be guided by "an imaginative 'heuristics of fear,'" which, by "replacing former projections of hope, must tell us what is *possibly* at stake, and what we must beware of." *Frankenstein*'s prophetic "view of nature" provides just such a proleptic heuristics of fear. By its very nature, prophecy will always be somewhat fragmented, so according to Jonas, we should abide by "the pragmatic rule to give the prophecy of doom priority over the prophecy of bliss."[13] *Frankenstein's* prophecy of technology's doom further proposes, from a nascent feminist perspective, that the patriarchal Christian religion, handed down by Milton, enables a view of both the natural world and women as resources for unlimited reproductive exploitation. By returning to and reinterpreting the prophetic language of Milton and the

Bible, *Frankenstein* demonstrates how Christianity and Western science similarly fuse women with nature in order to represent both as wild, mysterious places to the appropriated and exploited.

Taking on a more explicitly prophetic role in *The Last Man,* Shelley claims to be the inheritress of the Hellenic, prophetic power of the Sibyl. The preface recounts Mary and Percy Shelley's exploration of the labyrinthine cave of the Sibyl, where they discern passages that had been obscured by an earthquake and volcanic activity. In this forgotten passageway, the Shelleys discover the Sibylline leaves.[14] In an early recovery-reading of this neglected novel, Gilbert and Gubar argue that Shelley returns to the Sibyl's womb-cave for the birth of the text because "the womb-shaped cave is also the place of female power, the *umbilicus mundi,* one of the great antechambers of the mysteries of transformation" (95). The leaves of the Sibyl are scattered, so Gilbert and Gubar further read this text as "the story of the woman artist who enters the cavern of her own mind and finds there the scattered leaves not only of her own power but of the tradition which might have generated that power" (98). Although Kevin Hutchings's insightful ecocritical reading of this novel claims that *The Last Man*'s importance lies in its secular, materialist version of prophecy (as opposed to Christian prophecy), an ecofeminist reading would recognize this return to "a place of female power" as a form of ecofeminist spirituality based on a pre-Christian, mystical tradition.[15]

In her cave under the temple of Apollo, the Cumæan Sibyl held a unique position of female power among the Greek patriarchs as she alternately advised, opposed, and tricked both divine and worldly powers. Shelley adopts this female tradition of prophetic power, which is, moreover, intrinsically bound up with the natural world instead of separated from it. In a natural cave subject to the vicissitudes of geological change, a woman prophet literally writes on nature, creating the infamous Sibylline leaves.[16] In Percy Shelley's "Ode to the West Wind," prophetic authority is conceptualized as writing that finds its analogue in nature: "Drive my dead thoughts over the universe / Like withered leaves to quicken a new birth" (lines 63-64).[17] The withered leaves of Percy Shelley's famous poem are metaphors for loose-leaf paper, whereas Mary Shelley's sibylline version of the prophetic is a literal writing on the leaves in a place where the wilderness of nature and the culture of language are reconciled by female prophetic power. She writes,

> What appeared to us more astonishing, was that these writings were expressed in various languages: some unknown to my companion, ancient Chaldee, and Egyptian hieroglyphics, old as the Pyramids. Stranger still, some were in modern dialects, English and Italian. We could make out little by the dim light, but they seemed to contain prophecies, detailed relations of events but lately passed; names, now well known, but of mod-

> ern date; and often exclamations of exultation or woe, of victory or defeat, were traced on their thin scant pages.[18]

In this profound prophetic collapse of time, the leaves display ancient and modern languages that record past events and predictions of the future. As the author of the text, Shelley presents herself as the "translator" of the ancient tradition, "deciphering these sacred remains" that tell of the distant, twenty-first-century future (*Last Man,* 4).

In his germinal reading of the phenomenon of Romantic prophecy, Geoffrey Hartman suggests that the Romantic poet/prophet engages in a "mighty scheme not of truth but of troth—of trusting the old language, its pathos, its animism, its fallacious figures."[19] Appropriating her own version of this return to the "old language," Shelley's model of writing assembles the ancient female prophetic voices alongside the modern. In contradistinction to capitalist globalization (and these languages—Chaldee, Egyptian, Italian, English—are all languages of empire), the leaves further reveal the spatial and temporal connections of the globe in a version of globalization that displays, rather than homogenizes, the immense diversity of nature, language, and tradition. The knowledge inherited from the Sibyl's tradition of prophecy weaves a tale that powerfully critiques nineteenth-century British imperial power. As Alan Bewell points out, "Hers is the visionary task of writing the 'decline and fall of the British Empire,' proleptically, as a sibylline prophecy, a visionary post-colonialism."[20]

As Shelley's novelistic visionary postcolonialism adopts the voice of the Sibyl and re-visions Miltonic misogyny, Shelley's prophetic mode can be read as a spiritual ecofeminism that aims to discover and claim that "women were esteemed not only as mothers but as spiritual and political leaders as well."[21] The prophetic tone of both *Frankenstein* and *The Last Man* anticipates and perhaps even has influenced the prophetic rhetoric of contemporary environmentalism. "Ecological prophecy," Hutchings argues, "deploys its urgent message in order to warn humanity of the dire consequences facing nature and civilization should we fail to transform our social and economic practices."[22] Shelley's proto-ecological prophecies imagine the dire consequences of an identifiable masculine logic of domination over a feminized natural world.

"How dare you sport thus with life?": Shelley's Critique of the Masculine Logic of Domination

In the outer frame narrative of *Frankenstein,* a British man named Walton voyages into the perilous Arctic Circle in order to "satiate my ardent curiosity with the sight of a part of the world never before visited, and . . . tread a land never before imprinted by the foot of man" (*Frankenstein*, 7). Walton's desire to "tread," or make his mark, upon a virgin land mirrors the environmental ethics (or lack thereof) of his Gothic doppelgänger, Victor Frankenstein. As she introduces the characters of Walton and Victor by way of narrating their relationships with nature, Shelley calls attention to the masculinist psychosexual dynamics that motivate Enlightenment discovery and knowledge production, and further represents this knowledge production as a rupture of environmental integrity. The masculine logic of domination, according to Karen Warren, produces a web of oppressive conceptual frameworks that "have functioned historically to maintain, perpetuate, and 'justify' the dominations of women, other subordinated humans, and nonhuman nature."[23] *Frankenstein* repeatedly exposes this masculine logic of domination, beginning with Walton's desire to "tread upon" a virgin territory.

The logic of domination also characterizes the personality of Victor's favorite professor and mentor, Waldman. In his initial meeting with Victor, Waldman valorizes contemporary scientists who can "penetrate into the recesses of nature, and shew how she works in her hiding places. . . . They have acquired new and almost limitless powers" (*Frankenstein*, 28). Beyond connecting scientific discovery to an insatiable desire for power, here penetration into "the recesses of nature" equates the scientific mastery of nature with the sexual mastery of women. This mastery, moreover, is optimistically "limitless," revealing the capitalist, cornucopian view of nature that undergirds scientific experimentation and discovery. Using strikingly similar metaphors and vocabulary, Victor follows his mentor's example as he quests for ever greater penetration: "I pursued nature into her hiding places. Who shall conceive the horrors of my secret toil, as I dabbled among the unhallowed damps of the grave, or tortured the living animal to animate the lifeless clay?" (*Frankenstein*, 32). In this famous passage, Victor clearly collapses the female with the natural world as the object of scientific knowledge. Anne Mellor's feminist reading of *Frankenstein* has already implicitly excavated the proto-ecofeminist critique in Shelley's novel; she argues that this passage demonstrates how "uninhibited scientific penetration and technological exploitation of female nature is only one dimension of a patriarchal encoding of the female as passive and possessable, the willing receptacle of male desire."[24]

Mellor aptly analyzes how Shelley's "feminist critique of science" exposes the masculine psychosexual dynamics that motivate scientific discovery; an ecofeminist reading further attends to the way the passage above reveals that Victor's penetration of nature also exploits feminized and powerless nonhumans: animals and corpses. Victor's pursuit of nature into her hiding places requires the "torture of living animals." Here Shelley alludes to the vivisection of live animals, a practice about which there was great debate during her time because the surgery was done without anesthetic; vivisectionists, according to David Perkins, were considered by many to be "figures of horror."[25] Shelley intensifies this Gothic horror as Victor's scientific discovery further requires his intrusion into the "unhallowed damps of the grave"—unhallowed *because* of his intrusion and subsequent mutilation and manipulation of dead bodies. Like tortured animals, the dead cannot provide consent. Through his penetration of the grave, Victor disturbs the natural ecological cycle as he usurps the processes of decomposition in order to create life. Beyond equating the domination of women with the technological alteration of nature, this passage asserts that nonhumans, the ecological cycle, and women are similarly feminized objects of scientific mastery. In this way, Shelley's representation of the masculine pursuit of science anticipates Donna Haraway's list of interconnected terms that must be subordinated by Western science: "animal, nature, body, primitive, female."[26]

Like Haraway, Shelley further suggests the will to colonize and exploit the "primitive" motivates the scientific objectification and discovery. Victor dreams that through his ability to create life, "A new species would bless me as its creator and source; many happy and excellent natures would owe their being to me" (*Frankenstein,* 32). Part of Victor's motivation to gain esteem in science, then, amounts to a colonizing urge to rule over a new humanlike "species" that is not recognized as fully human. Anticipating the concerns of the ecofeminist physicist Vandana Shiva, who argues that "seed and women's bodies as sites of regenerative power are, in the eyes of capitalist patriarchy, among the last colonies," *Frankenstein* demonstrates the complicity of the scientific appropriation of reproduction with capitalist imperialism.[27]

Though Victor grasps the ability to appropriate reproduction, his creation, like so many colonial enterprises, turns out to be a "catastrophe." After seeing his creation, Victor laments, "the beauty of the dream vanished, and breathless horror and disgust filled my heart" (*Frankenstein,* 34). Anticipating the horror of the unintended consequences produced by technological, industrial, or colonial change, the prophetic tone of Shelley's novel also predicts the refusal of modern science to take responsibility for "cleaning up" the natural world after its alterations. Even though he abandons his creation, Victor is pursued and confronted by a living, speaking creature who asks, "How dare you sport thus with life?" (*Frankenstein,* 65). In this moment, not only does the creature confront his creator but also appropriated matter questions the scientist and the polluted environment turns against the capitalist: in short, in a reversal of the power dynamic at the heart of science, the object confronts the subject. After asking "How dare you sport thus with life?" the creature demands, "Do your duty towards me." *Frankenstein* thus becomes a tale about human responsibility. As Timothy Morton suggests, "*Frankenstein* is an ecological novel precisely not because it compels us to care for a preexisting notion of nature, but because it questions the very idea of nature." Once nature has been altered and even turned into a catastrophic monstrosity, rather than a longing for nostalgic restoration, "The task becomes to love the disgusting, inert, and meaningless."[28]

The creature demands that Victor create a female for him so that they can run off to the wilderness in South America. While engaging in the "filthy process" of creation a second time, Victor considers the unintended consequences: "Had I a right, for my own benefit, to inflict this curse upon everlasting generations?" (114). While ostensibly Victor's refusal to create a female stems from his interest in the welfare of "everlasting generations," a close reading suggests that he fears creating a female because, as Mellor points out, she might have the potential for "uninhibited female sexuality."[29] In addition to his fear of uninhibited female sexuality, the female's sexuality also implies that "a race of devils would be propagated upon the earth" (114). Victor thus destroys the female creature because he fears he will no longer have reproductive control over his species: the female creature's offspring would not bless him as creator. Unwilling to have anything less than complete reproductive control, Victor's ambition anticipates what Vandana Shiva has called "the ultimate ecological crisis," fabricated by the collusion of scientists and capitalists who have "torn apart cycles of regeneration, and forced them into linear flows of raw materials and commodities."[30] Victor destroys the female creature because of her capacity for a cycle of regeneration, which he had imagined would only flow linearly from him.

In *The Last Man,* the domination of nature transpires through equally passionate imperial conquest. Similar to the initial descriptions of Walton and Victor, Shelley's descriptions of the main male characters in *The Last Man* are based on their environmental ethics, or their conceptions of how the human and the nonhuman should interact. "Raymond was emphatically a man of the world," and as such, he "looked on the structure of society as but part of a machinery which supported the web on which his life was traced. The earth was spread out as a highway for him; the heavens built up as a canopy for him" (*Last Man,* 35). Raymond's emphatically Cartesian way of understanding the natural world as a vast machine full of resources for his benefit serves his individualistic, imperial ambitions; he declares, "my first act when I become King of England, will be to unite with the Greeks, take Constantinople, and subdue all Asia. I intend to be a warrior, a conqueror; Napoleon's name shall vail to mine" (44-45). Although Raymond's imperialist ambitions are, ostensibly, to spread political liberation and technological improvement,

Shelley's narrative clearly reveals Raymond's will to dominate both the natural world and the Asian other.

In contrast to Raymond's quest for authority over nature and society, "Adrian felt that he made a part of the great whole. He owned affinity not only with mankind, but all nature was akin to him; the mountains and sky were his friends; the winds of heaven and the offspring of earth his playmates" (35). Instead of androcentric domination, the character of Adrian senses what today's deep ecologists would call biospherical egalitarianism, a cooperative kinship with the nonhuman world around him.[31] By juxtaposing Raymond's mechanistic view of nature with Adrian's vitalist view, Shelley stages a debate between two different views of nature that translate into two different social and environmental ethics. In her analysis of the rise of Enlightenment science, Carolyn Merchant argues,

> The rise of mechanism laid the foundation for a new synthesis of the cosmos, society, and the human being, construed as ordered systems of mechanical parts subject to governance by law and to predictability through deductive reasoning. A new concept of the self as a rational master of the passions housed in a machinelike body began to replace the concept of the self as an integral part of a close-knit harmony of organic parts united to the cosmos and society.[32]

Adrian and Raymond clearly act out the debate Merchant describes: Raymond's mechanistic, individualistic view is pitted against Adrian's organic communalism. Given Adrian's more nurturing and feminine role—early in the text, Lionel refers to him as a "mother"—his older, organic way of nurturing the world with "ever greater care" is, in the logic of this novel, revealed as socially and morally superior to Raymond's selfish progressive view, even if it is finally politically ineffective.[33]

From the time that Raymond first took the office of Lord Protector to his conquering of the Greek state as his protectorate, Raymond's rule is characterized by an ethos of improvement, directed by progressive, "beneficial schemes." By building "canals, aqueducts, bridges, stately buildings, and various edifices for public utility," Raymond attempted to mold nature into a "mechanism" that, "once systematised according to faultless rules, would never again swerve into disorder" (82-83). After liberating Greece, Raymond's imperialist surge continues towards Constantinople, with a view to conquering Asia. His wife, Perdita, begs him to desist, his Greek soldiers refuse to enter the city with him, and finally, as he gets ready to enter the gates, "his very horse seemed to back from the fatal entrance; his dog, his faithful dog, lay moaning and supplicating at his feet" (156). Nevertheless Raymond enters Constantinople in order to plant a cross on the dome of St. Sophia, an important symbol in his crusade to liberate the world from the Turkish way of life, that "monument of antique barbarianism" (137). Upon entering the city, Raymond is crushed by a falling building in Constantinople; thus his wife, the Greek soldiers, and even his domesticated animals (in another constellation of the objects of knowledge production: woman/other/nonhuman) seem to have more wisdom than the conquering Raymond. As he enters the flaming, pestilent city, Raymond admits that he is "the victim of ambition." Like Victor Frankenstein, Raymond's ambition—"the prayer of my youth was to be one among those who render the pages of the earth's history splendid" (153)—not only destroys him, but destroys those around him.

After his death, Raymond returns to Lionel in a prophetic dream, "expanded into a gigantic phantom, bearing on its brow the sign of pestilence" (158). Raymond's conquest bears consequences not only for his family—Perdita commits suicide and their daughter Clara is left an orphan—but also for the entire human race: as his imperialist surge forces the West to encounter the East in the liminal space of Constantinople/Istanbul, the cultural contact zone turns into an epidemiological hot zone. *The Last Man* is "one of the first major works in the historical ecology of disease," Alan Bewell suggests, because "Shelley reflects on the important role empire has played in the spread of global diseases."[34] Imperial invasion allows the emergence of uncontrolled disease, and in Shelley's novel, this disease conducts a reverse invasion into the world of the colonizer. In other words, just as the goal of empire is rule over all, nature strikes back with its own unstoppable plague that conquers all, destroying the colonizer, colonized, and nations not even involved in the initial contact zone.

"Nature, our mother, and our friend, has turned on us a brow of menace": From the Angel to the Madwoman

In both *Frankenstein* and *The Last Man,* nature strikes back: Frankenstein's creature returns to confront his creator and the plague invades and conquers the globe. This apocalyptic imagination of nature's agency reflects the way Shelley anticipates a particularly ecofeminist view. "Ecofeminists have perhaps been the most insistent on some version of the world as active subject," Donna Haraway argues, and moreover, "acknowledging the agency of the world in knowledge makes room for some unsettling possibilities."[35] Unsettling the Wordsworthian green celebrations of a "nature [that] never did betray / the heart that loved her" and who leads humanity "from joy to joy,"[36] Shelley's gothic novels anticipate an ecofeminist imagination of nature as subject. Shelley imagines nature as woman (as does Wordsworth), yet Shelley's nature easily shifts from the joy-inducing, caretaking angel of the house to a volatile, monstrous madwoman with the power to seek violent revenge on those who will not care for her cooperatively.

This phrasing echoes Gilbert and Gubar's insight that nineteenth-century women writers "begin by alternately defining themselves as angel-women or as monster-women" (*Madwoman,* 44). Citing Sherry Ortner's breakthrough feminist analysis, "Is Male to Female as Nature Is to Culture?" Gilbert and Gubar suggest that representations of both motherly, angelic women and monstrous, mad women locate the female within *nature,* not culture; thus women must struggle with these social constructions of gender as they pen literary narratives. My ecofeminist rereading further asserts that Mary Shelley's "female pen" takes up this male construct of the angel/monster dualism and applies it directly to the natural world, thereby imagining nature's unsettling, feminist agency.

Even though nature finally takes on vengeful, monstrous qualities, at various points in both *Frankenstein* and *The Last Man* the female domestic sphere is associated with a localized pastoral ecotopia. Women in Shelley's novels conform with the woman as angel paradigm, and in both novels women repeatedly supplicate their husbands to return to or stay in a local environment: Elizabeth pleads with Victor to return home, Raymond's wife, Perdita, feels intense foreboding about his cosmopolitan ambitions, and Lionel Verney's wife, Idris, hugs, kisses, and weeps over an ancient oak tree in Windsor Forest. Women in these novels seem to be endowed with an innate sense of localized, domestic attachment; additionally there are moments when all the male characters look back with regret on leaving their native homes: Victor exclaims, "How much happier [is] that man who believes his native town to be the world" (*Frankenstein,* 31), and even Raymond admits, "I look back with regret to our tranquil life at Windsor" (*Last Man,* 144). Even though the way Shelley juxtaposes a female "ethic of care" for the environment with a male logic of domination may seem dangerously or naïvely essentialist, yet, perhaps because of her mother's insights about the cultural construction of gender, men too can exhibit an ethics of care. *The Last Man*'s Adrian is represented as "mother" who takes ever greater care of both humans and nonhumans, and Victor's brother Ernest decides to become a local farmer because "a farmer's life is a very healthy happy life; and the least hurtful or rather most beneficial profession of any" (*Frankenstein,* 39). By exposing the cultural construction of the masculine logic of domination, Shelley suggests that localized, domestic affections can serve as a feminist environmental ethics, and, moreover, therein lies an opportunity for social change because such an ethics is based on choice and gender performance, not biological sex.

In spite of the hints of domestic, pastoral harmony that might be attained through an agrarian localized economy, these moments are obliterated by the irreversibility of apocalyptic technological and imperial alterations of the natural world. Whereas the localized circle of destruction in *Frankenstein* destroys only those close to Victor, *The Last Man* takes on a wider political and environmental purview demonstrating the interconnections of all humanity with a global pandemic. Even when the protagonists who start the destruction repent and try to amend their ways, their world remains irreversibly altered.

After witnessing the destructive consequences of Raymond's imperial aggression, Lionel declares that England's quest for global domination and "improvement" should be abandoned: "Let us seek peace in our dear home, near the inland murmur of streams, and the gracious waving of trees, the beauteous vesture of the earth, and sublime pageantry of the skies" (*Last Man,* 171). Lionel's return to a domestic sphere safely nestled within the nationalistic icon of Windsor Forest is momentarily idealized as a "home" where humans can reinhabit an organic society, yet this ecotopian ideal is quickly overwhelmed by the plague that follows the repentant Lionel back to England, just as the creature pursues Victor. Almost immediately upon his return to England, Lionel is confronted with a side of nature that he had not anticipated:

> Nature, our mother, and our friend, has turned on us a brow of menace. She shewed us plainly, that, though she permitted us to assign her laws and subdue her apparent powers, yet, if she put forth but a finger, we must quake. She could take our globe, fringed with mountains, girded by the atmosphere, containing the condition of our being, and all that man's mind could invent or his force achieve; she could take the ball in her hand, and cast it into space, where life would be drunk up, and man and all his efforts for ever annihilated. (183)

Nature, gendered female, has transformed from a kind mother to a menacing figure with the agency for apocalyptic revenge. In a moment of humility, Lionel recognizes that humanity's Promethean efforts to "improve" and dominate the earth will be "for ever annihilated" if the natural world raises a mere finger in opposition.

In spite of Lionel's repentance and humility, the plague brings the commercial English economy to a standstill, instantly creating financial difficulty everywhere. At the same time, a reverse invasion of emigrants pours into the country. In response, the new leader of England, the bourgeois Ryland, abandons "his favourite scheme of equalization" as he realizes that he must confirm "manorial rights" so that they will be persuaded to return to their ethos of noblesse oblige and pay a 20 percent tax to sustain in order to subdue "the starving multitude that thronged around the palace of the Protectorate" (185). England must return power to the land-owning gentry, yet instead of effecting an overt, powerful hierarchy, this return to the land produces unprecedented social leveling and communal cooperation. Without imported food, the aristocrats must "give up their pleasure-grounds to the agriculturalist," and all classes must turn the soil and engage in subsistence farming. In spite of the numerous "beneficial schemes" that fueled England's industrial and capitalist progress, the plague's humiliating blow reveals that humanity cannot progress to a post-agricultural society. Thus as Lionel predicted, the natural world is confirmed in her power.

As a great leveler, the plague forces its survivors backwards from capitalism to feudalism, to agrarianism, and finally to a hunter/gatherer stage of society, with the exception that those who have survived the plague hunt and gather in the riches left by a society steeped in luxury.[37] In spite of the British government's heroic, humanitarian efforts to implement preventative measures and relieve suffering, a combination of the plague and natural disaster destroy the population. Lionel Verney is left alone as the last man. Even though he resembles the ideal, solitary, Romantic figure wandering through the landscape, Lionel's isolation is the consequence of an environmental disaster, not choice. He desperately seeks other humans while the entire earth seems forgetful of human habitation: the natural world overtakes cultural boundaries, weeds spring up in the uncultivated fields, and wild animals wander the city streets. Desperate for companionship, Lionel spies a peaceful flock of goats enjoying the thriving world around them, and he declares, "I will discipline my sorrowing heart to sympathy in your joys; I will be happy, because ye are so. Live on, ye innocents, nature's selected darlings; I am not much unlike you. Nerves, pulse, brain, joint, and flesh, of such am I composed, and ye are organized by the same laws. I have something beyond this, but I will call it a defect, not an endowment, if it leads me to misery, while ye are happy" (357-58). In the absence of human companionship, Lionel finds kinship with animals, and in the process he recognizes his commonality with all life on earth. In a momentary conversion to biocentrism, Lionel recognizes that the human species is not above all other species, and in fact, animals may instead be "nature's selected darlings."

Lionel's experience resonates with deep ecology's "ecosophical outlook," which, according to Arne Naess, "is developed through an identification so deep that one's *own self* is no longer adequately delimited by the personal ego or organism. One experiences oneself to be a genuine part of all life."[38] In a profoundly antihumanist move, the human capacity for thought is represented as "a defect, not an endowment." Yet this "ecosophical" recognition, like the previous one in Windsor Forest, turns out to be an illusion. Seeking community, Lionel approaches the goats and attempts to feed one of them.

In response to Lionel's pastoral care, the goat, "depressing his head, rushed at me with his horns" (358). In this startling and emotional scene, even Lionel's pastoral care is violently rejected as the world blissfully moves on in its own intelligence, both brutal and beautiful, dangerous and green, beyond human comprehension and reach.

In this way, Shelley's antihumanist view of apocalypse differs from most other depictions during this time. Although the "dismal science" of Thomas Malthus's *Essay on the Principle of Population* introduced an influential counter-Romantic conception of nature in which the power of population is always greater than the power of subsistence, he also argued that humans had the ability to prevent suffering and disease by implementing preventative checks on population.[39] Quite differently, Shelley imagines the complete destruction of a powerless humanity, even after the population has been reduced to far below the earth's carrying capacity. Whether in Lord Byron's "Darkness" or in John Martin's painting *The Last Man,* Romantic-era apocalyptic views generally depict the earth degrading alongside human population decline, yet Shelley's post-apocalypse imagines the earth continuing, even flourishing, without the human species, profoundly decentering both the Enlightenment and the Romantic conceptions of the human place in nature.

Although *Frankenstein* and *The Last Man* variously hint at the potential for harmonious organic pastoralism, they both abandon those hints in order to prophesy that certain modifications of nature and society are *irreversible,* and cannot be remedied by human intervention. Bereft of family and friends, Victor does not live to pass on his scientific secret, and Lionel heads off on a worldwide search for other humans, paradoxically venturing out on the same ocean that destroyed his two last companions. In this way, Mary Shelley's backwards movement in time, back to the pastoral in *Frankenstein* and radically back to a prehistorical state in *The Last Man,* is not Burkean but rather an anticipation of posthumanist ecofeminist ethos as articulated by Freya Mathews. Suggesting that even "eco-friendly" plans to build "a brave new world" amount to androcentric hubris, Mathews is in favor of allowing "an old world, a world unfolding naturally, redolent with meaning, beauty, and its own life and terms. The only way of achieving such a world, without engaging in further interventions, is, as I have explained, to let the present world grow old—to let the cities weather and fade, and the ivy creep up the walls."[40]

Shelley's profoundly antimodern view contests humanity's optimism in science, technology, and progress by imaginatively endowing the natural world with the agency of a "madwoman" capable of revenge. In this way, Shelley's view anticipates some of the most important rhetorical moves of contemporary environmentalists as they imagine epistemological alternatives to masculinist scientific discourse: Rachel Carson's influential chapter in *Silent Spring*, "Nature Fights Back," for example, insists that dominating nature with chemical pesticides amounts to "biocide" that destroys all life, or more recently, James Lovelock's "Gaia hypothesis" claims that the entire earth exists as a living, regulated system that will "revenge" itself on humanity if it continues to be unbalanced through Western industrial practices.[41] The feminist readings in *The Madwoman in the Attic* responded to the needs of its own era by helping women to identify the way they had been "penned in" by the narratives of patriarchal Western culture. Thirty years later, unprecedented species extinction, the increasing impact of global warming, and the dangerous toxic loads assaulting our bodies are all resounding calls for updated activist, feminist rereadings that might reveal the way a masculine logic of domination contributes to these problems. Although the prevailing theoretical and historical critical trends have nudged feminist criticism into an increasingly arcane academic sphere, if, following Gilbert and Gubar's model, feminist readings are again directed to a more general audience, then we may be able to develop a more informed sense of direction for activism on behalf of humans, animals, and the environment.

Notes

1. Sandra M. Gilbert and Susan Gubar, *The Madwoman in the Attic: The Woman Writer and the Nineteenth-Century Literary Imagination* (New Haven: Yale University Press, 1979), 220. Subsequent references will be given parenthetically.

2. Gayatri Spivak argues that "the emergent perspective of feminist criticism reproduces the axioms of imperialism. A basically isolationist admiration for the literature of the female subject in Europe and Anglo-America establishes the high feminist norm." Gayatri Chakravorty Spivak, "Three Women's Texts and a Critique of Imperialism," *Critical Inquiry* 12, no. 1 (Autumn 1985): 243. Spivak's critique directly attacks Gilbert and Gubar's readings of *Jane Eyre* and *Frankenstein.* In addition, Mary Jacobus argues against the naïve idea of "women's literature" because it neglects the textuality of sexuality. See Mary Jacobus, "Is There a Woman in This Text?" *New Literary History* 14, no. 1 (Autumn 1982): 117–41.

3. Sandra M. Gilbert and Susan Gubar, *The Madwoman in the Attic,* 2nd ed. (1979; New Haven: Yale University Press, 2000), xlii.

4. In the dialogue preceding the second edition of *Madwoman,* Gilbert admits that she continues to "share Adrienne Rich's 'dream of a common language' for criticism as well as for daily life." *Madwoman* (2000), xlii. Carolyn Merchant notes that the French writer Francoise d'Eaubonne used the term *ecofeminisme* in her book *Feminism or Death* (1974), in which she calls for an ecological revolution that "would entail new gender relations between women and men and between humans and nature." This point was taken up by American scholars, and "connections between women and nature and women and ecology were made in works by Sherry Ortner (1974), Rosemary Radford Ruether (1974), Susan Griffin (1978), and Carolyn Merchant (1980)." Carolyn Merchant, *Radical Ecology: The Search for a Livable World* (New York: Routledge, 2005), 194.

5. Greta Gaard and Patrick D. Murphy, introduction to *Ecofeminist Literary Criticism:*

Theory, Interpretation, Pedagogy (Urbana: University of Illinois Press, 1998), 12.

6. Anne Mellor, 'Making a `Monster': An Introduction to *Frankenstein*," in *A Cambridge Companion to Mary Shelley*, ed. Esther Schor (Cambridge: Cambridge University Press, 2003), 9.

7. Priscilla Wald, *Contagious: Cultures, Carriers, and the Outbreak Narrative* (Durham, N.C.: Duke University Press, 2008), 2.

8. With the rise of ecocriticism more generally, recent studies assert that the Romantics' work advocates proto-environmentalist "green" thought. Several studies have shown this connection, including Jonathan Bate, *Song of the Earth* (Cambridge: Harvard University Press, 2002), and James McKusick, *Green Writing: Romanticism and Ecology* (New York: Palgrave, 2000).

9. Mary Shelley, *Frankenstein*, ed. J. Paul Hunter (New York: W. W. Norton, 1996), 17. Subsequent references will be given parenthetically.

10. Shelley inherited her concerns about gender at least in part from her mother, Mary Wollstonecraft.

11. Anne Mellor, *Mary Shelley: Her Life, Her Fiction, Her Monsters* (New York: Routledge, 1989), 89.

12. Luc Ferry, *The New Ecological Order*, trans. Carol Volk (Chicago: University of Chicago Press, 1995), 77.

13. Hans Jonas, *The Imperative of Responsibility: In Search of an Ethics for the Technological Age* (Chicago: University of Chicago Press, 1984), x.

14. Gilbert and Gubar note that Percy, as male authority, must point out the leaves to Mary, which suggests her own inability to recognize literary maternity; yet perhaps this is a way in which Shelley has inherited her mother's refusal of gender essentialism, thus representing Percy Shelley as a mothering, nurturing figure (like Adrian in the novel) even though he is male.

15. Kevin Hutching reads the cave as part of a uniquely secular mode of this prophecy: "Thus the novel's Introduction subtly affirms the material—as well as visionary—value of earthly existence, challenging in the process the efficacy of an idealism based upon a dualistic conception of life" (241). Kevin Hutchings, "'A Dark Image in Phantasmagoria': Pastoral Idealism, Prophecy, and Materiality in Mary Shelley's *The Last Man*," *Romanticism* 10, no. 2 (2004): 228–44.

16. The Cumæan Sibyl, Marina Warner suggests, "exists as a Christian fantasy about a pagan presence from the past, and as such she fulfills a certain function in thinking about forbidden, forgotten, buried, even secret matters." Marina Warner, *From the Beast to the Blonde: On Fairy Tales and Their Tellers* (New York: Farrar, Straus, and Giroux, 1994), 11. This tradition of the Sibyl has also been appropriated by men. A famous example about which Mary Shelley would have known is S. T. Coleridge's volume of poetry entitled "Sibylline Leaves," published in 1817. In his preface, he states that he calls them Sibylline leaves "in allusion to their fragmentary and widely scattered state in which they have been long suffered to remain." S. T. Coleridge, *Sibylline Leaves: A Collection of Poems* (London: Rest Fenner, 1817), i.

17. Percy Shelley, *Shelley's Poetry and Prose*, ed. Donald H. Reiman and Neil Fraistat (New York: W. W. Norton, 2002), 221.

18. Mary Shelley, *The Last Man*, ed. Anne McWhir (Peterborough, Ont.: Broadview, 1996), 3. Subsequent references will be given parenthetically in the text.

19. In this quote, Hartman is discussing Wordsworth's *Prelude*. Geoffrey Hartman, "High Romantic Prophecy," *High Romantic Argument: Essays for M. H. Abrams*, ed. Lawrence Lipking (Ithaca, N.Y.: Cornell University Press, 1981), 38. Marina Warner argues the Sibyl is in a unique position to collapse history in a similar manner: "The Sibyl, as a cross-cultural symbol, necessarily denies historical difference; her words, originating in the past, apply to the rolling present whenever it occurs; however, the perceived fact of

her roots in the distant past adds weight to her message precisely because it is free of the historical context in which she uttered it; she was not fettered by historical time and place but could transcend it with visionary gifts." Warner, *From the Beast to the Blonde,* 71.

20. Alan Bewell, *Romanticism and Colonial Disease* (Baltimore: Johns Hopkins University Press, 1999), 297.

21. Spiritual ecofeminism has its problems, too, and Gaard goes on to summarize recent critiques of ecofeminism that make essentialist claims about the female connection to nature. Greta Gaard, *Ecological Politics: Ecofeminists and the Greens* (Philadelphia: Temple University Press, 1998), 39.

22. Kevin Hutchings, "The Modal Roots of Environmentalism: Pastoral, Prophecy, and Nature in Biblical and Early Romantic Discourse," *Genre* 35 (Spring 2002): 2.

23. Karen J. Warren, *Ecofeminist Philosophy: A Western Perspective on What It Is and Why It Matters* (Lanham, Md.: Rowman and Littlefield, 2000), 46.

24. Mellor, *Mary Shelley,* 115.

25. David Perkins, *Romanticism and Animal Rights* (Cambridge: Cambridge University Press, 2003), 15.

26. Donna Haraway, "The Dualism of Primatology," in *The Green Studies Reader,* ed. Laurence Coupe (New York: Routledge, 2000), 144–47.

27. Vandana Shiva and Maria Miles, *Ecofeminism* (Plymouth, U.K.: Zed Books, 1993), 25.

28. Timothy Morton, *Ecology without Nature: Rethinking Environmental Aesthetics* (Cambridge: Harvard University Press, 2007), 194–95.

29. Mellor, *Mary Shelley,* 120.

30. Shiva and Miles, *Ecofeminism,* 33.

31. See Arne Naess, "Ecosophy T.," in *Ecology, Community, Lifestyle,* ed. and trans. David Rothenberg (Cambridge: Cambridge University Press, 1989), 165–212.

32. Carolyn Merchant, *The Death of Nature: Women, Ecology, and the Scientific Revolution* (New York: Harper Collins, 1990), 214.

33. After Lionel comes under the tutelage of Adrian, he says, "I was a child lisping its devotions after its mother." Shelley, *The Last Man,* 22.

34. Bewell, *Romanticism and Colonial Disease,* 298.

35. Donna J. Haraway, *Simians, Cyborgs, and Women: The Reinvention of Nature* (New York: Routledge, 1991), 199.

36. William Wordsworth, "Lines Written a Few Miles above Tintern Abbey" (l. 121–24), William Wordsworth and S. T. Coleridge, *Lyrical Ballads* (New York: Routledge Classics, 2005), 160.

37. While the grave yawned beneath everyone, maturity and sexuality seemed to have stopped: "The world had grown old, and all its inmates partook of the decrepitude. Why talk of infancy, manhood, and old age? We all stood equal sharers of the last throes of time-worn nature. Arrived at the same point in the world's age—there was no difference in us; the name of the parent and child had lost their meaning; young boys and girls were level now with men." Shelley, *The Last Man,* 252. The "leveling" is so radical that not only are there no classes anymore, but neither age nor gender distinguishes one human from another.

38. Naess, "Ecosophy T.," 174.

39. See Thomas Malthus, *An Essay on the Principle of Population* (Oxford: Oxford University Press, 1999).

40. Freya Matthews, "Letting the World Grow Old: An Ethos of Countermodernity," *Worldviews: Environment, Culture, Religion* 3 (1999): 134.

41. Rachel Carson, *Silent Spring: Fortieth Anniversary Edition* (New York: Houghton Mifflin, 2002); James Lovelock, *The Revenge of Gaia: Earth's Climate Crisis and the Fate of Humanity* (New York: Basic Books, 2006).

5

Enclosing Fantasies

Jane Eyre

Madeleine Wood

> For the little drama enacted on "that day" which opens *Jane Eyre* is in itself a paradigm of the larger drama that occupies the entire book.[1]

Sandra Gilbert and Susan Gubar's observation from their chapter "Plain Jane's Progress: A Dialogue of Self and Soul" from *The Madwoman in the Attic* contends that Jane Eyre's red room scene establishes the symbolic pattern for the novel as a whole. Gilbert and Gubar claim that Jane's incarceration encapsulates the heroine's fundamental problem: the placing of an "anomalous orphan" within a society in which she has no place.

> And that Charlotte Brontë quite consciously intended the incident of the red-room to serve as a paradigm for the larger plot of her novel is clear not only from its position in the narrative but also from Jane's own recollection of the experience at crucial moments throughout the book: when she is humiliated by Mr. Brocklehurst at Lowood, for instance, and on the night when she decides to leave Thornfield. In between these moments, moreover, Jane's pilgrimage consists of a series of experiences which are, in one way or another, variations on the central, red-room motif of enclosure and escape. (*Madwoman,* 340-41)

This insight constitutes the interpretative foundation for my essay. Reading across Gilbert and Gubar's analysis, I highlight not only female empowerment and self-development but also self-enclosure. The concept of pilgrimage implies a sanctified journey that culminates in a blessed place: while Jane, as the writer of her own "autobiography," undoubtedly figures her story in these terms, in fact we see a compulsive motif of escape and return rather than progression. Brontë problematizes the concept of pilgrimage, asking us whether we can ever find a true resting place for our selves. Jane does not renounce her sense of self in the same way as do Charles Dickens's sacrificial heroines (for instance, Amy Dorrit and Florence Dombey), but she undoubtedly perpetuates the conditions that lead to her liminal social and psychological state. While the notion of "pilgrimage" provides the structural model for Gilbert and Gubar's analysis, my essay uses a traumatic model to reveal the lack of progression in Jane's journeying: she is caught within her own patterns of desire as well as by patriarchal structures. This concept is implicit within *The Madwoman in the Attic*'s exposition: the primary doubling of the self in the red room scene is symbolically echoed through the introduction of Bertha Rochester and Jane's own pervasive doubts prior to her wedding to Edward Rochester. These observations will be reconsidered, exploring how the red room episode establishes patterns of desire that repeat throughout the text. Jane's encounter with the "other" in the red room is not only with the unknown self but with the missing, and longed-for, father figure. Rather than seeing Jane's path through the novel as a progressive movement towards a predetermined goal, I see Brontë's story as inscribing a repetitive fantasy. By reevaluating *The Madwoman in the Attic*'s treatment of Jane Eyre through the concept of trauma, the nature of the "female imagination" in the nineteenth-century novel can likewise be reconsidered: she is enclosed not simply by male structures but by desire for the male figure. While Gilbert and Gubar's essay concludes with an optimistic reading of Jane and Rochester's isolated marriage at Ferndean, I argue that Brontë's decision to detach her protagonists from both social and familial structures means that their marriage becomes disturbingly utopian, in Thomas More's original sense of an impossible "no-place," rather than idyllic.[2]

The model of trauma implicit in this reading is Sigmund Freud's, taken from his writings of the 1890s, prior to the publication of *The Interpretation of Dreams*.[3] These theories work from the conceptual premise that an originary event, or "scene," creates a fundamental break in the subject's development, a break that can only make sense through the accumulation of secondary scenes that follow. Throughout the 1890s, Freud's trauma model became progressively more complex, moving beyond the single originary events explored by Josef Breuer in the case of "Anna O."[4] But the scenography of trauma slides under Freud's analytic technique: scenes proliferate, constantly referring back to an origin that can never be fully identified, and yet that is compulsively repeated. The "primal scene" emerges as both a product of fantasy *and* as a real event. The trauma is placed within the biographical time of the protagonist but exceeds this implied linearity: this temporal break is constitutive of the subject's construction of self and the emergence of a symptom or mode of fantasy. It is significant that the primal scenes created in Freud's early case histories are textual events, based upon processes of interpretation and free association. This does not invalidate Freud's emphasis on historicity: his fluctuating theorizations enable a space to emerge in which time can relate both to the subject and to the encounter with the "other."[5]

Throughout the 1890s, Freud increasingly located the etiology of pathological symptoms within the child: even in "The Preliminary Communication" (1892), Freud and Breuer tentatively identify childhood as a site of primary trauma, claiming that "quite frequently it is some event in childhood that sets up a more or less severe symptom which persists during the years that follow."[6] The beginning of a narrative, like the onset of a traumatic occurrence, is necessarily ruptured, a fiction within a fiction, as there can never be a "true" beginning or end. Peter Brooks argues that plot "puts time into motion and suspends it, in a single movement."[7] *Jane Eyre* is structured like a trauma through the originary scene in the red room in chapter 2. This scene interrelates the reality of the event with Jane's fantasy and retrospective narration, for as Gilbert and Gubar rightly claim, the childhood scene provides *Jane Eyre* with its narrative dynamism—childhood bears a privileged relation to the questions of subjectivity and identity that structure Brontë's novel. Carolyn Steadman has suggested that nineteenth-century culture often figured childhood as a site of loss; the child was perceived as a haunting presence within the adult.[8] Brontë's radical use of a first-person, retrospective narrator in *Jane Eyre* demonstrates her fascination with the resonant power of childhood experience, which never really goes away. *Jane Eyre* consistently belies Michael Wheeler's confident assertion that the narrative is "linear," that the reader traces "Jane's progress from location to location, [emphasizing] that hers is a spiritual journey or quest."[9] Instead, we can discover in the novel a series of disturbing returns and repetitions that establish the motif of feminine enclosure.

Jane Eyre is primarily concerned with the manifestations of patriarchy within specific *familial* structures. Jane's gothicized episode in the red room not only represents an enclosure within patriarchy, as Gilbert and Gubar suggest, but also involves an encounter with the shadowy absence-presence of her dead uncle Reed. Jane's longing for family is compressed into one emblematic scene that is quite complex, both in its originary status and its different repetitions. The first chapter of *Jane Eyre* is concerned with establishing Jane within a network of family relations in which she is excluded and despised.

This exclusion is taken to its logical extreme when Jane is incarcerated in chapter 2. Brontë depicts the Reed family as dysfunctional (to say the least), a site of violence, emotional manipulation, and misplaced affection (Mrs. Reed adores her vicious son, John). The Reeds are symbolically linked through their "unwholesome" skin and thick lips, although John reviles his mother for her "dark skin," "similar to his own."[10] Through this racial symbolism, Mrs. Reed and her son are able to represent both the violence and inhumanity of the slave driver *and* the degradation of the slave. This double figuration means that although it is Jane who is the obvious outsider or "alien" in the family (*JE,* 24), it is John Reed and his mother who are metaphorically correlated with otherness and aberrant desire. Questions of inside and outside, acceptance and expulsion are already obscured, and family ideals are irretrievably damaged prior to Jane's imprisonment in the red room. The suggested inferiority of mother and son is later reinforced by Bertha's own racial difference, replaying Jane's childhood associations. With these connections in mind, it is possible that Bertha represents not only the repressed double of Jane herself but the repudiated family connection between Jane and the Reed household. Tellingly, as an adult, Jane denies that she has any family; when Rochester asks if she has any uncles or aunts she replies, "None that I ever saw" (*JE,* 139).

Jane's incarceration in the red room—Gilbert and Gubar's "patriarchal death chamber" (*Madwoman,* 340)—changes her experiential relation to her family. It is, within itself, already a repetition of a potential alternative beginning, as her uncle Reed's final request for his wife to raise Jane as one of their own children took place in the red room (*JE,* 23). Mrs. Reed's betrayal is the fundamental question of Jane's childhood existence: "Yet in what darkness, what dense ignorance, was the mental battle fought! I could not answer the ceaseless inward question—why I thus suffered" (*JE,* 23). In the red room the father-daughter relationship is established as an ambivalent model of desire, providing Jane with the prototype for her relationships with all the male characters she encounters throughout the novel. The room is constructed as a symbolic encounter with paternity: as Gilbert and Gubar put it, the room is a specifically *male* space: it is "still" and "quiet," removed from the "nursery" and the "kitchen," the chatting of the servants and the disapproval of Mrs. Reed. It is a place of "secrets," containing "parchments," a "jewel-case" and a "miniature of [Mrs. Reed's] dead husband" (*JE,* 21). These carefully described details attest to a mystery within paternal authority, inscribed in unread documents and an unseen picture. The ghostly presence of Jane's uncle is an absence that contrasts with John Reed's excessive physical presence in chapter 1. The room is not only marked by symbolic representations of authority, with a "throne-like" chair by the head of the bed (*JE,* 21), but is metonymically connected to the vault in which Mr. Reed lay dead. As Jean Wyatt suggests, the scene in the red room is the "most forcible of [Jane's] confinements to the gender components of the patriarchal family."[11]

Despite this, Brontë creates a sense of sanctity, even blessedness: the bed is like a crimson altar, suggesting that a sacrifice has taken place in the betrayal of Jane and her uncle by Mrs. Reed; Jane's use of the word "tabernacle" implies that the bed and its past occupant had a sacred role in the household. The room is sensuous and luxurious, awash with a range of reds and pinks: the bed has impressive "mahogany pillars," "deep-red damask" curtains, and the carpet is red (*JE,* 20). The rich effect is softened by the room's "soft-fawn" walls, which have an almost coy "blush of pink" (*JE,* 21). The sensuality of Brontë's description problematizes the red room's perceived status as a grim patriarchal prison.

Just as Freud fluctuated between an emphasis on memory or fantasy in his theories of the 1890s, fifty years earlier Brontë also saw no need to choose. Jane confronts both the room and herself, and we are encouraged to look through the child's eyes as she peruses the space. Jane describes the wardrobe with its "subdued, broken reflections," the "muffled windows," and finally the "great looking-glass." At first the mirror merely perpetuates the emptiness and "vacant majesty of the room," until she "explored the depth it revealed." There is a fundamental doubleness to the affective atmosphere Brontë creates. As Gilbert and Gubar observe, the red room undoubtedly represents "the spirit of a society in which Jane has no place" (*Madwoman,* 340). However, it is also the first and only place she was ever loved: Mr. Reed may have been the "father who was not really her father" (*Madwoman,* 340), but his final words concerned her welfare (*JE,* 261). Later, on her own deathbed, Mrs. Reed recounts how her husband would have his little niece "brought continually to his bed-side" (*JE,* 261). The room is grim and enclosed, "a jail," but it dances with shadows and the indubitable memory of Mr. Reed's love (*JE,* 21, 23).

This shows unequivocally that love is both a male and female concern, both patriarchal and feminine (in the traditional sense): Mr. Reed's devotion to his sister and his sister's daughter rewrites the patriarchal house as one where shelter and protection can be found. This originary moment undermines any clear opposition between patriarchy and female identity. Later, it is Rochester's presence that makes Thornfield Hall a "home," even a "paradise" (*JE,* 276, 389), and despite the obvious charms of Diana and Mary's practical caretaking, it is St. John's presence that grants Moor House its magic and potency. In her account of the Rivers family, Jane consistently juxtaposes Diana and Mary's concerns for her well-being with St. John's more enigmatic, fascinating presence. The connection between patriarchal enclosure and love indicates the novel's process of double-think: despite Jane's restlessness and desire for freedom, she has an equally potent desire for love, which is relentlessly couched in relation to a male figure. The plot colludes on Jane's behalf: the inheritance from her powerful and protective uncle in Madeira grants her the financial independence to return to Rochester on her own terms, supposedly those of an equitable love.

In the red room, the wardrobe's broken reflections point toward the division of perception and identity, reinforced by the self-image presented in the mirror. Jane's perception of herself is uncanny, both other and same, seeming to reemerge from a time preceding the Reeds. She sees herself as a "strange" fairy-tale "little figure" from one of Bessie's stories, a "tiny phantom" who has returned to haunt the family (*JE*, 21). (The adult Jane's dreams of children echo this imagery with the "wailing" "baby phantom" who portends death and disgrace for the Reeds.) The way in which Jane perceives herself in the mirror creates a fragile unity; her strange self-image parallels the language Rochester uses towards her: she is unique, "imp-like" and "fairy-like." The red room scene constitutes a moment of empowering self-fashioning as well as self-perception, interrelating memory with the imagery that Jane, as an author, uses throughout her story. The seeming self-abnegation implied in Jane's view actually marks her out as seductively different as well as disturbingly foreign. It is Jane's sight of herself in the mirror that provokes her to consider her identity and position within the Reed family, and the idealization of fatherhood emerges as a distinct idea to Jane as a result of her incarceration:

> A singular notion dawned upon me. I doubted not—never doubted—that if Mr. Reed had been alive he would have treated me kindly; and now, as I sat looking at the white bed and overshadowed walls—occasionally also turning a fascinated eye towards the dimly gleaming mirror—I began to recall what I had heard of dead men, troubled in their graves by the violation of their last wishes . . . I wiped my tears and hushed my sobs; fearful lest any sign of violent grief might waken a preternatural voice to comfort me. (*JE*, 24)

There is a tension between the desires Jane harbors in fantasy and her practical realizations: the ghost of paternal love may initially be reassuring, but it may ultimately be terrifying, only "consolatory in theory" (*JE*, 24). Jane talks herself into fancying that the light passing over the window is "a herald of some coming vision from another world" (*JE*, 24). Although the chapter concludes with Jane fainting in "a species of fit" (*JE*, 25), she undoubtedly achieves a heightened sense of being from this episode. In chapter 4, Jane assumes Mr. Reed's absent—but still potent—paternal power to demand her rights from Mrs. Reed: "'What would uncle Reed say to you, if he were alive?' was my scarcely voluntary demand. I say scarcely voluntary, for it seemed as if my tongue pronounced words without my will consenting to their utterance: something spoke out of me over which I had no control" (*JE*, 36). From this point on, Jane's subjectivity is both a result of, and a breach with, paternal authority. Her experience in the red room leads to her continued rebellion at Gateshead, a replaying of the imagined conflict between Mr. and Mrs. Reed, and her departure to Lowood school.

Looking back at chapter 1, we first meet Jane enclosed in a window seat, shrouded with scarlet drapery, a "red moreen curtain" drawn close around her. This luxurious enclosure gives her a privileged view of the "winter afternoon" as well as providing her with a space in which to dream over Bewick's *History of British Birds:* "Folds of scarlet drapery shut in my view to the right hand; to the left were the clear panes of glass, protecting, but not separating me from the drear November day" (*JE*, 14). Jane reads Bewick with all the power of a child's imagination, creating a little theater in her mind with a series of "vignettes": each picture in the book tells a story (*JE*, 15). She imagines spectral and yet seductive "death-white realms" peopled with "phantoms" (*JE*, 15). Here her enclosure engenders her creativity: these dreamy images are clearly the basis for the otherworldly paintings Rochester examines later. This episode enriches our understanding of the way in which enclosure operates in *Jane Eyre:* self-willed as well as enforced, potentially liberating as well as stultifying. In the biography of her friend, Elizabeth Gaskell recounts how Brontë hid from other guests when visiting Plymouth Grove.[12] While Gaskell attributed this to shyness, it is tempting to note in this context how Jane similarly separates herself from the visiting gentry at Thornfield—and the series of contemptuous observations she makes to the reader from this shielded position. Placing herself behind a half-drawn curtain in the drawing room before the guests arrive after dinner, Jane coolly assesses the company as they enter one by one, criticizing Lady Ingram for her insupportable pride and (notably) her "inflated, darkened features" (*JE*, 195).

In *Reconstructing Desire: The Role of the Unconscious in Women's Reading and Writing,* Jean Wyatt identifies the basic fantasy structure of *Jane Eyre* as "being incarcerated in a patriarchal structure and burning it down in revenge."[13] As she herself observes, this statement needs qualification: diametrically opposed desires can undoubtedly coexist in both the unconscious of the individual and in the dynamics of a text. Wyatt limits this concept to the troubled nature of Rochester and Jane's relationship and its flirtatious father-daughter dynamic, but this notion can be extended effectively to the entire question of women's place within patriarchy; not only does Jane wish to burn down patriarchal structures, she wishes to exist within them, be accepted by them, and appropriate them. It is this fundamental ambivalence that leads to the novel's repetitive or traumatic symbolic structure. It is the feminine problem of *exclusion* that cannot be resolved.

The initial absence of the father figure, eerily resonant in the red room, is readdressed throughout the novel in Jane's relations with Mr. Lloyd, Mr. Brocklehurst, Mr. Rochester, St. John Rivers, and her absent uncle in Madeira: the primary affective problem—desirous fear connected to father or lover—is reinscribed throughout the novel. Gilbert and Gubar's claim that Jane makes a "mythical progress from one significantly named place to another" elides the processes of substitution through which each domestic location replays elements of the last, thus calling into question the whole concept of personal development and "independent maturity" espoused in *The Madwoman in the Attic* (*Madwoman*, 342, 350). The proliferating scenes that emerge following the primal red room scene show a reworking of the originary absence. In the childhood section, Mr. Lloyd and Mr. Brocklehurst operate antithetically, multiplying Jane's perceptions of paternity and masculinity. In a novel so concerned with equitable communication, it is critical that Mr. Lloyd is the first character to engage Jane in a "discourse" (*JE*, 35): he asks her what she wants from her life, even offering her the chance of being united with the unknown Rivers—her father's family; to each of his questions she "reflects" upon her answer (*JE*, 32-33). Jane rejects her chance to create new familial bonds in favor of the "complete change" offered by school (*JE*, 33). Mr. Lloyd also helps Miss Temple clear Jane of Mr. Brocklehurst's allegations at Lowood. But even this episode has unpleasant consequences: Miss Temple's authority is weakened as a result, and Jane once again is caught between the good "father" (Lloyd) and the bad "father" (Brocklehurst), just as she was drawn to memories of Uncle Reed's kindness but afraid of being visited by his ghost. Gilbert and Gubar have argued that Brocklehurst represents an aggressive "phallic" mode of patriarchy against Mr. Lloyd's gentleness as a physician (*Madwoman*, 344). Although the comparison is inexact, this antithesis prefigures Jane's choice between Rochester and St. John Rivers and illustrates the importance of male prototypes.

Talking over Jane's uncanny experience in the red room before her departure from Gateshead, Bessie and Abbott whisper to each other about the apparition of her uncle dressed in spectral white, with a great black dog beside him. This seems at first simply to reflect the servants' gratuitous relish for the supernatural, but it also provides the image for Rochester's own dramatic appearance in chapter 12—a crucial chapter in Jane's story. He is first seen with his black "lion-like" dog in the night, with the "moon waxing bright" (*JE*, 128); the "tramp, tramp" of his horse is reiterated twice in one paragraph, creating a sense of hyperawareness as well as waiting and longing: "In the absolute hush I could hear plainly [Hay's] thin murmurs of life. My ear too felt the flow of currents; in what dales and depths I could not tell: but there were many hills beyond Hay, and doubtless many becks threading their passes" (*JE*, 127-28). Rochester's introduction is critical in reaffirming the fundamental ambivalence of the novel's fantasy structure, but let's remember that chapter 12 opens with Jane's famous plea for liberty from Thornfield's roof and her impassioned discontent with her restricted lot:

> Women feel just as men feel; they need exercise for their faculties and a field for their efforts as much as their brothers do; they suffer from too rigid a restraint, too absolute a stagnation, precisely as men would suffer; and it is narrow-minded in their more privileged fellow-creatures to say that they ought to confine themselves to making puddings and knitting stockings, to playing on the piano and embroidering bags. It is thoughtless to condemn them, or laugh at them, if they seek to do more than custom has pronounced necessary for their sex. (*JE*, 125)

It is in this chapter, moreover, that the doubling between Jane and Bertha is firmly established. Jane paces the corridors, "backwards and forwards" like a caged animal, longing for "incident, life, fire, feeling" (*JE*, 125), foreshadowing Bertha's actions in the attic. It is in the second half of the same chapter that Jane's first meeting with her enigmatic master "marks with change" her "monotonous" life (*JE*, 132). The proto-feminist plea for liberty is answered with the appearance of a dark, brooding, Byronic hero (who falls under Jane's spell). Rochester is immediately struck by Jane's otherworldly aspect: "when you came on me in Hay Lane last night, I thought unaccountably of fairy tales, and had half a mind to demand whether you had bewitched my horse" (*JE*, 139). Rochester appears in the guise of the paternal ghost, and the encounter is initially staged in unambiguously supernatural terms—even Pilot is described hyperbolically as having "pretercanine" eyes (*JE*, 127). The bathetic moment when Rochester falls off his horse with a mild curse ("What the deuce is to do now?" [*JE*, 128]), repositions the male and female participants in Jane's—and the novel's—wishful fantasy. Instead of being rendered unconscious by the overwhelming possibility of the male presence, as she was in the red room, Rochester's accident contrives to manufacture a sense of equality that would otherwise be impossible. Gilbert and Gubar argue that Jane and Rochester "begin as spiritual equals"; but, in fact, Brontë never lets us forget what a tenuous construct this equality is, both in psychological and narrative terms. Rochester's fall in their first meeting prefigures his blinding and crippling when Bertha burns down Thornfield and Jane's own barely concealed delight at his physical and emotional dependence at Ferndean.

If we take equitable communication as the basis for Brontë's formulation of sexual equality, then the development of Rochester and Jane's relationship becomes further problematized. Jane describes herself as a vessel waiting to be filled with his conversation, she has a "keen delight in receiving the new ideas he offered, in imagining the pictures he portrayed, and following him in thought." Jane's potent imagination, apparent from the first chapter of the novel, now appears reduced to a function of Rochester's speech. She ceases "to pine after kindred" and "gathers flesh and strength" (*JE,* 166). Rochester's stories are filling the blanks of her existence, but she makes it clear to the reader that she herself "talks little" (*JE,* 166). It is within this context that Bertha sets fire to Rochester's bed. Alone in her own bed, musing on her attraction to her master, Jane hears Bertha's "demoniac laugh," seemingly at her bedside (*JE,* 167). Hastening to Rochester's bedchamber, she "baptizes" his couch to quench the flames (*JE,* 168), constructing her act as a ceremonial, even blessed, act of purification. If we accept the doubling between Bertha and Jane established in chapter 12, then this episode implies a trial by fire and water (further evoked in St. John *Rivers*), a symbolic ordeal through which Rochester must pass to become worthy of Jane's love; it is also, of course, a precursor of Bertha's destruction of Thornfield. By this symbolic token, Jane can seem to be both unconscious murderer and conscious savior, a conflict that leads to "delirium" and dreams of marriage: "Till morning dawned I was tossed on a buoyant but unquiet sea, where billows of trouble rolled under surges of joy. I thought sometimes I saw beyond its wild waters a shore, sweet as the hills of Beulah"—the Hebrew word for "married" (*JE,* 172).

The fact that the equality between Jane and Rochester is reliant on melodramatic contrivances of this sort belies the idealized reading of their relationship we find in *The Madwoman in the Attic.* Gilbert and Gubar oversimplify Rochester's games, claiming that Jane sees through his disguise when he dresses as a gypsy: "The implication is that he did not—or could not—[deceive her] because he respects 'the resolute, wild, free thing looking out of' Jane's eyes as much as she herself does" (*Madwoman,* 353). In this interpretation, Jane and Rochester's equality is paramount; but if we look back at the scene, there is an ambiguity ignored by Gilbert and Gubar. Rochester may not be able to play the role of the gypsy with Jane, but he plays an "unaccountable" role, one that is emphatically not his own (*JE,* 228). Jane is confused, disoriented, her sense of self undermined by his game and by his love: "Where was I? Did I wake or sleep? Had I been dreaming? Did I dream still? The old woman's voice had changed: her accent, her gesture, and all were familiar to me as my own face in a glass—as the speech of my own tongue" (*JE,* 227). Returning to the scene of the first fire, Brontë creates an edgy juxtaposition between Jane's reflection while she lies in her bed and Bertha's conflagration of Rochester's bedchamber to demonstrate the fragility of Brontë's ideological construction of "equality": when Jane is under threat of being possessed too fully by Rochester, her identity subsumed by his, the plot contrives (either through the intervention of Bertha or through more prosaic events) to undermine Rochester's overwhelming influence.

Despite the novel's games of equality, Jane emphasizes her lack of volition in her relationship with her master: "My master's colourless, olive face, square, massive brow, broad and jetty eyebrows, deep eyes, strong features, firm, grim mouth—all energy, decision, will—were not beautiful according to rule; but they were more than beautiful to me: they were full of an interest, an influence that quite mastered me,—that took my feelings from my own power and fettered them in his . . . He made me love him without looking at me" (*JE*, 198).

For all his manipulations and disguises, Rochester willingly shares more of himself and his history than does Jane. Through the repeated trope of "spiritual communication," Brontë subtly draws attention to Jane's own compromised attitude towards love, possession, and equality. In the engagement scene in the garden, Jane demands the equality she feels is her due and figures her speech as a divine communication: "It is my spirit that addresses your spirit; just as if both had passed through the grave, and we stood at God's feet, equal,—as we are!" (*JE*, 284). As the novel progresses, Jane seems to fear the loss of herself, the possessiveness, that this spiritual love could initiate. Her fear that her uncle Reed's ghostly voice may whisper words of comfort to her in the red room is later realized in the extraordinary telepathic exchange that takes place between Rochester and her. Her childhood fear is revealed as a wishful fantasy, but this magical event jars with Jane's ideals, as she prohibits Rochester from sharing the knowledge of it (*JE*, 497). In *Jane Eyre*, patriarchal figures are feared for their excess of social power. However, there is also a repetitive movement of gesturing towards, and then running away from, the male source of love: the pattern established in the red room. This, in itself, serves to trap Jane in the series of patriarchal enclosures identified in *The Madwoman in the Attic*.

If we read across the movement of the plot—"just reading" as Sharon Marcus terms it in *Between Women*—Jane's actions denote a strange stop-start movement that veers between paternal authority and romantic love.[14] The role of her absent uncle in Madeira is a case in point: fearing the vulnerability, possession, and degradation that her engagement to Rochester brings, she writes to her newly discovered uncle to make herself known to him:

> Glad was I to get him out of the silk warehouse, and then out of a jeweller's shop: the more he bought me, the more my cheek burned with a sense of annoyance and degradation. As we re-entered the carriage, and I sat back feverish and fagged, I remembered what in the hurry of events, dark and bright, what I had wholly forgotten—the letter of my uncle, John Eyre, to

> Mrs. Reed: his intention to adopt me and make me his legatee. "It would, indeed, be a relief," I thought, "if I had ever so small an independency; I never can bear being dressed like a doll by Mr. Rochester, or sitting like a second Danae with the golden shower falling daily round me. I will write to Madeira the moment I get home, and tell my uncle John I am going to be married, and to whom: if I had but a prospect of one day bringing Mr. Rochester an accession of fortune, I could better endure to be kept by him now." (*JE*, 301)

Jane's shift into the present tense in relating the progression of her thoughts brings a palpable sense of urgency to the event. Writing to her uncle leads directly (with a startling coincidence typical of the Victorian novel) to Richard Mason's prevention of the fraudulent marriage. From his deathbed, her uncle John "implored Mr. Mason to lose no time in taking steps to prevent the false marriage" (*JE*, 329). Once more a dying uncle saves Jane from a social fall, just as Mr. Reed did upon his own deathbed. Jane's bid for freedom from Rochester's oppressive attentions takes the form of an appeal to an absent father figure, who then "saves" her from her lover. The affective problem set up in the red room is repeated: Jane fears male power, desires love, and also desires the power that the male love object possesses. This complex psychological pattern operates alongside *Jane Eyre*'s proto-feminist social agenda.

As Gilbert and Gubar rightly demonstrate, as the wedding approaches, "Jane's anger and fear about her marriage intensify, she begins to be symbolically drawn back into her own past, and specifically [begins] to reexperience the dangerous sense of doubleness that had begun in the red room" (*Madwoman*, 357). The symbolic distance between Jane and Bertha reaches a crisis two nights before the wedding. Thinking of her union with Rochester, Jane imagines the life ahead of her as a "brook" running towards the "depths of the sea." "I thought of the life that lay before me—your life, sir" (*JE*, 314). She has two quasi-prophetic dreams. In the first, she carries a feeble child on a long road; Rochester is far ahead of her but she cannot reach him. In her second, she sees Thornfield as a ruin, and the child rolls from her clasp (*JE*, 314-15). The repeated figure of the child acts as a portent of doom but more specifically relates to Jane's own irretrievably damaged idea of family: Gilbert and Gubar describe the child as her "orphaned alter-ego" (*Madwoman*, 358). While she joyously reflects upon the prospect of being immersed in Rochester's life, she simultaneously fears the loss of her own self and the strange apparition of "Jane Rochester" (*Madwoman*, 359). It is entirely appropriate that it is within this context that Brontë creates a repetitive echo of the originary scene in the red room when Bertha enters Jane's room and puts on the "princely veil" Rochester has sent Jane from London. Bertha examines herself in the mirror, just as Jane did as a child, and finding the responding image equally disturbing, tears the veil into pieces. Bertha acts out a specifically female rage relating to the horror of being veiled behind a husband's identity. Her appearance can also be read as an uncanny reemergence of Jane's repudiated family life at Gateshead. The scene ends with Jane losing consciousness, "for the second time in my life—only the second time" (*JE*, 318), the first having been in the red room. Furthermore, Rochester's request to explain Bertha's appearance "a year and a day" after the wedding is carefully ironic. In common English law, a year and a day was the time in which a suspected murder had to be alleged; beyond this time a case could not be prosecuted.[15] The events preceding the wedding necessitate two kinds of reading; while we must undoubtedly recognize the symbolic role of Bertha acting out the violence and anarchy of Jane's repressed distress, on a simple narrative level, Jane herself acts on the selfsame distress and fear of degradation by turning to a male authority figure, her uncle John.

Jane Eyre evades the simple structure of an Oedipal love story: despite Rochester's fatherly persona, the vicissitudes of Jane's desires traverse the extended familial body represented by the Reeds and the Rivers. St. John's significance has often been overlooked by critics more attracted to the dark and brooding Rochester, but St. John nevertheless endows Jane's sanctuary, or "mooring," at Marsh End/Moor House with emotional and sensory potency. Jane observes St. John with fascination, noting the "frequent flash and changeful dilation of his eye," finding his own startlingly penetrative blue eyes "difficult to fathom" (*JE*, 391, 387). She figures their relationship as an exchange of looks: she "looked at him, as he looked at me, openly and without diffidence" (*JE*, 388). Jane systematically creates an opposition between St. John and Diana and Mary, and it is difficult to envisage how the sisters could function at all in the narrative without him. Despite St. John's apparent emotional frigidity, Jane's relationship with him is figured in the language of affect: he is not simply the antithesis of Rochester; he is a masculine mutation of Jane herself who takes self-control to an almost perverse level. He "rave[s] in his restlessness" just as Jane herself did pacing the roof of Thornfield. The parallel between them is revealed in Jane's description of his preaching: her heart is "thrilled," her "mind astonished" by his power, but she concludes that he, like herself, has not found the "peace of God which passeth all understanding" (*JE*, 393). St. John encourages Jane to "keep herself" financially, saying that "no service degrades" (*JE*, 390, 396). St. John is far from being the traditional oppressive patriarch; his insistence that female labor endows as much integrity as male labor is directly opposed to Victorian bourgeois notions of femininity and, indeed, contrasts strongly with the way Rochester forgets that Jane is his paid employee and then forbids her to continue to work as Adele's governess after their engagement (*JE*, 153).

It is through Jane herself that Moor House becomes another of the novel's domestic enclosures: after she receives the inheritance from her uncle John in Madeira, she exclaims joyously that she "is disposed to be as content as a queen" and rejects St. John's attempt to "stir" her "to restlessness" (*JE,* 436). By distributing her uncle's legacy between herself and her three cousins, Jane assumes the traditionally male role of head of the family, directly appropriating a form of patriarchal authority. Once she becomes financially independent, Jane has no wish to continue her work at Morton's school, wanting to be, in her own words, a "queen" at the center of a domestic establishment. Her passion for independence is transferred into a buoyant account of cooking and cleaning (*JE,* 435).

Her cousins give her "carte blanche" to refurbish Moor House "as I pleased" (*JE,* 436). Redecorating the house, Jane subconsciously re-creates the scene of her childhood trauma, the red room: "A spare parlour and bed-room I refurnished entirely, with old mahogany and crimson upholstery" (*JE,* 437). This strange but careful detail testifies to Jane's complex relation to patriarchal structures. The imposing visual influence of the red room is re-created in a disused room at Moor House, and the phantasmic power of Jane's childhood experience is reinscribed. Jane's reason for this act, even her understanding of it, is completely elided by the narrative voice. Her polite anger directed at St. John's "lack of gratitude" is provocative, and she addresses us directly to express her displeasure, saying, "Now, I did not like this, reader" (*JE,* 438). Jane arguably creates a masculine space for a man who has no interest in his own domestic authority. St. John's overwhelming influence only comes into play once he decides to groom Jane to become a missionary and his wife by teaching her Hindostanee (*JE,* 443).

St. John's pragmatic wish to marry Jane so that they can become fellow laborers in India undermines the temporary equilibrium Jane achieves at Moor House and the delicate placing of herself within Victorian bourgeois society: if she followed St. John, she would once again become an outcast from conventionality as well as placing herself under the auspices of a powerful and "relentless" husband (*JE,* 448). Speaking to Diana and Mary, she imagines that she would conceive a "strange, torturing, kind of love for him" if they were married, "because he is so talented; and there is often a certain heroic grandeur in his look, manner and conversation" (*JE,* 463). Her wavering under his "thrilling" speech creates a crisis that once again necessitates a potentially backwards motion: the return to Thornfield (*JE,* 447). Rochester's telepathic cry ("Jane! Jane! Jane!") rescues her from her near vow to marry St. John. Once again Jane veers between two male figures.

Brontë obscures these problems in Ferndean's soggy, "dank" dell (*JE,* 479), but Jane's last home brilliantly encapsulates the female problematic explored throughout *Jane Eyre.* Ferndean is a murky refuge in an "insalubrious" site (*JE,* 478), far away from society and her newly found family. Jane is reunited with a lover who has lost the masterful power that initially attracted her to him: "I saw a change: that looked desperate and brooding—that reminded me of some wronged and fettered wild beast or bird" (*JE,* 479). Brontë destroys her romantic, wandering Byronic ideal: Jane puts Rochester firmly in his domestic place, "rehumanising" him by brushing his wild hair (*JE,* 485). Rochester's blindness (far more than his maimed hand), constructs him as an object for Jane's uninterrupted observance and control, acting as his "prop" and "guide" (*JE,* 497): "I love you better now, when I can really be useful to you, than I did in your state of proud independence, when you disdained every part but that of the giver and protector" (*JE,* 494). The novel ends with a potentially distorted image of love: Jane's marriage is based not on spiritual equality but on Rochester's dependence. She does not confess that Rochester's spiritual cry saved her from marriage to St. John, which clearly prevents him from accessing the full resonance of what happened. Her reticence also conveniently conceals just how close she was to giving herself to another man. Carla Kaplan's argument that Jane's "autobiography" represents a search for an adequate listener is provocative in this context when we consider her final reticence towards Rochester; Kaplan argues that only a female reader or listener would enable Jane to fashion herself as an independent woman.[16]

Jane's ambivalent attitude to male love and masculine power is resolved in a claustrophobic pairing (one that Brontë has Lucy Snowe evade in *Villette* when Monsieur Paul disappears at sea). In *Jane Eyre,* Brontë's sharp realism is implicit in small and telling details: despite Adèle's "frantic joy" at being reunited with her adored governess (and probable father), Jane swiftly sends her back to boarding school: "I meant to become her governess once more; but I soon found this impracticable; my time and cares were now required by another—my husband needed them all" (*JE,* 499). Jane rejects Adèle, "the emblem of my past life" (*JE,* 320), instead choosing to "mother" her husband; Adèle is set upon a similar course to Jane herself as a young orphan (albeit at a better school).

In *The Madwoman in the Attic,* Gilbert and Gubar use Bertha Rochester as a figure for the female condition in patriarchal society: repressed, raging, and revengeful. In *Jane Eyre,* Bertha undoubtedly acts out the frustrated and repressed passion of the imprisoned woman, but, as we have seen, at Moor House Jane willingly encloses herself with all the pomp and state of patriarchal authority. The drama of "enclosure and escape" identified by Gilbert and Gubar is, in some ways, an accurate description of Jane's jerky progress, but by failing to note the ways in which desires, identifications, and fears become attached to the male figures, the two critics likewise ignore the way in which Jane perpetuates her own enclosure. Her movement through the novel can best be seen as a seesaw rather than a linear progression towards maturity. Through the originary scene in the red room and its strange repetitions throughout Jane's story, Brontë implies that women's place in patriarchy is even more complex than Gilbert and Gubar suggest. Jane's journey shows that enclosure can provide security, warmth, and its own domestic gods. This physical and emotional warmth is set against the oppressive determination of her character that is imposed on her by the majority of the male characters in her story. Jane resists this determination while also trying to find a secure place for herself within society. The central importance of two absent father figures, her uncle John Reed and her uncle John Eyre, exposes Jane's and the novel's reliance on the protective paternal ideal—an ideal that cannot realistically be relinquished if patriarchal society is to continue to operate. The "repetition-compulsion" that Freud identified as the dynamic basis for traumatic and obsessional neuroses underlies Jane's journey throughout Brontë's extraordinary novel.[17] The final scenes at Ferndean reveal the author's ambivalence concerning Jane's pilgrimage. The ending is more than a compromise: it is utopian, unworldly, and shaded in ambiguity.

Notes

1. Sandra M. Gilbert and Susan Gubar, *The Madwoman in the Attic: The Woman Writer and the Nineteenth-Century Literary Imagination* (New Haven: Yale University Press, 1979), 341. Subsequent references will be given parenthetically.
2. See Thomas More, *Utopia* (New Haven: Yale University Press, 2001).
3. Sigmund Freud, *The Interpretation of Dreams,* ed. and trans. James Strachey (London: Penguin, 1991).
4. Josef Breuer and Sigmund Freud, *Studies on Hysteria,* vol. 2 of *The Standard Edition of the Complete Psychological Works of Sigmund Freud,* ed. and trans. James Strachey (London: Vintage, 2001), 21–47.
5. In many of Freud's case histories, it is the compromising encounter with the adult other that constitutes the basis of the childhood trauma. For instance, in the case of "Emma," it is the sexual advances of a shopkeeper when she is only eight years old that precipitate the development of a repetitive trauma. The adolescent Emma fears that all shopkeepers look at her awry, and she will not enter shops alone (353–56). Sigmund Freud, "Project for a Scientific Psychology," in vol. 1 of *The Standard Edition,* 283–397.
6. Breuer and Freud, *Studies on Hysteria,* 5.
7. Peter Brooks, "Freud's Masterplot," *Yale French Studies* 55/56 (1977): 281.
8. Carolyn Steadman, *Strange Dislocations: Childhood and the Idea of Human Interiority* (London: Virago, 1995), 35.
9. Michael Wheeler, *English Fiction of the Victorian Period, 1830–1890* (Harlow, U.K.: Longman, 1994), 66.
10. Charlotte Brontë, *Jane Eyre* (London: Penguin Books, 1996), 16, 22. Subsequent references will be given parenthetically in the text.
11. Jean Wyatt, *Reconstructing Desire: The Role of the Unconscious in Women's Reading*

and Writing (Chapel Hill: University of North Carolina Press, 1990), 23–40, 32.

12. Elizabeth Gaskell, *The Life of Charlotte Brontë* (London: Dent, 1971), 379–80.

13. Wyatt, *Reconstructing Desire,* 33.

14. Sharon Marcus, *Between Women: Friendship, Desire, and Marriage in Victorian England* (Princeton: Princeton University Press, 1977), 75.

15. This law was not abolished until 1996 in the Law Reform (Year and a Day Rule) Act 1996. http://opsi.gov.uk/acts/acts1996/ukpga_19960019_en_1.

16. Carla Kaplan, "Girl Talk: *Jane Eyre* and the Romance of Women's Narration," *Novel* 30, no. 1 (Autumn 1996): 5–31.

17. See entries on "Compulsion, Compulsive," "Compulsion to Repeat," "Obsessional Neurosis," and "Trauma," in *The Language of Psychoanalysis,* ed. Jean Laplanche and Jean-Bertrand Pontalis, trans. Donald Nicholson-Smith (London: Hogarth, 1973).

6

Jane Eyre's Doubles?

Colonial Progress and the Tradition of New Woman Writing in India

Narin Hassan

Bertha Mason—the paradigmatic figure who frames and inspires Sandra M. Gilbert and Susan Gubar's *The Madwoman in the Attic*—represents female anger and confinement in their analysis of Brontë's *Jane Eyre* and other texts by nineteenth-century women writers. For Gilbert and Gubar, Bertha is "Jane's truest and darkest double," an embodiment of the suppressed rage experienced by silenced or marginalized Victorian women writers.[1] By emphasizing the patterns and metaphors that link Bertha with Jane's hidden rebelliousness, Gilbert and Gubar suggest a psychological and symbolic connection between the novelist, the heroine, and her "mad" exotic Other. Although some critics, such as Laurence Lerner, have argued that Bertha is a minor character, a sensational plot device undeserving of the symbolic weight of Gilbert and Gubar's analysis, their reading nevertheless opened the door to radical questions regarding the figure of the female writer and the production and reception of her work.[2] Their critique of *Jane Eyre* has provoked responses from a range of postcolonial critics, most notably Gayatri Spivak, who has argued that the native other is silenced through the emphasis on Bertha as a double or mirror for Jane. Spivak claims that Gilbert and Gubar's "emergent perspective of feminist criticism reproduces the axioms of imperialism" and that "isolationist admiration for the literature of the female subject in Europe and America establishes the high feminist norm."[3] *Jane Eyre* has since then become a central text for critics engaging with questions of race and empire in the context of Victorian culture. Suvendrini Perera, Susan Meyer, and Jenny Sharpe have noted the orientalist motifs in Brontë's novel and addressed Bertha as a "colonial other" representing not only feminist rebellion but also the anger of natives in Britain's vast empire.[4] While current feminist and postcolonial analysis of *Jane Eyre* is wide ranging in its scope, much of it is indebted to Gilbert and Gubar's initial efforts to recover a female history and analyze a neglected female literary tradition.

This essay traces the ways Gilbert and Gubar's feminist reading of *Jane Eyre* intersects with questions of identity and native subjectivity that concern postcolonial studies. I take as my focus a late-nineteenth-century autobiographical novel, *Saguna* (1887). Although this novel is set in India, it resonates with themes from *Jane Eyre* and provides a lens through which we can read native women's writing and its relationship to the English novel and empire. Written in English by an Indian woman writer, Krupabai Satthianadhan, *Saguna* is concerned with many of the issues that Gilbert and Gubar placed in the forefront of feminist reading in *Madwoman:* female confinement, the struggle for autonomy, creative resistance to dominant feminine roles and social expectations. The central character, Saguna, emerges as a "new" Indian woman, who struggles with the desire to study medicine while negotiating the burdens and expectations of colonial womanhood. Making use of Gilbert and Gubar's critical paradigm and building the process of historical recovery that their monumental work revealed, this essay complicates our reading of the Victorian female subject and her relationship to the native other by examining how the female tradition that Gilbert and Gubar address was translated—and perhaps extended—in the work of late Victorian Indian woman writers. Through a reading of *Saguna,* this essay will examine the ways that feminist identities in India were shaped by competing discourses in much the same way that they were in Britain, but also how progressive Indian womanhood was forged in the late nineteenth century and how women writers had to negotiate multiple influences and expectations—colonial, feminist, and nationalist—at once.

My reading of *Saguna* attempts not simply to trace unities or a set of interconnected themes that relate the work to Victorian novels such as *Jane Eyre.* Instead, I suggest that this particular novel provides one way to expand the boundaries of feminist reading and complicate our analysis of the native other. I read *Saguna* not as a derivative text inspired by Victorian fiction but as an example of an expanding tradition of women's writing that reveals the widening influence of nineteenth-century feminism and its engagement with colonialism. As such, my essay addresses some of the limitations of Gilbert and Gubar's approach by examining how a global exchange of feminist ideas took place in the nineteenth century; it also seeks to complicate

Spivak's notion of the "imperialist axiomatics" at play in works such as *Jane Eyre* by complicating our notion of the native subject and revealing how she simultaneously resisted, welcomed, and negotiated Western feminism and colonial reforms. As many critics have noted, Jane Eyre's feminist impulse often depends upon images of native seclusion; consider her claim, in a passage soon after her engagement to Rochester, that she will "preach liberty" and "stir up mutiny" to harem inmates and "those who have been enslaved" by their cultural traditions.[5] If such representations of native women support Jane's feminist progression, how can we read the work of native women who produced their own narratives of individual and cultural progress? While Gilbert and Gubar's representation of Bertha as Jane's double can be a troubling expression of Western feminism, we can also see a more complex version of doubling or mirroring at work in the production of *Saguna* in which the native subject both relies upon Western feminist ideals and tries to rework them within the contours of colonial and nationalist progress. Analyzing Satthianadhan's work is an opportunity to examine the complex negotiations between native women and their British counterparts while engaging with Gilbert and Gubar's exploration of a female literary tradition in the nineteenth century. This essay expands their analysis outside the borders of Western literary production and examines how native women's writing responded to such a tradition and to emerging feminist and colonial reforms.

Further, this essay attempts to unpack the unity of the terms "woman" and "nation" with which so many readings of colonialism engage. While women are often burdened as symbolic figures for cultural and national identity, they also negotiate their roles as such in complex ways. Reading Jane Eyre as a figure for English nationhood and Bertha as a figure of colonial oppression who represents racial or cultural difference is just one way of examining how the English novel engaged with the imperial project. Reading a text like *Saguna* reveals the multiple layers of identity that complicate our sense of woman and nation within empire itself. Saguna embodies a range of competing identities: she is from a Brahmin family that has converted to Christianity and she has privileged access to English books and a Western education. As many heroines of British novels, she struggles with the expectations of womanhood, and her novel presents the different forces she confronts as she negotiates a space for herself within a rapidly changing environment. Although her childhood and circumstances are very different from Jane Eyre's, she traverses and negotiates various spaces—domestic and public—and reveals the complexities of being a girl coming of age. She is, like Brontë's Jane Eyre and George Eliot's Maggie Tulliver, an intellectual aberration; her narrative is inspired and motivated by similar realities of female oppression and yet it wrestles with distinguishing itself from its English counterparts by providing access to an unsettled colonial landscape that is both liberating and confining.

Krupabai Satthianadhan (1862-96) wrote fiction, poetry, and advice literature; she published two novels and contributed to a range of Indian periodicals. As a late-nineteenth-century Indian Christian woman writer, Satthianadhan's work reveals the intercultural exchanges that had to be negotiated in the production of women's narratives not only from the perspective of British women but also from native women themselves. *Saguna,* her largely autobiographical novel, was first published serially in *Madras Christian College Magazine* in 1887-88 and then issued posthumously as a single-volume book by Srinivasa, Varadachari, and Company in 1895. The same press published her second novel, *Kamala,* in 1894 after its serialization during the same year in *Madras Christian College Magazine.* Satthianadhan began publishing articles on a range of topics, including female education and conversion to Christianity, in 1881 in papers, journals, and magazines, and these were compiled and published as a collection titled *Miscellaneous Writings* in 1896. Both her novels were written in English and later translated to Tamil. Satthianadhan appears to have enjoyed equal popularity among Indian and English audiences, and dedications and reviews of her work show that her novels were widely distributed at the time of publication.[6] In the introduction to her novel *Kamala* (1894), Mrs. H. B. Grigg writes, "Her writings seem even better known to English than to Indian readers, some of them having been reviewed in flattering terms in the leading English journals. Her Majesty the Queen Empress had recently accepted a copy of *Saguna* and was graciously pleased to request that any other work by the authoress should be sent to her."[7]

Satthianadhan also wrote a number of short stories. Six of these were published posthumously by her husband, Samuel Satthianadhan, and his second wife, Kamala, in their book *Scenes from an Indian Christian Life* (1899). These endeavors reveal her active engagement with the literary culture of colonial India, but, notably, she was also one of the first women accepted into medical programs in both India and England and she benefited from late Victorian efforts such as the Dufferin Fund, which focused increasingly upon educating Indian women in Western medicine. While Satthianadhan's work has been relatively unexplored, she is included in Susie Tharu and K. Lalita's encyclopedic volume *Women Writing in India* (1991), and her work has been reissued in recent editions by Chandana Lokuge, who applauds her as the author of "the first autobiographical novel in English by an Indian woman."[8] Recently, Satthianadhan has inspired attention from literary critics including Meenakshi Mukerjhee, Leslie Flemming, and Priya Joshi. While all of these critics examine the ways that Satthianadhan's work reflects the tensions of being caught between multiple communities, Joshi provides a particularly deft reading of the production and reception of Satthianadhan's writing and its participation in "complex and multiple transactions that simultaneously corroborated, challenged, and shaped some of the most intense issues surrounding narratives of nation, empire, gender, and the emergence of the English novel in India."[9]

The opening lines of *Saguna* reflect how the central character lives in a world of transition and progress in which she has to negotiate her identity within a national and political landscape in flux: "In the following pages, I shall in my own way try to present a faithful picture of the experiences and thoughts of a simple Indian girl, whose life has been highly influenced by the new order of things—an order of things which at the present time is spreading its influence to a greater or lesser extent over the whole of her native land."[10] Satthianadhan opens her book with a claim that emphasizes truth and accuracy at the same time it resists easy categorization and reveals Britain's influence over India. Saguna's narrative is inextricably bound to the larger national landscape and to the "new order of things," and it is the complexity of this new world that she has to negotiate. Through this introduction, Satthianadhan reveals the impact of colonial expansion upon the experiences of a young Indian girl, who quickly develops into an emblem of "New Womanhood" within her community through her educational successes and eventual acceptance to medical school. In a review in the *Daily Graphic,* Mary Billington observed Satthianadhan's place as a writer within this tradition: "*Saguna,* her first book, may be described as a study of the 'New Woman' as she is in Indian surroundings."[11] Along with Cornelia Sorabji, Toru Dutt, and Pandita Ramabai, she is one of the few Indian women who published in English during this period and were categorized as part of a female tradition. Reviewers described her writings as "truthful" authoritative accounts of native female life that compared "the native 'new woman' beside the old,"[12] and while a review of *Saguna* in *The Woman's Signal* compared her prose to Jane Austen's, it was also described as a valuable window for English readers into the intimate lives of Indian families: "whilst the style is the most remarkable part of the story, the most valuable part of it is the truthful picture which it represents of the *vie intime* . . . in Hindu and Christian families."[13] And yet, being a symbolic figure of "new womanhood" was not free of burdens: Satthianadhan's text reveals the ways that she has to satisfy and accommodate both Indian and English readers.

While the classic image of the New Woman of British fiction was one of unruliness—"New" womanhood challenged Victorian conventions—the "new woman" of India was instead imagined to support British intervention and colonial reform. She was a positive symbol of imperial progress, largely constituted by competing colonial and feminist desires and imagined to promote cultural exchange. As Susie Tharu and K. Lalita note:

> A powerful new female figure emerged in the nationalist imagination and can be encountered in text after text of the period. She was, in keeping with the now-naturalized Victorian ideals of domestic virtue, patient and long suffering. But the new woman was also self confident and autonomous, conscious of her power and of the strength she could find in tradition: a gentle but stern custodian of the nation's moral life. And this was a figure that dominated the literary imagination for several decades to come.[14]

Tharu and Lalita situate the emergence of this "New Woman" in the post-Sepoy rebellion period (1857), a time of active nationalist politics in India. They describe her as being caught between modernity and tradition. The "new" Indian woman had to uphold the moral and cultural history of India while participating in the educational and social reforms that colonial rule imposed.

Throughout the text, Satthianadhan represents a privileged Indian native life in constant negotiation with English models of selfhood that were expressed in Victorian British novels. Consider the following passage that displays Saguna's coming of age and her desire for independence and education. When Saguna discovers she will have the opportunity to study medicine with a "lady doctor," she claims,

> Just a minute before it had seemed as if there was nothing for me to do; now what a world of untried work lay before me, and what large and noble possibilities seemed to open out for me! I would throw aside the fetters that bound me and be independent. I had chafed under restraints and the ties which formed the common lot of women, and I longed for an opportunity to show that a woman is in no way inferior to a man. How hard it seemed to my mind that marriage should be the goal of woman's ambition, and that she should look pretty, and never know the joy of independence and intellectual work! The thought had been galling. It made me avoid men, and I felt more than once that I could not look into their faces unless I was able to hold my own with them. So, like a slave whose freedom had just been purchased, I was happy, deliriously happy. Some of my readers may be inclined to say that in recording these experiences I have given way to exaggeration. Let me assure you this is not the case. (*Saguna,* 131)

Saguna's desire for movement and education is much like Jane Eyre's, who also wishes to "go forth into [the world] to seek real knowledge of life amidst its perils" (Brontë, 116). Satthianadhan's rhetoric is also much like Brontë's when she expresses Jane's restlessness as a Victorian woman: "Women are supposed to be calm generally, but women feel just as men feel; they need exercise for their faculties, and a field for their efforts as much as their brothers do; they suffer from too rigid a restraint, too absolute a stagnation, precisely as men would suffer." (Brontë, 141). While Jane expresses the struggle of womanhood in Britain, Saguna celebrates the opportunities she has been given through colonial reforms in female education and imagines that an English education will pave the way for both her own future and the progress of a broader community of women who can see her as a model of progress. The passage above exemplifies the struggles of a young Indian girl to achieve independence in much the same way that Brontë's Jane Eyre does; Saguna, like Jane Eyre, suffers from the constraints of girlhood and uses the metaphor of slavery to describe the burdens of marriage and womanhood and the struggles of an intellectually stifled life. Further, Satthianadhan's writing evokes Brontë's through her use of rhetorical strategies that address the reader directly and establish a close relationship between reader and narrator. As the final lines of the quote above reveal, Satthianadhan writes her "autobiographical fiction" in a personal voice and forms alliances with her readers.

Like Jane Eyre, Saguna's distractions and escapes from the concerns of everyday life are through reading and the free exercise of the imagination. If Jane had the remote seas and Arctic wastelands of Bewick's *History of British Birds,* Saguna has English novels, and they fire her mind in a similarly exotic way: reading functions as a mode of possibility, not just because novels represent the far distance of England and English characters from her own life but also because they seem to articulate a widening sphere of potential growth from childhood. Brontë's *Juvenilia* is a world of fantasy for Saguna; while describing the open Indian landscape that her elder brother has the liberty to explore, she writes, "Ah it was lovely to visit the old Angria fortresses and the abodes of the sea pirates" (*Saguna,* 129). Satthianadhan suggests that through reading, England was itself a space of fantasy and possibility for colonial subjects. Novels are the one stable feature of Saguna's life, and English novels allow her to produce a private world of her making. Early in the text, Saguna discovers novels through her older friend Harni, who "talked English as her mother tongue, for she went to a European school" (*Saguna,* 79). Harni describes novel reading as an adult secret:

> "And what is a novel?" I said, afraid to show my ignorance and yet wanting to know what it was.
>
> "A novel! A book, you know, but you must not read one. Little girls should not read novels. It is different with me." (*Saguna,* 80)

When Harni tells Saguna about "a great secret"—that her mother has given her a novel to read without her father's knowledge—Saguna learns about the pleasures of creating "a world of her own making" (*Saguna,* 80). Although

Saguna's discovery of novels is punctuated by a warning that novels are inappropriate reading, significant encounters in her life include reading and books, and much of her education and identification with the various communities she inhabits intersect with novel reading. In a scene that echoes Jane Eyre's curiosity about Helen Burns's copy of *Rasselas,* Saguna encounters an Englishman who is surprised to see her tackling Spenser's *Faerie Queene:* "You are very clever to understand it. An English girl half your age would not understand it" (*Saguna,* 123). Satthianadhan produces what has now become a trope in postcolonial writing—depicting colonial subjects who as readers and writers of English excel the English themselves.[15] When Saguna enters a zenana missionary school, Satthianadhan provides a description of her advanced knowledge and interest in reading the history of Western civilization that suggests that Saguna knows more than her English counterparts:

> The first thing I was told in going to Miss Roberts'—for that was the name of the lady who took charge of me—was that I was a little girl; that in England girls of fourteen and fifteen were considered mere chits, and that I was to lay aside all solemnity of manner and behave as a girl. When it came to the lessons I was asked what I was learning.
>
> I said: "History, geography & c."
>
> "What in history?"
>
> "I have finished *Landmarks in the History of Greece* and I am reading—"
>
> "Greece! Greece! What have you to do with Greece?" I had loved this little book. It was like a story book, and I thought she would have been pleased, but she only murmured: "Well, I will see. I must get something more suited to you. What about English? Can you read fluently?"
>
> Longfellow's poems were put into my hand. The volume opened at "Pleasant it was when woods were green." I read this fast enough.
>
> "Too fast."
>
> "Oh, I know it by heart," I exclaimed, anxious to show my cleverness. I shut the book and repeated the whole thing to her. I had once learnt it in a fit of study, and it had given me much pleasure. (*Saguna,* 113-14)

The young heroine reads about both Greek and English history, and although her missionary education prepares her to "behave" like an English girl, she is still read by others as Indian. By the end of her narrative, Saguna claims, "I had been devouring with intense delight, George Eliot's works—once forbidden books" (*Saguna,* 160). While novels appear to be forbidden objects for Saguna and her friends, fictional texts allow them access to educational communities.

Writing appears to be the space through which Satthianadhan creates a world of her own making, as well. Through writing, Satthianadhan responds to the changing national and cultural landscape and produces meaning for the instabilities of her own subject position. While Brontë is an obvious influence in her novels, in her memoir, Elizabeth Grigg writes that Eliot and Kipling were two of Satthianadhan's favorite authors and that Tennyson's *The Princess* was one of her favorite poems.[16] Satthiandhan's depictions of Saguna's childhood often mimic Eliot's Maggie Tulliver, and her descriptions of girls' education (or lack of one) closely resembles the "School Days" section of *The Mill on the Floss* where Maggie's desire to read and learn is sacrificed for her brother's. While reading English texts certainly motivates Saguna to seek an alternative and "new" path as an Indian woman, such texts also demonstrate a broader patriarchal culture that both English and Indian women must transcend. Through the English texts available to her, Saguna imagines female liberation but also discovers that the limitations of girlhood expand beyond the borders of India. Thus, while Satthianadhan's narrative is complicated by colonial encounter, it can be read through Gilbert and Gubar's reading of the woman writer's internalization of confinement through reading and description of "the psychology of growing up female" (*Madwoman,* 121). In their analysis of Austen and romantic fiction, Gilbert and Gubar claim, "For even as she dramatizes her own alienation from a society she cannot evade or transcend, she subverts the conventions of popular fiction to describe the lonely vulnerability of girls whose lives, if more mundane, are just as thwarted as those they read about so obsessively" (*Madwoman,* 121). In Satthianadhan's narrative, English novels provide a model for the expression of female confinement and struggle at the same time as the novels themselves are imagined to provide solutions to the limitations of cultural traditions within India. Satthianadhan's text reveals the uneasy place of women within the negotiation of colonial progress and tradition.

Although much of *Saguna* celebrates English education as a form of access to freedom for young women, Satthianadhan subtly evokes questions of difference and discrimination between British and Indian communities to show that English is not necessarily a unifying language. Although British women often optimistically asserted English education as a cure-all for the ills and customs of India—Mrs. R. S. Benson claimed that "English is the one language that will enable them to have intercourse with Englishwomen from the Himalayas to Cape Comorin . . . it is language of their educated husbands and sons"[17]—Satthianadhan shows that distinctions of power within colonial India continued to be produced at the site of language. In a particularly striking scene, Saguna and her mother pay a visit to the missionary family in town, expecting a warm greeting as fellow Christians. Saguna describes hoping to befriend the young daughter at the missionary house through novels: "I asked her if she had any interesting story books to lend. She raised her eyebrows, and the next minute I felt the audacity of putting to her that question. She said, however, 'You read? *You* can't read what I read. You won't understand.' I said, 'I will try' but she immediately added that she never lent her books" (*Saguna,* 99).

Satthianadhan explores the riddles and complexities of language and the fraught relationship of Indian women and their access to English culture through language. Both of Satthianadhan's heroines use books as a means of escape; Kamala finds great pleasure in her father-in-law's sacred library and imagines that these books will allow her to escape the confines of her life. In *Saguna,* the significance of books is even more relevant, since Saguna's novel reading promotes her role as a misfit—Saguna's mother is repeatedly perplexed by her daughter's affection for English books (and the knowledge she gains from reading is described as a problem because she is a girl who will become too educated), but her English novel reading also provides her a space within reforming educational systems. Saguna describes her mother, "still full of the Hindu notions of things," responding to her "big books" and dictionaries: "my mother, good in her own way, thought that I would be terribly spoiled by having such freedom and learning things that were of no use to a girl" (*Saguna,* 20). Saguna both exposes and critiques the larger issues of colonial progress and education through these examples and, as Priya Joshi has also noted, her access to an English education renders her more of a misfit within Indian society.

Because Saguna's mother cannot find a proper place for her daughter within traditional Indian society, she takes her to a missionary school, hoping for a solution for Saguna's unusual zeal for reading. Here, the nuns are struck by her ability to learn, and in their search for a proper profession for Saguna, the "solution" they find for her zeal for learning is to prepare her for medical education. Satthianadhan's narrative challenges assumptions that women were not fit for medical work; *Saguna* captures the ways that within Indian culture, impressions of Western medical education were in transition. At a social gathering "consisting of natives and Europeans," Saguna claims, "I was introduced to people as a girl who was about to go to England. I was congratulated, and several times my ear caught half-whispered words of praise. I also heard remarks which were not so complimentary, and I noticed a surprised stare in the faces of a few, indicating doubts as to whether a native girl was capable of doing anything in the way of study" (*Saguna,* 146). Saguna represents the results of colonial medical reform and bears the burden of upholding the possibilities as a subject of scrutiny, and ultimately, her narrative shows how competing visions for Indian womanhood are negotiated. Under the direction of "Miss Roberts," she learns basic medical processes and begins tending patients. But her access to this education exposes the traditions of her native community more obviously, and Satthianadhan uses this opportunity to subtly critique both Indian and Western cultures and expose patriarchal constraints in both.

Saguna's access to privileged Western education complicates her already vexed position within the Indian community. Saguna is barraged by marriage proposals once she is accepted to medical school in England, and when a prospective Indian suitor suggests that she remain in India and become a wife, Saguna responds with a narrative that outlines her feminist desire for freedom and the limits of Indian culture. Saguna suggests that educated Indian men embrace English ideas but expect women to uphold tradition:

> "Married?" I said, catching his drift at last and astonished beyond words. "Married?" I repeated, while he smiled in a more insinuating manner, as if he was about to say: "Yes, what else can girls do? Marriage is the end of her learning." All his hidden sneers and veiled sarcasms flashed upon me. I felt how incapable he was of understanding us girls, and my tongue seemed to run away with me in the excitement of the moment, though I meant to be very cool. "Marriage is not the goal of every girl's ambition," I said. "It is really disgusting to see how many of you imitate the English in manners, dress and other superficial things without imbibing their liberal spirit—that spirit that gives to a woman equal privileges with man and credits her with noble and disinterested actions." (*Saguna,* 149)

Satthianadhan suggests that Western progress means female liberation but also complicates the position of intellectual and ambitious women within Indian society.

Ultimately, Saguna remains in India, and the conclusion of the novel ends with her, like Jane Eyre, managing to secure a position for herself in an Indian medical school and marry the Indian man of her choice.[18] While, as Gilbert and Gubar note, the marriage plot and fairy-tale associations are central to Jane Eyre's tale, Saguna's is one that neatly consolidates marriage into the conclusion as a solution to the psychological and physical struggle that has consumed much of the book. After describing a period of lengthy study, Saguna claims, "My health had become enfeebled, and I had gone back instead of advancing. The visit of a stranger had made an epoch in my life. It had given me a glimpse into a true and noble heart, shown me my own imperfections and want of strength" (*Saguna,* 158). This stranger, a fellow Indian Christian convert with an English education, becomes then a noble and guiding figure who with a "holy kiss" concludes her narrative with marriage and religious rebirth. While much of Saguna's narrative addresses the struggles of female independence, it is this romance that concludes the tale, and while Saguna describes her marriage to an Indian man as liberating, she also concludes by describing herself as a figure enfeebled and weakened by the urge to learn and negotiate an independent life. She is, like many of the characters Gilbert and Gubar confront, ultimately unable to dismantle patriarchal society and unable to bear and challenge the burdens of Indian womanhood alone.

While critics have examined Satthianadhan's novels and their reception within the context of the "woman question" in India, her other written work also addresses issues of female life, including female education and marriage rights, that comprised the focus of her fiction. While she may not have succeeded as a professional woman doctor (she did not complete her medical education due to illness), she continued to be influential as a voice for female education and reform through the production of shorter works that are compiled as her *Miscellaneous Writings.* Originally published in the journal of the National Indian Association known as the *Indian Magazine,* her articles, "Women's Influence at Home," "Home Training of Children," and "Female Education," all reveal how her vision of a progressive India relies upon the dissolution of a traditional past and reform that relies upon women: "the dust of ages must be swept away, the sleeping faculties awakened, and cultivated by careful education, the mind enlarged, and everything must be done to develop her powers, and bring out and strengthen the very best qualities in her" (*Miscellaneous Writings,* 9). Noting further that "what our women lack most is the freedom of thought and action" (9), in these works Satthianadhan places the domestic sphere at the center of national, religious, and cultural reform and emphasizes the importance of educated women as a force for change: "no home can be happy and cheerful without the guidance of a truly enlightened woman" (*Miscellaneous Writings,* 23). Such "enlightenment" is achieved through proper reading and through access to a Western knowledge and education.

While in her novels Satthianadhan evokes how such knowledge can complicate how Indian girls navigate their life choices and how they are read by others, in these critical works, Satthianadhan inflects ideals of Victorian feminism to interrogate the "degraded position of Indian women" and suggests that progress depends upon the expansion of Western colonial reforms. In her article "Hindu Social Custom," superstitious Hindu belief and tradition produces a metaphorical, ignorant Indian "madwoman": "born and bred in darkness and ignorance, cooped up in narrow homes, delighting in petty trifles, and unconscious of a better and nobler sphere of life in which they can move if placed under different circumstances, is it any wonder to see them so indifferent to the higher and more refined pleasures arising from perfect freedom and intellectual culture? . . . They are much to be pitied. It is only when education widens and enables them to compare and contrast their own condition with that of the women of other nations that they begin to feel for themselves and try to better themselves" (*Miscellaneous Writings*, 27-38). If in her novels Satthianadhan resisted simple categorization for the Indian tradition and exposed the complexities of a unifying notion of womanhood, in these later works, Satthianadhan suggests the inevitable continuation of India's relationship with Britain and confronts the residue of a colonial past, noting at one point that "India is still, as it were, a child, and she can by herself accomplish very little and it is our humble opinion that England and India ought to work together if anything good is to be achieved at all" (*Miscellaneous Writings*, 33).

Perhaps such claims emerge because Satthianadhan's popularity during the period depended upon her accessibility to English audiences and her ability to make her own image and that of her heroines palatable and useful to Western readers and to produce accounts of Indian life that drew the attention of English women and produced their sense of unity with their "Indian sisters." Mrs. R. S. Benson's preface to *Saguna* introduces Satthianadhan as an ideal "wife and mother, companion and friend." Benson describes her as an intellectually successful but suffering writer, and compares her to admired British women: "Like some of our own eminent women, she wrote latterly from a bed of sickness and suffering. So wrote Harriet Martineau and 'Carmen Silva.' So writes Florence Nightingale."[19] Since Benson appears unable to find models of Indian womanhood for Satthianadhan to follow, she relegates her to a set of Western models and prototypes. Discussions of Satthianadhan's role within public life offer similar professions of capabilities as a Westernized female reformer, highlighting her work in zenana schools for women and the various medical funds and schemes (largely organized by colonial reformers) provided in her name. The possibilities of Satthianadhan's role as a successful medical worker are described in the following contribution to Satthianadhan's "memorial" recorded in the 1894 publication of *Seguna:* "She was a most brilliant scholar in the medical college, and had health permitted, she would have qualified herself to render and succour to her suffering sisters."[20] The quote highlights the transformative role she could play in the suffering of other Indian women; Satthianadhan's imagined role as a female doctor mimics the construction of the British woman doctor abroad and assumes a distance between her and her "suffering sisters." While such portraits of Satthianadhan reveal the urge to place her within a common struggle of both British and Indian women, her texts reveal the desire to simultaneously align herself with colonial reforms and remind readers of an Indian experience that is distinct.

While Satthianadhan's early critics may have claimed her as an example of female reform in English colonial progress, her texts themselves reveal her uneasy position as simultaneously a figure of new womanhood and progress and cultural tradition. For Satthianadhan, supporting causes of reform that deal with the woman question in India meant negotiating her own Indian identity while embracing the progress that would break women from the bonds of a national and religious past. Such is the conflict still evident in our own feminist criticism. While the work of Gilbert and Gubar sought to recover a female tradition and expose the struggles of women writers, it also produced what Laura Chrisman terms "mythic essentialism," which many recent feminist and postcolonial critics have challenged.[21] The process of recovery that Gilbert and Gubar established has allowed for a broader range of women's writing to be addressed, and it is through such efforts that we can now read work by writers such as Satthianadhan and examine them through the complex lens of both feminist and postcolonial theory.

If Bertha Mason haunts *Jane Eyre* as a reminder of colonial oppression and female confinement, *Saguna,* too, is haunted by a looming figure of violence and metaphorical rage. The first chapter of the book tells us less about Saguna herself and focuses instead upon the description of a beautiful but ghostly landscape in the Deccan, the site of her family summer home. What haunts this landscape is the legend of a beautiful woman brought to an early death through the act of suttee. Satthianadhan's detailed description of this story is as follows:

> The story went that this woman was rich and beautiful, the wife of a banker. She was early taught by her father to read and write, and her learning was considered great. It was, however, the cause of her after-misfortune. People in their mysterious dread of learning then always held it unnatural for a woman to be clever or in any way learned. It was thought that the very power in her for acquiring knowledge was the gift of dreaded unseen agents, and she was supposed to hold conversation with spirits and to point out places where ancient treasures were hidden. This woman had the misfortune to lose her husband . . . and now that she had lost him she became the most accursed of women. The long pent up rage of the Brahmins, to whom this woman was detestable on account of her learning, now found vent in the form of cursing the unfortunate widow. She was accused of being in league with the evil spirits and of exorcizing *jadu* or sorcery on her own husband . . . she was dragged away from the corpse of her husband, people shouted in her ears that she was accursed, the white footed of the house, and her jewels were torn from her . . . the moment she rose and uncovered her head, which was looked upon as a sign of her willingness to become a suttee, and follow her husband to heaven, there was a great burst of joy . . . people had assembled from all quarters; and hither at the very last moment was brought the suttee in a deathlike swoon. . . . but sudden-

> ly a form was seen to bound through the fire and rush out with a shriek. The people in alarm fell back, and the form fled screaming to the hills. All the worst calamities, such as night blasts, death by lightning, and epidemics, that visited the surrounding villages were ascribed to her evil powers. Many are the stories told even now by the shepherd youths in their nightly gatherings round the blazing fire, about the solitary figure or unearthly noise heard at night. (*Saguna,* 24-25)

Framing her autobiographical fiction with the ghostly legend of a sacrificed woman, Satthianadhan offers a narrative that intersects individual identity with historical memory and legend. Satthianadhan suggests the impossibility of an Indian woman's autobiographical narrative apart from the dense and intertwined national, cultural, and religious history that she is part of. The text is haunted by the legend of the powerful but silenced woman, who though banished from society looms over the landscape as a ghostly reminder of female confinement and rage. Like Bertha, who looms in the attic and burns Thornfield in a metaphorical act of suttee, the figure of suttee in Satthianadhan's text frames the text and introduces us to the vexed position of women within India. Here, she is a haunting double who is a reminder of Indian's traditional Hindu past—a figure who both reminds Saguna of her cultural history and highlights the uneasy relationship of her intellectual progress in relation to it. The figure of suttee here reminds us that "New Woman" texts such as Satthianadhan's that attempted to "write back" to English audiences—and that, at the time, were so welcomed by European reformers—are also haunted by the specters of a traditional past.

Notes

1. Sandra M. Gilbert and Susan Gubar, *The Madwoman in the Attic: The Woman Writer and the Nineteenth-Century Literary Imagination* (New Haven: Yale University Press, 1979), 360. Subsequent references will be given parenthetically.
2. See Laurence Lerner, "Bertha and the Critics," *Nineteenth Century Literature* 44, no. 3 (1989): 273–300.
3. Gayatri Chakravorty Spivak, "Three Women's Texts and a Critique of Imperialism," *Critical Inquiry* 12, no. 1 (1985): 243.
4. See Suvendrini Perera, *The Reaches of Empire: The English Novel from Edgeworth to Dickens* (New York: Columbia University Press, 1991); Susan Meyer, *Imperialism at Home: Race and Victorian Women's Fiction* (Ithaca, N.Y.: Cornell University Press, 1996); and Jenny Sharpe, *Allegories of Empire: The Figure of the Woman in the Colonial Text* (Minneapolis: University of Minnesota Press, 1993).
5. Charlotte Brontë, *Jane Eyre,* (Harmondsworth, U.K.: Penguin, 1966), 297–98. Subsequent references will be given parenthetically.
6. In a number of favorable reviews, *Saguna* is described as being a particularly "truthful" account of native life, and one easily accessible to Western audiences. In the *Malabar*

and Travancor Spectator, a critic noted that "we fancy it is some English lady who has written the book, so charming it is to us," and in an 1890 review in *Harvest Field,* Satthianadhan is described as perfecting a traditionally Western autobiographical form: "It is a very significant fact that the most readable autobiography we have yet met with should come from the pen of 'A Hindoo Lady.' We trust that this very interesting story will meet with the large circulation it deserves."

7. Mrs. H. B. Grigg, "Memoir of Krupabai Satthianadhan," in Krupabai Satthianadhan, *Kamala: A Story of Hindu Life* (Madras: Srinivas Varadachari, 1894), i.

8. This is Chandana Lokuge's subtitle to the reissue of Satthianadhan's novel *Saguna.* The novel was originally published as *Saguna: The Story of Native Christian Life.*

9. Priya Joshi, *In Another Country: Colonialism, Culture, and the English Novel in India* (New York: Columbia University Press, 2002), 173–74.

10. Krupabai Satthianadhan, *Saguna: The First Autobiographical Novel in English by an Indian Woman,* ed. Chandana Lokuge (Oxford: Oxford University Press, 1998). Subsequent references will be given parenthetically in the text.

11. Review from *The Daily Graphic,* "Opinions of the First Edition," Krupabai Satthianadhan, *Miscellaneous Writings* (Madras: Srinivasa, Varadachari, 1896), 123.

12. Review from *The Queen* (London), "Opinions of the First Edition," Satthianadhan, *Miscellaneous Writings,* 118.

13. Review from *The Madras Mail,* "Opinions of the First Edition," Satthianadhan, *Miscellaneous Writings,* 119.

14. Susie Tharu and K. Lalita, eds., *Women Writing in India 600 B.C. to the Present,* vol. 1 (New York: Feminist Press, 1991), 173.

15. This image of colonial subject as reader of English books is prevalent in a number of postcolonial texts; see, for example, the characterization of Nyasha in Tsitsi Dangarembga's *Nervous Conditions* (London: Women's Press, 1988).

16. Grigg, "Memoir of Krupabai Satthianadhan," xxxvi.

17. R. S. Benson, preface to *Saguna: A Story of Native Christian Life* (1892; repr. Madras: Srinivasa, Varadachari, 1895), ix.

18. Both *Saguna* and *Kamala* have endings that evoke *Jane Eyre.* Although Kamala concludes with its protagonist choosing to remain a suffering widow (instead of marrying a second, more appropriate choice), she also discovers, after living a motherless life of hardship, that she is an heiress.

19. Benson, preface to *Saguna,* viii.

20. Krupabai Satthianadhan, *Saguna: A Story of Native Christian Life* (1892; repr. Madras: Srinivasa Varadachari, 1895), 238.

21. Laura Chrisman, "The Imperial Unconscious? Representations of Imperial Discourse," in Patrick Williams and Laura Chrisman, eds., *Colonial Discourse/Post-colonial Theory: A Reader* (New York: Columbia University Press, 1994), 502.

7

Revisiting the Attic

Recognizing the Shared Spaces of *Jane Eyre* and *Beloved*

Danielle Russell

To sail into uncharted waters is simultaneously invigorating and terrifying; the act of breaking free of convention is a perilous voyage. Possibility lies beyond the familiar shores, but so too does the burden of unforeseen responsibilities: the explorer by necessity begins to establish the parameters of the new territory. Sandra M. Gilbert and Susan Gubar embarked on just such a bold expedition with the launch of *The Madwoman in the Attic: The Woman Writer and the Nineteenth-Century Literary Imagination* in 1979. The literary world had never before encountered such a creative and politically invested critical study. Pushing against the limitations patriarchy imposed on their lives and scholarship, Gilbert and Gubar invoked a new literary tradition focused on the writings of long-neglected women writers. In the process, they became objects of both adoration and contempt—credited with wisdom and insightfulness, accused of naïveté and narrow-mindedness.[1]

The Madwoman in the Attic initially received qualified praise from academic and popular reviews, and it generated lively discussions about gender, tradition, and the relationship between an artist and her art. But a funny thing happened on the way to subsequent forums; the ground shifted and Gilbert and Gubar became the targets of heated debate. It was a development that caught them off guard in terms of its substance and tone. In the introduction to the second edition of *The Madwoman in the Attic* (2000), Gilbert expresses their surprise at the sniper fire: "Decades after we had the conversion experiences that issued in our first attempt to define *a* (if not *the)* female literary tradition, we were being accused of sins that in those early days we knew not of—essentialism, racism, heterosexism, phallologocentricism—accused, sometimes shrilly, by sister feminists and, sometimes patronizingly, by male quasi-feminists."[2] But *The Madwoman in the Attic* first appeared in a world that was just beginning to negotiate, in a sustained way, the meanings of "sexual politics" and systemic patriarchal oppression; "such nuances" of race, heterosexism, essentialism, and so forth, writes Gilbert, "may be precisely what we couldn't afford at a time when it was enough suddenly to see that there could be a new way of seeing" (*Madwoman*, xxiv, xxv). Subtlety and refinement are luxuries that can only follow the breaking of new ground and the formulation of new theoretical approaches.

In the preface to the first edition, Gilbert and Gubar explain that their work grew out of their teaching experiences. "Reading the writing of women from Jane Austen and Charlotte Brontë to Emily Dickinson, Virginia Woolf, and Sylvia Plath," the pair of instructors were "surprised by the coherence of theme and imagery . . . in works of writers who were often geographically, historically, and psychologically distant from each other."[3] The recurring patterns led Gilbert and Gubar to conclude, "The striking coherence we noticed in literature by women could be explained by a common, female impulse to struggle free from social and literary confinement through strategic redefinitions of self, art, and society" (*Madwoman*, xi-xii). A common impulse, resulting from a common struggle, unites the writings and experiences of women—an argument based on universalist assumptions. Because *The Madwoman in the Attic* sought to uncover a shared literary tradition for women writers, some critics accused Gilbert and Gubar of contrivance, selective analysis, and exaggeration. Detractors have pointed out that the study only addresses works by white women; that the readings of individual texts are open to other interpretations; and that there is a troubling focus on biography.

It is easy to make a case that the argument is flawed, and even the ambitious subtitle suggests the potential pitfalls of such a wide-ranging approach. *The Madwoman in the Attic* is not without its problems, but in the rush to condemn it, a valuable literary resource may be lost. A more reasonable, and reasoned, response, suggests William E. Cain, would be to "acknowledge that [the] work must be assessed and supplemented as its body of texts, and its terms and categories, are made more responsive to lesbian, minority, and ethnic literatures and as its ideas about authors and texts are refined."[4] From this vantage point, *The Madwoman in the Attic* can be read as a catalyst for the scholarship that followed its appearance. If there are unexplored factors (and clearly there are) that challenge the recurrence of "images of enclosure and escape" and "fantasies in which maddened doubles functioned as asocial surrogates for docile selves," do they undermine or enhance the "distinctly female literary tradition" theorized in *The Madwoman in the Attic*?

Madwoman, Race, and Feminism

One of the most widely recognized responses to *The Madwoman in the Attic* was Gayatri Chakravorty Spivak's "Three Women's Texts and a Critique of Imperialism," published in *Critical Inquiry* in 1985. Spivak takes issue with the treatment of the "cult text of feminism: *Jane Eyre*" and Gilbert and Gubar's failure to consider how Bertha Mason is "produced by the axiomatic of imperialism." Spivak takes exception to the reading of Bertha as "Jane's dark double," emphasizing the more complex role the character plays in the narrative. It is a provocative and clearly passionate piece with the potential to expand previous considerations of the novel. Spivak's hope "that an informed critique of imperialism, granted some attention from readers in the First World, will at least expand the frontiers of the politics of reading" has been answered many times over. Her brief essay has generated multiple responses and has been a remarkable catalyst for postcolonial readings. As Erin O'Connor observes, "Spivak's essay may be understood as a primal scene of postcolonial reading, the place where many of the guiding assumptions and logical premises of postcolonial thinking about Victorian fiction were born."[5] For O'Connor it is a disturbing development; as a scholar of Victorian literature, she views Spivak's work as an insidious threat: one with great influence but little substance. She points out that the essay is problematic, not in its theoretical focus but in its methodology. The point is well taken: Spivak fails to provide sustained evidence to support her assertions about Victorian literature (relying instead on sweeping generalizations), and her textual analysis of *Jane Eyre* is too brief and selective.[6]

O'Connor's article aggressively engages Spivak's essay and its influence on subsequent scholars. It is clear that O'Connor is personally and professionally invested in the debate. Spivak's essay, it should be noted, has its own political impulse. Gilbert and Gubar and the authors they discuss, in her assessment, are the privileged and powerful; Spivak aligns the version of feminism promoted in *The Madwoman in the Attic* with imperialist practices.[7] No doubt a critique of imperialism expands our understanding of nineteenth-century texts ("cult" or otherwise), but the reference to the "politics of reading" is apt: hidden power structures, covert and overt ideologies, and competing and frequently conflicting agendas are part of reading and criticism. And, as in politics, you cannot please everyone; every critical approach has built-in limitations and blind spots, and it can get ugly—witness the criticism directed at Gilbert and Gubar.

Has there ever been, indeed can there ever be, a single reading of a text encompassing all the concerns and anticipating areas of discussion that have yet to be articulated? In their discussion of *Jane Eyre,* for example, Gilbert and Gubar refer to Thornfield's attic as "a complex focal point where Jane's own rationality . . . and her irrationality . . . intersect" (*Madwoman,* 348). A space of conflicting and competing impulses, the attic externalizes Jane's internal struggles, and the focus is on Jane's perspective, not that of the imprisoned Bertha Mason. Spivak's postcolonial reading reconfigures the attic: from the vantage point of the imprisoned wife, the attic is a site of oppression and isolation. For Jane, the self-imposed isolation—she seeks out the solitude of the third floor—is invigorating; as Gilbert and Gubar assert, "She never . . . articulates her rational desire for liberty so well as when she stands on the battlements of Thornfield, looking out over the world" (*Madwoman,* 348). In the case of Bertha, solitude is neither a choice nor a temporary state; it is the result of domination by a more powerful other, her estranged husband. She is denied freedom of movement and "speaks" only through maniacal laughter and violent acts. Bertha's world is reduced to a room.

Jane and Bertha have undeniably different experiences in the third *story* of Thornfield, but Gilbert and Gubar show that, on a symbolic level, their feminine *stories* intersect. Each woman is "enclosed in the architecture of an overwhelmingly male-dominated society" (*Madwoman,* xi). On one level, they share the marginalized space symbolized by the attic, but Jane is afforded a degree of agency denied the first Mrs. Rochester. This relative privilege has made the attic a contested space. Gubar responds to Spivak's criticism in the introduction to the second edition of *The Madwoman in the Attic:* "According to this postcolonial perspective, *The Attic* of our title should be identified as the site of the disenfranchised Third World female character on the borders of, or outside, Western civilization, not as that of the relatively privileged First World heroine" (xxxvi). Need it be an either/or situation? The attic as a contested space can invigorate discussions of *Jane Eyre,* but the drive to recognize Bertha's suffering need not deny Jane's.

Casting Jane and Bertha in competing roles for critical attention impedes scholarship; in many ways, it is counterproductive. The dynamic between gender and race need not be configured as antagonistic (as it all too often is). Elsie B. Michie's assessment of Spivak's essay highlights the inherent problem with this approach: "In her reading of Brontë's novel, Spivak effectively turns the tables on those earlier feminist readers by bringing the occluded questions of race and imperialism to center stage." "Turns the tables" suggests one-upmanship and, as Michie points out, it is a flawed tactic: "the difficulty with such a critical gesture is, however, that when you foreground one set of images, others tend to move into the background and become invisible." Race supplants gender in Spivak's reading of *Jane Eyre.* In the process, Spivak becomes guilty of the same critical blindness of which she accuses Gilbert and Gubar. Jane *is* more privileged than Bertha, but to say that she is equal in status and power to Rochester or St. John Rivers would be a misstatement. Michie, tentatively, suggests that "Spivak does not ask, as I think she might, whether there is a difference between these explicitly masculine articulations of imperialism and the position of the feminine in the novel—a difference that, though it does not free the female characters or Brontë herself from the burden of imperialism, makes them differently complicit because their relations to the power structure of British society is different from that of figures like Rochester and St. John."[8] I would change the "might" to "should"—just as race must be considered in a reading of *Jane Eyre,* so too should gender. Systems of oppression are not mutually exclusive.

Susan Meyer takes the provocative position that an awareness of gender oppression was crucial to the consideration of racial oppression in the nineteenth century. She proposes that "since the gender positioning of British women writers required them to negotiate an association with 'inferior races,' their feminist impulse to question gender hierarchies often *provoked* an interrogation of race hierarchies." Meyer does not suggest that "an awareness of gender oppression has historically given women an easy, automatic comprehension of oppression on the basis of race or class." Instead, an interrogation of one system of oppression opened a space for the consideration of other systems of oppression. In Meyer's reading of *Jane Eyre,* the metaphor of race linking Jane and Bertha is significant because "the yoking between the two terms of the metaphor turns not on shared inferiority but on shared oppression."[9] Different experiences shape the lives of Jane and Bertha, but as women in a patriarchal society the pair share a commonality—other than Rochester. Jane's ability to articulate "her rational desire for liberty" stems, in part, from her movement on the battlements and her view of the world. The expanded attic—it bridges both the interior and exterior space—opens up the possibility of new perspectives on the issue of the shared experience of marginalization in a patriarchal society. Dialogue and debate can be invigorating; diatribes and denunciations are more likely to be debilitating. In the push to expose the gaps and biases in *The Madwoman in the Attic,* critics overlook a valuable paradigm for scholars interrogating the relationship between race and feminism.

Western feminism has increasingly been accused of privileging white, heterosexual, middle-class concerns. Women of different racial, cultural, sexual, and economic backgrounds may, as a result, opt to self-identify in a way that does not highlight gender as a central or unifying factor. The paradox of the timing is noted by Susan Gubar: "Race takes center stage in feminist criticism at precisely the moment when its fictiveness as a biological category has been fully demonstrated but also when its malevolence as a barrier to social justice has been fully documented." As a scientific category, race does not exist; as a social reality, however, it is very much alive. Siobhan B. Somerville concludes that race really reflects "a historical, ideological process rather than . . . fixed transhistorical or biological characteristics: one's racial identity is contingent on one's cultural and historical location." Identity thus has a greater range of possibilities than racial categories seem to suggest. The exchanges between different groups of feminists have been lively, sometimes painful, and above all, necessary. Struggles for justice must avoid the danger of overcoming one hierarchy only to impose another. Gubar observes that "gender analyses [have become] increasingly sensitive to the ways in which all rhetorics—including those dedicated to social justice—can be used and abused under a variety of complex circumstances."[10] Inadvertent omissions in theoretical approaches can have the same effect as deliberate dismissals: they result in gaps and silences and have the potential to alienate readers.

Bell hooks articulates just such a feeling of alienation in her work on race and feminism. *Ain't I a Woman: Black Women and Feminism,* published only two years after *Madwoman,* in 1981, compares the struggles of nineteenth-century black women against racial and sexist oppression with those of twentieth-century black women. Hooks notes that in the earlier period, equality movements were interconnected. Dissension, however, occurred when it became clear that one aspect would be privileged over the other. "Sisterhood" disintegrated when white suffragists obstructed the movement for black male enfranchisement. For hooks, the legacy of this division is that "contemporary black women could not join together to fight for women's rights because we did not see 'womanhood' as an important aspect of our identity. Racist, sexist socialization had conditioned us to devalue our femaleness and to regard race as the only label of identification. Consequently, when the women's movement raised the issue of sexist oppression, we argued that sexism was insignificant in light of the harsher, more brutal reality of racism." In the battle between racism and sexism, racism "wins" and women of color continue to lose when the problem is posited as an either/or situation. Permitting one aspect of identity to dominate to the exclusion of others proves to be a trap; racism and patriarchy put the black woman in a double bind. "Feminist analyses of biases in white, middle-class feminism," cautions Susan Lurie, "tend to produce a shift in critical attention from gender to other categories of analysis; the feminists under discussion emerge instead as agents of their race, class, and national positions."[11] While diversifying feminism signals progress, the subsequent loss of attention to the issue of gender also deserves consideration. Negotiating the conflicting expectations requires subtlety and perseverance.

Difference is all too often envisioned as division. Diversity is read as creating barriers. Lurie offers an alternative response: "Differences between women can be calibrated not only in terms of membership in different social categories (e.g., race, class, nation, sexuality), but also in terms of how female subordination is cohered in various contexts with different women's multiple other beliefs. Formulating difference between women in this way also can at one time ground feminist alliances across social boundaries in a shared opposition to such structures of domination and keep visible their different consequences at discrete cultural sites."[12] Acknowledging the diversity of identities opens up previously constricted categories; we need a process of accommodation fueled by mutual respect. The paradigm of intersectionality is useful. What once were viewed as separate sites of oppression—for instance, gender, race, class, ethnicity, sexuality—are increasingly being recognized as intersecting systems of oppression. This model allows for the recognition of commonalities without erasing differences. This approach to feminism emphasizes the movement's importance, its willingness to address challenging issues, and its malleability.

Gilbert and Gubar and *Playing in the Dark*

Thirteen years after the publication of *The Madwoman in the Attic,* Toni Morrison issued her own challenge to critics in *Playing in the Dark.* Morrison's interest was "the pervasive use of black images and people in expressive prose" and "the shorthand, the taken-for-granted assumptions that lie in their usage."[13] She confronted the unquestioned constructions of blackness in literature by directly challenging literary critics to incorporate race in a sustained way. Significantly, Morrison envisions the process as a discovery of "a wider landscape," of "space for discovery, intellectual adventure, and close exploration"; it is akin to "the original charting of the New World—without the mandate for conquest" (*Playing,* 3). The image is one of accommodation rather than conflict, but the metaphor is spatial, as are so many of Gilbert and Gubar's. Morrison draws "an instructive parallel" between "this willed scholarly indifference" to race and the "centuries-long, hysterical blindness to feminist discourse and the way in which women and women's issues were read (or unread)" (*Playing,* 14). This parallel helps to connect Gilbert and Gubar's feminism with Morrison's: the common experience of exclusion and neglect, the consistent failure to address depictions of race and gender in literature and literary criticism.

Another link between discussions of racism and sexism concerns the medium of the message; language is not a straightforward entity. Morrison expresses a frustration with the process of articulation. She asserts, "I cannot rely on these metaphorical shortcuts because I am a black writer struggling with and through a language that can powerfully evoke and enforce hidden signs of racial superiority, cultural hegemony, and dismissive 'othering' of people and languages which are by no means marginal" (*Playing,* x). For Morrison, language is not transparent; as a result she must grapple with its historical biases. Writing can be an act of complicity in this context. It is a concern about language and power that is also found in *The Madwoman in the Attic,* as is evident in the book's opening questions: "Is a pen a metaphorical penis?" "With what organ can females generate texts?" (*Madwoman,* 3). The two texts highlight the fact that language has been co-opted by oppressive rhetorics: racism and sexism. Both Morrison and Gilbert and Gubar interpret the writer's relationship to language as problematic. Having been denied the authority to engage in literary and critical debates in the past, writers—black and female—encounter linguistic conventions that function as barriers to creativity and clear communication.

At first glance, *The Madwoman in the Attic* and *Playing in the Dark* seem to have little common ground; Morrison's text is physically dwarfed by Gilbert and Gubar's tome (91 pages versus 719!). Gilbert and Gubar "were trying to recover not only a major (and neglected) female literature but a whole (neglected) female history" (*Madwoman,* xii). Morrison's interest is "the ways in which a nonwhite, Africanlike (or Africanist) presence or persona was constructed in the United States, and the imaginative uses this fabricated presence served" (*Playing,* 6). Gilbert and Gubar rely on biography in their analysis. They assert (to the dismay of scholars suspicious of the author as subject) that "by projecting their rebellious impulses not into their heroines but into mad or monstrous women . . . female authors dramatize their own self-division . . . [the double] is usually in some sense the author's double, an image of her own anxiety and rage" (*Madwoman,* 78). In stark contrast, Morrison insists that her "deliberations are not about a particular author's attitudes toward race. . . . In no way do I mean an investigation of what might be called racist or nonracist literature, and I take no position, nor do I encourage one, on the quality of a work based on the attitudes of an author" (*Playing,* 90). Morrison's critical eye is directed toward the text, not the author—a very different approach from Gilbert and Gubar's identification of the writer with the writing.

The two projects do spring from similar sources, since both works originated in the experience of teaching literature by women. In the effort to articulate their own critical responses to works of fiction, Morrison and Gilbert and Gubar encountered the inadequacies of mainstream theoretical approaches. *The Madwoman in the Attic* and *Playing in the Dark* share the conviction that the neglected and the unquestioned deserve, indeed demand, recognition. Morrison's interest "in how agendas in criticism have disguised themselves and, in so doing, impoverished the literature it studies" is mirrored in Gilbert and Gubar's efforts to recover a neglected female literary tradition (*Playing*, 8-9). *Playing in the Dark* reads as the first step in an ongoing project. Morrison "propose[s] some topics that need critical investigation," and they seem to take the form of a collective enterprise. The first topic is stated—"the Africanist character as surrogate and enabler"—followed by two questions and the (gentle) directive to "note, for instance, the way Africanism is used to conduct a dialogue concerning American space in *The Narrative of Arthur Gordon Pym*" (*Playing*, 51). The second topic is introduced in a similarly detached manner: "a second topic in need of critical attention is the way an Africanist idiom is used to establish difference or, in a later period, to signal modernity" (*Playing*, 52). It is followed by "we need to explicate" and the third and fourth topics are introduced with the phrase "we need" (in the space of two pages, "we need" appears four times). By incorporating guiding questions and the use of "we," Morrison invites the audience's participation; indeed she almost commands it through the insistence on a common need. It is a compelling strategy.

In several ways, *The Madwoman in the Attic* creates a less "intimate" reading experience than *Playing in the Dark*. Identification with the subject matter is not encouraged by the kinds of rhetorical strategies Morrison employs. The sheer size can be daunting, but of more significance is the difference in tone. Morrison's work, in part, grew out of a series of lectures; the conversational quality of the three chapters reflects its origins. Her claim of "an informal study" is somewhat disingenuous, but Morrison does allow questions to share an equal part in her discussion (*Playing*, 6). *Playing in the Dark* is presented as more of a catalyst for subsequent studies than a definitive statement about the Africanist presence in American literature. In contrast, *The Madwoman in the Attic*'s extensive study seems to fill in the literary gap that Gilbert and Gubar identify; that is, their authoritative stance can be viewed as closing down discussion rather than provoking new lines of inquiry. It is a troubling accusation, particularly in light of Gilbert and Gubar's efforts to (re)establish the authority of neglected authors. It is also too reductive.

Playing in the Dark helps to draw attention to one of the weaknesses of *The Madwoman in the Attic:* its failure to discuss race and its reproduction of stereotypes around blackness. In light of the work on the intersections of categories like class, ethnicity, gender, race, and so forth, *The Madwoman in the Attic* can also illuminate *Playing in the Dark*. An additional question for Morrison's project might be: does the Africanist presence (directly or indirectly) take a gendered position? That is, is there a masculine Africanist presence that is distinctive from a feminine one?[14] The distance between the two works is ultimately not as extreme as it may initially seem. Both were (and are) innovative and provocative challenges to traditional literary criticism; this shared impulse to denaturalize gender and race is a crucial one. By fusing the theoretical frameworks of the two texts, scholars can address what have tended to be separate threads of exploration; the result is a multifaceted reading that in turn can be the catalyst for other interpretations. In this context, a book that served to divide—*The Madwoman in the Attic*—is a vehicle for reconnecting feminists.

Shared Spaces: *Jane Eyre* and *Beloved*

Although 140 years separate *Jane Eyre* (1847) and Toni Morrison's *Beloved* (1987), these important works of fiction and the settings and central characters they bring to life reveal startling parallels—in fact, many instructors of women's literature courses place both books on the syllabus. The connections are all the more unexpected when drawing upon Gilbert and Gubar's work because they do not consider the implications of race in their work on women writers, while Morrison insists on its recognition in virtually all forms of contemporary discourse, insisting, as we have seen, that "the contemplation of this black presence is central to any understanding of our national literature and should not be permitted to hover at the margins of the literary imagination" (*Playing,* 6). Morrison issues a challenge to critics to incorporate race in a sustained way. The critical framework of *The Madwoman in the Attic* can accommodate such a modification. This new consideration is necessary for a number of reasons, in particular to achieve a more complex and compelling understanding of literature and to avoid the imposition of hierarchies. For example, Jennifer Devere Brody draws on Morrison's work in her study of Victorian culture, concluding that a "comparable 'real or fabricated Africanist presence' played a role in the construction of Englishness."[15] Although Morrison's focus is on American fiction, her insights transcend geographic boundaries. Rereading *The Madwoman in the Attic* in conjunction with *Playing in the Dark* supplements the text's original ideas with questions of racial identity. It also infuses Gilbert and Gubar's readings with a new energy and enhances their credibility as feminist critics.

Gilbert and Gubar assert that Jane Eyre's story provides a "pattern for countless others" as Jane's problems are "symptomatic of difficulties Everywoman in a patriarchal society must meet and overcome" (*Madwoman,* 339). Gender is the key factor in life experiences: the "problems encountered by the protagonist as she struggles from the imprisonment of her childhood toward an almost unthinkable goal of mature freedom" are specific to women

(*Madwoman*, 339). The ideology of patriarchy imposes a pattern of expectations and restrictions that the female protagonist must confront: oppression, starvation, madness, coldness, and an encounter with a double that represents socially unacceptable impulses such as rebellion and rage (*Madwoman*, 339). Given the work on the complexity of identity that has emerged in the decades following *The Madwoman in the Attic*, it seems unlikely that a single model could be applicable to "Everywoman."[16] I propose, however, that such a model can, with modifications and caution, be useful in discussions of texts outside the parameters of Gilbert and Gubar's study. The pairings of the central characters in *Jane Eyre* and *Beloved*—Jane/Sethe and Bertha/Beloved—are superficially incompatible: Jane is an orphan/governess/heiress while Sethe is an escaped slave/cook/murderess. Yet each woman struggles to find her own identity in the face of external pressures and internal doubts—Sethe's recognition that she is her "own best thing" is a variation of Jane's bold assertion of equality with Rochester. Furthermore, both women achieve unconventional but companionate relationships and a sense of contentment only after the deranged double is eradicated.

Florence Stratton's 1988 examination of the fiction of African women writers speaks to the continuing relevance of *The Madwoman in the Attic*. Surprisingly, Stratton discovered similar patterns to those outlined by Gilbert and Gubar "in the works of women at an even greater geographical, historical, and psychological distance" than the authors Gilbert and Gubar studied. She asks, "What can be said to link these two groups of women living in distinctly dissimilar cultural milieus? The most likely hypothesis is similarity of female psychological and artistic response to what, despite cultural specificity in its manifestations, is a cultural constant: patriarchy." Geographic, political, economic, and social differences are, to a large extent, transcended by the experiences of gender—not erased or deemed irrelevant, but overshadowed by gender issues. While Stratton is interested in exploring the "possibility of there being a female literary tradition that transcends all cultural boundaries," she wisely cautions the critic to be "neither indifferent to the culturally specific manifestations of patriarchy or any other cultural elements that a writer has incorporated into her text."[17] Drawing on the work of Gilbert and Gubar, Stratton makes a perceptive argument for its usefulness while mitigating its drawbacks. The "nuances" that were not possible in the urgency of *Madwoman*'s original manifestation must now be incorporated in all applications of its arguments. Armed with expanded perspectives of the theoretical debates that followed and, to some extent, grew out of *Madwoman*, the central pattern Gilbert and Gubar illustrate through their reading of *Jane Eyre* has the potential to open up new literary territory and unexpected connections. A comparison of *Jane Eyre*, as interpreted by Gilbert and Gubar, with Morrison's *Beloved* simultaneously exposes the gaps in their criticism and supports the utility of the pattern they outline.

The titles of the novels are telling: Brontë's fictional autobiography assures that we are reading Jane's story, while Morrison draws attention not only to the central figure of Sethe but to her murdered daughter, Beloved. Having lost her original name, the girl adopts the name that marks her grave; she is the spirit made flesh. Birth and death are linked in the concept, and conception of, Beloved. The price of the headstone is sexual exploitation, "ten minutes with her knees wide open as any grave . . . rutting among the headstones with the engraver."[18] At first sight of the young woman, Sethe has an uncontrollable need to relieve herself: "There was no stopping water breaking from a breaking womb and there was no stopping now" (*Beloved,* 51). It marks the murdered daughter's rebirth as a vengeful and uncomprehending figure. The child's original name is lost in the process but the new name suggests a relationship: to be called Beloved is to require someone to love you. Sethe's act is a desperate attempt to protect her cherished children; slavery distorts the mother's love, but it does not destroy it.

The choice of Jane Eyre's name (in her fictional autobiography) suggests self-fulfillment, autonomy. It is the assertion of individuality in defiance of a society that negated it at every turn by labeling her orphan, dependent, governess, plain. The impulse is similar to Beloved's quest for love and insistence on her right to exist in defiance of a society that deemed her property (and a mother who opted for death over enslavement). Jane, however, is afforded opportunities to develop her identity that the spirit-child is not. Beloved claims a name without substance; it is linked to her death rather than her life. As a matter of practicality, Jane's name improves her living conditions: St. John Rivers's discovery expedites Jane's inheritance. The fact that she is not called "Mrs. Rochester" can be construed as an attempt to emphasize a bedrock identity beyond a wife's. (It may also be a matter of practicality: such a title would raise the specter of the *first* Mrs. Rochester.) If Brontë's novel shines a clear light on the individual, Morrison's invokes the figure in the shadows: just as Jane's story is shadowed by Bertha's, Beloved's story is entwined with Sethe's.

Brontë's nineteenth-century story of a woman's struggle for autonomy is dramatically different from Morrison's twentieth-century depiction of the legacy of slavery. *Beloved* shifts in time but the main events happen between 1873 and 1874, the same century as *Jane Eyre* but decidedly different contexts. The pairings of the key female characters in the novels reinforce the differences: Jane the orphan, student, teacher, governess, heiress, wife, and mother has a more expansive experience than Sethe the slave, wife (albeit unofficial: the marriage cannot be legal given that the pair are deemed property—a more daunting legal impediment than Jane and Rochester face), mother, runaway, murderess, and cook. Bertha Mason's initial experiences as the daughter of a wealthy family afford more opportunities than Beloved's position as the daughter of an escaped slave, but both figures become victims of circumstances they cannot control—madness and the threat of slavery—and are isolated for their own "protection" by loved ones. Sethe's love, however disturbing, is unequivocal; at the sight of the slave catchers, she "collected every bit of life she had made, all the parts of her that were precious and fine and beautiful, and carried, pushed, dragged them through the veil, out away . . . where no one could hurt them . . . where they would be safe" (*Beloved,* 163). Sethe is motivated by genuine love and concern; the same cannot be said for Bertha's natal family or her husband, but her fate is also manipulated by intimate relations.

Racial differences create very different scenarios. Jane's independence is assured by the timely intervention of an inheritance: an inheritance that is the result of slavery.[19] Sethe's "freedom" is that of a fugitive and as such is highly tenuous. She enjoys "twenty-eight happy days" before the slave catchers appear; they are followed by "eighteen years of disapproval and a solitary life" (*Beloved,* 173). And yet, Jane and Sethe do struggle with the obstacles Gilbert and Gubar identify as common to "Everywoman" in a patriarchal society. Jane's oppression at Gateshead is echoed, and intensified, in Sethe's enslavement on the Sweet Home plantation. Jane is an anomaly at Gateshead—neither a useful servant nor an immediate family member—and as such, is never at home in this space. A rare feeling of "inexpressible relief, a soothing conviction of protection and security," comes to Jane after the red room incident; significantly it is inspired by the presence of a stranger—Mr. Lloyd—and not anyone "belonging to Gateshead . . . [or] related to Mrs. Reed."[20] Sethe also has a brief—and delusionary—feeling of comfort and safety while the Garners are in control, but once the Teacher and his nephews arrive the true nature of the slave plantation is revealed. Jane's experience of starvation at Lowood surfaces in Sethe's desperate flight for freedom. In each case, the physical starvation is temporary; the emotional deprivation, however, is more prolonged. The madness Jane encounters at Thornfield (in the form of Bertha and, to a lesser extent, her own infatuation with Rochester) and the coldness at Marsh End are overwhelmingly present in 124, the house her mother-in-law rents following Sethe's violent act. In Sethe's case, the madness is the nature of her interaction with Beloved and her psychological state after the second loss of the daughter. Withdrawing from life after Beloved's disappearance, Sethe's home is literally cold and she is emotionally frozen. The pattern of the female quest symbolized by the motifs Gilbert and Gubar isolate in their analysis of *Jane Eyre*—oppression, starvation, madness, coldness—matches Sethe's journey toward freedom and self-acceptance.

For Gilbert and Gubar, one of the central images in *Jane Eyre* is the red room. The childhood experience of being unjustly confined in an oppressive space resurfaces at key points in the novel. Gilbert and Gubar insist that "Jane's pilgrimage consists of a series of experiences which are, in one way or another, variations on the central, red-room motif of enclosure and escape" (*Madwoman,* 341). Jane is forcibly detained for daring to defend herself; at this point in her life, Jane's refusal to be a silent victim reinforces her vulnerability. Emotionally distraught and frightened, the child Jane is not equipped to resist. She is trapped in "a kind of patriarchal death chamber" that only exacerbates her feelings of alienation (*Madwoman,* 341). It is literally the death site of the (surrogate) father, Mr. Reed. Although the uncle's willingness to adopt Jane speaks to his compassion and kindness, she is terrified at the prospect of his "return."

Morrison incorporates a similar space in *Beloved.* The "keeping room" is a more complex site, and readers are provided with a variety of perspectives. For Sethe, it is "where she usually went to talk-think"; it opens a space for introspection (*Beloved,* 38). In this context, the keeping room has the potential to reinvigorate Sethe; it helps her to work through issues. Unlike Jane, Sethe chooses to enter, and is free to leave, the keeping room at any time. Enclosure is protective for Sethe; the room provides an escape from distraction. Denver, Sethe's youngest daughter, also views the room as a protective space. Fearing her mother's violent side, Denver believes the "only place she can't get to me in the night is Grandma Baby's room" (*Beloved,* 206). The keeping room, unlike the red room, seems to be a matriarchal space. The home itself belongs to an abolitionist brother and sister, but it has been transformed by Sethe's mother-in-law and is a maleless abode. Baby Suggs redesigns the home to reflect her newfound freedom. She "boarded up the back door that led to [the outside kitchen] because she didn't want to make that journey no more . . . if you want to get in 124 you have to come by her" (*Beloved,* 207). It is similar to Gilbert and Gubar's reading of Thornfield as "the house of Jane's life, its floors and walls the architecture of her experience" (*Madwoman,* 347). Baby Suggs literally transforms her dwelling. It provides, however, a false sense of security: slave catchers will appear without warning and the haunting legacy of life on the plantation will turn 124 into a haunted house.

In the case of Baby Suggs, contemplation becomes akin to suicide. Her spirit is broken by Sethe's desperate act and Baby Suggs opts for a withdrawal from society. As she informs her friend Stamp Paid, "What I have to do is get in my bed and lay down. I want to fix on something harmless in this world . . . Blue. That don't hurt nobody. Yellow neither" (*Beloved,* 179). Baby Suggs reduces her world to a single room and then further narrows her focus to one color at a time. Taking to her bed is Baby Suggs's act of surrender; the keeping room becomes her final enclosure—she only leaves it after her death. For a woman desperate for color, it is an odd choice. Sethe realizes "why Baby Suggs was so starved for color. There wasn't any except for two orange squares in a quilt that made the absence shout. The walls of the room were slate-colored, the floor earth-brown, the wooden dresser the color of itself, curtains white, and the dominating feature the quilt over an iron cot, was made up of scraps of blue serge, black, brown and gray wool. . . . In that sober field, two patches of orange looked wild—like life in the raw" (*Beloved,* 38). A somber space, the keeping room keeps Baby Suggs from reentering life. It fails to nourish her wounded spirit.

The keeping room is virtually devoid of color. In contrast, the red room is awash in a color: "swathed in rich crimson," the "scarlet darkness" Gilbert and Gubar describe has a vibrancy not found in the keeping room (*Madwoman,* 340). Red is, however, associated with Sethe's house. Paul D attempts to enter and encounters "a pool of red and undulating light that locked him where he stood" (*Beloved,* 8). A physical manifestation of the spirit world, Sethe reassures him that "it is not evil, just sad," but it is sadness with the potential to consume the house's inhabitants (*Beloved,* 8). Ultimately, the keeping room, like the red room, is "a kind of patriarchal death chamber" for Baby Suggs. The intrusion of the slave catchers obliterates any sense of autonomy. Baby Suggs cannot keep the men at bay—as she repeats to Stamp Paid, "They came in my yard" (*Beloved,* 179). The law is on the side of the men attempting to retrieve their "property."

The "central, red-room motif of enclosure and escape" Gilbert and Gubar identify in *Jane Eyre* is echoed in the keeping room in *Beloved* (*Madwoman,* 341). The domestic spaces have the potential to be suffocating, life-destroying, but they also have the potential to protect, to heal. Both Jane and Sethe are in desperate need of a true home, a chance to place themselves rather than be placed by others. It is significant that both characters end up in isolated dwellings—Ferndean and the exorcised 124—but are themselves no longer isolated—Jane has Rochester, Sethe has Paul D. Ferndean is physically isolated, but, like Thornfield before its destruction, it is further isolated by choice—the decision not to engage in social interactions is, in large part, self-determined (first by Rochester, and then by Jane and Rochester). Sethe's home is physically and socially isolated. The stigma of the murder turns a once thriving social space into a marginalized and feared dwelling (the timely intervention of the community, however, hints at a potential reconfiguration). Their journeys require Jane and Sethe to move through a series of houses that are not their own; autonomy and contentment are only possible when that externally created detachment is resolved. Focusing on Thornfield's "upper regions," Gilbert and Gubar interpret them as "symbolically miniaturiz[ing] one crucial aspect of the world in which [Jane] finds herself. Heavily enigmatic, ancestral relics wall her in; inexplicable locked rooms guard a secret . . . distant vistas promise an inaccessible but enviable life" (*Madwoman,* 348). The destruction of Thornfield then signals Jane's escape from obscurity (the "relics" the ancestor leave her are a fortune and a newfound family), secrecy (Bertha's death, oddly enough, brings her existence to the public light), and loneliness (the life she desired is now accessible)—all conditions created by her anomalous position in a patriarchal society.

Sethe is also an anomaly in a patriarchal society, but she must also grapple with systemic racism. Like Jane, Sethe struggles with obscurity, confinement, secrecy, and loneliness; unlike Jane, no rich ancestor intervenes to alleviate her suffering. The central address in *Beloved*—124—emphasizes the absence of the ancestor. Beloved is the missing third child but the break in the logical order of the numbers 1, 2, 3, and 4 reflects the disruption in the natural order of ancestors and descendents that resulted from slavery. The house is specifically haunted by the spirit of Beloved, but Baby Suggs points out, "Not a house in the country ain't packed to its rafters with some dead Negro's grief" (*Beloved,* 5). The impossibility of achieving a genuine home under slavery is painfully clear—it becomes a symbol of the "inaccessible but enviable life." In *Beloved,* the historical nightmare of slavery is a direct contradiction to the "home sweet home" motif. Sethe escapes from Sweet Home; while it was a relatively benign slave plantation during the master's life, one of its other survivors, Paul D, observes, "It wasn't sweet and it sure wasn't home" (*Beloved,* 14). The attempt to disguise the brutal reality behind a "homey" name is simply perverse. Nevertheless, the appeal of the home endures; Paul D's suggestion that she move her house "as though a house was a little thing—a shirtwaist or a sewing basket, you could walk off from or give away," horrifies Sethe (*Beloved,* 22). She has paid a high price for her home and, unlike Jane, Sethe has neither the means nor the opportunity to relocate.

Relocation is not a solution for Sethe in another sense: she cannot run from her past. After the second loss of her daughter, Sethe retreats to the keeping room. Seeing her in this space, Paul D is uncomfortable: "He knows what he is reminded of and he shouts at her, 'Don't you die on me! This is Baby Suggs' bed! Is that what you planning?'" (*Beloved,* 271-72). Paul D recognizes the seductive appeal of escape—the release from painful experiences—but manages to persuade Sethe that life—her life—has value. Healing requires that Sethe acknowledge and come to terms with the painful circumstances of her life. Beloved serves as the living embodiment of the past; Sethe's struggle to explain her choice to the uncomprehending and (understandably) hostile child-spirit is crucial to her own development.

For Gilbert and Gubar, the most important confrontation in *Jane Eyre* is "not with Rochester but with Rochester's mad wife Bertha"; it is an encounter "not with her own sexuality but with her own imprisoned 'hunger, rebellion, and rage'" (*Madwoman,* 339). The conflict with Rochester, while significant, pales in comparison with Jane's internal struggle. Bertha, "Jane's truest and darkest double," is the physical embodiment of the socially unacceptable emotions and impulses Jane has sought to repress: "the ferocious secret self" (*Madwoman,* 360). Like Sethe, Jane is haunted by her past; it intrudes at several points in the form of a phantom child. Jane's recurrent dream of a child, Gilbert and Gubar theorize, is a sign that Jane is being "symbolically drawn back into her own past, and specifically to reexperience the dangerous sense of doubleness that had begun in the red-room" (*Madwoman,* 357). The division between the past and present does not hold. In her sleep, the tenuous separation Jane has achieved is challenged. "The burden of the past," Gilbert and Gubar assert, "cannot be sloughed off so easily—not, for instance, by glamorous lovemaking, silk dresses, jewelry, a new name" (*Madwoman,* 358). Bertha is the obvious impediment to Jane's relationship with Rochester, but equally important is the "orphaned alter ego" Jane must carry "everywhere" (*Madwoman,* 358).

The past intrudes on the present with tragic consequences in *Beloved.* In a 1988 interview, Morrison expressed a concern with America's refusal to acknowledge its past: "We live in a land where the past is always erased and America is the innocent future in which immigrants can come and start over, where the slate is clean. The past is absent or it's romanticized. This culture doesn't encourage dwelling on, let alone coming to terms with, the truth about the past."[21] The myth of America cannot accommodate the brutal history of slavery. Rejecting a censored version of history, Morrison's work insists on recognition of the past. The necessity for acknowledging the past—both individual and collective—is a central concern in *Beloved.* Beloved becomes the living past, the lost daughter returned. She also embodies a past that is not hers. Neither Beloved nor Sethe experienced the forced relocation from Africa, and yet Beloved's descriptions of the "other place" incorporate scenes of life on the slave ships.[22] Beloved carries a past that is not directly her own into the present.

The confrontation with the double in *Beloved* and *Jane Eyre* is a confrontation with the past. Jane's double is a woman denied her own life by madness, marriage, and, indeed, by the shape of the narrative itself. Bertha is reduced to furtive incursions and a "preternatural . . . laugh" (*Jane Eyre,* 123). A haunting but unseen presence for much of the novel, Bertha becomes a more overt physical threat to Jane as it becomes clear that Jane and Bertha (or Jane/Bertha) cannot coexist; one must yield to the other. Similarly, Sethe's double—the daughter she murdered—is the spirit made flesh who asserts herself as a malevolent force. As Sethe's daughter, Beloved is an unusual double, but she (like Bertha) embodies the hunger, rebellion, and rage that Sethe has not acknowledged in herself. Beloved has been denied her life by slavery and her mother. Sethe hopes for a second chance with her daughter, free from the threat of slave catchers that made a mother's love take the form of infanticide. Beloved, however, has other plans. When she returns, the mother-child relationship is even further distorted, almost cannibalistic. Physical alterations in appearance signal the disturbed nature of the connection: "The bigger Beloved got, the smaller Sethe became; the brighter Beloved's eyes, the more those eyes that used never to look away became slits of sleeplessness. Sethe . . . sat in a chair . . . like a chastised child while Beloved ate up her life, took it, swelled up with it, grew taller on it" (*Beloved,* 250). Beloved feeds off of Sethe; she devours the life of the mother who took hers years ago. Bertha Mason Rochester is also construed as monstrous in *The Madwoman in the Attic*—a "mysterious specter, a sort of 'vampyre'"—but, in an odd way, she seems to serve as an agent for Jane: "What Bertha now does . . . is what Jane wants to do. Disliking the 'vapoury veil' of Jane Rochester, Jane Eyre secretly wants to tear up the garments. Bertha does it for her. Fearing the inexorable 'bridal day,' Jane would like to put it off. Bertha does that for her too" (*Madwoman,* 359). Bertha, however, remains an uncontrollable and destructive force with her own agenda: vengeance. In Morrison's novel, Beloved's desire for vengeance and Sethe's need for atonement converge in a deadly and disturbing confrontation that can only end in destruction.

As I have noted, Gilbert and Gubar assert that the key confrontation in *Jane Eyre* is between Jane and Bertha, between Jane and her repressed emotions. Sethe must also face disturbing emotions. Bertha and Beloved are driven by emotion—predominantly anger—and eager for vengeance. They act on impulse, not reason. Each is the embodiment of her society's fears: rampant passion, female sexuality, and importantly, the unrelenting anguish of a community haunted by the legacy of slavery (a clear fact in *Beloved* but a mere implication in *Jane Eyre*). Bertha and Beloved represent the uncontrolled—the spirited individual reduced to pure emotion and the pleasures of the flesh—and the uncontrollable—the spirit made flesh. As such, the narratives must eliminate them, but not before they leave an indelible mark on their counterparts.

Jane and Sethe grapple with different external pressures and internal doubts, and yet both characters achieve unconventional but companionate relationships and a sense of contentment only after the deranged double is eradicated. Gilbert and Gubar theorize that "when the Bertha in Jane falls from the ruined wall of Thornfield and is destroyed, the orphan child too, as her dream predicts, will roll from her knee—the burden of her past will be lifted" (*Madwoman,* 362). Bertha's death is necessary in a legal sense—Rochester must be free—but also in a psychological sense—Jane must be free of the conflicts that obstructed her relationship. For Gilbert and Gubar, Jane's "pilgrimage toward selfhood" actually ends at Marsh End with her rejection of St. John Rivers: "At that moment she had been irrevocably freed from the burden of her past, freed both from the raging specter of Bertha (which had already fallen in fact from the ruined wall of Thornfield) and from the self-pitying specter of the orphan child (which had symbolically, as in her dream, rolled from her knee)" (*Madwoman,* 368). Finding her voice (and spine!) frees Jane from Rivers's aggressive "courtship." Her insistence on her right to determine her own destiny opens Jane to Rochester's passionate cry. Wakening to "her own self, her own needs," Gilbert and Gubar conclude, liberates Jane, paving the way for an egalitarian relationship with Rochester (*Madwoman,* 368).

Waking from her nightmare proves to be much more difficult for Sethe. It is not a process she can complete on her own. Beloved has been a divisive presence in Sethe's life—chasing away her other children and lover—and the emotions concentrated in her memory have psychologically paralyzed Sethe. Beloved is driven away by the timely intervention of a female community: "The voices of the women searched for the right combination, the key, the code. . . . Building voice upon voice until they found it, and when they did it was a wave of sound wide enough to sound deep water. . . . It broke over Sethe and she trembled like the baptized in its wash" (*Beloved,* 261). The chorus of voices restores harmony but leaves Sethe despondent. Her hunger for her daughter's love and forgiveness, her futile rebellion against the cruel practices of slavery and rage at injustice nearly consume Sethe. It is not until Paul D opens Sethe's eyes to the crucial knowledge—"You your best thing, Sethe. You are"—that she is able to recognize her own value (*Beloved,* 273). In contrast, Jane's bold assertion of equality to Rochester—"my spirit . . . addresses your spirit, just as if . . . we stood at God's feet, equal—as we are!"—prefigures Bertha's removal (*Jane Eyre,* 284). Before Beloved's return, Sethe "had claimed herself. Freeing yourself was one thing [she discovered]; claiming ownership of that freed self was another" (*Beloved,* 95). The daughter's return blinds Sethe to that earlier awareness; she is caught in a new form of imprisonment in her relationship with Beloved. Sethe needs the love of others to release her. It is a collective, rather than an individual, struggle.

Jane Eyre is the triumphant story of an individual woman: Jane is the author of her own life. Bertha's story is situated on the fringes. Subsequent postcolonial readings of the novel have sought to move Bertha in from the margin, to address her function within the narrative with an awareness of power structures Gilbert and Gubar, for example, do not consider. It is a significant supplement to *The Madwoman in the Attic*'s theoretical approach. While Bertha is Creole[23] and not specifically black, the depiction of her, by both Brontë and Gilbert and Gubar, falls into what Morrison identifies as the "the pervasive use of black images" and "the shorthand, the taken-for-granted assumptions that lie in their usage" (*Playing,* x). To deem Bertha the "darkest double" is to perpetuate a literary technique that reinforces racial stereotyping (*Madwoman,* 360). Morrison's call to question this approach—to interrogate race and literary criticism—expands *The Madwoman in the Attic*'s insightful analysis on the systems of oppression that create and sustain patriarchy.

In contrast to the Jane/Bertha dynamic, the stories of Sethe and Beloved are interconnected. There is, however, a degree of uncertainty about Beloved's fate: "Disremembered and unaccounted for, she cannot be lost because no one is looking for her" (*Beloved,* 274). Beloved's story is submerged in fear and, unlike Jane, she does not narrate her own tale. In the final two pages of the novel, there is a repetition of the phrase "it was not a story to pass on." It is a haunting story, and despite these seeming disclaimers, it is a story that must be passed *on,* handed down, not passed *by* without recognition: Morrison's novel insists on recognition of the legacy of slavery and the reality of racism in the United States. The significance of the female community in Sethe's life must also be recognized. The women are compelled to act because they understand Sethe's struggle—comprehension leads to compassion. Paul D's love is also crucial; the shared experience of slavery, the ultimate form of racism, connects the pair, but gender differences remain. Thus any reading of *Beloved* must also acknowledge the reality of sexism.

Using a comparison of *Jane Eyre* and *Beloved* as a case study, it becomes clear that *The Madwoman in the Attic* continues to participate in current critical dialogues. To simply view Sethe's oppression in terms of race would be just as limiting as looking at gender in isolation. The point is addressed by Carolyn G. Heilbrun: "There is no universal woman subject, there is no sort of woman who can speak for others; certainly no white, heterosexual middle-class woman of European origin can speak for another woman who is none of these things. And yet, as Gilbert and Gubar seem to grasp and some of their female critics do not, beneath it all, women do have something in common, something that they do not have in common with men of the same race, class, sexual orientation, or national origin."[24] Rather than focusing on difference as a divider, feminist critics should keep those distinctions in sight while remaining open to commonalities. Patriarchy is an oppressive force for all women; acknowledging its influence need not negate extenuating factors like race, class, sexuality, or any number of variables that make us individuals. Race and gender do not have to be conceptualized as competing concerns.

The implicit challenge issued by *The Madwoman in the Attic*—to reconsider critical practices—has, in part, been lost in the backlash. Looking beyond the dismissive responses to the text, however, it is possible to envision a reenergized use of *Madwoman*. The paradigm Gilbert and Gubar extrapolate from *Jane Eyre* can accommodate the very factors critics derided them for neglecting. *The Madwoman in the Attic* remains a relevant and valuable resource once shortsighted biases are addressed. It is time to revisit the attic.

Notes

1. Some of the controversy is usefully summarized in Janet Gezari, "Sandra M. Gilbert and Susan Gubar's *The Madwoman in the Attic*," *Essays in Criticism* 56, no. 3 (2006): 264–79.

2. Sandra M. Gilbert and Susan Gubar, introduction to *The Madwoman in the Attic: The Woman Writer and the Nineteenth-Century Literary Imagination*, 2nd ed. (1979; New Haven: Yale University Press, 2000), xxiv, xxv.

3. Sandra M. Gilbert and Susan Gubar, *The Madwoman in the Attic: The Woman Writer and the Nineteenth-Century Literary Imagination* (New Haven: Yale University Press, 1979), xi. Subsequent references to this edition will be given parenthetically.

4. William E. Cain, introduction to *Making Feminist History: The Literary Scholarship of Sandra M. Gilbert and Susan Gubar*, ed. William E. Cain (New York: Garland Publishing, 1994), xix–xx. Subsequent references will be given parenthetically.

5. Gayatri Chakravorty Spivak, "Three Women's Texts and a Critique of Imperialism," in *The Feminist Reader: Essays in Gender and the Politics of Literary Criticism*, ed. Catherine Belsey and Jane Moore (New York: Basil Blackwell, 1989), 176, 180, 181, 195; Erin O'Connor, "Preface for a Post-Postcolonial Criticism," *Victorian Studies* 45, no. 2 (Winter 2003): 217–46.

6. Susan Meyer objects to Spivak's references to Bertha as both a white woman and a native: "Bertha is either native or not to suit Spivak's critiques. Thus it is by sleight of hand that Spivak shows feminism to be inevitably complicitous with imperialism." Meyer, *Imperialism at Home: Race and Victorian Women's Fiction* (Ithaca: Cornell University Press, 1996), 66. Carolyn Vellenga Berman, in *Creole Crossings: Domestic Fiction and the Reform of Colonial Slavery* (Ithaca, N.Y.: Cornell University Press, 2006), points out that "the crucial signifier in *Jane Eyre* is not 'native' but rather 'Creole'" (6).

7. Frank Lentricchia leveled a similar charge against Gilbert and Gubar's exclusions in terms of class: "The aristocratic social model simply saturates the analyses found in *The Madwoman in the Attic* and blinds its authors to any other sort of social experience and any other sort of literature not rooted in the English country house." Frank Lentricchia, "Patriarchy against Itself: The Young Manhood of Wallace Stevens," *Critical Inquiry* 13, no. 4 (Summer 1987): 782. Gilbert and Gubar responded to this charge (among others) in "The Man on the Dump versus the United Dames of America; Or, What Does Frank Lentricchia Want?" *Critical Inquiry* 14, no. 2 (Winter 1988): 386–406.

8. Elsie B. Michie, *Outside the Pale: Cultural Exclusion, Gender Differences, and the Victorian Woman Writer* (Ithaca, N.Y.: Cornell University Press, 1993), 12, 12–13.

9. Susan Meyer, *Imperialism,* 11, 66.

10. Susan Gubar, *Critical Condition: Feminism at the Turn of the Century* (Oxford: Oxford University Press, 1997), 21–22, 17. Siobhan B. Somerville, *Queering the Color Line: Race and the Invention of Homosexuality in American Culture* (Durham, N.C.: Duke University Press, 2000), 7.

11. Bell hooks, *Ain't I a Woman: Black Women and Feminism* (Boston: South End Press, 1992), 1; Susan Lurie, *Unsettled Subjects: Restoring Feminist Politics to Poststructuralist Critiques* (Durham, N.C.: Duke University Press, 1997), 2.

12. Lurie, *Unsettled Subjects,* 4.

13. Toni Morrison, *Playing in the Dark: Whiteness and the Literary Imagination* (New York: Vintage, 1992), x. Subsequent references will be given parenthetically in the text.

14. Ann Harris-Williams proposes that "whether intentionally or not, *Playing* engages Virginia Woolf's *A Room of One's Own* in a critical dialogue on the issues of otherness, color dichotomies, race and gender." Leaving aside the issue of intention, Morrison does not link the "otherness" of race with the "otherness" of gender in a direct way in *Playing in the Dark.* Harris-Williams, "Woolf and Toni Morrison: Moments from the Critical Dialogue," in *Virginia Woolf: Emerging Perspectives. Selected Papers from the Third Annual Conference on Virginia Woolf,* ed. Mark Hussey and Vara Neverow (New York: Pace University Press, 1994), 32.

15. Jennifer Devere Brody, *Impossible Purities: Blackness, Femininity, and Victorian Culture* (Durham, N.C.: Duke University Press, 1998), 11.

16. Debates about identity tend to take two broad approaches: essentialism (biology is the primary source of identity) and constructionism (systems of ideology and culture shape identity). Feminist discourse has mostly favored the latter since Simone de Beauvoir asserted, "One is not born, but rather becomes a woman." Beauvoir, *The Second Sex,* trans. H. M. Parshley (New York: Vintage Books, 1974), 301. Judith Butler has insisted that gender identity is "performatively constituted by the very 'expressions' that are said to be its result." We learn to perform our "appropriate" roles early in life. Butler, *Gender Trouble: Feminism and the Subversion of Identity* (New York: Routledge, 1990), 25.

17. Florence Stratton, "The Shallow Grave: Archetypes of Female Experience in African Fiction," *Research in African Literatures* 19, no. 2 (1988): 143, 144.

18. Toni Morrison, *Beloved* (New York: Plume, 1988), 5. Subsequent references will be given parenthetically in the text.

19. Meyer discusses the timing of the events in the novel; despite the vagueness, it is clear that they occur before the "full emancipation of the British West Indian slaves in 1838." The implication is that both Jane and Rochester gain fortunes derived from slave labor. It raises the issue of culpability, but the novel does not address the concern in a direct way. *Imperialism,* 70.

20. Charlotte Brontë, *Jane Eyre* (London: Penguin Books, 1996), 26. Subsequent references will be given parenthetically in the text.

21. Toni Morrison, "Living Memory," *City Limits* (March 31– April 7, 1988): 10–11.

22. For example, there are cryptic glimpses of the Middle Passage, the spirit world, and memories of Sethe. Morrison, *Beloved,* 210–13.

23. Berman provocatively argues that "since efforts to locate the Creole as either black or white meet with such textual resistance, the novel forces us to consider what Brontë stands to gain rhetorically from maintaining Bertha's racial ambiguity." "Perhaps," Berman proposes, "Bertha Mason becomes a more powerful synecdoche for the West Indies by encompassing Creoles of all classes—colonizers *and* colonized." *Creole Crossings,* 123–24.

24. Carolyn G. Heilbrun, foreword to *Making Feminist History: The Literary Scholarship of Sandra M. Gilbert and Susan Gubar,* ed. William E. Cain (New York: Garland Publishing, 1994), xiii.

8

The Legacy of Hell

Wuthering Heights on Film and Gilbert and Gubar's Feminist Poetics

Hila Shachar

Sandra M. Gilbert and Susan Gubar's analysis of Emily Brontë's *Wuthering Heights* (1847) in *The Madwoman in the Attic* (1979) remains one of the most influential interpretations of the novel. Under the title "Looking Oppositely: Emily Brontë's Bible of Hell," Gilbert and Gubar construct an analytical framework that presents Brontë's novel as an oppositional "bible" to Milton's patriarchal poetics in *Paradise Lost.*[1] "Milton's Bogey" (quoting Virginia Woolf) is the shadow of patriarchal assumptions and the inheritance of ideological models of gender which nineteenth-century women writers have inherited in that culture (*Madwoman,* 188). The feminist framework that Gilbert and Gubar provide for the novel has been discussed, extended, and contested by other feminist writers since the first publication of *Madwoman in the Attic,* providing a plural history of the critical reception of both Gilbert and Gubar's work and *Wuthering Heights.*[2] However, the purpose of this essay is not to revisit treatments of the novel in academic writing but rather to examine the relationship between the type of feminist poetics that Gilbert and Gubar help to shape and the reproduction of *Wuthering Heights* in popular culture, in the form of the novel's film adaptations. In these adaptations, we can locate the engagement with feminism beyond the pages of academic criticism. The films I examine form a type of ongoing cultural criticism of Gilbert and Gubar's feminist poetics.

It is important to point out however, that I am not working under the notion of direct or literal translation of Gilbert and Gubar's analysis of *Wuthering Heights,* but rather under the notion of cultural inheritance and a shared tradition. *Madwoman in the Attic* helped to shape both the feminist analysis of the novel and feminism as a critical discourse, and the films draw from a cultural history of evolving gender politics and feminism. I have found Gilbert and Gubar's analysis of *Wuthering Heights* to be relevant to many of the novel's film adaptations and believe that such relevance is due to the overall influence that Gilbert and Gubar have within feminism as a primary cultural discourse in Western culture. It is perhaps useful to approach Gilbert and Gubar's *Madwoman in the Attic* as not simply a specific set of analyses but also as a set of ideas and ideologies that participated in and helped to construct the feminist discourse with which the films engage.

At the heart of Gilbert and Gubar's analysis of *Wuthering Heights* lies the central supposition that the novel is a "myth of origins" (*Madwoman,* 292). Using the binaries of heaven and hell, innocence and experience, that are evident in both *Wuthering Heights* and *Paradise Lost,* Gilbert and Gubar argue that Brontë provides "a parodic, anti-Miltonic myth," in which "Heaven (or its rejection), hell, Satan, a fall, mystical politics, metaphysical romance, orphanhood, and the question of origins . . . cohere in a rebelliously topsy-turvy retelling of Milton's and Western culture's central tale of the fall of woman and her shadow self, Satan. This fall, says Brontë, is not a fall *into* hell. It is a fall *from* 'hell' into 'heaven,' not a fall from grace (in the religious sense) but a fall into grace (in the cultural sense)" (*Madwoman,* 303, 255). The notion that Brontë is rebelliously "looking oppositely" at her culture's norms and that the novel she has produced is tied to a narrative of myth is certainly not unique. Since its initial publication, *Wuthering Heights* has been the subject of much mythmaking, with various arguments that position the novel within a critical frame of mythical and rebellious storytelling.[3] What is new about Gilbert and Gubar's conceptual framework—indeed, in many subsequent feminist rereadings of *Wuthering Heights*—is linking the novel's supposed "mythical" status with overt feminist politics. In doing so, Gilbert and Gubar have contextualized *Wuthering Heights* in a specific social and cultural environment, helping to remove its problematic definition as a "transcendent" text while retaining the mythic aura that surrounds the novel in both critical writing and the popular imagination.

Many of the film adaptations of *Wuthering Heights* have inherited this logic of cultural interrogation and cultural myth, and display this inheritance with varying degrees of self-consciousness. Since the first publication of *Madwoman in the Attic* and the first feminist rereadings of *Wuthering Heights,* the legacy of presenting the novel as one of modern Western culture's most enduring myths has been inescapably bound up with issues of gender. Gilbert and Gubar's analysis of *Wuthering Heights* has helped to shape the reading of the novel through issues of gender and feminism. This positioning has also shaped the way it has been adapted on screen. In 1985, the French film director Jacques Rivette made an adaptation of the novel that seems to respond to feminist rereadings of the character of Catherine. In 1992, Peter Kosminsky's British production of *Wuthering Heights* presented a reaction to feminist discourse in the service of a masculinist poetics. And in 2003, MTV provided a version of *Wuthering Heights* that ironically reiterates the gender ideologies Gilbert and Gubar expose and dismantle, constructing a counter "myth of origins." These three films take us through three separate decades since the first publication of *Madwoman in the Attic:* an exploration of them is also an exploration of the continuing relevance of both the novel they adapt and Gilbert and Gubar's critical paradigm.

While the specific focus of this essay is on three particular films, the scope of *Wuthering Heights* adaptations is extensive. The novel has been a source of adaptation in a host of different media since the nineteenth century. Perhaps the most comprehensive work on the full scope of *Wuthering Heights* adaptations is Patsy Stoneman's *Brontë Transformations.*[4] Adaptations made in the 1970s and onwards show an awareness of the issue of gender, a trend that is arguably most evident in screen adaptations and one partly due to the influence of feminist discourse and rereadings of "canonical" English literature. The three films I have chosen for analysis here represent the diversity of responses to evolving gender politics and the discourse of feminism in distinct time periods and social contexts. As such, they are treated as cultural productions stemming from specific social, cultural, and ideological contexts rather than as exemplars of theoretical models of adaptation and film theory. This does not mean, however, that the films are not analyzed *as* films. In her exploration of *Wuthering Heights* film adaptations, Lin Haire-Sargeant notes that "Brontë's means to greatness were linguistic; the filmmaker's must be visual."[5] Just as Haire-Sargeant analyzes the visual representation of the novel on screen to explore the cultural evolution of the character of Heathcliff, I would like to analyze specific films to trace the cultural evolution of the novel through a feminist poetics—and feminist inheritance.

Jacques Rivette's French film adaptation of *Wuthering Heights, Hurlevent,* is perhaps one of the most subtle interpretations of the novel on screen.[6] As a multilayered film, gender is only one of many issues that are explored, but it is a significant one. Rivette's understated mode of storytelling requires a more probing manner of analysis. Ostensibly, his adaptation of *Wuthering Heights* could be read benignly due to the stark simplicity of his aesthetics.

His body of work as a whole, however, and his explicitly political comments about the role of cinema reveal a director who is sensitive to cultural modes of thought. For example, in some of his most political comments about cinema, Rivette says, "I truly believe that cinema's role is to disturb the audience, to contradict all ready-made ideas but even more those established patterns of thought that underlie those ideas. We have to stop the cinema being reassuring. . . . I believe more and more that the role of the cinema is to destroy myths."[7] This approach can be seen in his engagement with gender roles and the position of women in culture and society. Emmanuelle Béart, an actress with whom Rivette has worked in many of his films, has spoken of his particular sensitivity in representing women: "Sometimes I feel so fed up being the incarnation of someone else's fantasies! That's why I love Jacques—there's none of that sort of thing on in his films."[8] Instead, Rivette presents complex women, whose stories evolve from a decided context.

Rivette has always had a concern with the role of women in their immediate and wider cultural contexts, whether exploring a complex female friendship in *Céline et Julie vont en bateau* or critically representing the role of the female model and muse in *La Belle Noiseuse.* His French New Wave origins did not result in the misogyny apparent in the work of some of his New Wave counterparts. Rather, his style is a more sensitive probing of women's lives. What is also important about Rivette is that he has an interest in literary criticism and is perhaps the most "literary" of the original New Wave directors. In his understanding of both theoretical debates and the manipulations of film technique, Rivette creates multilayered films that require an audience to partake in the unraveling of metaphors and film surfaces. Rivette started his career as a critic, and his own films require an audience who will read the images before them in a critical spirit.[9]

Hurlevent moves the action of *Wuthering Heights* from an eighteenth- and nineteenth-century Yorkshire village to the rural French countryside of the Cévennes in the 1930s. The change in setting is particularly significant with regard to a previous adaptation of *Wuthering Heights,* made in 1939.[10] Directed by William Wyler and produced by Samuel Goldwyn in Hollywood's "Golden Era," the 1939 film is perhaps the best-known adaptation of the novel, one to which subsequent directors repeatedly return. Indeed, Rivette has admitted a dislike for the 1939 film and its "melodramatic" aesthetics. He noted that when making his own film, "I had a very strong memory of the Wyler movie—because I hate it . . . [it] makes no sense whatsoever with all those ball scenes sprinkled everywhere. In fact, they transformed it into an 'Emily Brontë and Jane Austen' production. Actually, *Wuthering Heights* is Wyler's movie, after a novel by Jane Austen!"[11] In many ways, *Hurlevent* could be read as a revision of the 1939 film through a feminist framework.

What becomes clear as the film progresses is that Rivette's own adaptation provides us with not only an altogether different aesthetic representation but also a different Catherine. In the various ball scenes Rivette refers to in Wyler's film, Catherine becomes a confectionary doll, dressed up in fancy gowns that explicitly highlight her role as feminine fetish. This misrepresentation is compounded by turning her character into a teasing vixen: rather than desiring to escape the enclosures of patriarchal households, she actively seeks them, along with the wealth and position they provide. The poetics of transcendence and identity so evocatively worked out in the novel through Catherine's complex relationship with Heathcliff are overturned in the 1939 film by a narrative of feminine containment.

In contrast, Rivette's Catherine is a subdued character. The intimacy with which Rivette presents her is unusual, for it signifies both her own sense of suffocation and frustration and Rivette's desire to understand her psychology in the specific context of her world. Rivette frames and follows her body with fascination throughout the film but not in a fetishistic way—she is neither a feminine spectacle nor the projection of "someone else's fantasies." Perhaps as a testimony to this lack of feminine stereotyping, Rivette avoids close-ups of her body and has simplified everything around her and on her: hair, clothes, manner of speech, environments. The aesthetics of stark simplicity represent a focus on the wider "frames" of society and culture rather than entrapping her in the limited frame of beautiful images. She is, in a way, simultaneously trapped within *and* transcendent of her immediate environment. Rivette's Catherine is a thorough engagement with Emily Brontë's own trapped and transcendence-seeking Catherine; his exploration of entrapment and transcendence with regard to female identity takes the issues Brontë raised in the nineteenth century into the twentieth century, as part of an ongoing discourse of gender politics. Similarly, his film is also a decided engagement with and extension of the kind of feminist analysis of the novel Gilbert and Gubar have helped to shape and the poetics of cultural myth. While his representation of Catherine is aligned with Gilbert and Gubar's argument that "given the patriarchal nature of culture, women must fall—that is, they are already fallen because doomed to fall" (*Madwoman*, 277), his interrogation of the mythology built around Catherine and Heathcliff as lovers implicitly questions the critical framework of positioning *Wuthering Heights* as a "myth."

For a film that partakes in "demythologizing" *Wuthering Heights, Hurlevent* tellingly begins with the much-mythologized realm of dreams. The film starts with Guillaume's (Hindley's) dream. In the first few images, we view Guillaume spying through large rocks at Catherine and Roch (Heathcliff) lying on top of a rocky hilltop. The scene before us recalls what Stoneman has succinctly termed the "hilltop lovers" motif in the 1939 film, with Catherine and Roch lying on top of large grey and white stones in a similarly sublime-looking natural environment that hints at transcendence.[12] Perhaps the most consciously constructed imagery in the 1939 film is the image of Catherine and Heathcliff sitting together side by side in a position of platonic love upon a hilltop representing the English moors, framed by the sky with all its connotations of eternity, and with gazes transfixed upwards in a transcendent unity. In contrast to scenes in other spaces where the camera is continually roving, moving, and searching as an active participant in the action of the film, shots of the landscape and of Catherine and Heathcliff on the "moor" are still for prolonged periods of time, as if Catherine and Heathcliff are posing for a photograph. The camerawork in these scenes evidences a distinct awareness of the power of the stylized image, frozen in time. Catherine and Heathcliff are almost aware that they are being watched, enacting a drama for an audience. The space of the landscape and the moors thus becomes implicated with a discourse of sublime spectacle. And this is not a spectacle that is constructed for its own sake; it is a spectacle that throughout the film is associated with the issues of canonical storytelling and a discourse of masculine transcendence. As the film presents Catherine as a betraying and materialistic woman, it simultaneously aligns Heathcliff's masculine and existential drama with the sublime poetics of the moors.

Rivette's echo of the trope of the hilltop lovers is not an homage to the 1939 film, but rather a "misuse" of the imagery and its transcendent politics. In Rivette's film, there is no staged posing and flourish of romantic music but rather the movement of writhing bodies locked in an embrace and a natural silence that ensures the audience can hear all the sighs emanating from their bodies. Rivette also frames the scene within a narrative of voyeuristic spying that is uncomfortably intimate and sexual. Catherine lies beneath Roch in an embrace that signals sexual awakening and bodily desire. Her position hints at the physical power that Roch has over her in the sexual act, and the overarching frame of her brother spying on their passionate encounter renders the scene menacing; the female body is both literally and metaphorically "beneath" male power and under the control of masculine surveillance. Adding to this menacing overtone, Guillaume picks up a large rock to throw at them. However, another man, whom we later learn is Catherine and Guillaume's father, stops him from throwing the rock by looming over him as a guilty conscience. The three men metaphorically surround Catherine when she is in a position of vulnerability and exposed sexuality. With the image of Catherine lying beneath Roch and closely watched by her brother and father, Rivette introduces the themes of female containment, surveillance, and suffocating intimacy that are explored throughout the film. Just as importantly, he introduces these themes within the context of a dream, ironically highlighting how such aspects of feminine experience are based on a false version of "reality" and determined by the logic of a particular context rather than "truth."

Catherine's body will be the subject of containment and surveillance throughout the film, as she experiences her domestic environments as intimate prisons. Catherine's body is not her own in this male fantasy that presents it as an object of contestation between men, each of them wishing to leave their imprint on it as a symbol of their own desires, their own sense of who she should be and to whom she "belongs." Guillaume's dream enacts dramas of control between father, son, and brother, with the female body acting as the object upon which such networks of power are played out and exposed. In this opening sequence, Rivette sets the scene for his questioning of "those established patterns of thought," those ideologies of gender that encompass the female body in Brontë's text and in his own culture. The sense of discomfort and unease in the dream sequence works to negate the "reassuring" discourse of the hilltop lovers and instead focuses attention on the politics of power inherent in Catherine's relationship not only with Roch/Heathcliff but with all the men in her life.

Rivette's revision of the politics of the hilltop lovers motif is explored during another sequence in the film where Catherine defies her brother's punishment of confinement in her room. As she escapes her room and runs with Roch across a hilly landscape, the camera pans out and startling music blares in unison with their running bodies. The sudden change in the camerawork and the sudden introduction of music that breaks the harsh silence of the film signal a change of tone from menacing intimacy to exuberant freedom. Valérie Hazette argues that the "only concession to lyricism" in the film "can be found in the magical accents of *Le mystèrie des voix bulgares*, a Bulgarian choir's album that Rivette discovered thanks to Willy Lubtchansky in the early 1980s. Their voices echo at some key, epiphanic moments—when, for instance, Roch and Catherine, in a state of utter happiness, dash across the *Garrigue*."[13] It is the film's only concession to a type of lyricism, but whether or not it comes at a moment of "utter happiness" is contestable. Like the music itself, the scene is more complex.

In its loud, drawn-out notes and amalgamation of a variety of human voices, the music is at once joyous, rebellious, and melancholy. The voices of the women in the choir are tinged with a wailing gypsy sadness that speaks of a community of female voices singing in sympathy and empathy with Catherine's bid for freedom. As if colluding with the music, the camera pans out and gives Catherine and Roch space within the confines of its gaze, moving away from their bodies and from the confining intimacy within which Catherine was locked only moments ago. As it pans out, we view Catherine and Roch dwarfed by a wild landscape. Rivette is here using the romanticism of the imagery of the hilltop lovers that has become such a familiar trope of any adaptation of *Wuthering Heights*. However, his romanticism exists within a certain frame of meaning that curtails its transcendent overtones in the service of exposing how the politics of transcendence stems from an overarching discourse of female limitation and frustration. The scene reads as Catherine's desire for transcendence and freedom rather than a lovers' narrative of unified subjectivity. This becomes even more apparent when Catherine and Roch eventually run in opposite directions and the camera remains on Catherine rather than Roch, who momentarily disappears from our view.

Rivette's romanticism must also be read in the context of the proceeding scene where, after a short period of play on the landscape, Catherine and Roch enter the space of the woods. The landscape of the woods is presented as a menacing and threatening place as we enter a fairy tale space laden with the familiar fairy tale tropes of female victimization and blood. I believe that part of the logic behind Rivette's sudden romanticism in the midst of the stark simplicity of much of the film is to self-consciously highlight the mythic status of the hilltop lovers motif and thereby insert Catherine into a logic of inherited and repeated cultural discourses of subjectivity and gender. The mythic status of the familiar imagery is similar to the spaces and recurrent tropes found in many traditional fairy tales.

As Catherine runs ahead of Roch in the woods and comes to spy on the Landon (Linton) children playing tennis, she is caught by the claws of a trap meant to capture wild animals. Once she enters a mythic, fairy tale space, Catherine becomes a stereotypical fairy tale girl, forcibly held by patriarchal culture. Rivette mirrors the manner in which Catherine is caught in the novel—instead of being seized by the Lintons' dog, Skulker, her foot bleeds from the trap—and how this signifies a type of "fall" from childhood to adulthood. Gilbert and Gubar argue that in the novel,

> Catherine's fall . . . is caused by a patriarchal past and present, besides being associated with a patriarchal future. It is significant, then, that her problems begin—violently enough—when she literally falls down and is bitten by a male bulldog, a sort of guard/god from Thrushcross Grange. Though many readers overlook this point, Catherine does not *go* to the Grange when she is twelve years old. On the contrary, the Grange seizes her and "holds [her] fast," a metaphoric action which emphasizes the turbulent and inexorable nature of the psychosexual *rites de passage Wuthering Heights* describes . . . (*Madwoman,* 271)

Rivette's conversion of the space of entrapment from the landscape of the moors to the forest signifies both an awareness of the type of argument Gilbert and Gubar explore in their analysis of Catherine's "fall" into womanhood in the novel, and an extension of such an argument by the mingling of Catherine's experience with fairy tale tropes and fairy tale spaces. Wendy Swyt has written that the space of the woods or the forest in traditional fairy tales is a psychosexual site that is often menacing and threatening to the fairy tale girl, who must lose her innocence and her subjectivity.[14] One such example is Little Red Riding Hood, who becomes the object of patriarchy upon her walking the forest path. Indeed, in *The Trials and Tribulations of Little Red Riding Hood,* Jack Zipes explores the significant gender politics evident in the fairy tale.[15] Destined to become either a victim to be consumed where her body is her own enemy or the object of patriarchy to be saved by the huntsman, only to be returned to the culture that entrapped her in the first place, Little Red Riding Hood's entrance into the space of the forest is a fall into patriarchal femininity.

Similarly, the symbolic nature of being "caught" and bleeding is a typical motif of fairy tales where girls fall by the pricking of fingers and other such accidents. As Gilbert and Gubar rightly point out with regard to Catherine, "Such bleeding has sexual connotations, especially when it occurs in a pubescent girl" (*Madwoman,* 272). The fact that Rivette chose such a young actress to play Catherine highlights her vulnerability and fall into womanhood. The message is clear: under the "established patterns of thought" of her culture, Catherine is doomed to enter a mythical space of femininity that sees her body as a prison of objectivity and her role in culture in relation to the desires of the men in her life. The fact that he mingles Catherine's fairy tale "fall" with the culturally mythic space of the hilltop lovers indicates a subtle yet telling criticism of the manner in which the romantic discourse that has been built around *Wuthering Heights* has often been used against a politics of female transcendence and in the service of patriarchy.

Rivette explores, perhaps more than any other director of *Wuthering Heights,* the hell that is patriarchal culture. His revisionary Catherine closely follows Gilbert and Gubar's own analysis of Catherine as a woman who "falls" into culture and where the "heaven" of this culture is really a prison-like hell. Similarly, he self-consciously highlights how the story of *Wuthering Heights* has become a mythic tale, comparable to traditional fairy tales. However, Rivette also asks questions of his own, for he "looks oppositely" at a previous and iconic adaptation of the novel that delights in the heaven of culture. By turning a critical eye upon the 1939 film's representation of Catherine and use of the poetics of transcendence in the form of the hilltop lovers motif, Rivette also implicitly interrogates Gilbert and Gubar's own legacy of interpreting the novel in mythologizing terms. It is as if Rivette is saying that the problem with defining *Wuthering Heights* as a myth of any kind—whether a Hollywood myth or a feminist myth—is the romanticization that often comes with such a definition and that works to obscure, rather than highlight, the novel's politics of gender. Instead, in his harsh and simple aesthetics, Rivette dispels the mists of myth that surround the novel in both critical discourse and popular culture by revealing that a prison is a prison and hell is hell. Rivette's ironic revelation of the dangers of the myth is consistent with Gilbert and Gubar's feminist poetics.

If Rivette is skeptical of the myth of transcendence in *Wuthering Heights,* Peter Kosminsky's 1992 adaptation of the novel fully revels in it. Kosminsky's film, *Emily Brontë's Wuthering Heights,* is a British production that casts Ralph Fiennes as Heathcliff and Juliette Binoche as Catherine and is one of the few adaptations of the novel that tackles the novel's second generation.[16] Nevertheless, it is Catherine and Heathcliff who dominate the film, representing a metaphysical and transcendent lovers' discourse that ultimately facilitates a masculinist poetics. While Catherine is given a relatively strong persona, there is a decided focus on Heathcliff, which displays a rereading of feminist discourse and a reaction to the politics of feminism.

In many ways, Kosminsky's representation of Catherine and Heathcliff is reminiscent of Gilbert and Gubar's analysis of Catherine's "heaven" as a "delightful," "energetic," and natural realm that stands in antithesis to the order of patriarchal culture (*Madwoman,* 255). In the numerous scenes of Catherine and Heathcliff frolicking on the moors and playing together at Wuthering Heights, Kosminsky constructs a visual representation of rebellious and energetic lovers who break the religious, ideological, and cultural boundaries surrounding them. Binoche enacts Catherine in an overtly physical manner that recalls Brontë's own Catherine as "always going—singing, laughing, and plaguing everybody who would not do the same."[17] Binoche's literalization of Catherine's behavior in the book speaks volumes on the screen as her skin is flushed from exercise and her mouth always ready with giggles and songs. She is a visual representation of the rebellious female energy associated with feminist poetics and a physical manifestation of Gilbert and Gubar's interpretation of Catherine as "never docile, never submissive, never ladylike" but rather a "raw, uncultivated being" who is full of "creative energy" (*Madwoman,* 265, 266). In contrast, Heathcliff, while equally rebellious in behavior, is represented in a subdued manner as the typical brooding male. His brooding masculinity highlights the vivid energy and restless physicality of Catherine, who seems like a wild spirit, happiest in her natural environment.

This is a rare representation of Catherine, as her wild and restless energy in the novel has typically been interpreted in a more "tamed" manner. For example, the 1939 film's Catherine is like an ice queen in her still and silent beauty, highlighting her role as an object to be looked upon. Ironically, Rivette's desire to steer away from this feminine spectacle also results in a subdued Catherine, although the effort is ostensibly to suggest her interiority. Kosminsky's Catherine is an energetic creature who displays this energy either overtly as a young woman or as a seething mass of emotions lying beneath the surface when she is superficially subdued by her role as the lady of Thrushcross Grange. Like Gilbert and Gubar, Kosminsky interprets Catherine's change in behavior upon entering the space of the Grange as a reverse "fall" from hell into heaven. We view a change from childish energy, happy laughter, and singing to a consciously repressed hysteria. In his representation of Catherine and in his scenes of Catherine and Heathcliff acting out their youthful and chaotic energy through their various games, Kosminsky provides us with a thorough representation of Gilbert and Gubar's notion of Catherine's "heaven."

However, while the 1992 film displays a similar reading of Catherine to Gilbert and Gubar, the film's gender politics is deeply ambivalent. On the one hand, it seems to champion rebellious female energy, yet on the other, this female energy is often overshadowed by the discourses it helps to create. Kosminsky's emphasis on Catherine's wild physicality is constructed in the service of an overarching discourse of the hilltop lovers, representing a transcendent and "natural" model of love and desire that is pitted against the artificial world of culture and its constraints. Furthermore, this discourse of the hilltop lovers is ultimately aligned with Heathcliff's desires and identity as he enacts an existential drama tied to issues of masculinity. The film provides a rereading of the notion of Catherine's hellish heaven through a focus on masculinity rather than femininity.

For example, one of the most striking and visually memorable scenes in the film occurs when Catherine and Heathcliff wander a particularly spectacular landscape specifically chosen for its visual potency—Kosminsky shot the landscape scenes of the film on location in the moorlands of North Grassington in Yorkshire.[18] Catherine and Heathcliff walk upon huge white stones that are interspersed with Gothic-looking trees. Their dark clothing and hair stand out against this backdrop, and the enormity of the stones coupled with the overwhelming whiteness create an atmosphere of poetic sublimity and transcendence. The camerawork and positioning of Catherine and Heathcliff is also telling: at one point, the camera focuses on them standing in a strikingly similar position to Catherine and Heathcliff in the 1939 film. In a direct visual homage to Wyler's film, Catherine and Heathcliff are positioned side by side, with heads inclined in the same direction and with gazes transfixed upward as they are framed by the landscape and sky. While this mirroring of the 1939 film's aesthetics works to construct an image of the transcendent hilltop lovers, it is also distinctly linked to Heathcliff, for it comes at a moment when he seems to prophesy Catherine's future:

> CATHY: Who sent you?
> HEATHCLIFF: Nobody.
> CATHY: Was it a bird, or a tree, or the wind?
> HEATHCLIFF: I don't know.
> CATHY: Do you know anything?
> HEATHCLIFF: Can you talk to trees? Touch the wind? Let's send your spirit into that tree and make it talk to us.
> [An eerie music begins to emanate from the tree they both gaze at, as Heathcliff seems to bid it to move and "speak." The crows in the tree flee in fright.]
> HEATHCLIFF: Listen, they're calling your name.
> CATHY: How did you do that?
> HEATHCLIFF: I can do lots of things.
> CATHY: What things?
> HEATHCLIFF: Stand up. Now close your eyes. If, when you open your eyes, the day is sunny and bright, so shall your future be. But if the day is full of storms, so shall your life. Now, open your eyes.

As Catherine opens her eyes, the camera focuses on their unified gazes, with their bodies pressed together, and lingers on this image as if to jolt a knowing audience with the memory of Wyler's film. However, as Heathcliff begins to look in the opposite direction, trouble looms, for the sky is no longer clear but stormy and their gazes are no longer unified but discordant. Catherine, aware that his gaze has been diverted, shifts to look in that direction, too, only to gaze fearfully at the stormy sky and utter, "What have you done?" As Stoneman rightly points out, this added scene, "which has no precedent in Emily Brontë's text, undermines the famed oneness of the lovers by making it appear that Heathcliff has 'written' Catherine's life."[19] I would argue that it also undermines the potency of Catherine's rebellious female energy and instead constructs such an energy as in the service of more dominant discourses of being: her alignment with nature facilitates Heathcliff's more dominant characterization throughout the film. If Catherine is the daughter of nature and a hellish heaven, Heathcliff is its "master." As Catherine later betrays the ethos of rebellious nature by being girlishly wooed by Edgar and entering his world of culture and finery, Heathcliff remains the one constant in the film as a tall, dark, and commanding figure of nature who is both physically and metaphorically akin to the dark trees that sparsely populate the landscape he once inhabited with Catherine. The film depicts Heathcliff as writing Catherine's life through his control of nature and through its focus on him as the one constant character throughout the narrative. Kosminsky's film is primarily Heathcliff's story.

The focus on Heathcliff is telling in light of the context of the 1990s. Claire Monk writes,

> To an almost unprecedented extent, 1990s British cinema seemed preoccupied with men and masculinity in crisis. . . . This post-feminist male panic, and the resultant mix of masculinist reaction and masculine self-scrutiny, have been the defining influences shaping the dominant images of men produced in the British cinema's intensified attention to men and should not be read as denoting a progressive, liberalising or egalitarianising shift in the gender and sexual politics of British cinema or society. What was new about this preoccupation with men was its self-consciousness, its confessional and therapeutic impulses (its admission of male neediness and pain) and its attentiveness to men and masculinity as subjects-in-themselves. However, the emergence of this impulse within the mainstream of British cinema at the moment when the fallout of post-industrialism and Thatcherism collided with the gains of feminism, produced a strand of male-focused films whose gender politics were more masculinist than feminist.[20]

Kosminsky's Heathcliff is both a product and symptom of his times. The film's focus on Heathcliff signals another avenue through which masculinity is explored in this period. In fact, the film's Heathcliff seems to negotiate (if not deny) Gilbert and Gubar's feminist legacy.

Gilbert and Gubar's analysis of the novel links the dichotomy between nature and culture along gender lines where nature is a decidedly female presence that informs Brontë's "anti-Miltonic myth": women are "Fal'n by mistaken rules" of culture (*Madwoman*, 251). In turn, the 1992 film also "looks oppositely" at the feminist legacy it has inherited. The realignment of nature as a masculine rather than feminine space reveals an uncertainty about men's position in a postfeminist world, where patriarchal culture has been a continual object of attack and interrogation. However, this appropriation of the feminist legacy once again pushes the female subject to the margins and appropriates her hellish heaven as a distinctly masculine space. If men have fallen from their lofty seat of assumed subjectivity into the politics of gender, then one form of recuperation of this subjectivity is via the appropriation of the discourses that led to this fall. The film is also a myth of origins: it is a myth of the "new" modern man who has to rewrite the script of power and negotiate his position in a postfeminist world where the laws of culture are continually interrogated. Nature is perhaps a fitting refuge, as it is for Catherine in the novel.

There are other layers of meaning at work here, as this focus on Heathcliff places him within a distinctly Romantic framework. The sense of "oneness" between self and the natural landscape speaks of a Romantic discourse of being that locates a transcendent identity in the eternity of nature and, perhaps more importantly, in a specifically English landscape. What is striking about the film's construction of Heathcliff as mystically at one with nature is how it appropriates a feminist poetics in a manner similar to the way that the Romantic authors of the eighteenth and nineteenth century appropriated feminine sensibilities in the service of masculine subjectivity. As Anne K. Mellor has argued,

> By taking on the feminine virtues of compassion, mercy, gentleness and sympathy, the male Romantic poets could speak with ultimate moral as well as intellectual authority. Endowed with feminine empathy or what Keats called "negative capability" and Percy Shelley the "instinct and intuition of the poetical faculty," the male poet becomes in Shelley's *Defense of Poetry* a mother while the work of art becomes "a child in the mother's womb." Having given birth to poetry . . . the male poet becomes the hero of the modern age. . . . Such poets "are the unacknowledged legislators of world." By usurping the mother's womb, life-giving power, and feminine sensibilities, the male poet could claim to be God, the sole ruler of the world.[21]

Similarly, it is possible to read the fascination with Heathcliff as a master of nature as a reaction to a postfeminist and postindustrialist world. Kosminsky constructs Heathcliff as an archetypal Romantic hero akin to the poets whom Shelley labeled "the unacknowledged legislators of the world." Not only has he usurped nature, but, in taking control of it and Catherine's life, Kosminsky's Heathcliff has usurped the female womb by being the sole origin of creativity and life. Gilbert and Gubar's analysis of *Wuthering Heights* provides an important framework of interpretation that seeks to recuperate female stories from the margins and bring them into the center. The 1992 film adaptation of the novel pushes these female narratives and the female author back to the margins by revealing that at the heart of the narrative lies a masculine author who has control over both nature itself and its "daughter." Heaven becomes another form of Miltonic hell.

The Heathcliff that the film presents reveals a complex engagement with the inheritance of feminist discourse. The film is not simply an adaptation of the novel but also an adaptation of the theoretical models through which it has been interpreted. Gilbert and Gubar's interpretation of a hellish heaven and a myth of origins endures in complex and varied ways. While Rivette examines hellish culture only to reveal the danger of the myth, Kosminsky expands this myth by reworking hellish heaven as an inherently masculine space in which masculine power reasserts itself. In doing so, Kosminsky metaphorically rewrites Gilbert and Gubar's myth of origins and changes the ending of Heathcliff's "battle" (*Madwoman,* 292-98). If in the novel Heathcliff "fails because in stories of the war between nature and culture nature always fails" (*Madwoman,* 298), then in Kosminsky's film he "wins" through his alignment with a nature that is employed in the service of patriarchy rather than against it.

MTV's *Wuthering Heights* updates the novel by setting it in modern-day California: Wuthering Heights is transformed into a secluded lighthouse called "The Heights" located in an isolated seaside landscape.[22] Directed by Suri Krishnamma and made in 2003, the film uses young actors, clearly cast to market the film to MTV's target audience. Despite the modernization of the story as a teen drama (Heathcliff becomes Heath, a young rock star) and despite the change of setting and landscape, the film still constructs ideological discourses similar to those found in other screen adaptations of the novel. In particular, the seaside landscape is represented in a manner similar to "the moors" in other adaptations.

A discourse of the hilltop lovers is also constructed in this film, with numerous scenes of Cate (Catherine) and Heath wandering a seaside landscape with towering cliffs that are meant to convey the transcendent nature of their love. These scenes evidence a cultural touchstone of familiarity in which the imagery of lovers wandering any sort of sublime landscape is inescapably tied to the screen adaptation of *Wuthering Heights* as an image that summarizes the novel's "meaning." The film has clearly inherited the Romantic scenery from previous adaptations of *Wuthering Heights.* Similarly, it has inherited the gender politics. However, like its previous adaptations, the 2003 film is also a product of its times. What is actually achieved in this film, whether consciously or unconsciously, is a reversal of Gilbert and Gubar's feminist poetics and rewriting of their framework of an oppositional bible and anti-Miltonic myth in the context of a postfeminist society and culture. If Gilbert and Gubar argue that Brontë looks oppositely at her culture's inheritance of gender, the 2003 film looks oppositely at its own society's legacy of feminist politics and reconstitutes Victorian domesticity and motherhood through a rewriting of the hilltop lovers motif and the character of Catherine.

In their analysis of *Wuthering Heights,* Gilbert and Gubar argue that if "Heathcliff is Catherine's almost identical double, Catherine II is really her mother's 'non-identical double'" (*Madwoman,* 298). "Where, for instance, Catherine Earnshaw rebelled against her father, Catherine II is profoundly dutiful. . . . Catherine II is a cook, nurse, teacher and housekeeper. In other words, where her mother was a heedless wild child, Catherine II promises to become an ideal Victorian woman, all of whose virtues are in some sense associated with daughterhood, wifehood, motherhood" (*Madwoman,* 299). In their conception of Brontë's "myth,"

> There was an Original Mother (Catherine), a daughter of nature whose motto might be "Thou, Nature, art my goddess; to thy law / My services are bound." But this girl fell into a decline, at least in part through eating the poisonous cooked food of culture. She fragmented herself into mad or dead selves on the one hand (Catherine, Heathcliff) and into lesser, gentler/genteeler selves on the other (Catherine II, Hareton). The fierce primordial selves disappeared into nature, the perversely hellish heaven which was their home. The more teachable and docile selves learned to read and write, and moved into the fallen cultured world of parlors and parsonages, the Miltonic heaven which, from the Original Mother's point of view, is really hell. (*Madwoman,* 303)

The 2003 film provides a directly oppositional myth to the one that Gilbert and Gubar set out in their analysis, with the "Original Mother" becoming her nonidentical double. While Cate/Catherine is at the heart of the myth in the film, as she is in Gilbert and Gubar's conceptual framework, all the characters are depicted, in some form or another, as rotating around the central myth of motherhood and domesticity or, perhaps more correctly, the lack of both.

All the young characters in the film experience the lack of a clearly defined domestic space and instead are depicted as seeking it in various other places through drugs, music, sex, and relationships. The film stands as an indictment of contemporary families, in which the patriarchal order has been broken by irresponsible mothers. One of the themes interrogated throughout the film is the issue of Cate's mother leaving her family and thus destroying the unity of the home. Cate and her brother, along with "orphan" Heath, are emblematic children of the modern age, who have no home due to the selfish desires and irresponsible freedoms of neglectful mothers. It is significant that the space of Wuthering Heights is transformed into a towering (and overtly phallic) lighthouse that stands against a barren landscape. Perhaps as a symbol of lost femininity and motherhood, one of the rooms in the Heights bears the remnants of Cate's mother, where she painted a portrait of a woman, perhaps herself, on the ceiling of the room. When Heath is rescued by Cate's father and brought to the Heights, one of the first things Cate reveals to him is the portrait, telling him that her mother painted it. Her father responds, "She did, just before she left."

The figure of this woman seems to haunt the house. Cate's father dies while staring at the painting, Cate cries to the painting after his funeral, and the painting is the focus after she and Heath consummate their relationship, linking their close relationship to a desire for family and their own lost mothers. The moralistic undertone in the film is that if Cate's mother had not left, these orphaned children would not consume themselves, and everyone around them, in destructive relationships. The freedoms of individual self-expression and reconceptualization of the patriarchal family that have been fought for, and, to some extent, won, by feminist discourse are here considered selfish disregard for the necessary cohesion of traditional family life and traditional feminine roles. Cate's mother, the flighty artist, is the "daughter" of Gilbert and Gubar's feminist poetics. The implicit argument throughout the film is that feminist politics have created a "fallen" world of irresponsible femininity, due to the freedoms that have accompanied the interrogation of traditional female roles. The anti-Miltonic myth has become a reality—and a hellish one at that.

However, the film's own myth seems to redeem contemporary femininity through its rewriting of feminist poetics and its turning of Cate/Catherine into her nonidentical double. While much of the film seems to indict modern femininity, the last few scenes and the ending recast woman in her forgotten Victorian role of motherhood. The culmination of the film's action begins in the rocky cave by the seashore in which Cate and Heath used to play as children, an allusion to Catherine's fairy cave in the novel:

> I see in you Nelly . . . an aged woman—you have grey hair, and bent shoulders. This bed is the fairy cave under Penistone Crag, and you are gathering elf-bolts to hurt our heifers; pretending, while I am near, that they are only locks of wool. That's what you'll come to in fifty years hence; I know you are not so now. I'm not wandering, you're mistaken, or else I should believe you really *were* that withered hag, and I should think I *was* under Penistone Crag, and I'm conscious it's night, and there are two candles on the table making the press shine like jet.[23]

Catherine utters these words in her marital bed at Thrushcross Grange, pregnant and dying. Like Catherine in the novel, Cate seeks her cave at a moment when she is about to give birth and die. However, unlike Brontë's Catherine, Cate's cave is not a symptom of her desire to escape from the confines of her marriage bed and her maternal body but rather a form of domestic reconstitution. Throughout the film, the cave is a symbol of Cate and Heath's "orphan" status and their desire to construct a "family" of their own through each other and the enclosed space of the cave. As Cate lies dying and in labor in the cave, her "ghost" runs to Heath in the Heights and tells him to come find her. Heath rescues her and brings her back to the Heights to give birth to a baby girl who is most certainly Heath's child rather than her husband's. After the birth, Cate dies and the last scene of the film is her ghost standing on top of the lighthouse, watching over Heath and their daughter as they play together. Against a background of tender music, Cate's ghost speaks the following words to her daughter: "I once dreamt of getting away from the Heights, but now I know I was meant to stay. To see you grow up, my daughter. In this lighthouse, on the edge of the ocean, no matter what the future holds, I'll always be there, watching over you."

The sublime imagery of transcendence that accompanies these scenes is similar to the 1992 film, in the sense that the large cliffside rocks, the towering structure of the Heights, and the camera's closing in on and fixation with shots of the ocean and the birds in the sky construct a discourse of hilltop lovers. The camerawork in the last scene is similarly uncomplicated in the sense that the camera looks up at Cate's ghost to create the feeling that Cate is looking down upon the domestic scene before her, highlighting her transcendent position. These last scenes mingle the transcendent oneness of Cate and Heath (there are numerous shots of them wandering the landscape) with a domestic politics, highlighting the film's implicit final message: domesticity, family, and, above all, motherhood, are in fact ultimately more transcendent than sexual love and individual desire.

Cate here becomes Catherine's nonidentical double as a domesticating force that reinstates the boundaries of family and constructs a home through her overarching presence. In other words, she becomes an ideal emblem of Victorian femininity. Like Catherine II, Cate creates a domestic space where there is none and does so through the use of her own body. In casting aside her selfish desire for escape, expressed throughout the film, and realizing that her function is in fact to become a symbol of eternal motherhood, Cate "redeems" modern femininity from its "fallen" status of individuality and reconstructs it as a Victorian ideal of, in Gilbert and Gubar's apt words, "selfless" femininity, "with all the moral and psychological implications that word suggests" (*Madwoman,* 21). Cate's sacrifice of her individuality is highlighted by her ghost's crucifixion-like position on top of the lighthouse as she watches her daughter. Once-selfless femininity has been restored, the social environment of the Heights is changed from a barren, motherless space of selfish desires and violence into a happy, productive world of domestic unity. Furthermore, the film elevates this neo-Victorian femininity to the realm of sublime transcendence by linking it with a discourse of eternal nature, "on the edge of the ocean." The 2003 film's use of the hilltop lovers motif is ultimately in the service of rendering Victorian femininity a natural and transcendent discourse of being.

What the film also provides through the last image of Cate's domestic and domesticating ghost is a metaphorical rewriting of Gilbert and Gubar's own feminist analysis of the novel through an altogether different "myth of origins." Cate's ghost, guarding her daughter and the domestic ideal as a figure of eternal motherhood, is a direct antithesis to her own mother's ghost, represented by the painting in the Heights. The painting is a symbol of artistic and individual expression where female identity is not constructed in relation to other people and other things but in relation to the creative process and one's individual identity. Cate's self-sacrificing ghost casts her mother's anti-domestic ghost into the margins and initiates a contemporary "myth of origins" where neo-Victorian femininity rises from the ruins of postfeminism. Rather than the "fierce primordial selves" disappearing "into nature," the "Miltonic heaven" instead *becomes* nature; that is, becomes a transcendent "truth" while the Original Mother is cast aside as the product of destructive ideology that abandons the rightful laws of both motherhood and nature. The film rewrites hellish heaven as a new form of Miltonic heaven and thereby looks oppositely at both Brontë's original Catherine and Gilbert and Gubar's feminist legacy.

These three films provide a compelling picture of the continuing relevance of Gilbert and Gubar's *Madwoman in the Attic* in the cultural afterlife of *Wuthering Heights.* If *Wuthering Heights* continues to exert a fascination in Western culture through its various adaptations, it also continues to raise critical debates about its meaning. The competing, dissenting, and supporting voices that have been heard since the publication of *Madwoman in the Attic* can also be heard across the spectrum of popular culture through a wider engagement with gender politics. The films represent the need to listen to the voices beyond the pages of academic writing and to trace the legacy of feminist theory in various forms of media. If the afterlife of *Wuthering Heights* on film has shown anything, it is that such plural voices will continue to speak on screen and that Gilbert and Gubar's "bogey" roams the moors along with Catherine and Heathcliff.

Notes

1. Sandra M. Gilbert and Susan Gubar, *The Madwoman in the Attic: The Woman Writer and the Nineteenth-Century Literary Imagination* (New Haven: Yale University Press, 1979), 248–308. Subsequent references will be given parenthetically.

2. For feminist rereadings of Gilbert and Gubar's *Madwoman in the Attic,* including their particular analysis of *Wuthering Heights,* see William E. Cain, ed., *Making Feminist History: The Literary Scholarship of Sandra M. Gilbert and Susan Gubar* (New York: Garland, 1994); Patsy Stoneman, ed., *Emily Brontë: A Reader's Guide to Essential Criticism* (Houndmills, Basingstoke, U.K.: Macmillan, 2000), 155–83; and Toril Moi, *Sexual/Textual Politics: Feminist Literary Theory* (London: Routledge, 1988), 57–69.

3. For example, see Sidney Dobell, "The Stamp of High Genius" (1850), and W. C. Roscoe, "Dark, Intense, Powerful" (1857), in *Emily Brontë: Wuthering Heights,* ed. Miriam Allott (Houndmills, Basingstoke, U.K.: Macmillan, 1992), 57–59 and 70–73; Virginia

Woolf, "*Jane Eyre* and *Wuthering Heights*" (1925), in *The Norton Anthology of Literature by Women: The Tradition in English,* ed. Sandra M. Gilbert and Susan Gubar (New York: W. W. Norton, 1985), 1348–49; David Cecil, "Emily Brontë and *Wuthering Heights,*" in *Early Victorian Novelists: Essays in Revaluation* (London: Constable, 1934), 161–69; Stevie Davies, *Emily Brontë: The Artist as a Free Woman* (Manchester: Carcanet, 1983), 97.

4. Patsy Stoneman, *Brontë Transformations: The Cultural Dissemination of* Jane Eyre *and* Wuthering Heights (London: Prentice Hall/Harvester Wheatsheaf, 1996). For a comprehensive index of *Wuthering Heights* adaptations, see pp. 292–324.

5. Lin Haire-Sargeant, "Sympathy for the Devil: The Problem of Heathcliff in Film Versions of *Wuthering Heights,*" in *Nineteenth-Century Women at the Movies: Adapting Classic Women's Fiction to Film,* ed. Barbara Tepa Lupack (Bowling Green, Ohio: Popular Press, 1999), 168.

6. *Hurlevent,* screenplay by Pascal Bonitzer, Suzanne Schiffman, and Jacques Rivette, dir. Jacques Rivette, prod. Martine Marignac, La Cécilia, Renn Productions, Ministère de la Republique Française, 1985.

7. Rivette is quoted in Peter Harcourt, "On Jacques Rivette," *Ciné-Tracts* 1, no. 3 (1977–78): 52; Jacques Rivette, "Time Overflowing," *Cahiers du Cinema* 204 (1968): n.p. This article was part of an interview with Rivette that was conducted on July 27, 1968, by Jacques Aumont, Jean-Louis Comolli, Jean Narboni, and Sylvie Pierre and translated by Amy Gateff.

8. Emmanuelle Béart quoted in Richard Porton, "Acting as the Joy of Discovery: An Interview with Emmanuelle Béart," *Cineaste* 29, no. 1 (2003): 17.

9. For studies on Jacques Rivette and the French New Wave movement, see James Monaco, *The New Wave: Truffaut, Godard, Chabrol, Rohmer, Rivette* (New York: Oxford University Press, 1976); Richard Neupert, *A History of the French New Wave Cinema* (Madison: University of Wisconsin Press, 2002). Geneviève Sellier provides a particularly illuminating discussion on the role of women in French New Wave cinema in her article, "Gender, Modernism, and Mass Culture in the New Wave," in *Gender and French Cinema,* ed. Alex Hughes and James S. Williams (New York: Berg, 2001), 125–37. For further discussions on Jacques Rivette's background, see Monaco's and Neupert's works. Saul Austerlitz also briefly discusses Rivette's love of criticism in relation to his filmmaking in his biographical article, "Jacques Rivette," *Senses of Cinema* 24 (2003): n.p.

10. *Wuthering Heights,* screenplay by Ben Hecht and Charles MacArthur, dir. William Wyler, prod. Samuel Goldwyn, United Artists, 1939.

11. Valérie Hazette, "*Hurlevent:* Jacques Rivette's Adaptation of *Wuthering Heights,*" *Senses of Cinema* 29 (2003): n.p.; Rivette quoted in Hazette, "*Hurlevent,*" n.p.

12. Stoneman, *Brontë Transformations,* 116. It should be noted that Stoneman's discussion of the "hilltop lovers motif" throughout *Brontë Transformations* is not simply in relation to the 1939 film but also includes an analysis of numerous other adaptations in which this motif features. Wyler's 1939 film, however, is perhaps the best-known *Wuthering Heights* adaptation in any media, and therefore the imagery that it constructs has retained a particular hold in the popular imagination regarding the novel's "meaning." *Brontë Transformations,* 126–34.

13. Hazette, "*Hurlevent,*" n.p. The *Garrigue* is a scrubland in the regions of Provence and Corsica in France.

14. Wendy Swyt, "'Wolflings': Angela Carter's Becoming-Narrative," *Studies in Short Fiction* 33, no. 3 (1996): 315.

15. See Jack Zipes, ed., *The Trials and Tribulations of Little Red Riding Hood* (New York: Routledge, 1993), 1–15 and 17–90. In Zipes's studies, he also raises issues of gender and sexual politics in traditional fairy tales and the role of women in patriarchy. See Jack Zipes, *Breaking the Magic Spell: Radical Theories of Folk and Fairy Tales* (London: Heine-

mann, 1979), and *The Brothers Grimm: From Enchanted Forests to the Modern World* (New York: Routledge, 1988).

16. *Emily Brontë's Wuthering Heights,* screenplay by Anne Devlin, dir. Peter Kosminsky, prod. Mary Selway, Paramount, 1992.

17. Emily Brontë, *Wuthering Heights,* ed. Ian Jack (New York: Oxford University Press, 1998), 36.

18. Zoë Heller, "Sexy, Witty, Spooky, and Wet," review of *Wuthering Heights* directed by Peter Kosminsky, *The Independent on Sunday,* November 10, 1991.

19. Stoneman, *Brontë Transformations,* 210.

20. Claire Monk, "Men in the '90s," *British Cinema of the '90s,* ed. Robert Murphy (London: BFI, 2005), 156–57. The issues that Monk discusses here are also raised in Brian McFarlane, "The More Things Change . . . British Cinema in the '90s," *The British Cinema Book,* ed. Robert Murphy (London: BFI, 2001), 277.

21. Anne K. Mellor, *Romanticism and Gender* (London: Routledge, 1993), 23–24.

22. *Wuthering Heights,* teleplay by Max Enscoe and Annie de Young, dir. Suri B. Krishnamma, MTV, September 14, 2003.

23. Brontë, *Wuthering Heights,* 108.

9

The Veiled, the Masked, and the Civil War Woman

Louisa May Alcott and the Madwoman Allegory

Keren Fite

Though written thirty years ago, *The Madwoman in the Attic* is still a highly influential text in feminist discussions of the woman writer's authority. In her discussion of Sandra M. Gilbert and Susan Gubar's feminist poetics, Rita Felski suggests that the madwoman has become a significant allegory of female authorship, "yoking together spatial imagery, psychological diagnosis, and linguistic analysis . . . creat[ing] new ways of seeing, casting familiar works of literature in a startling yet compelling light."[1] Felski points out the construct of the feminist literary critic embedded in the madwoman allegory: the critic is portrayed as either a diligent archeologist or as an avid detective, "burrowing through the layers of language to uncover muffled traces of female identity and desire . . . decipher[ing] the covert marks of the female psyche."[2]

Feminist literary criticism of the works of Louisa May Alcott is highly influenced by Gilbert and Gubar's allegory of the madwoman. In their attempt to "uncover muffled traces of female identity," feminist critics of Alcott's literary works either focus on her gothic thrillers as courageous manifestations of female rebelliousness or stress the subterranean gothic elements in her domestic works.

An earlier version of this paper was presented at the Annual Conference of the North American Society for the Study of Romanticism: "'To Keep Bright the Devil's Door Knobs': Louisa May Alcott's Revision of the Transcendental Poet Genius Ideal," Montreal, August 16, 2005.

This essay will point out the narrow perspective the madwoman allegory imposes on Louisa May Alcott's literary corpus. The first section will discuss the prevalent metaphors feminist critics "uncover" in Alcott's works and point out the various ways these metaphors echo the madwoman allegory. This section will also explore Gilbert and Gubar's explicit construction of the woman artist according to the Romantic male model of authorship and will point out the ways this construct limits the scope of the feminist discussion of Alcott's literary corpus. The second section will present Louisa May Alcott's revision of the transcendental poet-genius ideal, an ideal that was highly influenced by the Romantic male model of authorship. Focusing on Henry David Thoreau's *Walden* in conjuncture with Louisa May Alcott's *Little Women,* the second section points out the ways in which Alcott criticizes and revises the transcendental poet-genius ideal, and suggests a broader perspective on Alcott's concept of the artist in general and the artist heroine in particular.

The Madwoman Allegory and Louisa May Alcott's Authorial Image

In "*Little Women:* Alcott's Civil War," Judith Fetterley points to the discrepancy between Alcott's domestic works and her gothic thrillers, arguing that it is "hard to reconcile the authorial image inherent in *Little Women* with the personality capable of the sensational *Behind A Mask.*"[3] Trying to reconcile the disparity between the children's friend and the creator of the lurid, Fetterley invokes the Civil War as a metaphor to illustrate an internal conflict between overt domestic values and covert gothic rebelliousness. The Civil War metaphor echoes Gilbert and Gubar's allegory of the madwoman: the socially conventional narrative that defines a girl's process of maturation and progress in terms of matrimony and motherhood is condemned as overt "little womanhood," while the alternative rebellious narrative of a tomboy growing into a creative woman writer who dares to imagine sensational stories, financial independence, and a life of happy spinsterhood is the covert, subversive narrative. Fetterley points out that "Jo's rebellion is neutralized . . . [she is taken] out of her boots and doublet and her misguided male-identification . . . into her role as a future Marmee," consequently arguing that as a writer, Alcott betrayed her own values in compromising her vision of Jo as a rebellious creative female. Fetterley seems to expect Jo to represent Alcott's personal choice not to marry and finds merit only in what she terms *Little Women*'s covert rebelliousness against a conventional, nineteenth-century domestic script: "it is to Alcott's credit that at least covertly if not overtly she recognized that the sugar plum was the poison."[4]

Also baffled by the incongruence between Alcott's domestic and gothic works, Angela M. Estes and Kathleen Margaret Lant wonder how to reconcile Alcott's avid interest in the violent and gory gothic with her proliferate, tame children stories.[5] Estes, Lant, and Fetterley need a homogeneous, coherent critical narrative that smoothly explains Alcott's experiments in a variety of genres. The difficulty is not with the author's experimentations but with what these feminist critics experience as her inconsistent representation of the woman artist. Fetterley founds her explanation on historical context: the Civil War is both a historical event in the background of *Little Women* and a powerful metaphor that encapsulates the literary daughter's dilemma. Estes and Lant base their explanatory narrative of Alcott's seeming authorial contradictions on a sociocultural context. Estes and Lant suggest that Alcott not only accepted the transcendental ideal of self-reliance but also believed in women's rights to exercise self-exploration. However, the ambiguities embedded in Transcendentalism, coupled with Alcott's astute awareness of the potentially harsh social censure against an overtly liberated woman, lead her to refrain from expressing her liberal views openly.[6]

Very similar to Gilbert and Gubar's characterization of the woman artist as a social rebel perpetually at odds with her society, forever in conflict with herself for rejecting socially accepted scripts of femininity, Estes and Lant argue that in *Little Women* "there is not only evidence of ambivalence but also *covert* manipulation of the text by Alcott in order to disguise the fate of her experimental, self-reliant heroine." To uncover the "covert manipulation of the text," Estes and Lant cast Jo in the role of "the madwoman in the attic," Alcott's alter ego whom she must destroy, while performing the role of a keen-eyed detective "uncovering muffled traces of female identity and desire." Estes and Lant identify in *Little Women* a surface narrative that conveys the acceptable female sphere, and a simultaneous subtext that discloses the woman writer's drive towards self-assertiveness.[7]

Published under a pseudonym two years prior to the publication of *Little Women, Behind a Mask* depicts the ironic and darker aspects of domesticity. Its protagonist, Jean Muir, an embittered actress, plays the role of her life when she overtly poses as a young governess while covertly attempting to secure her social and economic future through marriage with a rich man. For many feminist critics, *Behind a Mask* has come to represent its author's lifelong dilemma between domesticity and self-assertive creativity. Identifying *Behind a Mask* as a self-reflexive literary work, "[an] art about art," Fetterley argues in "Impersonating *Little Women:* The Radicalism of Alcott's *Behind a Mask,*" that the mask, or rather the position "behind a mask," is "the metaphor which makes sense of [Louisa May Alcott's] career" in particular and reveals the logic behind the female writer's conflicted authorship in general.[8]

Like her protagonist, Alcott is able to point out the wrongs of domesticity but cannot openly rebel against its confines. Fetterley points out the dangers of the overt masquerade the woman author must undertake: impersonating the "angel in the house" may result in a devastating loss of the author's "true story." Echoing the madwoman allegory, Fetterley suggests that excessive masks and storytelling may lead to self-fragmentation and an inevitable loss of identity. The madwoman who angrily rebels against the wrongs of domesticity is entrapped in a scheme of lies to the degree that she cannot see the truth anymore.[9]

The question of the woman writer's "true" style and the extent to which the female author is able to master her mask of propriety is also discussed in Teresa A. Goddu's *Gothic America: Narrative, History, and Nation.* Goddu argues that Alcott's sentimental style was a mask the author mastered in order to ensure her economic success. Unfettered by a "true" style, Alcott is free to manipulate the literary market. Ultimately, however, the mercenary impulse gets the better of its master, imprisoning Alcott in a golden cage. Goddu argues that Alcott's sentimental style served as a mask that covered her economic ambition. However, her economic success doomed Alcott to perpetual imprisonment within her mask of sentiment.[10] Criticizing *The Madwoman in the Attic,* Goddu suggests that despite its revisionary reading of the female gothic in terms of female identity, Gilbert and Gubar's germinal work confines the female gothic within the private sphere, exclusively viewing it in psychological terms. Goddu argues that locating the female gothic in relation to the nineteenth-century American marketplace would expose the economic concerns, anxieties, and dislocations of the commodity culture. Furthermore, Goddu suggests that the sentimental and the gothic are not contradictory but rather interdependent, complementary genres since both are commercial and female. In this sense the two genres function like the dark/light women doubles that populate gothic thrillers: the "light" sentimental veils the maneuvers of the "dark," gothic-like commodity culture.[11]

Both Goddu and Fetterley consider Jean Muir as an alter ego of the author who created her. Fetterley identifies the radicalism of *Behind a Mask* in the final revelation that Jean Muir has behaved according to the competitive, ruthless laws of the male marketplace: "the desire to win, the desire for revenge, the desire to manipulate, dominate, and control . . . Jean stands revealed as the culture's ultimate monster: a man herself, she has treated men like women." However, when she discusses *Behind a Mask* as a reflexive meditation of art on art, Fetterley points out that as an actress Jean is not independent of the roles she performs: "so systemic is the confusion between mask and self that the concept of identity becomes meaningless."[12] Jean's absence of identity reflects her author's inability either to know who she is or to tell her "true" story. The sentimental genre is a mask revealed, but not conquered, by the gothic horror. Focusing on Alcott's artful manipulation of the literary market, Goddu views the sentimental form as a veil, mystifying the gothic horror of the marketplace. The fluidity of nineteenth-century American commodity culture is exposed through Jean Muir's absence of self, consequently leading to the inevitable, symbolic "murder" of the rebellious woman: "The ending of the tale . . . contains Jean's threat when it reveals not that the little woman hides a market monster, but that the veiled lady is imprisoned in the role of sentimental woman." Goddu argues that the sentimental re-veiling in Alcott's gothic exposes the horrific reality that "even the most expert market magician must remain imprisoned behind the veil of sentiment."[13]

In this sense, Goddu expands rather than revises the underlying assumptions Gilbert and Gubar present in *Madwoman in the Attic.* The rebellious madwoman not only exposes the domestic confinement but also reveals the anxieties and dislocations of nineteenth-century American commodity culture. Very similar to Gilbert and Gubar's assertion that the madwoman must be killed, Goddu points out that the talented, manipulative Dark Lady must die. However, while Gilbert and Gubar argue that the death of the madwoman marks the female author's potential release, Goddu realistically suggests that the Dark Lady must die in order to enable her threat to be socially contained. Her confinement metaphorically marks the female author's imprisonment within marketplace considerations. Jean's theatrical manipulations successfully place her in the leading role of the Coventry household. However, once she secures her economic and social future, she must relinquish her rebelliousness: the Dark Lady must concede herself to a death-in-life existence of little womanhood. In line with Gilbert and Gubar's assumption that the madwoman is the woman writer's alter ego, Goddu, like Fetterley, considers Jean Muir a powerful illustration of Alcott's literary career. Echoing Gilbert and Gubar's madwoman allegory and Fetterley's mask metaphor, Goddu presents the veil as a symbolic sign of the talented author whose mastery of the literary marketplace ultimately confines her to a gilded cage: "Like [her] veiled ladies . . . Alcott [was] bound by the market even as [she] manipulated it. The veil, which simultaneously masks and emphasizes the market economy, is the sign of [her] mastery and of [her] slavery."[14]

In *Writing Women's History,* Margaret J. M. Ezell rightly points out that in *The Madwoman in the Attic* Gilbert and Gubar "characterize the female writer . . . as an individual at odds with her society and with herself because her creative drives require her to resist accepted 'feminine' roles."[15] Reviewing the construction of anthologies of women's writing, Ezell notes that Anglo-American feminist literary critics' image of the woman writer tends to conform to the Romantic concept of the artist. In this sense, instead of suggesting a new feminist poetics, the madwoman allegory that views the female author in terms of an alienated Romantic figure actually constructs the female artist according to a Romantic male image of authorship. Identifying Milton's Eve as "akin to Satan the Romantic outlaw," Gilbert and Gubar forcefully argue that the woman writer is similar to the Romantic poet:

> Certainly, if both Satan and Eve are in some sense alienated, rebellious, and therefore Byronic figures, the same is true for women writers as a class . . . educated to submission, enjoined to silence, the woman writer, in fantasy if not in reality, must often have "stalked apart in joyless revery" . . . Feeling keenly the discrepancy between the angel she was supposed to be and the angry demon she knew she often was, she must have experienced the same paradoxical double consciousness of guilt and greatness that afflicts both Satan and . . . [the Byronic hero].[16]

In modeling the woman writer after the alienated Romantic Poet, the influential madwoman allegory is actually a model of exclusion. The construct of the female artist as rebellious madwoman rejects any woman who feels comfortable with her conventional social role as daughter, wife, and mother and who dares to celebrate domesticity. Discussing Emily Dickinson's decision to lock herself into her room, Gilbert and Gubar mockingly refer to the "Mrs. Sigourneys" as "lady poets": artistic amateurs for whom "writing verse became a genteel accomplishment . . . an elegant hobby like sketching, piano-playing, or needle-point." The fact that these women turned their literary talent into a profitable career is a repellent proof of "the mercenary auction of the mind of man" (*Madwoman,* 559). Dickinson's choice of isolation over fame and fortune is hailed by Gilbert and Guber as "a passionate renunciation of the self-assertion lyric poetry traditionally demands, and at its most ironic a seemingly demure resignation to poetic isolation or obscurity" (*Madwoman,* 564). In line with the paradoxical nature of the madwoman allegory, Dickinson praises the pleasures of such painful renunciation while simultaneously secretly expressing angry self-assertion. Dickinson's poetic heroism is celebrated as "sumptuous destitution": "ambivalently [expressing] affirmed sensuality she is determined to indulge even in her poverty" (*Madwoman,* 564). In this discussion, as in most of the discussions in *The Madwoman in the Attic,* the woman artist is constructed according to the Romantic ideal of male authorship: a mystified genius who looks inward for his powers and inspiration, a hermetic recluse isolated from social and economical spheres, a suffering rebellious demigod who practices art as a spiritual vocation, untainted by mercenary marketplace considerations.

Explaining the constrained perspective of the madwoman allegory by pointing to the danger embedded in literary critics' need to search for signs of commonality in women's writing, Rita Felski observes that critics often search for "patterns, conventions, and clusters of themes that span multiple works and can tell us something revealing about a certain sensibility, worldview or historical moment." As an allegory of authorship, the madwoman has inspired critics, yet it has also imposed a "provisional coherence onto a shifting sea of writing."[17] In many senses, feminist critics' treatment of Louisa May Alcott's life and literary work illustrates how the madwoman allegory has turned into a "hard-and-fast-assertion," a powerful all-inclusive affirmation that imposes a narrow construct of a universal "true" female artist, consequently offering a limited and limiting interpretation of literary works by women writers.[18] The scope of Alcott's literary work is too complex to fit nicely into the construct of the rebellious Romantic outlaw who sacrifices herself on the high altar of her creative genius, secretly exercising strategies of duplicity to ensure her anguished survival. Furthermore, Alcott's novels and short stories only partially fit the feminist construct of the Female Romantic or Poetess tradition. This feminist construct celebrates the woman artist's difference and the aesthetic uniqueness deriving from the domestic sphere. In dismissing the Female Romantic as "amateur," Gilbert and Gubar ignore women writers who considered writing their profession. In this respect Alcott is an interesting case in point. Quite different from Gilbert and Gubar's reference to Alcott as "a talented girl . . . try[ing] her luck at journalism, fiction-writing, even poetry" (*Madwoman,* 558), Alcott was an ambitious writer who treated her art both as profession and vocation. While meticulously documenting her growing income from literary publications, Alcott also professed a rejection of sentimental "gush." Furthermore, Alcott explicitly expressed her commitment to the antislavery movement and to the women's cause, consequently publishing explicitly political works and public letters to promote social reform.[19]

Writing within the social and cultural context of Transcendentalism—whose poet-genius ideal parallels to a great extent the Romantic notion of the suffering artist at odds with society—and astutely aware of the literary marketplace that demanded gothic and sentimental works, Alcott is neither the oblivious amateur nor the mercenary hypocrite. It would be unwise to attempt to replace one all-inclusive allegory with another. Alcott's literary corpus is a quilt-like narrative that is pieced from a wide range of contradictory cultural and psychosexual scripts. In her works, Alcott revises the transcendental poet-genius ideal while simultaneously criticizing the "gush" of sentimentality that was prevalent during the nineteenth century. She does not construct her artist heroines according to one mold but rather presents a varied array of creative women's process of trial and error, a lifelong struggle for actuating a self that is mutually intertwined with, rather than estranged from, community. Henry David Thoreau's mythic Artist of Kouroo and Louisa May Alcott's famous Jo March serve as examples.

"Though an Alcott I Can Support Myself": Louisa May Alcott's Revision of the Transcendental Poet Genius Ideal

Though every prominent Transcendental thinker wrote about art and the artist, there are nuances and discrepancies in Ralph Waldo Emerson, Margaret Fuller, Henry David Thoreau, and Bronson Alcott's definition of the artist and the practical implementations of art in life. Exploring *Walden* (1854) and *Little Women* (1868), two autobiographical *künstlerromane* depicting the education and rise of a young artist, will enable a presentation of Alcott's criticism and revision of the Transcendental poet-genius ideal. The ideal in general, and Thoreau's concept of the perfect artist-genius in particular, can be regarded as a philosophical and cultural script she negotiates, criticizes, and revises throughout her various depictions of artist heroines.[20]

In his conclusion to *Walden,* Thoreau presents the parable of the Artist of Kouroo, a mythic artist who devotes his life to the creation of a perfect wood staff, oblivious of time and untouched by the mundane aspects of life: "in an imperfect work time is an ingredient, but into a perfect work time does not enter . . . it shall be perfect in all respects, though I should do nothing else in my life." The parable suggests that art is an intuitive and spiritual vocation and an artist is a person whose "singleness of purpose and resolution" transcend the material and temporal aspects of life to make "a new system . . . a world with full and fair proportions."[21]

While the parable of the Artist of Kouroo depicts the artist as an aloof creator, untouched by the torments of time and talent, an inspired demigod who creates a complete masterpiece without having to go through the agonizing process of learning, erring, and evolving into an artist, Alcott's *Little Women* depicts the labor and loss embedded in the process of becoming an artist. Contrary to Amy, who proclaims "talent isn't genius, and no amount of energy can make it so. I want to be great or nothing,"[22] Jo does not strive for greatness but rather endeavors to make her art meaningful to her familial community. Reading the conflicting criticism following the publication of her first novel, Jo exclaims, "how can [criticism help me] when it's so contradictory that I don't know whether I have written a promising book, or broken all the Ten Commandments." Summing up her literary lesson, Jo ironically proclaims the practical usefulness of lack of genius: "not being a genius, like Keats, it won't kill me" (*Little Women,* 271-72).

Little Women does not depict the woman artist's creative process in the romanticized, transcendental terms of a genius-poet hero, but rather in practical daily experiments. Quite differently from the autonomous Artist of Kouroo who establishes a "fairer, and more glorious" new tradition with the creation of his staff, Jo explores her independent artistic voice with an "up again and take another" spirit, until she manages to marry tradition and autonomy. While with the parable of the Artist of Kouroo, who "made no compromise with Time," Thoreau suggests that a work of art derives solely from its creator with no influence of historical conditions and personal circumstances, Alcott describes Jo's literary labors as a series of "tumbles down the beanstalk": a work of art is the product of the artist's complex negotiations of personal aspirations, familial conditions, commercial tastes and demands, and social constraints. Each fall serves as an educational turning point on Jo's continuing literary quest: "The novel disaster quenched [Jo's] courage for a time, for public opinion is a giant which has frightened stouter-hearted Jacks on bigger beanstalks than hers. Like that immortal hero, she reposed a while after the first attempt, which resulted in a tumble, and the least lovely of the giant's treasures . . . But the 'up again and take another' spirit was as strong in Jo as in Jack" (*Little Women,* 345). Jo's first "tumble down the beanstalk" results in the understanding that a writer cannot please everyone's tastes. Her second fall leads to a realization that "character is a better possession than money, rank, intellect or beauty" (*Little Women,* 353). Jo finally finds her style when she writes "with no thought of fame or money, [putting] her heart into [her story]" (436). Here Alcott mildly echoes Thoreau's harsh criticism against mercenary capitalism and his adamant call for a morally meaningful labor that disciplines the mind:

> I respect not his labors, his farm where every thing has its price; who would carry the landscape, who would carry his God, to market, if he could get any thing for him; who goes to market *for* his god as it is; on whose farm nothing grows free, whose fields bear no crops, whose meadows no flowers, whose trees no fruits, but dollars; who loves not the beauty of his fruits, whose fruits are not ripe for him till they are turned to dollars. Give me the poverty that enjoys true wealth. (*Walden,* 196)

Jo's agonizing loneliness at the end of *Little Women* is relieved by her parents, who sustain and support her personal quest. Jo can be regarded as an illustration of an investigation into the two extremes the madwoman allegory suggests: writing sensation stories allows Jo to experiment in monster-like creativity, while attempting to replace Beth in the family home is an experiment in angelic domesticity. Between these two extreme cultural scripts, Jo finds her individual voice and offers a third model that combines creativity, paid labor, and community: "I've known [poverty] long enough to lose my dread, and be happy working for those I love . . . I may be strong-minded, but no one could say I'm out of my sphere now, for woman's special mission is supposed to be drying tears and bearing burdens. I'm to carry my share, Friedrich, and help to earn the home" (*Little Women,* 480). Unlike the Artist of Kouroo, Jo has to confront giants from within in the form of her uncontrollable anger and burning creative fits, and from without in the form of contradictory public opinion. Like Jack who finally destroys the giant with an ax he receives from his mother, with the help of parents and a future husband, Jo manages to find peace within her inner and outer conflicts and contradictions.[23]

While the narrator of *Walden* proclaims "the man who goes alone can start to-day; but he who travels with another must wait till that other is ready . . . I should not consciously and deliberately forsake my particular calling to do the good which society demands of me" ("Economy," 72), Marmee teaches her young women artists that "it is better to have a few duties, and live a little for others" (*Little Women,* 117). In contrast to the poet-hero's solitary deliberate living and explicit intention to become the independent "builder of his temple," the "sculptor of his own flesh and blood," the artist heroines in *Little Women* live and create within a community that incorporates a complex array of contradictions. As Anne Douglas points out, the narrative depicts the four girls' arduous endeavor to balance each member's right to independence with her allegiance to the cohesion of the family, leading to a final balance in which no member may express herself completely, yet everyone can express herself in part.[24]

While *Walden* perceives domestic labor as the toil and detail that fritter away life, *Little Women* presents domestic duties as a woman's labor of love: the honest mud-sweeping that molds character, and nourishes worthy art, deriving out of and sustained by life and community.[25] Alcott does not romanticize the woman artist's labor of love. *Little Women* depicts the obtrusiveness and drudgery of domestic duties. In her depiction of Meg's married life and motherhood, Alcott portrays the confinements of domesticity: "in America . . . girls early sign a declaration of independence, and enjoy their freedom . . . but the matrons usually abdicate with the first heir to the throne, and go into a seclusion . . . they are virtually put upon the shelf" (*Little Women,* 388). However, *Little Women* also presents the ways in which the domestic community sustains the artist heroine. When Jo "falls into a vortex," she is "unconscious of want, care or bad weather." However, when she emerges from her "vortex fit," she is "hungry, sleepy, cross or despondent," in urgent need of recovery and nourishment by her family (265-66).

Describing Meg's married life, *Little Women*'s narrator contrasts Meg's unrealistic determination "to be a model housewife," with the realistic assertion "it is a world of disappointments" (*Little Women,* 273, 275). Meg's attempt to produce the perfect homemade preserves on her own is presented as a useless struggle: "Meg wrestled alone with the refractory sweetmeats all that hot summer day, and at five o'clock sat down in her topsy-turvy kitchen, wrung her bedaubed hands, lifted up her voice, and wept" (*Little Women,* 275).

This far-from-perfect performance is made worse by John's innocent attempt to cash in on Meg's hubristic declaration "my husband shall always feel free to bring a friend home whenever he likes" (*Little Women,* 275). Walking into the domestic confusion and despair, John resigns himself to Thoreauvian simplicity—"give us the cold meat, and bread and cheese"—only to meet Meg's horror at the "promiscuous lunch" (*Little Women,* 277, 278). Meg's tragicomic adherence to unrealistic, abstract models of "angelic" perfection is contrasted with Jo's comic kitchen fiasco:

> [Jo] did her best alone, and discovered that something more than energy and good-will is necessary to make a cook . . . "Well, they can eat beef and bread and butter if they are hungry; only it's mortifying to have to spend your whole morning for nothing," thought Jo, as she rang the bell half an hour later than usual, and stood hot, tired and dispirited, surveying the feast . . . Poor Jo would gladly have gone under the table, as one thing after another was tasted and left. . . . She turned scarlet, and was on the verge of crying [when] the comical side of the affair suddenly struck her, and she laughed till the tears ran down her cheeks. (*Little Women,* 115-16)

Contrasting perfect models with open-minded experimentation, the two scenes juxtapose transcendental rigid adherence to abstractions with a willingness to experiment and err. Meg's homemade-preserves disaster suggests that principles of perfection may lead to a lonely crash, while Jo's kitchen fiasco presents a practical realization that gradual learning and eloquent bearing of domestic burdens are the makings of an artful way to create beauty out of life's details.

Both *Little Women* and *Walden* are fictitious representations of their authors; their multilayered narratives portray some of the conflicts their creators confronted throughout their lives as artists in "grey Concord." In a letter written to Lucy Brown a few months before joining his father's pencil-making business, Thoreau rebelliously proclaims his uselessness, comparing himself to an exiled god: "I am as unfit for any practical purpose, I mean for the furtherance of the world's ends, as gossamer for ship timber . . . [I] can sympathize with god Apollo, who served king Admetus for awhile on earth."[26] In his allusion to Apollo, a herdsman for Admetus, Thoreau foreshadows the drudgery of piecing together mosaics from his journal to form *Walden:* a meticulous construction obscured under the transcendental rhetoric of inspiration. In two separate letters written to her parents, Alcott rejects the Transcendental poet-genius ideal, replacing her father's model of a destitute poet-genius with a community-conscious woman artist: "I am very well and very happy. Things go smoothly, and I think I shall come out right, and prove that though an *Alcott* I *can* support myself."[27] In 1856 she wrote, "It's clear that Minerva Moody is getting on in spite of many downfalls, and by the time she is a used up old lady . . . she may finish her job and see her family well off."[28] In her allusion to Minerva, the patron of the art of weaving, the goddess who was never a child, leaping from her father's head full grown and armed, Alcott conveys her lifelong battle with the triple bind of duty, artistic ambition, and womanhood. The voice of the writer, who considered her great artistic achievement as "sculpting" herself into a good daughter, is echoed in Jo's conscious understanding that a woman artist does not transcend art in life, like a poet-genius. Neither madwoman nor angel, Jo transforms life's burdens into aesthetic creations.

Notes

1. Rita Felski, *Literature after Feminism* (Chicago: University of Chicago Press, 2003), 65.

2. Ibid., 69. *The Madwoman in the Attic* has been criticized from various other perspectives. See also Toril Moi, *Sexual/Textual Politics* (London: Routledge, 1985); Nina Baym, "The Madwoman and Her Languages: Why I Don't Do Feminist Literary Theory," *Tulsa Studies in Women's Literature* 3, no. 1–2 (Spring–Autumn 1984): 45–59; Marta Caminero-Santangelo, *The Madwoman Can't Speak: Or Why Insanity Is Not Subversive* (Ithaca, N.Y.: Cornell University Press, 1998).

3. Judith Fetterley, "*Little Women:* Alcott's Civil War," in *Little Women and the Feminist Imagination: Criticism, Controversy, Personal Essays,* ed. Janice M. Alberghene and Beverly Lyon Clark (New York: Garland, 1999), 27–42.

4. Ibid., 39, 40.

5. Angela M. Estes and Kathleen Margaret Lant, "Dismembering the Text: The Horror of Louisa May Alcott's *Little Women,*" *Annual of the Modern Language Association Division on Children's Literature Association* 17 (New Haven: Yale University Press, 1989), 99.

6. Ibid., 99–100.

7. Ibid., 121 n. 2, 101.

8. Judith Fetterley, "Impersonating *Little Women:* The Radicalism of Alcott's *Behind a Mask,*" *Women's Studies* 10, no. 1 (1983): 12, 2.

9. Fetterley's assertion that the masked woman may be lost in her deception is shared by Gail K. Smith who argues that Louisa May Alcott's gothic narratives suggest that "deception is the essence of womanhood . . . self and mask are ultimately indistinguishable." Gail K. Smith, "Who Was That Masked Woman? Gender and Form in Louisa May Alcott's Confidence Stories," in *American Women Short Story Writers: A Collection of Critical Essays,* ed. Julie Brown (New York: Garland, 1995), 57.

10. Teresa A. Goddu, *Gothic America: Narrative, History, and Nation* (New York: Columbia University Press, 1997), 117.

11. Ibid., 96, 94.

12. Fetterley, "Impersonating," 11–12, 13.

13. Goddu, *Gothic America,* 124, 125.

14. Ibid., 130.

15. Margaret J. M. Ezell, *Writing Women's Literary History* (Baltimore: Johns Hopkins University Press, 1993), 26.

16. Sandra M. Gilbert and Susan Gubar, *The Madwoman in the Attic: The Woman Writer and the Nineteenth-Century Literary Imagination* (New Haven: Yale University Press, 1979), 203. Subsequent references will be given parenthetically.

17. Felski, *Literature after Feminism,* 93.

18. The madwoman allegory includes several influential assumptions concerning the woman artist. My discussion here illustrates how the madwoman allegory has become a feminist construct of the woman artist as a Romantic outlaw. Elsewhere I discuss the dichotomy between the woman artist's "true" rebellious self and her "false" socially tame self. See Keren Fite, "Wrestling with the Angel in the House, Slaying the Monster in the Attic: The Artist Heroines in Louisa May Alcott's 'Psyche's Art' and *Little Women,*" in *Auto-poetica: Representations of the Creative Process in Nineteenth-Century British and American Fiction,* ed. Darby Lewes (Lanham, Md.: Lexington Books, 2006), 75–92. I also examine the centrality of anger in the woman artist's creative life in "'From Savage Passion to the Sweetness of Self-Control': Female Anger in *Little Women* and 'Pauline's Passion and Punishment,'" *Women's Writing* 14, no. 3 (December 2007): 435–48.

19. Viewed from this perspective, Alcott's more political works may fit Anne Mellor's "Female Poet" construct. See Anne Mellor, "The Female Poet and the Poetess: Two Traditions of British Women's Poetry 1780–1830," *Studies in Romanticism* 36, no. 2 (1997): 261–76. For a survey of the Female Romantic tradition, see Laura Mandell, "Introduction: The Poetess Tradition," in *The Transatlantic Poetess* 29–30 (February–May 2003), *Romanticism on the Net,* http://www.erudit.org/revue/ron/2003/v/n29/007712ar.html.

20. As a historical movement, Transcendentalism was active from the mid-1830s to the late 1840s. However, transcendental ideas became part of New England culture and continued to be influential throughout the nineteenth century.

21. Henry David Thoreau, *Walden,* ed. Jeffrey S. Cramer (New Haven: Yale University Press, 2004), 326–27. Subsequent references will be given parenthetically.

22. Louis May Alcott, *Little Women* (New York: Viking Penguin, 1989), 405. Subsequent references will be given parenthetically.

23. Jo's "tumble down the beanstalk" can also be seen as an illustration of Alcott's revisionist mythmaking. Here it is used to present Alcott's revision of the transcendental poet-genius ideal. See Fite, "Wrestling with the Angel in the House."

24. Ann Douglas, introduction to Louis May Alcott, *Little Women* (New York: New American Library, 1983), vii–xxvii. Reprinted in *Little Women and the Feminist Imagination: Criticism, Controversy, Personal Essays,* ed. Janice M. Alberghene and Beverly Lyon Clark (New York: Garland, 1999), 56.

25. In "Psyche's Art," Alcott explicitly suggests that "moulding character is the highest sort of sculpture." Psyche Dean's process of maturation into a sculptress is depicted through taking on the burden of domestic work, thus paying "the price of [artistic] success in patience and privation, labor and hope." Louisa May Alcott, "Psyche's Art," in *Alternative Alcott,* ed. Elaine Showalter (New Brunswick, N.J.: Rutgers University Press, 1988), 207–26.

26. Henry David Thoreau, *The Correspondence of Henry David Thoreau,* ed. Walter Harding and Carl Bode (New York: New York University Press, 1958), 47; Walden Woods Project, Thoreau Institute, Online Research Resources http://www.walden.org/Institute/thoreau/writing/correspondence/Correspondence.html.

27. Louisa May Alcott, *The Selected Letters of Louisa May Alcott,* ed. Joel Myerson and Daniel Shealy (Athens: University of Georgia Press, 1995), 26.

28. Ibid., 113.

10

Sensationalizing Women's Writing

Madwomen in Attics, the Sensational Canon, and Generic Confinement

Tamara Silvia Wagner

When Sandra Gilbert and Susan Gubar directed new attention to nineteenth-century women writers in 1979, they firmly linked together the representation of the confined Victorian antiheroine, the iconic madwoman in the attic as her double, and the female novelist's self-conscious engagement with her own marginalization. This linkage has become one of the major premises of discussions of Victorian literature by women and in particular of their contributions to midcentury sensation fiction. What has been seen as the genre's underpinning interest in domestic confinement has marked it out as intrinsically subversive, even proto-feminist. Yet this focus has further marginalized an array of domestic women writers, including until very recently Margaret Oliphant, Eliza Lynn Linton, and Charlotte Yonge. Nicola Diane Thompson has provocatively asked of the ideological limitations in feminist recuperative work, "What, for example, do you say about a conservative woman novelist like Charlotte Yonge once you've discovered her?"[1] Precisely the incorporation of new fictional paradigms into domestic realism, however, singles out the most revealing cases of the intricacies of popular Victorian women's writing. Yonge adapted literary sensationalism to serve a religious agenda, and in the process engendered alternative forms of representing domesticity, the heroine's struggles within its confines, and, most intriguingly perhaps, easily sensationalized emotional distress at home. That much of the rediscovery of nineteenth-century women writers can be, to a decisive extent, conducted via a remapping of the sensation novel's cultural impact does more than simply testify to the genre's range and adaptability. In disclosing important interchanges between sensationalism and domestic realism, the transformative deployment of sensational elements by domestic, even notoriously antifeminist, novelists not only asks for but helps to facilitate a reassessment of popular fiction and the centrality of women's writing within its development, reception, and reworking.

Far from presenting placidly subdued heroines—proverbially suffering in stillness—such ambiguously anti-sensational novels by domestic women writers minutely delineate intensive emotional experience and its symptoms. The poignancy of their delineation, I wish to argue, counters the absorption of any emotional experience into the general sensationalization of the mundane that characterizes the sensation genre's domestic Gothic. A much-needed reconsideration of their critical engagement with what could loosely be termed emotional instabilities and their containment therefore also offers a crucial opportunity for a renewed evaluation of the impact Gilbert and Gubar's work has had on the making of a sensational canon of women writers. This canon itself needs to be carefully reappraised to do justice to its various, at their best epistemologically sophisticated, exponents. If their invocation of cultural anxieties about socially constructed madness has formed a defining element of Victorian sensationalism, then these alternative takes on divergent reactions to the "abnormal" evince the complexities of contending discourses on normalcy and their fictionalization. Yonge's treatment of emotional distress and its perception in an often unforgiving society may first and foremost continue to serve a specific agenda, and yet it also illustrates her ambiguous reuse of the sensational in depicting domestic ideals in danger of collapse. It is not only that her treatment of intersecting emotional, mental, and spiritual uncertainties becomes increasingly more sympathetic and less rigidly tied to either religious doctrine or an easy identification with current medical claims. This rejection of a medicalization of emotion offers an important alternative approach to sensation fiction's investment in clinical discourses.

In order to trace Yonge's continued concern with protracted emotional distress, I shall focus on its changing representation in her midcentury works. There is a perceptible shift from her fiction of the 1850s to that of the early-1860s. *The Castle-Builders; Or, The Deferred Confirmation* (1854) is notorious for promoting doctrine so explicitly that it overshadows the plot more than any other of Yonge's novels. It firmly identifies expressions of "low spirits," including their poetic expression, with spiritual carelessness. By contrast, *The Young Step-Mother; Or, A Chronicle of Mistakes* (1861) leaves its original didactic agenda behind fairly quickly to delineate instead the slow, laborious, almost belated, recognition of what are variously—and with a significant amount of ambiguity—termed the combination of "hereditary low spirits, a precocious mind, a reserved temper, a motherless home."[2] In drawing on the extensive oeuvre Yonge produced as a dedicated Tractarian writer, I also seek to highlight the urgent need to fill in the gaps in part created by agenda-driven omissions (such as the absence of writers with a different agenda) in feminist recuperative work. The aim of what must necessarily remain only a sketch for a larger reappraisal of current canons of women's writing is therefore twofold: the opportunity for a reassessment of sensational formulae in Victorian domestic fiction is illustrated by the changing approaches to emotional distress in Yonge's novels.

Beyond Sensational Canon Formation

Although Gilbert and Gubar initially referenced sensational novelists only very briefly when they set out to stress the association of women's writing in general with transgression, the critical recuperation of the Victorian sensation novel has since rendered the genre a watershed for literary representations of normalcy as a cultural construction. The shifts across fluid lines of demarcation, the very porosity of such boundaries, and above all, the threat of the transgressing element's containment have been shown to drive the plots of the most influential sensation novels in a continuation of a "feminine Gothic" tradition. Confinement has been the overarching metaphor, and its literalization the recurring, unifying narrative strategy. Bertha Mason, in Charlotte Brontë's *Jane Eyre* (1847), forms a projection of Jane's desires as well as fears: a more extreme, literalized, version of her "anomalous, orphaned position in society, her enclosure in stultifying roles and houses, and her attempts to escape through . . . madness."[3] Sensational antiheroines are more likely to resemble Bertha herself, as they struggle against being confined, literally or metaphorically. It is therefore not surprising that incarceration in a "home," a disconcerting euphemism for an insane asylum, forms the most memorable and pervasive topos of Victorian popular culture: it is an ironic manifestation of insanity's domestication in the nineteenth century. Janet Oppenheim speaks of "the widespread Victorian anxiety about unlawful confinement, in both private and public institutions," and Winifred Hughes's *The Maniac in the Cellar: Sensation Novels of the 1860s* pivots on sensational invocations of incarceration within the house. Such a policing of the abnormal constitutes a central part of the sensation genre's domestic Gothic, a bringing home of the threats of the outside world (and its institutions, including doctors ready to institutionalize the "abnormal"). In its inversion of domestic ideologies, it functions at once as a double of, and an analytic lens for, a revaluation of the ideal home.[4]

The Victorian sensation novel can be seen to emerge from domestic realism in two complementary ways: the domestic may fail as the promised refuge or, more invidiously, it can breed danger in the very confinement it offers. Accounts of the sensation craze's development have begun to stress the ways in which it critically interacted with the prevalence of domestic fiction, even as it fed on ideals of domesticity by aiming to explode them. As Pamela Gilbert puts it, the "rhetoric of inviolable British domesticity becomes both the parent and opponent of sensation fiction." Karen Chase and Michael Levenson similarly suggest that in sensation fiction, the "Victorian investment in family life unfolds in the awareness that at any moment it can turn into the antifamily of popular sensation." More recently, Andrew Maunder has stressed that the sensation novel was certainly much more than a "riposte to the dominance of the domestic novel." On the contrary, the simultaneity of domestic realism and sensationalism in the popular book market created a two-way process of interchange. Sensational accounts of the domestic located the Gothic at home, in middle-class households. Since this creation of a domestic Gothic hinged on sensationalizing the familial and familiar, the home itself was increasingly featured as a threatening as well as a threatened space. Deliberately anti-sensational writers reacted in markedly critical ways to current discourses, and this included the reworking of their prevalent literary representations. It is consequently crucial to consider the changing depiction of emotional turmoil, beyond the confines of the sensational canon, as more than simply influenced by the growing craze in sensation at the literary marketplace.[5]

What are now generally considered the seminal sensation novels of the 1860s clearly link together domestic confines, female transgression, and discourses on insanity. Wilkie Collins's *The Woman in White* (1860) and Mary Elizabeth Braddon's *Lady Audley's Secret* (1862), as well as a subplot in her first novel, *The Trail of the Serpent* (1860), accentuate the instability of identity by firmly connecting it to the experience or, even more decisively, the allegations of madness. Charles Reade's *Hard Cash* (1863) pivots on a young man's incarceration in a private asylum as a case of "lovesickness" and "monomania" (obsessions that include a "little delusion" about his father's schemes) that enables the father's continued speculations with his children's money.[6] Symptomatically, it is his association with a "feminine" sensitivity that renders the son's commitment so easy: he is a "bloke [who] really has awful headaches, like a girl" (*Hard Cash,* 33), is suspected of shedding tears at college, and sobs heartrendingly in the asylum, while composing pleading messages written in blood, until rescued by his fiancée's booby brother. The containment of unwanted family members, instigated by greedy relatives who have a financial interest in the policing of mental health, is admittedly already threatened in Dickens's *David Copperfield* (1850). It presents the largely comical figure of Mr. Dick in what John Reed has called "an amusing, if not medically convincing picture of benign lunacy growing out of a shock to a good man's sensitive nature and resulting in an *idée fixe,* both pathetic and diverting." In the wake of the "sensational sixties," however, opposing constructions of sanity become central to the plot. In Braddon's *Lady Audley's Secret* and Collins's *The New Magdalen* (1873), decisions about who is consigned into medical care for mental instability is a question of social and familial power, while Collins's *The Law and the Lady* (1875) and Braddon's *The Fatal Three* (1888) both track the spectrum of what is termed, in an invocation of newly fashionable clinical terminology, "latent insanity."[7]

Beneath the angry exposure of easily manipulated medical ideas of emotional experience runs an internalized and therefore much more invidious apprehension of diagnosable instabilities. As it is put in *Lady Audley's Secret,* in what has become an iconographical representation of the Victorians' struggle with the shifting definitions of normalcy, "How many minds must tremble upon the narrow boundary between reason and unreason, mad today and sane to-morrow, mad yesterday and sane to-day."[8] The fluctuations of instability engender a threat that can be exploited for its sensational potential in complementary ways that match the two sides of the sensation novel's domestic Gothic. Notably, the almost laconic statement on insanity's pervasiveness towards the end of Braddon's novel is not so much concerned with fear of madness itself as with the social dangers presented by its possible disappearance or disguise. It is not about being sane today and no more tomorrow, but on the contrary, about being insane one day, but sane again the next, locked up or at large with apparently no traceable history of insanity and hence a threat to the established confines of society.

In *Victorian Psychology and British Culture,* Rick Rylance refers to a shift in nineteenth-century diagnoses of mental pathology. Opposed to the "all-or-nothing game" that assumed that insanity was either all there or not there at all, a new conception of self developed that was "inherently more complicated and unstable." Rylance mentions Bertha Mason as the most famous literary example of the lunatic as an easily demarcated social pariah.[9] Rochester, we remember, is tricked into marrying into a family of concealed lunatics and idiots, yet the deception is symptomatically kept up only in Spanish Town, Jamaica, in an exoticized, colonial space. In mid-Victorian sensation novels, the emergent concept of concealable, latent, or temporarily abeyant insanity becomes a conduit for social anxieties. This is how Lady Audley notoriously abjures any responsibility for her crimes, including the attempted murder of her husband when his return threatens to jeopardize her social position. It remains unclear whether she is right in claiming this "excuse." As an obliging physician puts it to facilitate her exportation to a private asylum abroad, "The lady is not mad; but she has the hereditary taint in her blood. She has the cunning of madness, with the prudence of intelligence. I will tell you what she is, Mr. Audley. She is dangerous!" (*Lady Audley's,* 379). Earlier conceptualizations are specifically addressed and refuted. A visit to her mother, confined in an asylum, radically revises the future Lady Audley's original perceptions of madness, but an additional irony rests in her continued reliance on similarly outmoded concepts of its transmission:

> This visit served at least to dispel the idea which had so often terrified me. I saw no raving, straight-waist-coated maniac, guarded by zealous jailers, but a golden-haired, blue-eyed, girlish creature, who seemed as frivolous as a butterfly, and who skipped toward us with her yellow curls decorated with natural flowers, and saluted us with radiant smiles, and gay, ceaseless chatter. . . . Her madness was a hereditary disease transmitted to her from her mother, who had died mad. (*Lady Audley's,* 349-50)

It is the literary image of Bertha Mason that is rehearsed and dispelled here. In its place, angelic appearance may mask encroaching or fully fledged insanity and, in Lady Audley's appropriation of this camouflage, a dangerous criminality. Whereas the split image highlighted in *The Madwoman in the Attic* is literalized by the doubling in Brontë's novel, its two sides are the more disconcertingly fused in Braddon's. Jane Eyre, in the famous red room scene, sees a reflection in the mirror that foreshadows the madwoman's appearance: with "glittering eyes of fear moving where all else was still, [her mirror-image] had the effect of a real spirit." Bertha, locked into her red room, becomes this spectre. The pairing of "the angel in the house" and "the madwoman in the attic" may have had a long history, yet in female sensation fiction, it is often the more disconcerting for being internalized as well as carefully concealed. Lady Audley's portrait (locked up in her private rooms) brings out her hidden demonic qualities. The "wax-dollish young person . . . with flaxen ringlets and a perpetual giggle" is revealed as "fiendish" by her own "likeness": "It was so like, and yet so unlike. . . . My lady, in his portrait of her, had something of the aspect of a beautiful fiend" (*Lady Audley's,* 33, 70-71). As Elaine Showalter has already argued, *Lady Audley's Secret* rewrites *Jane Eyre* by making the "demure little governess" the bigamist. In this sensational inversion of the "post-Jane" heroine, the villainess is the central protagonist, whereas socially confirming female characters pale in comparison.[10]

Gilbert and Gubar did much more than simply point out an intriguing doubling, however. The creation of "doubles as monster characters who shadow angelic authors and mad anti-heroines who complicate the lives of sane heroines" articulated an encompassing negotiation of a duality or duplicity that could be seen to link together a "female literary tradition" (*Madwoman*, 80). The feminist recuperative work undertaken in the 1970s embraced such expressions of split images, projections, and the literalization of women's confinement in the marginal spaces of the house. In *A Literature of Their Own: British Women Novelists from Brontë to Lessing* (1977), Showalter pointed out the twofold projection of Jane Eyre onto Bertha Mason and Helen Burns, who dies as an adolescent, a spiritualized epitome of the angelic female protagonist. Such "implied and explicit connections to Victorian sexual ideology" helped to formulate "the deadly combat between the Angel in the House and the devil in the flesh." But it was Gilbert and Gubar, Janet Gezari stresses in a recent assessment, who "were the first to unite the angel and the madwoman [to] applaud her expressive transgressions, and identify her with the woman writer." Bertha Mason has since become "the most famous 'madwoman in the attic' of women's literary history," as Susanne Becker puts it in *Gothic Forms of Feminine Fictions.* This "resonant 'madwoman in the attic'" provides "a clue to the attractions of gothic form for feminine fictions."[11]

A by-product of the craze for sensation among critics has been a tendency to equate midcentury women's writing with the sensational, however. Much has been written on the paradigms of a feminine Gothic as it became reworked in the "sensational sixties." Lyn Pykett has pointed out that male and female novelists drew on the traditions of late-eighteenth-century Radcliffean Gothic. Its Victorian versions "enacted, and, simultaneously, or by turns, managed and recontained [women's] fantasies of escape from the physical and psychological confinements of the domestic and conventionally defined femininity." Despite continued disputes about the possibility of demarcating a "female imagination" or marking out "gendered" writing, the Victorian sensation novel is now widely acknowledged, discussed, and taught as a "feminine" genre in which women writers predominated, whereas thirty years ago references to this forgotten category were almost completely confined to one or two works by Wilkie Collins. This shift has led to the reprinting of a range of novels by Braddon, Ellen Wood, and more recently, Rhoda Broughton, Florence Marryat, or Ouida. Conversely, sensational elements have been traced in fiction by canonical realist writers. Winifred Hughes suggests that "even Trollope and Eliot began to incorporate recognizably sensational elements into their own portrayals of everyday life."[12]

What is often underestimated is the extent to which Gilbert and Gubar already pointed out the significance of such generic interchanges or slippages.

Their analysis of George Eliot's supernatural novella *The Lifted Veil* (1859) thus importantly instigated the inclusion of neglected, even obscure, works by a canonical woman writer identified with realism. Criticized precisely for this use of an obscure text in the late 1970s, a decade later, it could be termed yet another standard reading of women's "hysterical dilemma" under patriarchy, as it was put in a 1989 review essay on recently published feminist studies. But whereas Eliot's supernatural text therein became coupled with such likewise quickly standardized depictions of "hysteria" or "neurasthenia" as Charlotte Perkins Gilman's "The Yellow Wallpaper," Gilbert and Gubar had not only focused on Eliot's use of clairvoyance as a metaphor for the male protagonist's "feminine" qualities (and hence the intriguing projection of a "feminine" dilemma onto the hero), but also linked it specifically to Braddon's representation of "exceptional insight, with resultant duplicity" in Braddon's *Lady Audley's Secret* as well as to Jane Eyre's preternatural hearing in one of the most sensational moments in Brontë's novel.[13]

But if Gilbert and Gubar on the whole applied their analysis of recurring tropes and figures primarily to realist—and chiefly canonical—fiction, the sensation genre has now become indisputably canonical, and current reassessments have begun to probe its impact on the Victorian novel at large. Noncanonical examples of domestic realism are read through the lens of sensation fiction, allowing us also to reconsider the initial pairings in *The Madwoman in the Attic.* In a recent study, Marlene Tromp analyzes in detail "tensions in the boundaries between the sensational and the real, the moral and the depraved," in Oliphant's *Salem Chapel* (1863), and June Sturrock terms both Oliphant's novel and Yonge's *The Trial* (1864) "quasi-sensation novels" that move "beyond the private realm of the family chronicle to take on many of the horrific, extreme, and mysterious trappings of the sensation novel." In short, to draw on what literary sensationalism had to offer had quickly become an attractive strategy. Yet, as Sturrock adds, Yonge responded to trends in fiction by exploiting them "for both didactic and for market purposes." So, far from merely using what had become popular formulae to appeal to a wider readership, otherwise markedly different novels traded on them as much to reflect current social and cultural anxieties as to promote diverse agendas. Now it is time to follow up on the analysis of the transformation of such nonrealist, sensational, elements within the works of emphatically domestic women writers.[14]

Yonge was not alone in appropriating sensational elements for religious fiction. Felicia Skene, for example, resorted to sensationalism in *Hidden Depths* (1866) to create a social-problem novel that combined a polemical reaction to the Contagious Diseases Acts of 1864 and 1866 with both Tractarian doctrine and sensation. As Lillian Nayder puts it in her introduction to a recent reprint, Skene extends "the moral boundaries of sensation fiction, using it to convey an orthodox Christian message" while simultaneously transcending the political limits of religious fiction. It is in the same vein that Yonge brings "a moral and spiritual purpose to sensation fiction," yet unlike Skene, she concentrates on securely bourgeois or gentry households. Her narratives are emphatically domestic, infused by the need to sustain ideals of a happy home, with all its traditional hierarchies, despite the (sensationalized) fissures that are shown to threaten it. In this, her fictionalization of conflicts at home renders the adaptation of sensationalism within the confines of domestic realism more prominent, disclosing flows of influence that have hitherto been neglected in dismissals of Yonge's conservative antifeminism.[15]

It is crucial, therefore, to get away from the rehearsal of inherited categories. This is the rigidity Thompson deplores: "Victorian and modern critics" alike, she writes in *Victorian Women Writers and the Woman Question,* "tend to label works by women novelists according to their apparent position on the woman question, creating such categories as domestic novels, sensation novels, and New Woman novels." In this taxonomy, Yonge features regularly as an example of "the other side in the debate." Yet as Emma Liggins and Andrew Maunder point out in a recent special issue of *Women's Writing,* there is finally recognition "that we cannot just dismiss mid-Victorian popular fiction by women as conservative or formulaic junk, which lacks intellectual depth or is insufficiently 'feminist.'" At the same time, we cannot simply sidestep Yonge's commitment to family values that can appear virulently antifeminist. Talia Schaffer importantly cautions that we need to go beyond mere rediscovery that takes previous neglect as its main premise, which may end up "flattening out" complicated sets of representations to defend "the apparently hopelessly popular author." Recent criticism suggests that it is Yonge's religious orientation that makes her epistemologically self-reflexive, and that "the limitations and errors of Yonge's worldview" should not "disqualify her from consideration as a serious moralist." Similarly, it has been remarked that her narratives are replete with children who have either psychological or physical problems and rarely "emerge into adulthood without a crisis or a struggle of some kind," which denotes Yonge's feelings about extensive families as essentially contradictory. An analysis of her representation of suffering at home discloses an intense engagement with emotional turmoil beyond the generic confines of sensational canon formation.[16]

Out of the Attic: Beyond "the Spring of Spirits"

Yonge adapted popular formulae to promote a particular ideology: Tractarian doctrine. As Catherine Sandbach-Dahlström put it nearly twenty-five years ago, "It has often been said of Charlotte Yonge that she was chiefly successful in combining her religious message with a portrayal of empirical reality—that is to say, in comparison with other writers of religious fiction." John Keble, Yonge's literary as well as religious mentor, had notably cautioned her against introducing explicit preaching into her fiction. Yonge's introduction of spiritual subjects can consequently appear "coded" or "oblique." Discussing domestic realism, Vineta Colby has similarly suggested that Yonge "was the novelist who most gracefully converted the tractarian impulse into novels of family life" because her idealism was practically oriented, concerned with "her characters' problems of daily living far more than with their problems of dogma and ritual." Although Colby acknowledges that Yonge's fictional families were, despite all their "apparently idyllic blessings, [shown to be] plagued with pain and sorrow," prevalent preconceptions have continued to focus on her seemingly idyllic domesticity. In 1975, David Brownell described the commonly perceived boundaries of her world: "One boundary of Yonge's created world is established by the subjects that she will not treat. Like Austen, whom she greatly admired, Yonge prefers to let other pens dwell on guilt and misery. She will not study attractive sins or sinners, ministers delinquent in their duty, or subjects such as hereditary insanity which readers with such family problems may find too painful."[17]

Although Yonge's fiction features sinners of various kinds and even convicted criminals, they really cannot be said to share the attractiveness of a Count Fosco or a Lady Audley. Neither is there a place for such controversial topics as Skene was to treat. Pain, guilt, and misery of all kinds, however, are pervasive. Indeed, they structure her novels. They are central to the heroines' growth, to what has been seen as their minutely detailed, sympathetically presented albeit ultimately policed struggles against the very ideals her novels set out to endorse.[18] More importantly, the presence of pain illustrates communal interdependence, as Martha Stoddard Holmes has recently shown: Yonge may at times seem to push "the overt Christian message that disability is not an affliction but a blessing," yet she also presents "disability and mutual dependency as pervasive social goods." Misery, moreover, has to be dealt with at home, where it often also originates. Its fictional treatment, I wish to suggest, becomes significantly inflected by reactions to the sensation genre's appropriation of clinical discourses.[19]

In a counterpoise to sensation fiction's investment in sudden fits of emotional display and the acts of passion they may cause, Yonge concentrates almost invariably on protracted suffering. As it is put in an aside in *Hopes and Fears* (1860), it is "when the world supposes the sorrow to be over, and ordinary habits to be resumed" that real need for sympathy arises. Suicidal impulses can be evoked with great poignancy but seldom result in self-destruction. Nor are they subservient to detective plots as they often are in sensation novels, and hence the detailing of emotional distress can be accorded more space. Thus, in *The Trial* (1864), Leonard Ward's wrongful conviction for murder occurs early on in the plot, and the real culprit's death abroad releases him to the aftereffects of three and a half years of penal servitude. The trial scenes themselves certainly are "resolutely downplay[ed]," yet this is in order to foreground subsequent struggles.[20] In a similar vein, *The Clever Woman of the Family* (1865) shows that "recovery is often more trying than illness" as it describes the heroine's "excitement of nerve [and] morbid fancy," a "weary air of depression, too wistful and startled even to be melancholy repose," the result of "shattered nerves" after her nonetheless salutary humiliation at a public trial. Altogether, the main interest rests in "low" or "depressed spirits," although their impact on, or realization of, sensitive, spiritually intense characters tracks a revealingly changing spectrum of approaches.[21]

In *The Castle-Builders*, the heroine's problems can admittedly be traced all too directly to the delay of their confirmation. What Robert Wolff has praised as the novel's redeeming feature—its "vivid sketch of the terrible boredom . . . , what later generations would call neurasthenia and depression"—becomes obscured by concerns with doctrinal differences. Yonge here seems to ignore Keble's warning against too much discussion of doctrine. Her preface to *The Two Guardians* (1852) further sums up the "principle" *The Castle-Builders* had been meant to illustrate: "the instability and dissatisfaction of mind occasioned by the want of a practical, obedient course of daily life; with an especial view to the consequences of not seeking strength and assistance in the appointed means of grace." The resolution, in short, is anticlimactic to underscore the ease with which distress could have been prevented altogether. What are shown to be lapses from grace double as easily diagnosable symptoms: Emmeline fails to resist the temptation both of attending Roman Catholic mass (ostensibly for the music) and of identifying with Tennyson's Mariana in his eponymous poem of 1830. An exemplary clergyman symptomatically treats her experience of world-weariness as something "put on for the sake of poetry."[22] When she attempts to describe her misery by stating that she feels "like Mariana in the moated grange," sympathy collapses with a jarring abruptness:

> "My dear Emmie, I only want you to get rid of what is nonsense, and put on for the sake of poetry, and then perhaps we may be able to see what is the matter. I know you are unhappy and out of spirits, but at the same time you think it is a very fine thing to be weary of the world, and, till we get to your real self, I don't know how to talk to you."

> "You think all I have said affectation," said Emmeline, a good deal hurt.
> "No, by no means all, and quite unconsciously, but when we come to Mariana—" (*The Castle-Builders,* 279)

This is in pointed contrast to the evocation of Tennyson's Mariana in popular sensation fiction. More important still, it markedly differs from Yonge's own later accounts of emotional distress. In *The Castle-Builders,* clergymen may be called in like doctors to deal with world-weariness by highlighting the primacy of another world, yet no such easy resolution can be achieved in her subsequent works. Even in her most successful, emphatically domestic, family chronicle *The Daisy Chain* (1856), the neglect of Norman May's protracted experience of a "depression [that] was not wilful repining" after he witnesses the carriage accident that kills his mother and permanently injures his father and eldest sister is condemned as a recipe for brain fever. In a startling rejection of religious observance as refuge, he becomes "lounging, listless and forlorn, through the weary day, not always able to go out with his father, and on Christmas Day unfit even for church" (1: 152). Valerie Sanders lists Norman among a series of youngsters who suffer neglect in boisterous families, indicating that they can be very dysfunctional. Yet Sanders perhaps somewhat unfairly maintains that Norman "easily goes to pieces under pressure."[23] It is vital to note with what poignancy such familial neglect is evoked throughout Yonge's fiction. The novel's sequel, *The Trial,* identifies Leonard's low spirits with "Norman's dejected hopelessness" after his own ordeals at the same age: "'He is just the age that our Norman was.' That was the key to a great deal. Ethel knew that her father had never admitted any of the many excuses for the neglect of Norman's suffering." It is one of the most explicit acknowledgments of inadvertent emotional neglect at home.[24]

But if Leonard and Norman recover to become missionaries, *The Young Step-Mother* uncompromisingly rejects religious ritual as a "talisman" against low spirits, and this denotes the novel as Yonge's most skeptical treatment of various apparent solutions. Realizing that her birth in a remote area in India meant that she was only privately baptized, Sophy Kendal hopes that this may account for her recurrent low moods. She needs to be cautioned to "not think of [religious ritual] like a spell" (*Step-Mother,* 172). Neither a renewed baptism nor confirmation can act "like a charm, which will save you all further trouble with yourself," nor should it be regarded "in the light of a talisman" (*Step-Mother,* 179, 172). Instead, Sophy's hope is mercilessly undercut by her father's belief that her "tempers" are simply constitutional:

> "Ah! my child, I am afraid the tempers are a part of your physical constitution," he returned, mournfully. "You mean that I am like you, papa," said

> Sophy. "I think I might at least learn to be really like you, and if I must feel miserable, not to be unkind and sulky! And then I should leave off even the being unhappy about nothing."
>
> Her eyes brightened, but her father shook his head sadly, and said, "You would not be like me, my dear, if depression never made you selfish. But," he added, with an effort, "you will not suffer so much from low spirits when you are in better health, and able to move about." (*Step-Mother,* 174)

The Young Step-Mother exhibits an almost clinical interest in possibly hereditary moods and their increasingly sensationalized function in fiction. It not only provides Yonge's most extensive account of "being unhappy about nothing" by divorcing this sympathetically evoked experience from both, in modern parlance, posttraumatic reactions (exhibited by Leonard and Norman) and spiritual crises. It explores the treatment of sensitive temperaments at home and in society through a doubling of the high-spirited titular stepmother and her misunderstood, seemingly simply morose, stepdaughter. Albinia Ferrars marries Edmund Kendal, recently left a widower with three children, aged eleven to thirteen. His "melancholy is one of his charms in her eyes" (*Step-Mother,* 2). With an ironic reference to the proliferating governess novel, she is likewise "eager at the notion of being governess to the girls" (*Step-Mother,* 1). It is hardly surprising, therefore, that her brother and his wife fear her exploitation as "a maid-of-all-work" (*Step-Mother,* 94). The novel's early chapters focus primarily on the young stepmother's difficulties, which intriguingly become projected onto the almost preternatural influence of her new home's undoubtedly unhealthy pond. Even before the outbreak of typhus that carries off the first Mrs. Kendal and some of her children, all their English-born offspring die in infancy. Despite her emphatically buoyant spirits, Albinia becomes infected by an oppression that tries her "nerves and spirits" (*Step-Mother,* 102).

It is a domestic horror that even Albinia's embarrassed dismissal of a "duck pond [as] a funny subject for sentiment [and] spectres" cannot erase: "In truth, the terror, half real, half imaginary, had been a sorer burthen than all the positive cares for those unruly children, or their silent, melancholy father" (*Step-Mother,* 101-2). It is "a spectral haunting fancy that sickness lurked in the heavy, misty atmosphere" (*Step-Mother,* 24). Her nightmares of the four dead babies become exacerbated by the "awe" she feels at the eldest surviving child's "dim superstitious terror" of his dead twin brother's last call to him, which he believes means that he shall die young as well (*Step-Mother,* 53). It is part of the "chronicle of mistakes" indicated in the subtitle that Albinia fails in converting this terror into "a blessed and salutary restraint" (*Step-Mother,* 53). Having the pond drained additionally alienates the youngest stepdaughter, Sophy, since she associates it with the memory of her dead elder brother.

The pond's identification with Sophy's moods, moreover, undercuts the ostensibly salutary effects of a clinical approach, of a clearing up of the pond and the spread of morbidity it stands for: "Her voice was less hoarse and gruff since the pond had been no more, and she had acquired an expression, so suffering, so concentrated, so thoughtful, that, together with her heavy black eyebrows, large face, profuse black hair, and unlustrous eyes, it gave her almost a dwarfish air, increased by her awkward deportment" (119).

Mirrored by the pond, this is a deep, outwardly opaque sensitivity that her stepmother notably fails to fathom. As Sanders points out, Albinia considers her own family, the Ferrars, "as both morally and physically superior to the listless Kendal family into which she marries," yet this is, in fact, her main fallacy. Evincing her belief in the concept of hereditary sensitivities or temper, Albinia even coins the term "Kendalism" to describe "those troublesome Kendal feelings that always demonstrated themselves in some perverse manner," including in her own young children when they are at their most introspective (*Step-Mother,* 518, 510). In this, the novel is unequivocal in asserting the moral effects of affliction. Albinia is "unchecked" and "irresponsible" because she has "not previously been chastened by a life-long affliction" (*Step-Mother,* 116). As a salutary experience, it is in important contradistinction to the diagnosis of depression as a "morbid" or "clinical" condition. Although this at first sight implies the concept of suffering as a blessing, the novel's force rests in the sympathetic delineation of misunderstood unhappiness. Albinia is conscious that her "likings had taken a current absolutely contrary to all her preconceived notions" as she feels she ought to credit Sophy more for "her sullen truth," instead of basking in her sister's indiscriminate display of affection only because she is "superior in temper, amiability, and all the qualities that smooth the course of life" (*Step-Mother,* 74, 212). Unchecked, this more amenable temper notably leads to frivolity and an unhappy marriage. It is yet another instance of Albinia's inadvertent mismanagement.[25]

The heroine's replacement midway through the novel testifies the most forcefully to its defense of misunderstood sensitivity. What disqualifies Albinia is her "spring of spirits" (*Step-Mother,* 150). Sophy's reticence not only brings out Albinia's inability to recognize either her worth or her suffering but prevents any alignment with paraded sickliness as a symptom of goodness or femininity. Not only is Sophy's "awkward deportment" and suffering expression registered as a form of ugliness (*Step-Mother,* 119), but she self-consciously divorces the symptoms of her emotional suffering from what she pinpoints as the privileges often accorded to physical affliction. Thus, shortly after accidentally dropping her baby brother in an attempt to carry him off to exhibit him to some gossipy neighbors of whom her stepmother disproves (and hence in a fit of defiance), Sophy faints in church. It transpires that she suffers from a spinal complaint that has been causing her long-suppressed pain. Albinia blames herself for her neglect, yet as Sophy pointedly puts it, she "can't be forgiven only because [she is] ill" (*Step-Mother,* 142).[26]

A proliferation of subplots serves to underline this point. The vicar's invalid wife, a "little, clever, fairy-looking woman," may seem an awkward stereotype, "with her playful manner, high spirits, keen wit, and the active habits that even confirmed invalidism could not destroy" (*Step-Mother,* 42), yet she stands in a line of important opposites. Sophy's struggles with the emotional turmoil created by a disappointment in love—a disappointment, moreover, largely created by her stepmother's misguided encouragement of her passion for an indiscriminately friendly Irish clerk—also contrast sharply with her brother's selfish passion for a governess and his resentment of his parents' interference: "he lay about on the grass in doleful dejection, studied little but L.E.L., lost appetite, and reproachfully fondled his cough" (*Step-Mother,* 277). Once he lies dying abroad after proving himself by saving a relative's life in the Crimean War, he leaves off the habit of making the most of physical weaknesses: "How differently Gilbert wrote when really ill, from his desponding style when he only fancied himself so" (*Step-Mother,* 470).

This is the key to the novel's exploration of emotional distress and its "symptoms": "One good thing about Sophy [is] that she will never talk her feelings to death" (*Step-Mother,* 209, 230). Significantly, this is not suppression but the reticence of a (like the pond) "deep" temperament. Her "apparently cold, sullen, impassive spirit" is long unrecognized by a stepmother absorbed in her "cherished vision" of the "education of 'Edmund's children'" (*Step-Mother,* 577, 128). If the pond's opaqueness already reflects the difficult realization of Albinia's vision and serves as the mirror image of what needs to be recognized as Sophy's "low spirits, far more than temper" (*Step-Mother,* 156), its erasure expresses the dangers of containment or depletion. More than the draining of the pond, removing associations with a moated grange, the circumvention of the attic further realizes Yonge's remapping of the imagery of emotional distress, including literary traditions of melancholia and their sensationalization at midcentury. In an additional opposition of physical and emotional affliction, an invalid grandmother literally upsets domestic arrangements. Sophy is threatened with banishment into the attic until her father gives up his study—his own untouchable refuge—since "she must have some retreat" (*Step-Mother,* 210). Albinia notably counters that seeking solitude "did [him] no good," and therefore "letting these fits have their swing [cannot be] good for Sophy" either, yet her father not only insists that they "must not be harshly treated" but also rejects all "compulsion," including banishment into the margins of the house (*Step-Mother,* 210-211). Sophy's converted morning room is to offer a retreat that is nonetheless at the domestic center.

Throughout Yonge's fiction, invalids are moved from the hidden spaces of the household into the drawing room, where they become the center of "dyads of care," as Stoddard Holmes has convincingly argued. Comparatively little has been made of Yonge's treatment of emotional or mental forms of "affliction," although her novels of the 1860s increasingly focus on the effects of their neglect, often in juxtaposition with physical illness. In *The Daisy Chain,* it is understandable that Norman's shock is undervalued at a general moment of family crisis, but in its replication in *The Trial,* there is less excuse for "medical harshness" (*Trial,* 40). After his anticlimactic release from prison, Leonard suffers from "the remains of morbid oppression," and it takes Dr. May a painfully long time to acknowledge "the temptation to us doctors to ascribe too much to the physical and too little to the moral" (*Trial,* 387, 370). As Oppenheim has pointed out with reference to Dr. John's admission that "medicine can give nobody good spirits" in Brontë's *Villette* (1853), this is "a confession, needless to say, that came more easily to fictitious than to practicing medical men." Given Yonge's noted submission to patriarchal authority, this resistance to medical opinion may seem remarkable, yet it is an essential part of her assertion of the primacy of spiritual strength so that "if body and mind come out unscathed, it is the soundness of the spirit that has brought them through" (*Trial,* 372). The end of *The Trial* highlights this function of her religious orientation: "Mind and body may be hurt, and it is not possible to know one's mind from one's soul while one is alive, but as long as the will and faith are right, to think the soul can be hurt seems to me like doubting our Protector" (*Trial,* 374-75).[27]

This resistance to the medicalization of emotional or spiritual difficulties informs Yonge's most self-reflexive reworking of expected plotlines. As *The Young Step-Mother* negotiates various approaches to protracted emotional distress, it intriguingly posits an alternative to the conventional marriage plot as a narrative solution. Sophy's disappointment has "an entirely contrary tendency on her" instead of acting as the "trouble . . . proverbially the most hardening and exacerbating" (*Step-Mother,* 579). She survives lovesickness in a final disruption of her stepmother's simplistic surmises. They boil down to a quickly rehearsed and as quickly dismissed sensational plotline: "Illness—brain-fever—permanent ill-health and crushed spirits—nay, death itself she augured—and all—all her own fault!" (*Step-Mother,* 564). Instead, Sophy becomes "sweet and gentle towards all" (*Step-Mother,* 579). At the same time, there is no succumbing to resignation through physical repining, no cloistering of the disappointed heroine. On the contrary, the transformation of her morning room into a center of larger communal and familial interests generates a coming away from the threats of the attic and the pond. It is a resolution that needs neither a contrived marriage ending nor a medicalized "recovery" from sensitivity. In fact, if feminist suspicions of the "fragile, pale, ethereal, . . . in some sense 'sick,'" heroine have edged out a wealth of Victorian women writers, their complexities deserve another look. Far from not fitting the paradigms outlined by Gilbert and Gubar's germinal work, they lead us back to the initial, long-ignored combination of canonical and noncanonical, realist and sensational as well as more generally supernatural texts in *The Madwoman in the Attic.* Most significantly, they show that the structure of doubling and projection in nineteenth-century women's writing was remarkably adaptable as well as pervasive.[28]

Notes

1. Nicola Diane Thompson, "Responding to the Woman Question: Rereading Noncanonical Victorian Women Novelists," in *Victorian Women Writers and the Woman Question,* ed. Nicola Diane Thompson (Cambridge: Cambridge University Press, 1999), 2.

2. Charlotte Yonge, *The Young Step-Mother; Or, A Chronicle of Mistakes* (Gloucester, U.K.: Dodo Press, n.d. [1861]), 135. Subsequent references will be given parenthetically.

3. Sandra M. Gilbert and Susan Gubar, *The Madwoman in the Attic: The Woman Writer and the Nineteenth-Century Literary Imagination* (New Haven: Yale University Press, 1979), 341. Subsequent references will be given parenthetically.

4. Janet Oppenheim, *"Shattered Nerves": Doctors, Patients, and Depression in Victorian England* (Oxford: Oxford University Press, 1991), 10; Winifred Hughes, *The Maniac in the Cellar: Sensation Novels of the 1860s* (Princeton: Princeton University Press, 1980), passim. Gilbert and Gubar's *Norton Anthology of Literature by Women* (New York: W. W. Norton, 1985) features more specific references to sensation fiction as "a newly viable—and popular—genre in which [women] could work" (185). I shall come back to the significance of their inclusion of George Eliot's *The Lifted Veil.*

5. Pamela Gilbert, *Disease, Desire, and the Body in Victorian Women's Popular Novels* (Cambridge: Cambridge University Press, 1997), 2; Karen Chase and Michael Levenson, *The Spectacle of Intimacy: A Public Life for the Victorian Family* (Princeton: Princeton University Press, 2000), 7; Andrew Maunder, "General Introduction," *Varieties of Women's Sensation Fiction: 1855–1890,* vol. 1, ed. Andrew Maunder (London: Pickering and Chatto, 2004), xi.

6. Charles Reade, *Hard Cash* (London: Chatto and Windus, 1863), 259. Subsequent references will be given parenthetically.

7. John Reed, *Victorian Conventions* (Athens: Ohio University Press, 1975), 202. Wilkie Collins, *The Law and the Lady* (London: Penguin, 1998), 264. In a reworking of Collins's detective plot involving a husband accused of having murdered his first—suicidal—wife, Braddon's version sees him confined in an asylum abroad for a year, part of which he spends in a "cage." *The Fatal Three* (Stroud, U.K.: Sutton, 1997).

8. Mary Elizabeth Braddon, *Lady Audley's Secret* (Oxford: Oxford University Press, 1998), 205. Subsequent references will be cited parenthetically.

9. Rick Rylance, *Victorian Psychology and British Culture* (Oxford: Oxford University Press, 2000), 114.

10. Charlotte Brontë, *Jane Eyre* (New York: Everyman, 1991), 1: 11; Janet Gezari, "Sandra M. Gilbert and Susan Gubar's *The Madwoman in the Attic*," *Essays in Criticism* 56, no. 3 (2006): 264; Elaine Showalter, *A Literature of Their Own: British Women Novelists from Brontë to Lessing* (Princeton: Princeton University Press, 1977), 165. Compare also Showalter's analysis of "the densely symbolic red-room" (*Literature,* 114) and *Madwoman,* 473.

11. Showalter, *Literature,* 113; Gezari, "Sandra M. Gilbert," 264; Susanne Becker, *Gothic Forms of Feminine Fictions* (Manchester: Manchester University Press, 1999), 10.

12. Lyn Pykett, "Sensation and the Fantastic in the Victorian Novel," in *The Cambridge Companion to the Victorian Novel,* ed. Deirdre David (Cambridge: Cambridge University Press, 2001), 198; Hughes, *Maniac,* 70. Showalter refers to discomfort "with the notion of a 'female imagination'" (*Literature,* 12). On the evolution of a "sensational criticism," see Anna Maria Jones's introduction in *Problem Novels: Victorian Fiction Theorizes the Sensational Self* (Columbus: Ohio State University Press, 2007).

13. Betsy Draine, "Refusing the Wisdom of Solomon: Some Recent Feminist Literary Theory," *Signs* 15, no. 1 (1989): 155; Gilbert and Gubar, *Madwoman,* 473.

14. Marlene Tromp, *The Private Rod: Marital Violence, Sensation, and the Law in Victorian Britain* (Charlottesville: University Press of Virginia, 2000), 161; June Sturrock, "Murder, Gender, and Popular Fiction by Women in the 1860s: Braddon, Oliphant, Yonge," in *Victorian Crime, Madness and Sensation,* ed. Andrew Maunder and Grace Moore (Aldershot: Ashgate, 2004), 74, 76; June Sturrock, "Sequels, Series, and Sensation Novels: Charlotte Yonge and the Popular Fiction Market of the 1850s and 1860s," in *Part Two: Reflections on the Sequel,* ed. Paul Budra and Betty A. Schellenberg (Toronto: University of Toronto Press, 1998), 105. Sturrock suggests that as "a committed Anglo-Catholic propagandist," Yonge "might hardly distinguish between these two purposes" ("Sequels," 110).

15. Lillian Nayder, "Introduction to *Hidden Depths,*" *Varieties of Women's Sensation Fiction: 1855–1890,* vol. 4, ed. Lillian Nayder (London: Pickering and Chatto, 2004), xii.

16. Thompson, "Responding," 7; Barbara Dennis, introduction to *Reform and Intellectual Debate in Victorian England,* ed. Barbara Dennis and David Skilton (London: Croom Helm, 1987), 14–15; Emma Liggins and Andrew Maunder, "Reassessing Nineteenth-Century Popular Fiction by Women, 1825–1880," *Women's Writing* 11, no. 1 (2004): 5; Talia Schaffer, "British Non-Canonical Women Novelists, 1850–1900: Recent Studies," *Dickens Studies Annual* 37 (2006): 336. In "Women and Domestic Culture," Schaffer warns against the pitfalls of traditional "advocacy feminism," which "like Foucaldian criticism, risks incorporating all artifacts into pre-set narratives that may flatten out what is actually a much more complicated set of representations" (*Victorian Literature and Culture* 35, no. 1 [2007]: 386). Gavin Budge, "Realism and Typology in Charlotte M. Yonge's *The Heir of Redclyffe,*" *Victorian Literature and Culture* 31, no. 1 (2003): 201, 197; Maria Poggi Johnson, "The Reason for What Is Right: Practical Wisdom in John Keble and Charlotte Yonge," *Literature and Theology* 20, no. 4 (2006): 390; Valerie Sanders, "'All-sufficient to one another'? Charlotte Yonge and the Family Chronicle," in *Popular Victorian Women Writers,* ed. Kay Boardman and Shirley Jones (Manchester: Manchester University Press, 2004), 107.

17. Catherine Sandbach-Dahlström, *Be Good Sweet Maid: Charlotte Yonge's Domestic Fiction* (Stockholm: Almqvist and Wiksell International, 1984), 1; Barbara Dennis, *Charlotte Yonge (1823–1901): Novelist of the Oxford Movement* (Lewiston, N.Y.: Edwin Mellen, 1992), 2, 56; Vineta Colby, *Yesterday's Woman: Domestic Realism in the English Novel* (Princeton: Princeton University Press, 1974), 186–87; Colby, *Yesterday's Woman,* 200; David Brownell, "The Two Worlds of Charlotte Yonge," in *The Worlds of Victorian Fiction,* ed. Jerome H. Buckley (Cambridge: Harvard University Press, 1975), 168.

18. As Margaret Mare and Alicia Percival put it, "Fortunately, her characters usually got beyond their creator's conscious control, and, impelled by some inner necessity, developed as they would" (*Victorian Best-Seller: The World of Charlotte M. Yonge* [London: George G. Harrap, 1947], 5). Sandbach-Dahlström similarly suggests that "at an imaginative level Charlotte Yonge, as implied author, has access to patterns of thought and feeling that do not accord with the ideology she sets out to preach" (*Be Good Sweet Maid,* 107).

19. Martha Stoddard Holmes, *Fictions of Affliction: Physical Disability in Victorian Culture* (Ann Arbor: University of Michigan Press, 2004), 51–52. In "Victorian Fictions of Interdependency: Gaskell, Craik, and Yonge," Holmes similarly applies a disability studies model to suggest that such fictions of interdependency "engage disability as a force that brings people into a wide range of complex relationships" (*Journal of Literary Disability* 1, no. 2 [2007]: 30).

20. Charlotte Yonge, *Hopes and Fears* (London: John W. Parker and Son, 1860), 1: 155; subsequent references will appear parenthetically. Budge, "Realism" 204. Differentiating between the sensational elements the novel takes up (murder, trials) and those it rejects (female dissidence), Sturrock suggests that the novel "masculinises" its central murder trial by avoiding putting women in the dock: "Reluctant to address commonplace female fictional delinquency (bigamy, adultery), Yonge turns to violent crime, and keeps herself in the current market with a brutal murder" ("Murder," 75).

21. Charlotte Yonge, *The Clever Woman of the Family* (Peterborough, Ont.: Broadview, 2001), 373, 442, 435, 436. Subsequent references will appear parenthetically. Even though the inherited "Morville temper" renders the hero of *The Heir of Redclyffe* (1853) Byronic until he learns to control such fits of temper, it is as much characterized by "his depression" as by any violent outbursts: he has "an air of sadness and depression" that makes him seem "unstable" (Yonge, *The Heir of Redclyffe* [London: Duckworth, 1964], 152, 191, 223).

22. Robert Lee Wolff, *Gains and Losses: Novels of Faith and Doubt in Victorian England* (New York: Garland, 1977), 126, 122–23; Charlotte Yonge, *The Two Guardians* (New York: Appleton, 1871), 4; Yonge, *The Castle-Builders; Or, The Deferred Confirmation* (New York: Appleton, 1855), 279. Subsequent references will appear parenthetically.

23. Charlotte Yonge, *The Daisy Chain* (McLean, Va.: IndyPublish, n.d.), 1: 153, 138–39; subsequent references will appear parenthetically. Sanders, "All-sufficient," 100. Sanders suggests that especially "physically weaker children go under, with too much schoolwork and pressure to win scholarships, or succeed musically" (98); the casualties include Norman May in *The Daisy Chain* as well as both Felix and Lance Underwood in *The Pillars of the House* (1873).

24. Charlotte Yonge, *The Trial* (Doylestown, Pa.: Wildside, n.d.), 52, 36. Subsequent references will appear parenthetically. Sensational writing translates the suicidal self-abandonment encapsulated in Tennyson's iconic poem into fiction. In Braddon's *John Marchmont's Legacy* (1863), Mariana's "moated grange" becomes the disappointing realization of the heroine's castles in the air and an apt image of both her own and the antiheroine's sense of confinement.

25. Sanders, "All-sufficient," 96.

26. Discussing the alterations between the narrative's original serialization and its publication in book form, Amy de Gruchy stresses that in both versions Sophy is "a girl of great integrity, intelligence and learning," yet in the serial she is also a gifted writer and comic actress, which accords her even more centrality. "*The Young Stepmother*—The Serial and the Book," *Review of the Charlotte Mary Yonge Fellowship* 3 (1996): http://www.dur.ac.uk/c.e.schultze/review/review.html.

27. Holmes, "Victorian Fictions," 35; Charlotte Brontë, *Villette* (Oxford: Clarendon, 1984), 261; Oppenheim, *Shattered Nerves,* 116. This rejection of medical conceptualizations of "low spirits" and the "shattered nerves" that came to be diagnosed as neurasthenia later in the century proposes alternative interpretations of emotional experience and its evaluation. For a detailed discussion of *The Trial,* see Tamara S. Wagner, "Depressed Spirits and Failed Crisis Management: Charlotte Yonge's Sensationalisation of the Religious Family," *Victorians Institute Journal* 36 (2008): 275–302.

28. Gilbert and Gubar, *Norton,* 170. While it has been remarked that Yonge's creation of marriageable invalided women explodes "the pervasive Victorian (and later) message that disabled girls do not marry, in the process offering a commentary on the limitations and possibilities of marriage as an institution" (Holmes, "Victorian Fictions," 30), here Yonge moves further to suggest an alternative for women: a fulfilled life.

11

Ghosts in the Attic

Gilbert and Gubar's *The Madwoman in the Attic* and the Female Gothic

Carol Margaret Davison

Nearly thirty years after its initial publication, Sandra M. Gilbert and Susan Gubar's *The Madwoman in the Attic: The Woman Writer and the Nineteenth-Century Literary Imagination* (1979) remains an influential and groundbreaking work of feminist literary criticism. Despite the problems attendant on the application of a critical master theory to a broad cross-section of literary texts, the major insights of *Madwoman* still stand up under scrutiny. Indeed, its sixteen chapters devoted to the principal canonical works of the nineteenth century produced by women writers are rare in their sustained and cogent analysis and rich evidentiary detail. As reflected in the existing critical literature and relevant discussion groups, *Madwoman* has been, and remains, valuable to scholars in the fields of Victorian literature and women's studies. As Solveig C. Robinson has noted, *Madwoman*'s "influence can be traced through many branches of contemporary critical thought and in many works on the history and psychology of nineteenth-century literature."[1] Its impact on feminist literary criticism has been especially pronounced: the idea that women's texts are palimpsests, encoding doubleness in the form of a dominant and a muted story, has left a particularly indelible stamp on the field of women's studies.

Significantly, despite its innumerable points of contact with and tremendous relevance to Gothic studies, Gilbert and Gubar's landmark work has been generally ignored by specialists in that field. In the rare instance where it has been recognized, the response has been either one of celebration or indictment. Susanne Becker, for example, takes her cue from Margaret Atwood in her interpretation of the "madwoman in the attic" as an "attractive" figure for inclusion in what she calls "feminine fictions" as she encodes both imprisonment within and liberation from sociocultural constraints as played out in narrative.[2] At the other end of the critical spectrum, Alison Milbank condemns *Madwoman* as exemplifying what she calls a "male" Gothic paradigm in its orchestration of "narrative tropes of penetration into a secluded and privileged interior—here Western literary history—by a deliberately transgressive protagonist—itself, or the woman writer—who in turn seeks release from the limits to her identity fashioned by society, history and morality."[3]

I will return to Milbank's provocative yet problematic assessment of *Madwoman*'s driving paradigm in due course. It is my contention that *Madwoman* is principally a study of nineteenth-century *female* Gothic whose recognition by contemporary Gothicists would enrich, among other things, their understanding and conception of the Gothic's historical trajectory.[4] Perhaps most telling is the use of Gothic-inflected tropes that pepper Gilbert and Gubar's second chapter, "Infection in the Sentence: The Woman Writer and the Anxiety of Influence." Likewise, the "curious collocation" between the Gothic and contemporary critical theory that has been identified by David Punter in such key works as Jacques Derrida's *Spectres of Marx* (1993) and cited as evidence of literary criticism getting unobjectively "too close to its subject matter" is also on exhibit in *Madwoman* and bears special consideration in the light of their gender-aware enterprise.[5]

Like Bloom's theory on the anxiety of influence, Gilbert and Gubar also produced a work of "literary psychohistory" that exhibits a tremendous anxiety of influence on at least two major counts.[6] First, they fail to recognize the centrality of the female Gothic to the female literary "tradition" they identify that defies illness-inducing "male mimicry" (*Madwoman*, 71). They specifically neglect the works of Ann Radcliffe and *The Mysteries of Udolpho*, but their madwoman (and Charlotte Brontë's) is Radcliffe's long-lost daughter. Especially due to the Gothic's long-standing association with women readers and writers and Gilbert and Gubar's feminist agenda, the selection of the female Gothic as their primary heuristic template is an extremely canny choice. Second, despite their acknowledgment of Ellen Moers's category of the female Gothic, coined in an article in 1974 in the *New York Review of Books* and more popularly disseminated in 1976 in her *Literary Women*, they also perpetuate some of the biases upheld by the 1970s literary critical establishment that denied the Gothic any authority and vilified and marginalized it as a peculiarly "feminized" form.[7] One of the foremost questions that arises, therefore, is why Gilbert and Gubar especially shy away in *Madwoman* from the concept of the *female* Gothic. They mention it only once in relation to the works of George Eliot and fail, in that instance, even to define or discuss the term (*Madwoman,* 445). Exploration of the ghosts of literary/critical foremothers in *Madwoman*'s figurative attic may provide some clues as to the reasons and possible strategy underpinning this elision. In the final analysis, a certain irony may be said to obtain in Gilbert and Gubar's promotion of the recognition of literary foremothers—also a central component of the female Gothic plot—in the light of their own act of disregarding certain key "foremother" texts.

Intersections of Gender and Genre

Ellen Moers coined the term "female Gothic" in her 1974 article in reference to a mode of literature, emerging in the eighteenth century, that tapped women's fears about sexuality and childbirth.[8] Such feminist-based theorizing, focused on the intersections between gender and genre, occurred over the course of the next decade in relation to other literary and critical categories. Theorists of the female bildungsroman, for example, began to demonstrate how gender was a vital component in that genre. Elizabeth Abel, Marianne Hirsch, and Elizabeth Langland in *The Voyage In: Fictions of Female Development* (1983) argued that the notion of development and the ideal of success were gender-contingent, and that men and women were impeded, judged, and nurtured in radically different ways. Gender was an extremely "pertinent category" that modified "every aspect of a particular *Bildungsroman*: its narrative structure, its implied psychology, its representation of social pressures."[9] Taking their cue from Moers, theorists of the female Gothic like Juliann Fleenor and Joanna Russ likewise called attention to the fact that women's generally repressed fears and desires—Gothic's twin fascinations—were socially contingent and differed dramatically from those of their male counterparts.[10]

The Madwoman in the Attic was at the forefront of these noteworthy developments in genre theory. Although they selected the potent narrative figure of Charlotte Brontë's Bertha Rochester, the so-called madwoman in the attic, as the basis for their theoretical paradigm, Gilbert and Gubar were implicitly engaged in genre theory. Their generically expansive, broad-based study sought to examine the "contradictions of genre and gender" and worked from the articulated premise that "most Western literary genres are . . . essentially male—devised by male authors to tell male stories about the world" (*Madwoman,* 67). Gilbert and Gubar assume the role of the paradigmatic pseudo-detective female Gothic protagonist in their attentiveness to such aforementioned contradictions and their elucidation of decidedly female stories within a patriarchal literary tradition.

Jane Eyre was doing double duty in much literary criticism of the 1970s as both the prototypical Victorian female bildungsroman and as a female Gothic novel. Contrary to Jerome Beaty's 1977 claim that "discussions of *Jane Eyre* and genre usually center on the Gothic," the novel's place as a bildungsroman was also a key point of discussion.[11] Gilbert and Gubar's choice of *Jane Eyre* was particularly apt given its dual nature and the fact that the bildungsroman constituted the preeminent novelistic genre in the Victorian era upon which they focus their attention.

The Gothic may be said to be, as I have argued elsewhere, the bildungsroman's dark mirror.[12] These two forms are not as distinct as might be supposed. While both the female Gothic and the bildungsroman concentrate on a young woman's rite of passage into womanhood, her vexed experiences of love and romance, and her ambivalent relationship to the multifaceted ideology of femininity, particularly the constraining roles advocated for women and the joint institutions of marriage and motherhood, the female Gothic deploys the supernatural for political ends. As Eugenia C. DeLamotte explains in *Perils of the Night: A Feminist Study of Nineteenth-Century Gothic,* "The 'fear of power' embodied in Gothic romance is a fear not only of supernatural powers but also of social forces so vast and impersonal that they seem to have supernatural strength." Paternal/patriarchal authority and institutions come under especially intense scrutiny in the female Gothic. More specifically, in the words of James P. Carson, the female Gothic "focuses intensely on a violation of just those ideals of sociability and rational intercourse that the Enlightenment prized and promoted." The female Gothic, however, often renders the violation of such ideals in veiled, sexualized terms, in keeping with the nature of the threats experienced by women. Although they are generally rendered in more implicit, subtle ways, Ann Radcliffe's terrors "are the specifically female terrors of physical assault: terrors, as has been often observed, that woman authors of sentimental and gothic novels do not explicitly chronicle, unlike novelists such as Samuel Richardson or Matthew 'Monk' Lewis who permit scenes of sexual assault and counsel the restitution of Lucretia." As Sybil Korff Vincent extrapolates, the female Gothic "expresses conflicts within the female regarding her own sexuality and identity, and uses a highly stylized form and elaborate detail to effect psychic catharsis."[13]

The most significant component in the female Gothic's cathartic process is the stylized space in which it occurs—the domestic sphere, a symbolically loaded, psychically resonant site associated with familial inheritance.[14] If a single trope is obsessively reiterated in the female Gothic as crystallizing the experience of female terror, that trope is the confined woman. The sense of oppressive and invariable confinement so plagues the protagonist's course in this genre that D. A. Miller labels it the "feminine carceral." In such texts, as DeLamotte cleverly states, women "just can't seem to get out of the house."[15] While the house is such a central image in women's novels generally, it assumes a more symbolically charged dimension in Gothic fiction. According to Eva Figes, "In the clear light of the courtship novel it represents security and status. The house of the bridegroom, into which the heroine will move after marriage, is always of prime importance. . . . But in the Gothic novel the house changes from being a symbol of male privilege and protection conferred on the fortunate female of his choice, to an image of male power in its sinister aspect, threatening and oppressive."[16]

Kate Ellis concurs, claiming that the home represented in the female Gothic is "the place from which some (usually 'fallen' men) are locked out, and others (usually 'innocent' women) are locked in." Especially in its capacity as a "nighttime house," this locale "admits all we can imagine into it of the dark, frightening, and unknown." It is not surprising that the popular conception of the haunted house sees its origins in this Enlightenment-based literary form, and assumes an especially powerful signification in this branch of the dark romance.[17]

Women writers of the female Gothic hijacked the form for their own ends at a noteworthy historical moment—namely, when the rising middle classes were in the process of "renovating" both the domestic sphere and the institution of marriage. The domestic sphere was fast becoming a gendered site of consumption as opposed to production during this era and a middle-class patriarchy was attempting to put women, quite literally, in their place. Such a monumental alteration of women's position in the domestic economy was profound in its consequences as it divested them of any possibility of obtaining power in the marketplace. Women's economic role, as Dorinda Outram has noted, was increasingly replaced by an emotional one during this era. Drawing upon the Gothic genre, which explored the dark side of modernity, the female Gothic advanced a gender-aware commentary on modern institutions by way of a point-blank portrait of domestic relations.[18] As DeLamotte relates, "Women's Gothic shows women suffering from institutions they feel to be profoundly alien to them and their concerns. And those institutions were all too contemporaneous with the lives of the women who wrote and read Gothic literature in the 1790s and early 1800s: the patriarchal family, the patriarchal marriage, and a patriarchal class, legal, educational, and economic system."[19] The female Gothic castle/house mirrored woman's "ambivalent experience of entrapment and longing for protection" within these institutions. Front and center in the female Gothic is the idea, as Tamar Heller has nicely observed, of "the house *as* institution."[20]

The seemingly exaggerated themes and threats of incarceration, violation, and death often cryptically articulated in the female Gothic are rendered more comprehensible when one considers that the domestic sphere was where most middle- and upper-class women of the late eighteenth and early nineteenth centuries spent the majority of their lives. It was also the site where many died in childbirth. These anxieties were further compounded by the fact that women of the era were both commodified and rendered *femmes couvertes* under established law. As the jurist William Blackstone described the doctrine of coverture in his *Commentaries on the Laws of England* in 1765, "The husband and wife are one person in law; that is, the very being or legal existence of the woman is suspended during the marriage, or at least is incorporated and consolidated into that of the husband: under whose total protection and cover, she performs everything."[21] E. J. Clery further details, "Among the real consequences of this principle were the following: the husband took control of the whole of his wife's property, past, present and future; he had sole rights over their children; a married woman could not enter into any legal agreement or lawsuit on her own behalf; she could not bring proceedings against her husband in common law; and, since her 'very being' was suspended, she no longer held property in her own person, Locke's minimum condition for civil rights."[22] As these descriptions make clear, women assumed the status of their husbands' property, an ironic (and sinister) development at a time when men were engaged in establishing their democratic rights. In stark contrast, women's autonomy and identity were being entirely denied, leaving them at the mercy of their husbands. While companionate marriage, the new middle-class ideal, was based in theory on affection, mutual concerns, and sympathy, the wife remained subordinate to her husband under law. The romantic ideal treacherously disguised the existing reality where women remained powerless handmaidens to men.

Such a complex and weighty sociohistoric backdrop not only informs the female Gothic, it is equally relevant to Gilbert and Gubar's *Madwoman,* especially the figure of the madwoman herself and her doppelgänger, Jane Eyre, Rochester's wife-in-waiting. Indeed, key female Gothic tropes and dynamics are writ large in *Madwoman*'s driving theoretical paradigm. Gilbert and Gubar's master theory combined the female Gothic's most potent motifs: self-divided women authors who were labeled freakish, "unsexed," or "fallen," who penned palimpsestic works containing ambivalent (conformist yet rebellious) female doppelgängers "trapped in the architecture—both the houses and the institutions—of patriarchy" (*Madwoman,* 63, 85). They claim that "dramatizations of imprisonment and escape are so all-pervasive in nineteenth-century literature by women that . . . they represent a uniquely female tradition in this period" (85) and "spatial constrictions" such as those in the works of Ann Radcliffe are found regularly in novels of manners, domestic tales, and lyric poems (85). This universalizing overtly and problematically denies Radcliffe's act of fostering a literary tradition and her hugely influential role on her eighteenth- and nineteenth-century literary daughters. Radcliffe's "melodramatic dungeons," as Gilbert and Gubar call them, serve, however, as the principal source of the "obsessive imagery of confinement" they identify in women's writing (83, 65). Bringing the key informing motif of Charlotte Perkins Gilman's "The Yellow Wallpaper"—a work examined in Gilbert and Gubar's theoretical framework—to bear on *Madwoman,* the figure of Ann Radcliffe may be obscured but she is nonetheless discernible in every page.

Although Radcliffe is not positioned as a primary entry point into their study, she is unarguably *the* principal foremother of Gilbert and Gubar's theoretical paradigm. In this occlusion, Gilbert and Gubar resist acknowledging Michel Foucault's claim in his 1969 article "What Is an Author?" that Ann Radcliffe served as "the founder of a discursive practice that had an impact well into the nineteenth century and beyond."[23] Radcliffe is a fitting foremother for the literary tradition identified by Gilbert and Gubar because she was conscious of the gendered nature of literary genres. In her posthumously published essay, "On the Supernatural in Poetry" (1802; 1826), she distinguishes between two types of Gothic—*terror Gothic,* which she tacitly associates with her own work, and *horror Gothic,* which she associates with the much more sensational work of Matthew Lewis. While she characterized the former as "feminine," intended to expand the soul by bringing it into contact with sublime objects of terror, the latter was more "masculine" as it focused on encounters with graphically detailed mortality. In Radcliffe's words, "Terror and horror are so far opposite, that the first expands the soul, and awakens the faculties to a high degree of life; the other contracts, freezes, and nearly annihilates them."[24]

Radcliffe is also suitable as a foremother for *Madwoman* because of the battles she fought on behalf of women writers to legitimate their enterprise. The Gothic was viewed "as an impassioned, and hence suspect, subliterary form" largely because it was perceived as "feminized": the majority of its producers and consumers were women. But Radcliffe established a standard and a new formula that garnered immense respect and a larger, broader readership, earning her titles such as "the Shakespeare of Romance Writers," "Queen of the tremendous," and "the first poetess of romantic fiction." Perhaps with the astute advice of her legally trained husband, William, a newspaper proprietor who had been trained at Oxford's Inner Temple, she also made a noteworthy amount of money from her writing. Her "extraordinary contract" of £500 for *The Mysteries of Udolpho* in 1794 "exactly doubled the previous highest copyright fee for novels known to us." She followed this up with £800 for *The Italian* in 1797. Radcliffe presents "a successful case study," therefore, of how women writers could navigate "a course between erudition and popular appeal to address the new inconsistently-educated mass audience." The tremendous popularity of her novels inspired a slew of imitators—predominantly women—who have since been accused of plunging her work into disrepute. Annette Cafarelli has called attention to the gender-based biases against Radcliffe, whereby the profusion and redundancy of her imitators drew her work into discredit while their "carloads" of imitators contributed to the reputations of various male writers.[25]

That Ann Radcliffe early on redirected the Gothic's lens to the figure of the persecuted heroine who risks incarceration, madness, and even death in the domestic sphere testified to her canny abilities to seize an opportunity to strategically (because covertly) register women's concerns. Due to its commercialized character, low cultural status, and structural openness, the novel in general, and the Gothic novel more specifically, offered women writers a unique venue in which to engage in a variety of important cultural debates. As Gary Kelly has cogently argued, subsequent to its establishment as a distinct literary type in the 1790s the Gothic novel became a dialogical "field of struggle" where "individual works . . . often seem[ed] to be in dialogue and dispute with one another—not so much taking up successful devices of a predecessor as redeploying those devices, or deploying different ones, to counter the predecessor's cultural politics."[26] The female Gothic ratcheted this up a notch by speaking back to the Gothic "mainstream" from a specifically gender-aware perspective. As such, Radcliffe initiated more than a purely *aesthetic* revolution, as Wylie Sypher has erroneously claimed. Rather, she was at the forefront of what Gary Kelly has rightly characterized as a "middle-class *cultural* revolution."[27]

In their consideration of the exact nature and source of the subversive "female" plot they identify, one that calls into question the patriarchal status, Gilbert and Gubar wonder, "What is this other plot? Is there only *one* other plot?" (*Madwoman,* 75). The plot derives, as I am suggesting, from the female Gothic as conceived and fostered by Ann Radcliffe, a form in which those women writers examined in *Madwoman* were well versed, as seen by the numerous "Gothic closets"[28]—subplots marked by Gothic conventions and tropes—found in their works. There were, in short, certain important literary foremothers, like Radcliffe, who were not as obscure as Gilbert and Gubar suggest in *Madwoman.* Their critical act of reconsidering and reconnecting with women's literary history of the nineteenth century nevertheless engaged in the process of reclamation that preoccupied much second-wave feminist scholarship. This reclamation process intriguingly paralleled that of such female Gothic heroines as Emily St. Aubert in *The Mysteries of Udolpho,* whose intrepid acts of exploring and deciphering the tragic, mysterious, and repressed histories of their foremothers are fundamental to their journeys towards self-knowledge. Indeed, in the tragic tale in *Mysteries* of Signora Laurentini, a passion-driven woman turned criminal whose act of murder ultimately results in her overwhelming remorse and madness, Radcliffe offers up the mother of Charlotte Brontë's impassioned Bertha Rochester.

In identifying and theorizing about the ingredients comprising the female Gothic plot, Gilbert and Gubar significantly advance the work of *Madwoman*'s other critical foremother, Virginia Woolf. In *A Room of One's Own* (1929), Woolf argues that women writers "had no tradition behind them, or one so short and partial that it was of little help." "For we think back through our mothers," she says, "if we are women."[29] Just as the women writers Gilbert and Gubar consider were not entirely aware of the numerous influences at play in their works (John Milton was not the only poet to cast a shadow) neither were these feminist critics entirely aware of their own influence in their "epic struggle with nineteenth-century literary tradition."[30] Indeed, only now in the light of the expansive field of Gothic studies may the full extent of that genre's influence on *Madwoman* be recognized.

Conversely, many of Gilbert and Gubar's insights have fed into female Gothic scholarship without being openly acknowledged. Whether or not the Gothic was a conscious or unconscious focus, Gilbert and Gubar's decision not to foreground it was smart given the contentious nature of that form in the 1970s. Battles remained to be fought to acknowledge the Gothic as a legitimate domain of scholarship worthy of academic attention. Further, the idea of there being a Gothic *tradition* was an even more contentious issue that would involve numerous lengthy debates. Especially in terms of the female Gothic, those debates are ongoing. They are particularly explosive around the designation of the very category: many critics have undermined it—as they have several of *Madwoman*'s underpinning theoretical foundations—as essentialist and prone to universalizing women's experiences.[31]

Ironically, in identifying the nineteenth-century woman writer's agenda in *Madwoman,* Gilbert and Gubar simultaneously articulate their own feminist agenda of conforming to yet subverting established literary standards and obscuring but not obliterating their most radical impulses and influences. Perhaps the most substantial ghost in *Madwoman* is that female pseudo-writer otherwise known as the literary critic who was engaged in the late 1970s in the dual action of supporting and subverting a (then) putatively patriarchal institution known as the university. They render this agenda especially clear in their celebration of Bertha Rochester and her irrepressible radical incursions into a privileged male sphere, a process Alison Milbank characterizes as "male Gothic." While the suggestion that Bertha is aware of a privileged male sphere in Brontë's novel is disputable, and offers up an example of contemporary theory being problematically foisted onto past texts, it positions Bertha Rochester as a true sister-in-arms to contemporary feminist critics.[32] That Gilbert and Gubar were engaged over a century later in enacting such incursions, albeit in another domain, raises the spectre that a certain misogyny still underpinned the culture. Like key works of contemporary criticism such as Jacques Derrida's *Spectres of Marx*, *Madwoman* exhibits what Punter has described as "the curious collocation" between the Gothic and contemporary critical theory, a phenomenon for which Punter advances various speculations, among them the idea that contemporary theory is, like the Gothic, haunted by a history resistant to both understanding and change. The sins of the fathers may not only be visited upon the sons—one of the key mantras of the Gothic[33]—but they may be perpetuated by them.

From the critical distance of thirty years, Gilbert and Gubar's *Madwoman* may be described in its influences as a Chinese-box of feminist literary criticism that, in its objectives and results, is mixed: in certain of its prejudices, it is decidedly of its time. It constitutes a pioneering work in the truest sense as it lay the groundwork for future developments in the examination of the intersections of gender and genre. Only in retrospect can literary critics see the broad swath of critical land carved out by its two gifted authors. The tendency in recent years of third-wave feminists and poststructuralist/deconstructionist critics has been to scoff at and undervalue such scholarship, to demean it as closed-minded, archaic, myopic, and "essentialist" in that it universalizes female identity and experience. While such an inclination has resulted in some provocative scholarship and the development of some useful theoretical paradigms, it is also arrogant and itself myopic. Indeed, this response is akin to laughing at the inventor of writing implements whose experiments gave us the tools with which to write. Although their tools might require reconsideration and refinement, we would be inarticulate without them, these, our foremothers who helped to liberate "successive scholars from the 'anxiety of authorship' they so carefully illuminate."[34]

Notes

1. Solveig C. Robinson, "*The Madwoman in the Attic*," in *The Victorian Literature Handbook*, ed. Alexandra Warwick and Martin Willis (London: Continuum, 2008), 121.

2. Susanne Becker, *Gothic Forms of Feminine Fictions* (Manchester: Manchester University Press, 1999), 10–11. I will take up the possible reasons for this lack of acknowledgement in due course. What I am *not* suggesting is that *Madwoman* is an actual work of Female Gothic. Such a ludicrous suggestion was made by Robert J. C. Young, "Freud's Secret: *The Interpretation of Dreams* was a Gothic Novel," in *Sigmund Freud's The Interpretation of Dreams: New Interdisciplinary Essays,* ed. Laura Marcus (Manchester: Manchester University Press, 1999), 206–31. Young suggests Freud "pulled off . . . a fictional coup, unparalleled in literary history" for he produced "a [Gothic] novel that pretended to be a real work of scientific psychology" (208, 206–7). Tipping his hat to "his greatest literary precursor, the Romantic Gothic writer Thomas De Quincey," Freud created, according to Young, a work whose real project was "to make the reader undergo an experience—typically, a frisson of horror or of sexual excitement" (213, 217).

3. Alison Milbank, "Milton, Melancholy, and the Sublime in the 'Female' Gothic from Radcliffe to Le Fanu," *Women's Writing* 1, no. 2 (1994): 143.

4. The Gothic, as Robert Miles argues, has long been viewed as "a feminized form" often decimated by male critics. In his words, "The bibliographical evidence strongly supports the thesis that the marginalization of the Romantic novel is connected with the form's capture by women writers." Robert Miles, "What Is a Romantic Novel?" *Novel* 34, no. 2 (2001): 181. Anti-Gothic commentary during the Gothic's heyday was centered on its moral nature and served to normalize "an emerging middle-class literature at the expense of a feminized popular culture." Bradford K. Mudge, "The Man with Two Brains: Gothic Novels, Popular Culture, Literary History," *PMLA* 107, no. 1 (1992): 99. The involvement of women in the literary marketplace was increasingly associated both "with illicit pleasure and . . . economic gain." Mudge, "Man with Two Brains," 96.

5. David Punter, "Introduction: The Ghost of a History," in *A Companion to the Gothic,* ed. David Punter (Oxford: Blackwell, 2000), ix.

6. Sandra M. Gilbert and Susan Gubar, *The Madwoman in the Attic: The Woman Writer and the Nineteenth-Century Literary Imagination* (New Haven: Yale University Press, 1979), 46. Subsequent references will be given parenthetically.

7. The broad-spectrum definition of the Female Gothic offered up by Gary Kelly in the introduction to his excellent six-volume series devoted to the Female Gothic describes it as "a species of Gothic fiction from the decades just before and after 1800, written by women, featuring female protagonists in certain situations, with appropriate settings, descriptions and plots, using distinctive kinds of narrations, and with distinctively feminine and feminist interests and tendencies, specific to that time, but of continuing interest to women and feminists now." Gary Kelly, ed., "General Introduction," in *Varieties of Female Gothic,* vol. 1 (London: Pickering and Chatto, 2002), xiv. With the exception, possibly, of some Radcliffean Gothic copycats like Anthony Holstein and others who penned their works anonymously, this is generally true for the era Kelly examines—namely, "the decades just before and after 1800" (xiv). The idea that the female Gothic belongs exclusively to women writers has been disputed in recent years. Tamar Heller, for example, has written an in-depth study devoted to Wilkie Collins's use of female Gothic tropes, and Alison Milbank has examined its appropriation by various Victorian male writers. More contemporary male writers of the female Gothic include William Faulkner ("A Rose for Emily") and Iain Banks *(The Wasp Factory).*

8. Ellen Moers, "Female Gothic: The Monster's Mother," *New York Review of Books* (March 21, 1974): 24–28.

9. Elizabeth Abel, Marianne Hirsch, and Elizabeth Langland, eds., *The Voyage In: Fictions of Female Development* (Hanover, N.H.: University Press of New England, 1983), 9.

10. See their works in Juliann E. Fleenor's anthology devoted to the new category, *The Female Gothic* (Montreal: Eden Press, 1983).

11. Jerome Beaty, "*Jane Eyre* and Genre," *Genre* 10 (1977): 619. The single major exception in this regard was Moers who, when she does step beyond the eighteenth century, fails to mention *Jane Eyre* in her consideration of the female Gothic. Instead, she takes Mary Shelley's *Frankenstein* as the key example of that genre.

12. See my essay on *Great Expectations,* where I argue that the connections and tensions between the bildungsroman and the Gothic are actually rooted in their conventions, ideological makeup, and the context of their almost simultaneous emergence in literary history as expressions of and responses to the advent of modernity. Carol Margaret Davison, "The Ghost of Genres Past: Theorizing the Gothic in the Victorian Novel," *Leeds Working Papers in Victorian Studies* 6 (2003): 23–40. See also Franco Moretti, *The Way of the World: The Bildungsroman in European Culture* (London: Verso, 1987), and Paul A. Cantor and Michael Valdez Moses, "Teaching *Frankenstein* from the Creature's Perspective," in *Approaches to Teaching Shelley's Frankenstein,* ed. Stephen C. Behrendt (New York: Modern Language Association, 1990). The difference between the Gothic novel that works out of the bildungsroman tradition and the "traditional" bildungsroman is predominantly in the nature and significance of the process whereby the protagonists arrive at the final state of spiritual and material fulfillment. I suggest labeling Gothic works "dark *Bildungsromane*" as they generally involve highly stylized rites of passage and oneiric narrative landscapes that serve to register deep-seated desires and anxieties fundamental to the development of self and national identity.

13. Eugenia C. DeLamotte, *Perils of the Night: A Feminist Study of Nineteenth-Century Gothic* (Oxford: Oxford University Press, 1990), 17; James P. Carson, "Enlightenment, Popular Culture, and Gothic Fiction," in *The Cambridge Companion to the Eighteenth-Century Novel,* ed. John Richetti (Cambridge: Cambridge University Press, 1996), 266; Annette Wheeler Cafarelli, "How Theories of Romanticism Exclude Women: Radcliffe, Milton, and the Legitimation of the Gothic Novel," in *Milton, the Metaphysicals, and Romanticism,* ed. Lisa Low and Anthony John Harding (Cambridge: Cambridge University Press, 1994), 98; Sybil Korff Vincent, "The Mirror and the Cameo: Margaret Atwood's Comic/Gothic Novel, *Lady Oracle,*" in *The Female Gothic,* ed. Juliann E. Fleenor (Montreal: Eden Press, 1983), 158.

14. Houses in general, and not just within the confines of the female Gothic genre, have a variety of psychic resonances; one of the major insights of *Madwoman in the Attic* was applying the "poetics of space" to Victorian women's domestic spaces, in particular. See chapter 2, "House and Universe," in Gaston Bachelard, *The Poetics of Space,* trans. Maria Jolas (Boston: Beacon Press, 1969).

15. D. A. Miller, "*Cage aux Folles:* Sensation and Gender in Wilkie Collins's *The Woman in White,*" *Representations* 14 (1986): 121; DeLamotte, *Perils,* 10.

16. Eva Figes, *Sex and Subterfuge: Women Writers to 1850* (New York: Persea Books, 1982), 74.

17. Kate Ellis, *The Contested Castle* (Urbana: University of Illinois Press, 1989), ix; Norman N. Holland and Leona F. Sherman, "Gothic Possibilities," *New Literary History* 8, no. 2 (1977): 282; Peter Fritzsche, "Specters of History: On Nostalgia, Exile, and Modernity," *American Historical Review* 106, no. 5 (2001): 1616.

18. Pam Morris, "General Introduction," in *Conduct Literature for Women,* ed. Pam Morris (London: Pickering and Chatto, 2005), 1: xi; Dorinda Outram, *The Enlightenment* (Cambridge: Cambridge University Press, 2005), 85; Fred Botting, *Gothic* (London: Routledge, 1996), 2.

19. DeLamotte, *Perils,* 152.

20. Roberta Rubenstein, "House Mothers and Haunted Daughters: Shirley Jackson and Female Gothic," *Tulsa Studies in Women's Literature* 15, no. 2 (1996): 312; Tamar

Hellar, "*Jane Eyre,* Bertha, and the Female Gothic," in *Approaches to Teaching Brontë's Jane Eyre,* ed. Diane Long Hoeveler and Beth Lau (New York: Modern Language Association, 1993), 51; my emphasis.

21. Quoted in Diane Long Hoeveler, *Gothic Feminism: The Professionalization of Gender from Charlotte Smith to the Brontës* (University Park: Pennsylvania State University Press, 1998), 6.

22. E. J. Clery, "The Politics of the Gothic Heroine," in *Reviewing Romanticism,* ed. Philip W. Martin and Robin Jarvis (New York: St. Martin's Press, 1992), 78.

23. Michel Foucault, "What Is an Author?" *The Foucault Reader* (New York: Pantheon Books, 1984), 114. Gilbert and Gubar do acknowledge Radcliffe's place in the rise of the English novel: "Indeed, beginning with Aphra Behn and burgeoning with Fanny Burney, Anne [*sic*] Radcliffe, Maria Edgeworth, and Jane Austen, the English novel seems to have been in good part a female invention" (*Madwoman,* 540).

24. Ann Radcliffe, "On the Supernatural in Poetry" (1826), in *Gothic Documents: A Sourcebook 1700–1820,* ed. E. J. Clery and Robert Miles (Manchester: Manchester University Press, 2000), 168. For more detail on the distinction between terror and horror Gothic narratives, see Botting, *Gothic,* 71–80.

25. Mudge, "Man with Two Brains," 93; Nathan Drake, *Literary Hours: or Sketches, Critical, Narrative, and Poetical* (1800; New York: Garland Publishing, 1970), 1: 359; review of *The Italian* by Ann Radcliffe, *Analytical Review* 25 (1797): 516; Walter Scott, "Ann Radcliffe," *Sir Walter Scott on Novelists and Fiction,* ed. Ioan Williams (London: Routledge and Kegan Paul, 1968), 103; Caroline Franklin, Emma Clery, and William Edvers Garside, eds., *Authorship, Commerce and the Public: Scenes of Writing, 1750–1850* (London: Palgrave Macmillan, 2002), 13; Montague Summers, *Essays in Petto* (Freeport, N.Y.: Books for Libraries, 1967), 17; Cafarelli, "How Theories," 93; Robert Donald Spector, *The English Gothic: A Bibliographic Guide to Writers from Horace Walpole to Mary Shelley* (Westport, Conn.: Greenwood, 1984), 13; Cafarelli, "How Theories," 92.

26. Kelly, *Varieties,* xxxi. "The Gothic mode by the 1790s is entering the proto-generic phase, and becoming recognizable as a distinct literary type. By the early 1800s it will be legitimated, if not respectable, simply by virtue of its undeniable existence. Whatever the critics and moralists thought, the literature of terror was not going to go away." E. J. Clery, *Women's Gothic: From Clara Reeve to Mary Shelley* (Devon, U.K.: Northcote House, 2000), 32.

27. Wylie Sypher, "Social Ambiguity in the Gothic Novel," *Partisan Review* 12 (1945): 56–57; Kelly, *Varieties,* xxviii; emphasis added.

28. I discuss elsewhere what I have called Victorian "Gothic closets" as incorporating one or several characteristics of the traditional Gothic novel without adhering strictly to the conventions of that genre. See Carol Davison, "The Ghost of Genres Past: Theorizing the Gothic in the Victorian Novel," *Leeds Working Papers in Victorian Studies* 6 (2003): 23–40.

29. Virginia Woolf, *A Room of One's Own* (London: Hogarth, 1929), 114.

30. Milbank, "Milton," 143.

31. Avril Horner and Sue Zlosnick, "Female Gothic," in *Teaching the Gothic,* ed. Anna Powell and Andrew Smith (London: Palgrave Macmillan, 2006), 109. With regard to the theoretical history of the category Female Gothic, see the special issue of *Women's Writing* 2, no. 1 (1994) edited by Robert Miles, as well as the double issue of *Gothic Studies* 6, no. 1 (2004) edited by Andrew Smith and Diana Wallace.

32. Milbank, "Milton," 143. I have discussed Bertha's relationship as Jane Eyre's "sister-in-arms" in my essay devoted to the postcolonial Gothic and *Jane Eyre.* See Carol Davison, "Burning Down the Master's (Prison)-house: Revolution and Revelation in Colonial and Postcolonial Female Gothic," in *Empire and the Gothic: The Politics of Genre,* ed. Andrew Smith and William Hughes (London: Palgrave Macmillan, 2003), 136–54.

33. Punter, *Companion*, ix. From the Gothic's inception in 1764 with Horace Walpole's *The Castle of Otranto,* its driving theme has been inheritance in its various manifestations—moral, spiritual, financial. The succinctly and specifically identified "useful moral" of that novella, as articulated by Walpole himself in the preface to the first edition, is that "the sins of the fathers are visited on their children to the third and fourth generation." Horace Walpole, *The Castle of Otranto* (Oxford: Oxford University Press, 1996), 7.

34. Robinson, "*Madwoman,*" 121.

12

Elizabeth Gaskell

A Well-Tempered Madness

Thomas P. Fair

Through its insightful scrutiny of language and allusion, Sandra M. Gilbert and Susan Gubar's *The Madwoman in the Attic* dissects Victorian women authors' repressed madness and anger as a coded response to exploitation, domination, marginalization, and economic dependency.[1] Gilbert and Gubar's investigations of canonical works by Charlotte Brontë, Jane Austen, and George Eliot posit a feminine imagination operating from within a prison of gender and sexuality in order to subvert patriarchal oppression. Initial critical reception generally perceived the work as an apt continuation of Kate Millett's groundbreaking *Sexual Politics* (1968) and as an important progression from feminist literary criticism begun by Patricia Meyer Spacks, Ellen Moers, and Elaine Showalter.[2] But Gilbert and Gubar's approach also raised controversy among feminist critics: *Madwoman* was received as both persuasively argued and unpersuasively monolithic. Nina Auerbach, for example, claimed that Gilbert and Gubar's "rich compendium of images, fears, and dreams of power that haunted nineteenth-century women writers is a definitive, if not totally consistent, study of the mythos of subversion out of which the woman's tradition arose." Auerbach's reservations about the book's limitations, though, were shared by other critics. *Madwoman,* she wrote, "posits a patriarchal oppressor who is more gargantuan than any I have ever met, in the nineteenth century or our own."[3] Did *all* Victorian women writers register anger and rebellion against a titanic patriarchal oppressor?

Perhaps because Elizabeth Gaskell takes a less adversarial and more elusive position, one that places her outside the main critical direction taken in *The Madwoman in the Attic,* she is notably absent from Gilbert and Gubar's monumental work.[4] Deirdre d'Albertis argues in *Dissembling Fictions: Elizabeth Gaskell and the Victorian Social Text,* that Gaskell "is written out of *Madwoman in the Attic* because she in no way resembles their preferred type of the angry Romantic artist."[5] Exploring the possibilities for freedom and self-expression for a woman in the domestic sphere of the emergent middle class, Gaskell avoided the potentially reductive relationship of a female author's struggle against her male precursors or her characters' endeavors against the limiting and debilitating patriarchy noted in *Madwoman.* An interpretation of Gaskell's novels against Gilbert and Gubar's critical assertions challenges their analysis of the restrictions and obstacles faced by female characters in the work of Victorian women writers. Although historically and culturally Gaskell's female protagonists must contend with a social environment that, in part, contains oppositions identified and detailed by Gilbert and Gubar,[6] Gaskell's fictional environments reflect several complex, competing relationships—class, economics, and gender—more intricate than those identified in *Madwoman.* Operating within realistic and conventional social models of marriage and family to demonstrate the range of possibilities for a woman's fulfillment, Gaskell often balances, either internally or externally (and with equal success), a rebellious individual with a conventional figure. Gaskell *appears* to be reinforcing the hegemonic paradigm when, in fact, she is subverting it to allow her rebellious heroines agency and the opportunity to fashion their own success from within the system that would attempt to contain them within its traditional boundaries. In this essay, I want to reinsert Elizabeth Gaskell into the discussion of the nineteenth-century woman writer's literary imagination: Gaskell's portrayals of women's psychological, domestic, and political stratagems temper the madness of their revolt and should be read as an imperative alternative to the oppressed and enraged madwoman.

Often marginalized as a quaint chronicler of village life and manners, Gaskell actually promotes a complex vision of domestic relationships with an intricate interplay of individual desires and traditional demands. This complicated, multifaceted aspect of Gaskell's novels is the focus of Felicia Bonaparte's *The Gypsy-Bachelor of Manchester* (1992) in which she offers an interesting but speculative biographical investigation of Gaskell's work. Bonaparte's argument segments Gaskell's personality and writing into that of a sentimental and traditional "Mrs. Gaskell" and that of a fully realized if not feminist author, a "demon" reminiscent of Gilbert and Gubar's madwoman.[7] The psychological suppositions and the absence of a domestic and social-cultural context so integral to Gaskell's writing, however, significantly undercut Bonaparte's overall analysis. Gaskell's presentation of female consciousness in relation to patriarchal authority functions within an ambiguous if not elusive framework that simultaneously reflects and subverts common tropes identified as part of the Victorian hegemony. Her stance balances and accommodates the demands placed upon her as a Victorian woman and as an individual responding to a variety of personal and political concerns that relate to broad and complex social issues. Rather than choose from resignation, revolt, or madness, individuals in Gaskell's novels endeavor to attain sexual and social autonomy within a variety of contexts. In Gaskell's life and her novels, she recognizes the socially determining power of economics, but she does not accept economic status as solely an issue of gender.[8] She also rejects working from a position of destructive confrontation, opting instead for a subtler approach of negotiation rather than open conflict.

Gaskell reworks the term "patriarchy" in such a way that it functions as enemy neither to woman nor worker; her position thus reshapes and reexamines feminist suppositions found in *The Madwoman in the Attic.* For example, Gaskell offers alternative views of patriarchal figures: a guiding and protective paternal figure on a personal, industrial, or political level, functioning as a caring and supportive father, or a compliant husband/lover who follows his wife's wishes and shares his life and position with her. In *Mary Barton* (1848), *North and South* (1854), and *Wives and Daughters* (1866), fathers never actually assume a repressive or dictatorial position; similarly, husbands learn to embrace a marital vision of mutuality. Moreover, challenging the chiefly antagonistic relationship between women and a patriarchal authority present in Gilbert and Gubar's assessment, Gaskell occasionally acknowledges positive aspects of patriarchy, such as a husband's protective role, and also criticizes oppressive and dehumanizing beliefs that limit a woman's individuality and are typical of prevailing social codes. Gaskell emphasizes the need for her heroines to act despite the so-called confines of their "sphere" rather than to remain immobilized by their disadvantages.[9] While she recognizes the power of masculine authority in a character such as John Thornton in *North and South* (or patriarchal law in general), she favors adaptation, even deception, as an enabling action for her female characters: Molly Gibson may choose to comply with the restrictions imposed by a patriarchal system; Hyacinth Clare may manipulate and deceive; Cynthia Kirkpatrick may revolt.

Illustrative of Gilbert and Gubar's restrictive critical approach, their discussion of Charlotte Brontë's *Shirley* (1849) iterates thematic strands Gaskell introduced a year earlier with *Mary Barton* and further examines in *North and South;* yet their analysis creates a limited interpretation of both character and conflict, neglecting to consider the range of options Gaskell presents.

In their examination of Brontë's novel, Gilbert and Gubar establish the metonymic relationship connecting both the female protagonists' and the workers' encounters with a patriarchal industrial society: Shirley's "experience of her gender as it is circumscribed by available sexual roles gives her insight into the misery of the poor" (*Madwoman,* 387). Significantly, Gilbert and Gubar's analysis moves the examination of the text beyond overt economic and political parallels between the workers and the women to an investigation of the psychological complexities women encounter when seeking agency in a restrictive system. Forced to act only in gender-appropriate roles despite her money and strength of character, Shirley chooses an ultimately limiting marriage to Louis Moore, proof, according to Gilbert and Gubar, that "the only 'happy ending' for women in [Brontë's] society is marriage": we are never allowed to forget "that marriage is a suspect institution based on female subordination" (*Madwoman,* 395).

An alternative presentation of feminine destiny clearly manifests itself in a careful consideration of *Mary Barton* and *North and South.* While these works reveal Gaskell's realistic understanding of the problems created by rapid industrialization and its confrontation with existing English social structures, they also examine female agency and the "fate" of marriage as increasingly significant issues. Gaskell's investigations of power distributions within the domestic sphere anticipate Nancy Armstrong's *Desire and Domestic Fiction: A Political History of the Novel* (1987), which investigates the ways in which gender difference began to obscure class difference and nineteenth-century domestic fiction neutralized class struggle by replacing that struggle with gender conflict.[10] Armstrong uses Foucault's analysis of sex, sexuality, and power to locate power in domestic space, acknowledging Gilbert and Gubar's figure of the madwoman as only a single dimension of a complex social struggle, as Gaskell clearly demonstrates. Similarly, Hilary Schor's *Scheherezade in the Marketplace* (1992) touches on the recognizable parallel Gaskell introduces in her industrial novels between political relationships and romance.[11] Following Armstrong's argument about the replacement of class conflict with domestic struggle, Schor posits that Gaskell frames the conventional "marriage plot" as a means of resisting a dichotomous choice and accurately recognizes that Gaskell does not scorn marriage as either support for a patriarchal system or a means of repressing transgressing females but sees it as a point of political critique and a potential redefinition of gender-determined roles.

Gaskell's first novel, *Mary Barton,* demonstrates a developing feminine consciousness defining itself amid the industrial conflicts simmering between workers and owners. Initially, Gaskell focused on the industrial paradigm and titled the novel *John Barton,* until her editor, Edward Chapman, convinced her to change both the title and focus: from a sociopolitical examination of industrial issues, the novel was edited to explore a domestic theme and private relationships.[12] Although, in this case, Gaskell's investigation of women's issues lacks her characteristic coherence, Mary Barton's story provides ample evidence of the "struggles of female individuality in a male dominated world."[13] With behavior reminiscent of conventional domestic tragedy, Mary mistakenly defines her sense of individuality in economic terms dominated by a materialistic and social class emphasis. Her developing romance with young Henry Carson appears as neither sexual nor romantic but defined by the economic advantages associated with such a relationship—Mary pictures herself at leisure with the Carson sisters or returning by carriage to Miss Simmonds's shop to buy expensive gowns.[14] Despite the apparent harmlessness of such fantasies, the potential danger of materialistic aspirations emerges in the presence of Mary's Aunt Esther, the "fallen woman" whose similar desires lead to her seduction and downfall.[15] Such seduction is even more tangible in the form of Mrs. Carson, the mill owner's wife who was herself a factory girl and escaped working-class poverty through marriage. Gaskell challenges and subverts commonly held notions of self-fulfillment through romance with her suggestion that economic influences shade popular perceptions of love and that choosing and acting responsibly earns self-fulfillment.

Although the novel's strongly patriarchal framework suggests that wealth produces power and agency while poverty produces limitations and marginalization, Mary's story provides evidence of women's agency within a restraining patriarchal context. Flirting earlier with a romantic but restrictive resolution, Gaskell rejects a possible union between Mary and Harry Carson. Rather than focus on the marginalization and impotence Gilbert and Gubar emphasize in their treatment of *Shirley,* Gaskell focuses on Mary's empowerment and ultimate success. Mary's conflicting character traits further complicate the readers' perceptions of her as Gaskell's assertion of a new female consciousness. While Mary often acts bravely and independently, at other times she is emotionally overcome or even faints. Although initially appearing to approximate Gilbert and Gubar's critical stance of a woman's limited, nurturing role when she presents Mary as a conventional Victorian image, a woman demonstrating a self-effacing willingness to assist others, Gaskell imbues this situation with a more assertive sense of responsibility and urgency as Mary assumes the domestic duties in the care of her father, administers to members of the Wilson family through the series of tragedies that befall them, and later attends upon both her dying father and Aunt Esther.

In strong contrast to this traditional portrayal, a brave, capable and determined Mary eventually emerges to prove Jem Wilson's innocence. Her journey to Liverpool and her search of the dockyards for Will Wilson reveal individual power and potential for action in a public forum, one dominated by patriarchal expectations in contrast to actions solely related to the "hearth," so widely identified and illustrated in Coventry Patmore's "The Angel in the House" (1854-1862). Mary's revolt is embodied by her refusal to wait patiently for others to resolve the conflict and her willingness to confront possible danger and act directly and definitively. Although *Mary Barton* fails, perhaps, to establish a clearly defined, entirely innovative perception of women, the novel succeeds in raising questions about Victorian assumptions pertaining to acceptable female behavior through Mary's independent actions, assertiveness, and rejection of feminine passivity. Mary "awakens" to her true love for Jem prior to the accusation that he murdered young Carson, and she "works" at achieving her goal, undertaking unusual efforts to attain Jem's freedom. Her eventual marriage to Jem may be a conventional choice, but, for Mary, it is a desirable goal and not merely an accommodation of contemporary values. Notably, Mary's actions toward attaining that marriage are exceedingly unconventional. Gaskell employs Mary's endeavors to assert a central concept of her vision: marriage can be a fulfilling experience rather than automatic and repressive marginalization. The acquisition of a new life for Mary and Jem lacks melodramatic simplicity and arrives at the end of a complex and realistic process of maturation. Her choice of marriage to Jem is not the result of limited possibility but rather of a developing moral understanding—a new knowledge of her obligations to others and the emptiness of her earlier frivolous desires.

Published serially in *Household Words* in 1854, *North and South* returns both to the industrial issues raised in *Mary Barton* and to a more extensive examination of a developing feminine consciousness. In this novel, Gaskell presents a sophisticated analysis of the industrial issue, one that rejects simple oppositions to reveal complex and at times paradoxical relationships from the perspective of the mill owners, the workers, and the female protagonist. Gaskell advances beyond the parallel relationship between women and workers that Gilbert and Gubar investigate in Brontë's *Shirley* (*Madwoman,* 375) to weave together metonymically the public and the personal as both mill owner John Thornton and minister's daughter Margaret Hale learn about opposing sides of the labor issue and the social inequities that separate them. *North and South* examines how the challenges of an emerging industrial society affect the established social and gender expectations of a woman's identity. Gaskell mitigates the potential radicalism of her position both with her focus on individual development instead of universal or class application and with her combination of established values with innovation. Margaret Hale emerges not so much as a "madwoman" as a woman who exhibits a controlled and determined response to conventional gender demands.

North and South opens with a prenuptial party and an ironically critical examination of marriage, conventional female stereotypes, and the social values connected to marriage as an expected, accepted, and defining source of female identity. Margaret's close relationship with her cousin Edith creates a particular focus on Margaret's single status, and the striking contrast in expectations and behavior between them situates Margaret outside conventional ideals, signaling the beginning of Margaret's independence. Their physical appearance is likewise significantly different and contrasted: Edith appears as "a soft ball of muslin and ribbon, and silken curls," while Margaret is a "tall, stately girl of eighteen."[16] Edith's doll-like appearance supports conventional female stereotypes of softness and vulnerability in contrast to Margaret's strength and maturity. A quietly determined Margaret further places herself outside conventional tastes and expectations through her preference for a "calm and peaceful time" (*North and South,* 12) before her marriage rather than a period of celebratory parties and functions. Notably, Margaret does not dismiss marriage as a probability; she instead redefines her approach to it. Shortly after her return to her parents in Helstone, Margaret must act on her convictions regarding marriage and its economic and social components. Edith's new brother-in-law, Henry Lennox, proposes to her, and her immediate refusal without consideration of material benefits reveals her desire for a relationship beyond traditional expectations: "she could have loved him had he been but different, with a difference which she felt, on reflection, to be one that went low—deep down" (*North and South,* 31). Margaret's decision to reject her cousin's example establishes her growing awareness of her independence from typical gender expectations that privilege convention over emotion. Her rebellion in this case is not against marriage as much as it is against assumptions that material and social advantages are acceptable or even adequate reasons for a woman's acquiescence.

The complications in Margaret's later relationship with industrialist John Thornton, who sees her as a potential wife because of her regal appearance and assertive nature, create alternative perceptions of personal relationships and marriage. Thornton's mother responds with conventional maternal suspicion, perceiving all of Margaret's actions as intentional designs to attract and entrap her son; however, Margaret's aloof and critical manner fails to conform to Mrs. Thornton's desire for a demure and properly subordinate wife for John. As in *Shirley,* Margaret knows that an angry mob of striking workers is approaching Thornton's home; however, instead of only allowing her to observe, as Brontë's characters do, Gaskell empowers Margaret with decisive action. While Mrs. Thornton and her daughter remain secluded in the house, Margaret's impulsive defense of Thornton in their confrontation with the mob locates Margaret solidly outside the common expectations of a woman of her class and background. In contrast to *Shirley,* where from the safe position of the rectory window, Caroline Helstone and Shirley Keeldar can only hear and not see the workers approach Robert Moore's mill, Gaskell has her protagonist act in a defining moment, which further confirms Mrs. Thornton's perceptions of Margaret's intent.[17] Despite unanimous consensus of all observers as to the significance of Margaret's action, she determinedly asserts that she acted solely out of responsibility and not affection. Refusing Thornton's unexpected proposal and rejecting conformity to gender and class expectations, Margaret again privileges her emotions above the overt economic and social advantages a marriage to Thornton could provide.

As evidence of her inclusive presentation of gender roles, Gaskell also suggests a more conventional aspect to Margaret's character as she cares for her invalid mother and her working-class friend, Bessy Higgins. When Margaret emerges in a seemingly stereotypic role of caregiver, Gaskell's characterization echoes the marginalized female role so often criticized in *Madwoman.* However, the context in which Margaret operates as caregiver challenges a reading of her actions as conventional and, instead, proves her bravery, independence, strength, and determination. She attends to her mother as a dutiful daughter, and, to protect her father, she also assumes many of the responsibilities that traditionally would fall to him. After she receives her mother's negative prognosis from the doctor, Margaret is anxious to protect her father from worry and refuses to allow the news to overcome her emotionally. She operates as a locus of strength in the household, supporting both parents. Following up on an invitation, Margaret also sets aside her elevated sensibilities, as well as her class distinctions, and journeys into the working-class section of Milton Northern, specifically, to the home of Bessy Higgins.[18] Margaret's personal interaction, primarily as a caregiver with the Higgins family and later the Boucher family, provides intimate knowledge of working-class conditions atypical for a young woman of her social class.[19] Margaret's movement within and without gender norms gains her firsthand experience and expanded understanding of the industrial conflict and establishes her as a more independent and influential character than either of the heroines in *Shirley.*

Margaret ventures through a series of personal deprivations and challenges to establish her strength of character, and through these trials, Gaskell redefines standards for the Victorian woman. Both of Margaret's parents die, and her exiled brother Frederick fails to gain legal reinstatement and rejects all further attempts for his possible return to England; these events contribute to Margaret's isolation, challenging her strength of character as well as her determination to be independent. Comforted by her father's close friend Mr. Bell and by her Aunt Shaw, Margaret faces the temptation of remaining in the comfort and safety of her aunt's house in London and returning to predictable social conventions. Margaret also soon inherits Mr. Bell's fortune, including the property Thornton leases. Her new economic status qualifies her as a participant in, not just an observer of, the social interactions and expectations, such as marriage, characteristic of her Aunt Shaw's milieu. Recognizing her situation, Margaret reflects "that she herself must one day answer for her own life, and what she had done with it; and she tried to settle that most difficult problem for women, how much was to be utterly merged in obedience to authority, and how much might be set apart for freedom in working" (*North and South,* 377). In a final parallel to *Shirley,* Gaskell reverses Shirley Keeldar's inability to effect change or operate in a male setting with her fortune. Demonstrating a strong sense of determination and claiming a mutual position in business affairs, Margaret directs Henry Lennox to draw up the appropriate papers, and she presents Thornton with a legal contract and loan offer to save his business herself. Once again, Gaskell's representations resonate with concepts examined in contemporary analysis. Mary Poovey's *Uneven Developments: The Ideological Work of Gender in Mid-Victorian England* (1988) presents an Althussarian concept that ideology masks actual conditions, presenting limited or repressive conditions as reasonable and desirable while the inherent conditions subvert the concealing ideology as shifts occur in the acquisition of power and control.[20] Similarly, Margaret and Thornton appear restricted by conventional courting assumptions; however, the shift in economic and social status redefines the nature of their relationship and imbues Margaret with power.

The rapidly following romantic conclusion to Margaret and Thornton's relationship, a fact made necessary by editorial restraints from *Household Words,*[21] still asserts mutual understanding as the basis of the relationship, not the concession or subordination Gilbert and Gubar investigate (*Madwoman,* 395). Ultimately, Margaret and Thornton exhibit a partnership that is intellectual and emotional as well as financial. Gaskell destabilizes common premises about relationships between public and private, society and self. Perceiving the two spheres as inextricably entwined, Gaskell clearly demonstrates the connection between society and self to be less metonymic and more individualistically complex. Her female protagonist emerges as an economic and emotional partner, literally and figuratively, with the novel's strongest paternal figure. The rebellious nature of Margaret's earlier stance on marriage shifts to that of a "peaceful" partnership.

Gaskell moves from the examination of a woman's attempts at self-definition within an industrial context to a broader examination of gender definition, especially the tensions and conflicts typically characteristic of the middle-class ethos. The time, place, and layered social structure of *Wives and*

Daughters anticipate George Eliot's *Middlemarch* (1871); both texts examine similarly situated female characters and the possibilities of marginalization and agency these women confront as they attempt to define themselves in a strongly patriarchal society. In their analysis of Eliot, Gilbert and Gubar posit that Dorothea's marriage to Casaubon holds her in "sterile submission to male force," and both Rosamond and Dorothea "can only express their dissatisfaction with provincial life by choosing suitors who seem to be a possible means of escaping confinement and ennui" (*Madwoman,* 505, 514). Gaskell's characters rebel against their marginalization and a prevalent "male force" by working the system; Hyacinth Gibson exploits and manages the domestic sphere to her full satisfaction. Eliot is less interested in the political reality of Rosamond Vincy's marriage to Lydgate than she is in the elevated aspirations of Dorothea Brooke (or even of Lydgate). Elizabeth Langland notes, "In contrast to her contemporaries Elizabeth Gaskell and Margaret Oliphant, George Eliot depicts society's discursive practices not as integral to the construction of meaning and identity but as a constricting force to be transcended, something to be penetrated by distinction of mind."[22] Gilbert and Gubar's discussion of George Eliot particularly emphasizes the opposing issues at the center of *Middlemarch,* such as how a woman is to satisfy her ambition for accomplishment "outside a certain circle of wife and mother."[23] The many romantic and marital pairings in the text offer a rich, complex variety of relationships to examine. However, Gilbert and Gubar's approach limits the discussion to oppressive gender identities; they fail to consider revising the standards or finding alternatives to them.[24] Conversely, in *Wives and Daughters,* Gaskell emphasizes the nature of the relationship between the individuals involved, conceding that an alteration in society's view of marriage, however desirable, lies outside the power of any two individuals to change beyond their relationship to each other. Gilbert and Gubar also suggest that behaviors of submission and dissimulation have significant currency as they permit women to function within a patriarchal system; such submission replaces individuality with proscribed identities—a point Gaskell rejects categorically.

Departing from the melodramatic realism characteristic of her earlier work, in *Wives and Daughters* Gaskell creates a slightly skewed view of the prevalent paternalism in the pre-reform pastoral village of Hollingford. Against this enhanced patriarchal setting, Gaskell depicts the lives of Hyacinth Clare Kirkpatrick Gibson, Molly Gibson, and her antithetical stepsister Cynthia Kirkpatrick. Molly's actions appear as the period's typical fictional female experience of maturation and self-discovery, ultimately leading to marriage with a romantically appropriate male; yet, while she claims some agency in her conventional choices, she is not the novel's subversive protagonist. Both young women operate in a marginalized territory of little power and social influence. Cynthia rejects Molly's choice of social identity and subsequently emerges as the novel's subversive protagonist as she asserts an identity that provides her with greater control in her marriage and frees her from Hollingford's social limitations. Gaskell contrasts Hyacinth Kirkpatrick Gibson's manipulation of prevailing marital boundaries with Molly Gibson's life, thereby reinforcing hegemonic expectations of both a woman's social role and marriage in general. Interestingly, Hyacinth (Molly's stepmother and Cynthia's mother) acts as a bridge between the expectations for women, represented by Molly, and the subversion of those assumptions, represented by Cynthia.

In *Bearing the Word: Language and Female Experience in Nineteenth-Century Women's Writing* (1986), Margaret Homans focuses on Gaskell's development beyond the limitations of Gilbert and Gubar's assessment. Her analysis ultimately suggests that Gaskell incorporates tropes characteristic of masculine discourse into her writing and creates a different speech mode that blends the opposing figurative masculine and literal feminine into a new form, one that offers alternative perspectives to normative situations.[25] Using Cynthia Kirkpatrick's character and story to offer a subversive approach to both marriage and a customary social identity, Gaskell challenges the hegemony and its dictates. Amplifying paternalistic social roles and feminine limitations, the "homey" village description of the cottages with the portrayal of the "housewives" making breakfast for the "breadwinners" undercuts the quaintness of the village and emphasizes distinctly separated identities and tasks.[26] Representative of the dangers inherent in an apparently "benign" patriarchy is Mr. Gibson's "loving" repression of his daughter Molly: regardless of his affection for her, his desire to limit her education and his unease about her aspirations resonates with the existing social views limiting and marginalizing women.[27] Gibson's directions to Molly's governess, Miss Eyre, emphasize a strongly marginalized view of women's ability despite the established love he has for his daughter: "Don't teach Molly too much; she must sew, and read, and write, and do her sums; but I want to keep her a child, and if I find more learning desirable for her, I'll see about giving it to her myself. After all, I'm not sure that reading or writing is necessary . . . we must yield to the prejudices of society, Miss Eyre, and so you may teach the child to read" (*Wives,* 46). Molly's own determination helps her avoid the archaic marginalization her father planned for her, for "only by fighting and struggling hard . . . bit by bit Molly persuaded her father to let her have French and drawing lessons." Gaskell proceeds to expand Molly's intellectual revolt; Molly reads "every book that came in her way, almost with as much delight as if it had been forbidden" (*Wives,* 46). Significantly, her early revolt and claim for equal education undercut and challenge the later perception of Molly's conformity and establish her choice over submission. Commenting on Molly's determination, Miss Eyre reflects on her home experience and alludes to the evils that befall an ungovernable temper, further defining a women's place as one that provides no sense of self or redress for injustice, simply acquiescence (*Wives,* 47). Gaskell sets up the elder Miss Eyre in opposition to the youthful Molly, thus representing Victorian conventions against the emergent self-empowering female. Later in the novel, Gaskell reminds the reader of the dominant restrictive principles of marriage inherent in this system through comments of the local lord's wife, Lady Cumnor, to Cynthia Kirkpatrick: "You must reverence your husband, and conform to his opinion in all things. Look up to him as your head, and do nothing without consulting him . . . Keep strict accounts; and remember your station in life" (*Wives,* 602). By this point, however, Gaskell has carefully constructed an ironic and subversive response that challenges and redefines many of the elements in Lady Cumnor's lecture through Cynthia's choice of a husband and the agency she maintains after she marries.

In Hyacinth Gibson, Gaskell combines both the economic determinants associated with class and the gender-based assumptions typical of the society to examine the ways both limit women's attempts at self-determination. Hyacinth, economically and socially battered by society's limitations, determinedly plots her course through those options that remain open to her. Hired as a governess to Lord Cumnor's daughters (a fact that denotes limited economic choice), Hyacinth loses further personal identity when she is called simply "Clare." The continued use of "Clare" by Cumnor's grown daughters reinforces the idea that her marginalized identity is because of her social rank. Her earlier marriage to Mr. Kirkpatrick is readily seen as an attempt to improve her lot and escape the limitations of an unmarried governess by becoming the wife of a curate "who was of a very good family" (*Wives,* 21). Mr. Kirkpatrick's poverty and early demise thwart Hyacinth's plans at improvement, as does her current position of headmistress of a failing school in Ashcombe. Hyacinth's economic difficulties drive her back to the ignominious "protection" of Lady Cumnor and her daughters, who take it upon themselves in a sort of noblesse oblige to "find out some way of helping her to a livelihood without parting her from her child" (*Wives,* 12). Staying at the Towers, the Cumnor estate, Hyacinth encounters a lost Molly Gibson, an encounter that eventually provides the next opportunity for Hyacinth's attempt to achieve greater autonomy.

Hyacinth is quite mindful of her limited position: she is determined to improve it but cautious not to offend her social superiors while she "enjoys" their patronage. Her mannerisms while at the Towers model the proper degree of subservience expected of one from a lower class. Knowing how to behave within the system does not mean a complacent acceptance of it, and Hyacinth, while recognizing the limitations of her economic sphere, uses her connection to the Cumnors as a potential means of advancing herself. Eager to attain her own agency, economic security, and a respectable social position for herself and her daughter, Hyacinth perceives marriage to Gibson as a means of achieving these goals. Most telling of Hyacinth's motivations is her fervent desire to reclaim her name and thus her identity. The fact that Lady Cumnor and her daughters previously called and continue to call her by her surname grievously wounds her pride. The use of the surname alone renders her as a commodity rather than a person (or if a person, not one of much worth). Whatever marginalization marriage may contain, employment as a governess is worse, as it offers no authority, control, or independence in adult social spheres, public or private. Rejecting the Cumnors' use of "Clare," she exclaims to Gibson, "Call me Hyacinth—your own Hyacinth. I can't bear 'Clare,' it reminds me of being a governess, and those days are all past now" (*Wives,* 108). Although her decision to marry and become "Mrs. Gibson" challenges the sense of individualism in her exclamation, Hyacinth reclaims her name and her sense of agency in her role as wife.

Her marriage to Gibson clearly defines a pragmatic approach to procuring an acceptable social position within the highly embedded patriarchal social structure of Hollingford. Her calculations may challenge the accepted portrait of the demure female, but she is no more calculating than Mr. Gibson with his pragmatic reasoning. Evidence of Hyacinth's successful social advancement emerges in a sardonic moment as Hollingford's middle-class matrons comment on the improvement of Hyacinth's dresses since her marriage to Gibson: "I remember the time when Mrs. Kirkpatrick wore old black silks, and was thankful and civil as became her place as schoolmistress . . . she's all dressed in pearl-grey satin now!" (*Wives,* 282). Gaskell's exploration of the economic, social, and cultural obstacles Hyacinth has to face creates a realistic context for evaluating a form of agency within accepted marital bonds and against which to examine the emerging lives of Molly Gibson and Cynthia Kirkpatrick.

Molly Gibson's kindness and sensitivity establish her as an alternative to Mrs. Gibson's version of wife and mother and add another layer of complexity to Gaskell's investigation and definition of female roles within a marriage. Molly's selfless involvement with the various needs of the Hamley family enables Gaskell to examine the established domestic concept of woman as nurturer and caregiver. Assisting Mrs. Hamley, Molly receives the direct influence of a woman who is virtually the opposite of her stepmother. Mrs. Hamley is a quiet, self-effacing, nurturing model who reflects conventionally ascribed ideals defining a woman's role in marriage: Mrs. Hamley appeases the often gruff squire, worries excessively as she attends her ineffectual son Osborne, and places her own health and needs below her family's needs and the household's requirements. Significantly, along with this traditional representation, Gaskell also offers a subtler component to the conventional image to strengthen her depiction of a woman's importance and agency within a marriage. She attributes the deterioration of Hamley Hall to Mrs. Hamley's death, suggesting that her management and guidance significantly directed not only the predictable domestic issues but also the entire hall's management—her death literally affects the hall to its very foundation. Describing the general disintegration of the estate, the narrator comments of the squire that "his wife had urged him to take advantage of the proffered loan. But now that she was no longer there to encourage him, and take an interest in the progress of the work, he grew indifferent to it himself" (*Wives,* 245). Ironically and in a manner consistent with Gilbert and Gubar's criticism of female destruction through male expectations, Gaskell traces the deterioration and eventual death of Mrs. Hamley to her self-denial and her perpetual accommodation of the squire's needs. Forsaking her "sociable pleasure in the company of her fellows in education and position" because of the squire's dislike for her friends, Mrs. Hamley fades: "deprived of all her strong interests, she sank into ill-health; nothing definite: only she was never well" (*Wives,* 43). After Mrs. Hamley's death, Molly dutifully follows her self-sacrificing precedent by attending to the Hamley family's needs. Through Molly's eventual collapse from exhaustion, Gaskell fully recognizes the debilitating demands conventional expectations place upon women, a point shared with Gilbert and Gubar, and rejects the inevitability of such a narrowly defined, dangerous role with Molly's removal from the hall.

Gaskell redefines the Victorian female paradigm represented in Molly Gibson as Molly continues her intimate connections to the Hamley family, especially in her support and admiration of Roger Hamley. The mutual connection between Molly and Roger, evident from the novel's early stages, becomes more complicated with Cynthia's arrival and begins to define the connection differently: Molly's adoration of Roger continues while his perception of Molly as a sister is reinforced. Later stunned by Roger Hamley's proposal to Cynthia, Molly displays the Victorian woman's expected degree of self-sacrifice as she struggles to maintain control despite her disappointment and sense of loss (*Wives,* 364). Maintaining purity of thought and repressing her physical attraction for Roger, Molly expresses her love for him by playing his advocate in all things and claiming at one point to Cynthia, "I don't think you value Roger as you ought" (*Wives,* 394). Eventually, Molly's perseverance results in her union with Roger; however, despite the eventual marriage, Gaskell creates a character whose judgment and understanding exceed those of a typical heroine and who redefines the traditional as a choice, not an inevitability. Molly desires to support and assist Roger and regards such a role as significant rather than marginalized; however, close consideration of Molly's conventional representation also accentuates the independent and even transgressive nature of Cynthia Kirkpatrick's choices.

From her introduction, the French-schooled Cynthia Kirkpatrick seems a displaced foreign element whose worldly experience strongly contrasts to the placid patriarchy of Hollingford. Initially regarded as an outsider, Cynthia demonstrates proper deference, quick conversation, and pleasant demeanor, all of which quickly win the general approval of Hollingford society. Cynthia's calculated and self-serving behavior eventually achieves her economic and social needs with a minimum of self-denial and sacrifice and becomes Gaskell's major challenge to the customary tropes of women's marginalization identified in *Madwoman.* Unquestionably, Gaskell manipulates certain contrasts between Cynthia and Molly to amplify Molly's "traditional" feminine stereotypes.[28] However, through her creation of the provocative and unconventional Cynthia, Gaskell challenges accepted norms regarding "proper" behavior, marriage, and feminine identity, especially in her examination of Cynthia's relationships with Robert Preston, Roger Hamley, and Walter Henderson. Eventually, Cynthia may follow protocol through marriage, but as the novel ends, her position is one of power and control, not marginalization.

Through Cynthia's relationship with Robert Preston, Lord Cumnor's land agent, Gaskell investigates economic and sexual forces as determinants in a woman's life and examines the potential for scandal and social disaster. Lacking family money, Cynthia finds her options severely limited by her gender—a fact recognized and exploited by Preston. Although she immaturely accepts a gift of money to join her friends (typical behavior for a sixteen-year-old), Cynthia finally recognizes Preston's predatory intent and applies herself to retracting her promise to marry him. Cynthia's ability to work within a limited situation to repay her debt to Preston and extricate herself from any obligation to him clearly demonstrates character strength. Notably, Cynthia is aware that as much as Preston speaks of his great love for her, his obsessive behavior and his adamant refusal to accept her rejection reveal his controlling nature. His offer of marriage provides the possibility of economic security and middle-class social acceptance but at the cost of personal freedom.

Cynthia's subsequent involvement with Roger Hamley develops Molly's forbearance and self-sacrifice and allows Gaskell to reexamine the commonly accepted notion that elevated social position and a gentlemanly partner always provide a basis for an appropriate marriage. The initial connection between Cynthia and Roger arises from a predictable male response to Cynthia's beauty and her engaging manner with men, the only powers she appears to possess. Infatuated with her appearance and pressured by his new position and imminent departure for Africa, Roger arranges a tentative connection, enabling Cynthia to act freely in the present while allowing for a change of mind at a later date. While holding onto the best marital opportunity she has received thus far, Cynthia recognizes drawbacks to the situation and allows herself the freedom of investigating other possibilities. As desirable as the connection to a country squire's family might be, it is not the aristocratic Cumnors. Moreover, the restraint and isolation characteristic of a country squire's life are unequivocally antithetical to Cynthia's sophisticated character. Although her "mad" insistence on refusing the term "engagement" may seem questionable and evidence of superficial egotism, Cynthia retains her agency and finds her best marital option. Through the complexity of Cynthia's behavior, Gaskell questions socially accepted values associated with privileging a self-effacing love like Molly's to the realistic practicality of Cynthia's design. Additionally, Cynthia's perceived malfeasance regarding her "pledge" to Roger is generated by melodramatic convention and popular romantic sentiments that overlook the businesslike, masculine tropes Cynthia uses to create the qualifications for the "arrangement" to which Roger agrees.

Gaskell's realistic rendering of Cynthia's character—her emotional piques, flirtation, deceptions, and irresponsibility—qualifies Cynthia for "madwoman" status as it enhances the goodness and moral strength of Molly's character. Significantly, despite Cynthia's flaws, Gaskell deploys a radical claim for women's agency in marriage through Cynthia's declaration of how marriage will accommodate *her* needs instead of how *she* will accommodate hegemonic expectations: "I'm glad to be free. I dreaded Roger's goodness, and learning, and all that. It was not in my way, and I don't believe I should have ever married him . . . I know he could not have made me happy, and I don't believe he would have been happy with me . . . I would rather be a governess than married to him. I should get weary of him every day of my life" (*Wives,* 561). Through Cynthia's declaration, Gaskell reveals new territory, one not seen in *Madwoman,* in which a woman marries according to her desires, not because it is expedient.

Walter Henderson presents a far more suitable partner for Cynthia and her aspirations than the robust adventurer that Roger becomes. In fact, marriage to Roger would require Cynthia's subordination to the demands of his exploration and his commitments to the scientific community—areas towards which she has no inclination. Cynthia's interest in London's fashionable social scene, as well as that of Paris and other European centers, is not part of Roger's world of African exploration. Gaskell creates in Henderson the best combination of qualities for Cynthia's husband. Described as handsome,

Henderson operates in the social milieu Cynthia desires, has a respectable profession of barrister-at-law, enjoys the benefits of a "private fortune," and is considered "good tempered and kind" (*Wives,* 598). Moreover, Henderson is keen to please Cynthia, who finds him quite tractable and makes her as "happy as she could be" (*Wives,* 598). Most significantly, Gaskell again suggests that mutual understanding, acceptance, and a freedom from enforced marginalization are fundamentally necessary to meaningful marriages when Cynthia admits she told Henderson about her past and "He liked me just as I was" (*Wives,* 597). While seemingly conventional in her choice to marry, Cynthia accommodates her interests; she does not repress them. Cynthia's fate reveals Gaskell's support for the character's choices: rather than being punished for her refusal to accept and adapt to the established feminine identity, Cynthia achieves a notable degree of agency and thus success. With Henderson, Cynthia gains financial security and higher social status than would have been possible with either Preston or Roger, and she is also able to follow her ambitions without repressive constraint.

Throughout *Wives and Daughters,* Gaskell investigates several representations of women's marginalization in a strongly paternalistic society. She initially examines this idea within the traditional framework of marriage as the era's defining identity for every woman of every class; even Lady Cumnor brings Lady Harriet into contact with a desirable suitor. Marriage in this period is often criticized for the sublimation of a woman's identity to that of her husband and the actual loss of what little agency she possesses as a single woman.[29] In *Wives and Daughters,* however, Gaskell posits alternative views that recognize the reality of the social scene and subvert common marital concepts to suggest different possibilities. Hyacinth Clare Kirkpatrick Gibson illustrates the economic hardship and social relegation a widow experiences and argues for a practical marriage to a practical man like Mr. Gibson. Carefully selecting her choice of husband and situation, Hyacinth constructs and manages a pleasant and relatively free existence for herself within her marriage. Likewise, in her lengthy relationship to Roger Hamley, Molly Gibson most closely epitomizes the Victorian paradigm of female virtues—altruistic self-sacrifice, purity of spirit, and moral integrity—ultimately earning her the reward of marriage to her heroic male counterpart. Gaskell's greatest challenge to conventional assumptions about women and marriage emerges through the story of Cynthia Kirkpatrick. Throughout the novel, Cynthia suffers exploitation, evades obligation, sidesteps formal commitment, and orchestrates her marriage to a prominent, wealthy, attractive, and tractable husband. While she risks marginalization through marriage and thus dependence on her husband, she carefully selects and manipulates her opportunities. Through her equally careful use of her sexuality, she revises the usual distribution of power to establish her control and agency within the marriage.

Elizabeth Gaskell's examination of marriage and of the associated expectations of women's agency in *Wives and Daughters* subverts contemporary Victorian perceptions of these topics; it also challenges modern critical arguments claiming primarily the negative and repressive nature of conventional Victorian marriage and gender definition. While recognizing the reality of the marginalization facing women, Gaskell argues that such a fate is not inevitable. Molly Gibson, in her love and support for Roger Hamley, comes closest to fulfilling the general concept of the ideal of a nurturing, self-sacrificing woman, but the depth of Roger's love suggests a union of similar souls, not the subordination of one to the other. Deirdre d'Albertis has remarked, "If Cynthia provides the locus for a reading of Gaskell's text as subversive of masculine discourse, Molly represents a powerful opposing tendency in the same novel: her learning allows her to emulate revered male teachers, even as she denigrates her own capacities and achievements as their obedient student."[30] Alternatively, Hyacinth's experiences demonstrate how economic restraints create a marginalization universally more repressive and damaging than the potential marginalization marriage may impose. Her marriage to Gibson provides her with greater security, status, and agency than she previously experienced. Finally, Cynthia's character flaws may prevent her from classification as a typical Victorian heroine; however, her refusal to follow established expectations blindly, in both behavior and role, challenges the validity of these assumptions of "goodness." Gaskell acknowledges that marriage is a virtually inescapable necessity for social mobility in Victorian society; yet, more importantly, through Cynthia, Gaskell also demonstrates that complete, or at least near complete, agency for women is entirely possible within a marriage. In the conclusion of *Wives and Daughters,* Gaskell provides an alternative reading to situations Gilbert and Gubar's analysis would present as untenable.

Elizabeth Gaskell's novels explore a rapidly developing feminine consciousness struggling to assert itself within the limitations of Victorian patriarchy. Close comparison of the issues and solutions generated by Elizabeth Gaskell's perception with the interpretations developed by Gilbert and Gubar reveals the rich diversity of women's options explored in Gaskell's works. *The Madwoman in the Attic* offers significant, original insight into the feminine consciousness of several nineteenth-century women writers; however, the authors' omission of Elizabeth Gaskell's work and its response to the patriarchal expectations and restraints of the Victorian hegemony reveals Gilbert and Gubar's incomplete assessment of the period's feminine consciousness. Gaskell injects the concepts of accommodation and redefinition into the examination of female agency central to most nineteenth-century women's writing and advances the basis for critical assessment: her even-tempered contribution offers women the possibility of "sanity" in place of "madness" in their confrontation with the often debilitating impositions of Victorian patriarchy.

Notes

1. Sandra M. Gilbert and Susan Gubar, *The Madwoman in the Attic: The Woman Writer and the Nineteenth-Century Literary Imagination* (New Haven: Yale University Press, 1979). Subsequent references will be given parenthetically.

2. See, for example, Nina Auerbach, review of *The Madwoman in the Attic* by Sandra M. Gilbert and Susan Gubar, *Victorian Studies* 23, no. 4 (Summer 1980): 505–7; and Helene Moglen, review of *The Madwoman in the Attic,* by Sandra M. Gilbert and Susan Gubar, *Nineteenth-Century Fiction* 35, no. 2 (September 1980): 225–29.

3. Auerbach review, 505, 506.

4. Deanna L. Davis provides an excellent overview of the feminist critical response to Gaskell and her work in "Feminist Critics and Literary Mothers: Daughters Reading Elizabeth Gaskell," *Signs* 17, no. 3 (1992): 507–32.

5. Deirdre d'Albertis, *Dissembling Fictions: Elizabeth Gaskell and the Victorian Social Text* (New York: St. Martin's Press, 1997), 169.

6. Moglen review, 226–27.

7. Felicia Bonaparte, *The Gypsy-Bachelor of Manchester: The Life of Mrs. Gaskell's Demon* (Charlottesville: University of Virginia Press, 1992), 15.

8. Jenny Uglow, *Elizabeth Gaskell: A Habit of Stories* (London: Faber and Faber, 1993), 201.

9. Elizabeth Langland, *Nobody's Angels: Middle-Class Women and Domestic Ideology in Victorian Culture* (Ithaca, N.Y.: Cornell University Press, 1995), 114.

10. Nancy Armstrong, *Desire and Domestic Fiction: A Political History of the Novel* (New York: Oxford University Press, 1987), 10.

11. Hilary Schor, *Scheherezade in the Market Place: Elizabeth Gaskell and the Victorian Novel* (New York: Oxford University Press, 1992), 121.

12. Elizabeth Gaskell, *The Letters of Mrs. Gaskell,* ed. J.A.V. Chapple and Arthur Pollard (Manchester: Manchester University Press, 1966), 56. See Catherine Gallagher, *The Industrial Reformation of English Fiction* (Chicago: University of Chicago Press, 1985), for an examination of the shifting narrative modes Gaskell incorporates.

13. Shirley Foster, *Victorian Women's Fiction: Marriage, Freedom, and the Individual* (Totowa, N.J.: Barnes and Noble Books, 1985), 145.

14. Elizabeth Gaskell, *Mary Barton* (Harmondsworth, U.K.: Penguin, 1996), 160. Subsequent references will be given parenthetically.

15. Schor, *Scheherezade in the Market Place,* 34.

16. Elizabeth Gaskell, *North and South* (New York: W. W. Norton, 2007), 7, 11. Subsequent references will be given parenthetically.

17. Terry Eagleton, *Myths of Power: A Marxist Study of the Brontës,* 3rd ed. (1975, 1988; Basingstoke, U.K.: Palgrave Macmillan, 2005), 48.

18. Ibid., 65.

19. Dorice Williams Elliott, "The Female Visitor and the Marriage of Classes in Gaskell's *North and South,*" *Nineteenth-Century Literature* 49, no. 1 (1994): 22. Elliott

presents an insightful study of class interactions and Gaskell's reworking of period concerns over the advisability of visitations to the working-class poor.

20. Mary Poovey, *Uneven Developments: The Ideological Work of Gender in Mid-Victorian England* (Chicago: University of Chicago Press, 1988), 3.

21. Elizabeth Starr, "'A Great Engine for Good': The Industry of Fiction in Elizabeth Gaskell's *Mary Barton* and *North and South*," *Studies in the Novel* 34, no. 4 (2002): 393.

22. Langland, *Nobody's Angels*, 206.

23. Michael Cohen, "Reform, Rescue, and the Sisterhoods of *Middlemarch*," *Victorian Literature and Culture* 21 (March 1993): 91. Cohen's essay significantly connects the female characters in Eliot's *Middlemarch* to similar characters in the works of Austen, Gaskell, Dickens, and Collins.

24. Ibid., 475.

25. Margaret Homans, *Bearing the Word: Language and Female Experience in Nineteenth-Century Women's Writing* (Chicago: University of Chicago Press, 1986), 11.

26. Elizabeth Gaskell, *Wives and Daughters* (New York: Barnes and Noble, 2005), 6. Subsequent references will be given parenthetically.

27. Suzy Clarkson Holstein, "Finding a Woman's Place: Gaskell and Authority," *Studies in the Novel* 21, no. 4 (1989): 380–88.

28. Homans, *Bearing the Word*, 257–58. Homans examines several levels of similarity between Molly and Cynthia.

29. Phillipa Levine, "'So Few Prizes and So Many Blanks': Marriage and Feminism in Later Nineteenth-Century England," *Journal of British Studies* 28, no. 2 (1989): 161.

30. D'Albertis, *Dissembling Fictions*, 157.

13

Mimesis and Poiesis

Reflections on Gilbert and Gubar's Reading of Emily Dickinson

Lucia Aiello

"I'm Nobody! Who are you?"

In the opening chapters of *The Madwoman in the Attic*, Sandra M. Gilbert and Susan Gubar trace the genealogy of the metaphor of literary paternity, and explain how patriarchal ideology has penetrated almost every aspect of literary production throughout the ages. In their view, not only does the masculine perspective connote traditional ways of understanding poetry, it also configures the power relationship between the author and the characters he creates, female characters included. Consequently, women wishing to "attempt the pen" have had to master great anxieties, above all what Gilbert and Gubar—following the Bloomian model of literary history—have famously defined as "the anxiety of authorship." While endorsing Gilbert and Gubar's major argument concerning the debilitating effects that the intrinsic misogyny of the Western literary tradition has had on women wishing to "attempt the pen," this article takes issue with the implications their theoretical underpinnings have for the analysis of Emily Dickinson's poetry. In particular, I suggest that the extensive application of their theoretical model to both prose and lyric works by nineteenth-century women writers appears, after nearly thirty years, debatable.[1] Their gendered version of the Bloomian theory of literary history does not sufficiently account for the implications that these women's use of different literary forms have for the deployment of their coping strategies. The lack of differentiation in the analysis of the literary forms that these women writers favored carries with it at least two major consequences. First, the interpretation of women's literary history as the enactment of strategies of survival and rebellion against patriarchal literary authority, disregarding the artistic form they decide to engage with, tends to emphasize the mimetic over the poietic as a mode of characterizing women's relationship to their artworks. Second, such an excessive reliance on the mimetic as a category for understanding narrative strategies in women's literary works leads Gilbert and Gubar to explain the innovative elements at the level of form as the direct expression of the artist's personality or her psychic disposition. In their interpretative scheme, women's art appears as a coping mechanism, whereby women's enactment of their subordination partially compensates for the profound distress caused by the fact of experiencing their creativity as a form of illness.

These points require further explanation. Basing their analytical method on the reading of "metaphors in an experiential way," Gilbert and Gubar suggest that nineteenth-century women writers "act out male metaphors in their own texts, as if trying to understand their implications."[2] Thus, in their study, writing is presented as a sort of therapeutic action that women undertake in order to project outwards the tensions and anxieties emerging from their idiosyncratic, almost schizophrenic, relationship to the literary work of art. In addition, taking at face value patriarchal definitions of the aesthetic, Gilbert and Gubar interpret male literary works as the enactment of grandiose dreams of virility, sexual potency, and domination. Only occasionally do they admit that the rhetoric of virile domination might diverge dramatically from the truth content of overconfident male writers' literary works.[3] The end point of this theoretical path is a binary version of literary history, characterized by male self-assertion on one side and by timid, self-effacing, and guilt-ridden female incursions into the alien territory of literature on the other. These traits, in their opinion, have characterized literary history from Aristotle to Ruskin:

> Defining poetry as a mirror held up to nature, the mimetic aesthetic that begins with Aristotle and descends through Sidney, Shakespeare, and Johnson implies that the poet, like a lesser God, has made or engendered an alternative, mirror-universe in which he actually seems to enclose or trap shadows of reality. Similarly, Coleridge's Romantic concept of the "human imagination or esemplastic power" is of a virile, generative force which echoes "the eternal act of creation in the infinite I AM," while Ruskin's phallic-sounding "Penetrative imagination" is a "possession-taking faculty" and a "piercing . . . mind's tongue" that seizes, cuts down, and gets at the root of experience in order "to throw up what new shoots it will." (*Madwoman,* 5)

It might be worth deconstructing this binary. In the first instance, it should be noticed that, although the trajectory from the Aristotelian to the Romantic concept of poetry is inflexibly marked by the "phallic-sounding imagination," changes occur that have a significant impact on determining the kind of legacy that women writers inherit and with which they engage. As Hans Robert Jauss makes clear, one way of distinguishing the modern from the ancient and medieval world is by registering the shift in the conception of artistic poiesis: "From a making which the perfect antedates as a model to be imitated, to a creation which itself produces the perfect (or, expressed differently, the beautiful appearance of perfection)."[4] The poet as the imitator of nature and creator of "shadows of reality," historically gives way to the poet as the maker of a reality all of its own and, if not superior, at least on an equal stand with God.

Even acknowledging the inherited concept of the poet as the projection of a masculine way of understanding creativity, the implications of this change in emphasis from mimesis to poiesis are relevant for understanding nineteenth-century women's relationship to literary creation. As do other women writers of this period, Emily Dickinson inherits a version of poetry heavily centered on a godlike masculine image of the self. Thus, the major problem she has to face is the dislodgment of this godlike poetic self from the house of poetry. This problem, however, has connotations that are peculiar to her engagement with the poetic form and thus are not always applicable to the works of women who expressed themselves in the novelistic form. Gilbert and Gubar, on the other hand, submit the formal concerns these women's works arouse to biographical explanations, and read their works as a reflection of the difficulties they experienced as artists. Ultimately, they interpret nineteenth-century women's novels and poems as the enactment of these women's condition of self-denial.

Dickinson is not exempt from such treatment. Her "self-effacing" poems are seen as the further demonstration of her inability to assert her feminine self in the public sphere. For the sake of their argument, Gilbert and Gubar set up an equivalence in which male self-assertion corresponds to an aesthetic of domination, while female self-effacement and social timidity corresponds to an aesthetic of renunciation. Although this correspondence might be instrumental in defining the role women writers were allocated in patriarchal literary history, it does not facilitate the comprehension of Dickinson's intricate poetry. By interpreting her poetry as the enactment of her personal situation, Gilbert and Gubar suggest that Dickinson's dismissal of publishers and her long seclusion are symptomatic of her fear of confronting the public as well as of her now much-investigated semi-psychotic condition. In their reading, they counterpoise Walt Whitman's poetic celebration of his own subjectivity (*Madwoman,* 556) to Dickinson's self-restrained "I'm Nobody":

I'm Nobody! Who are you?
Are you—Nobody—Too?
Then there's a pair of us?
Don't tell! They'd advertise—you know!

How dreary—to be—Somebody!
How public—like a Frog—
To tell one's name—the livelong June—
To an admiring Bog!
J288 (1861) / Fr260 (1861)[5]

In their view, this poem is emblematic of "the fundamental alienation a woman (especially, perhaps, a woman poet) feels from her 'own' name: it is not hers to risk, not hers to publicize, not even hers to immortalize." The conclusion is that "in Dickinson's case, . . . the literary consequences of being Nobody were far-reaching indeed, ranging from a sometimes grotesquely childlike self-image to a painfully distorted sense of size, a perpetual gnawing hunger, and even, finally, a deep confusion about identity" (*Madwoman,* 555). However, if one interprets the "childlike self-image" and the "confusion about identity" not as "metaphors in an experiential way," but as experiments in poiesis, then the innovative value of Dickinson's poetry becomes powerfully visible and the assertiveness of her new poetics forcefully accomplished.

In *Emily Dickinson and Her Contemporaries: Women's Verse in America, 1820-1885,* Elizabeth Petrino argues that in order to fully appreciate Dickinson's "inspired and original verse," one has to read her decision not to publish as "a defiant act that rejected the standards for women writers in this period." By viewing Dickinson against the shared culture and literary tradition, Petrino goes beyond Gilbert and Gubar's biographical approach and brings to the surface the more original aspects of her poetry: "Although Gilbert and Gubar's approach has been instrumental in defining a female literary tradition, I would also argue that we need to investigate Dickinson's poetry more fully with respect to the literary achievements of her sister poets."[6] It could be argued even further that if one regards Dickinson as a "consummate poet," her poetry could be viewed against the literary achievements of controversial male poets such as Friedrich Hölderlin and Paul Celan, who translated into German twelve poems by Dickinson.[7]

Following up on Petrino's point, then, Dickinson's *Nobody* could be interpreted as the woman poet's discovery that poetry is mainly concerned with the *impossibility* of self-assertion, and that the confident "I am" of the male lyrical tradition is nothing other than the parody that mocks the whole project constructed around the idea of subjectivity. However, while for the post-Romantic male poet such a discovery is the source of his disenchantment and melancholy attitude, it is in this parodic discrepancy that the woman poet operates. In contrast with this falsely confident image of a *Somebody,* Dickinson productively opposes a *Nobody* whose contours are configured in and through the making of the poem. Therefore, more than a retreat into a "negative identity," as suggested by Roland Hagenbüchle, Dickinson's *Nobody* performs the function of disconnecting the inherited concept of subjectivity from burdensome metaphysical and semantic connotations. In other words, Dickinson's refusal to be *Somebody,* rather than indicating her "choice to leave her self totally undetermined as a reflection of the unknowable mythical You," and therefore her inward surrender to "self-negating imperatives," could be read as the ground where multiple determinations of an alienated concept of subjectivity become graspable even across genders.[8] Only in the openness of such a multiplicity of determinations is the encounter with an anti-mythical "you" imaginable. It is not accidental that Nobody's first confrontation in the poem is with another Nobody, not with a Somebody, and that the poetic "I" imagines itself in the company of an equal ("Then there's a pair of us?"). Through the destabilization of the inherited version of subjectivity, Dickinson's poetry exposes the linguistic idiosyncrasy underpinning women poets' relationship to the most masculine form of art, lyric poetry. The woman poet cannot inhabit a language that expresses the singularity of the masculine experience without feeling displaced. For Dickinson, therefore, the distance between the lyrical subject and her own sense of poetic self is constitutive of her poetic experience as a woman poet. The poetess who speaks in the language of the Other is concretely exploring an alien territory and opening up the possibility that this territory might be inhabited by "translating" poetically her experience of displacement and alienation.

Experiments in Poiesis

> Dickinson's life itself . . . became a kind of novel or narrative poem in which, through an extraordinarily complex series of manoeuvres, aided by costumes that came inevitably to hand, this inventive poet enacted and eventually resolved both her anxieties about her art and her anger at female subordination. Her terse, explosive poems are therefore, in a sense, the speech of a fictional character. . . . Indeed, understood as an elaborate set of dramatic monologues, her poems constitute the "dialogue" in an extended fiction whose subject is the life of that supposed person who has christened herself variously, Emilie, Daisy, Brother Emily, Uncle Emily, and simply Dickinson. (*Madwoman,* 583)

In the conclusive chapter dedicated to Emily Dickinson, Gilbert and Gubar argue that by transforming her life into a verse drama, Dickinson manages to transcend the "double bind" of the woman poet: "on the one hand, the impossibility of self-assertion for a woman, on the other hand the necessity of self-assertion for a poet" (*Madwoman,* 584).[9] In their view, Dickinson's poetry can be interpreted as a sort of versified biography, configured according to the aesthetic canon of the Romantic tradition (612, 648-50). In their analysis, there are frequent comparisons with, and references to, William Blake (587, 594, 603), to the "Gothic Romance" into which supposedly she turned her own life (594), and to "Romantic inspiration" (649). Their reading of Dickinson's relationship to poetry as a fictional enactment helps us appreciate the full extent of her dedication to poetry. Nevertheless, it is less helpful when dealing with the innovative force of Dickinson's poems. By framing her poetic endeavor within the Romantic tradition, Gilbert and Gubar fundamentally see Dickinson's poetic talent expressed in the mimetic reproduction of experience by means of the "dramatic monologue" (589).

In his influential study *The Poetry of Experience* (1957), Robert Langbaum designates the translation of experience into the sympathetic perspective of the dramatic monologue as a primary distinctive category between modern (Romantic) lyric poetry and classical drama. In Langbaum's definition, the poetry of experience privileges the lyrical moment as a "movement for its own sake," where values are not judged in the light of a meaningful unfolding of events but are turned into "biographical phenomena, manifestations of a life which as life is self-justifying." Langbaum indicates the evocation of a higher form of experience as the unifying purpose "from the romantic poems of Wordsworth and Browning, with their individualized speakers and objects, to the symbolist poems of Yeats and Eliot, with their archetypal speakers and objects."[10] Chronologically, Dickinson could be included in this list. However, reading her poems as poetry of experience is as perplexing as interpreting her poetic corpus as the versified expression of her singular experience of self-imposed seclusion. Such a reading fails to appreciate that, at a very fundamental level, Dickinson's poetry ponders on the validity of lived experience as an epistemological category. In other words, many of her poems reflect on the possibility that the linguistic articulation of experience via the poetic form inevitably casts doubts on the validity of the experiential moment as the poet's access to a higher truth. The distance that the poetic form establishes between the poetic "I" and lived experience in fact renders definitions of Dickinson's art as the poetic expression of her *subjectivity* problematic. I suggest that in her poetry the poetic "I" speculates on the impossibility of accounting for *any* lived experience in an unmediated way.

By turning Dickinson's relationship to her art into a self-perpetuating narrative of survival and renunciation, Gilbert and Gubar mitigate the disruptive potential of Dickinson's rebellion. In spite of their disorientation in front of Virginia Woolf's silence on Emily Dickinson (silence motivated either by ignorance or—one could equally argue—by incomprehension),[11] the two critics base their analysis of women's poetry, Dickinson's included, on the Woolfian model of the woman poet, Judith Shakespeare. In Woolf's story, Judith is the great playwright's imaginary sister who, because she is a woman, cannot pursue her much desired literary career. A close reading makes it clear that Judith's self-denial is not just the result of the abuse to which she is subjected. Judith is caught in the paradox of having to create art in the language and forms conceived by her putative brother/oppressor. In other words, Judith's unachievable aesthetic ideal is in fact her brother's, and this prevents her from becoming the paradigmatic woman poet. Instead, she is a hybrid, a male poet in feminine clothes. A different reading of Dickinson's poetry might suggest that Dickinson is not concerned with the possibility of becoming a Judith Shakespeare, namely a woman who is destined to artistic and personal self-denial. On the contrary, the first task she undertakes is to get beyond what could be termed as the Judith Shakespeare syndrome, and to dissolve the marriage between poetry and the individual voice of the (male) poet.

The configuration that Gilbert and Gubar give to self-assertion moves within the contours of a masculine idea of the self and of poiesis, in relation to which women poets cannot but experience the burden of their own inadequacy. When the two critics maintain that "for Dickinson, indeed, art is not so much *poesis*—making—as it is *mimesis*—enactment, and this is because she believes that even consciousness is not so much reflective as it is theatrical" (586), they decidedly bind Dickinson and her work to Judith Shakespeare's stifled condition. In their view, Judith/Emily's isolated sparks of rebellion and poetic innovation only demonstrate the "psychic splits" she endured and partially overcame through her enactments. As Gilbert and Gubar observe, "Despite her secret sense of election, Dickinson understood the social requirements, masquerading as cosmic laws, which obliged every woman in some sense to enact the role of Nobody" (588). In this perspective, Dickinson's poetic beginnings are interpreted as the childlike enactment of a father/daughter relationship (587). This "child mask enabled her . . . to write a great deal of astonishingly innovative poetry—poetry full of grammatical 'mistakes' and stylistic eccentricities such as only a mad child could write" (591). Dickinson's attentive and playful examination and handling of words is imputed to her "impersonation of a child's naiveté" (593). Even in later years, Gilbert and Gubar argue, Dickinson's "poetic questionings of language and experience remained childlike in their perspective of Awe but darkened and became severer" (593). Her poetic experiments of the 1860s are interpreted as strategies that convey "what she defines as her rejection by that masterful male adult world of 'Day' to whose Requirements she has, with conscious and distinctly unchildish obstinacy, refused to rise" (594). Her metaphorical blindness "seems to have functioned in part as a castration metaphor" (595). Her poetic development is understood as the painful descent from agoraphobia to claustrophobia, into madness.

As stated previously, recent readings of the poems have revealed that Dickinson's poetic "mistakes and eccentricities" are in fact emblems of the poet's incursions into a zone from which she, as a woman poet, does not feel estranged. Her investigation of the potentialities of the poetic word emerges out of her consciousness of the impossibility of channeling the poetic word into the mimetic enactment of an individual state or condition. This can be better understood if one contests not only the idea that the dramatic monologue conveys lived experience, but also that it is indistinguishable from that drama that the life of the poet is. Yet the distinction between the drama that takes place in the privacy of the human heart and the one that is enacted in front of an audience (whether real or imaginary) is quite sharp in "Drama's Vitallest Expression":

> Drama's Vitallest Expression is the Common Day
> That arise and set about Us—
> Other Tragedy
> Perish in the Recitation—
> This—the best enact
> When the Audience is scattered
> And the Boxes shut—
>
> "Hamlet" to Himself were Hamlet—
> Had not Shakespeare wrote—
> Though the "Romeo" left no Record
> Of his Juliet,
>
> It were infinite enacted
> In the Human Heart—
> Only Theatre recorded
> Owner cannot shut—
> *J741 (1863) / Fr776 (1863)*

Gilbert and Gubar read this poem as the demonstration of Dickinson's "theatrical," "mimetic" enactment of the "supposed persons" she imagines being in her poetry. However, as Páraic Finnerty suggests in *Emily Dickinson's Shakespeare,* this poem cannot but register the fact that "for the speaker, that which is most personal in the human experience is still unrecorded; although Shakespeare and his characters have examined the vast spaces of the heart, there remains something to be written about." There is a singularity about the drama of the human heart, which words are inadequate to express. Shakespeare's dramas and Dickinson's poems can only gesture towards, and reflect on, this characteristic of the human condition: "This returns us to Dickinson's use of Hamlet's 'wavering'—he 'wavers for all of us,' not only between life and death, but because his struggles evoke those private experiences that are inexpressible and ungraspable."[12]

The interpretation of Dickinson's poetry as the moment of self-conscious externalization of her intimate drama entails the reflective moment. In "Trying to Think with Emily Dickinson," Jed Deppman demonstrates "how important the category of thought was for Dickinson and how committed she was to certain projects of thinking."[13] *Thinking,* for Dickinson, is the only option she has to turn the inadequacy of language into an empowering process, a possibility. Thought is a weapon and her thoughts concerning Life, Death, I, Immortality, and so forth, are the result of a complex elaboration on the distance that the poetic form establishes between language, experience, and meaning. Thus Dickinson's handling of words might indeed be regarded as "childlike," to use Gilbert and Gubar's expression, if with this term one refers to the playful element involved in presenting the poetic word in a myriad of new combinations and associations. However, Dickinson's reflection on the poetic use of words, far from being the fruit of naïve childish language games, elicits further questions concerning their potential. For example, the poetic status of words such as "wife" and "woman" is not commensurate with the mimetic enactment of the condition of wife and woman. The poetic transposition of these words is in and of itself a kind of reflection on their status in the ordinary language. These words bear witness to their inadequacy to give full individuation to the common day "drama" while they poietically project the possibility of an alternative based on the consciousness of this inherent lack. In "I'm 'wife'—I've finished that," the conflict between two very different conditions of being a wife is located within the same signifier, that is, the word "wife":

I'm "wife"—I've finished that—
That other state—
I'm Czar—I'm "Woman" now—
It's safer so—

How odd the Girl's life looks
Behind this soft Eclipse—
I think that Earth feels so
To folks in Heaven—now—

This being comfort—then
That other kind—was pain—
But why compare?
I'm "Wife"! Stop there!
J199 (1860) / Fr225 (1861)

It should not go unnoticed that the word "wife" is spelled in different ways throughout the poem. In the first line, wife is spelled with the small "w," while in the last line of the poem, the word begins with the capital letter. Between these two, there stands the word "Woman," oddly juxtaposed to the word "Czar," and counterpoised to the word "Girl." The poem therefore presents an internal movement that discloses the multiple potential of these words. In this perspective, the simple binary that Gilbert and Gubar construct around the two concepts of renunciation and self-assertion is complicated by the possibility of inversion of traditional hierarchies and established power relationships. To a wife, the girl's life looks "odd"; however, the wife's life is a comforting, "safer" "soft eclipse." The "eclipse," although "soft," arouses in the wife a tinge of envy for the girl's life, which, however, is characterized by "pain." The Czar status applies to the Woman, not to the Girl, and it is in the passage from Girl to Woman that the transition from wife to Wife is sanctioned. The poetic "I" is persistent in almost every line of the poem and stands as a principle of non-identification and first condition of multiple identities. It is in this obstinate differentiation that one can detect the poetic transposition of Dickinson's personal confrontation with the masculine poetic tradition. As Gilbert and Gubar concede, "Rather early in her life as an artist, Dickinson must have half-consciously perceived that she could avoid the necessity of renouncing her art by renouncing, instead, that concept of womanliness which required self-abnegating renunciation" (*Madwoman*, 590). In this act, they see also a gesture of sexual self-denial, whereby the asexual (childlike) consoling "election" of the artist supplants the suffocating adulthood of the woman (591). However, this perspective leads to the underestimation both of Dickinson's project and of her "astonishingly innovative poetry," which in Gilbert and Gubar's interpretative scheme finds only a random justification.

On the other hand, Dickinson's engagement with poetry can plausibly be portrayed as a challenge to the male concept of subjectivity at the core of the masculine lyric form. Her "White Election," far from being an asexual possibility of childhood, is grounded on the supreme awareness of having reached the core of the forbidden area upon which the image of subjectivity is grounded. Dickinson is not just an observer at the gates of poetry but the acute manipulator of words and forms. By acknowledging the otherness of the poetic word vis-à-vis the feminine experience, she undermines directly its patriarchal authority. She recognizes that, in order to confront the constitutive insufficiency of the word, she must dwell in an area of risk and possibility that the composite dialectic of prose does not allow for:

I dwell in Possibility—
A fairer House than Prose—
More numerous of Windows—
Superior—for Doors—

Of Chambers as the Cedars—
Impregnable of Eye—
And for an Everlasting Roof
The Gambrels of the Sky—

Of Visitors—the fairest—
For Occupation—This—
The spreading wide of narrow Hands
To gather Paradise—
J657 (1862) / Fr466 (1862)

Poetry offers such a possibility, especially to the female artist, who, in the formal organization of her work, recognizes and registers the exclusion of the feminine experience from the poetic word. It is therefore as a woman poet that Dickinson divests crucial words, tainted with this exclusion, of their traditional metaphysical connotations and transforms the mimetic experience of renunciation into a poietic act, one that creates the conditions for previously inconceivable combinations. As Gilbert and Gubar admit, "In her hands, words are examined, handled, tasted, fondled with ironic Awe" (593). It does not come as a surprise, then, that in this ironic examination, words such as Day and Midnight, or Light and Darkness, display a prismatic ambivalence that cannot simply be ascribed to Dickinson's "gothic" enactment of her inner conflict between the impossibility of renunciation and the inevitability of it. The ambiguity of Dickinson's poetic word might in fact be one of the "Requirements" to accomplish her poetic mission:

She rose to His Requirement—dropt
The Playthings of Her Life
To take the honorable Work
Of Woman, and of Wife—

If ought She missed in Her new Day,
Of Amplitude, or Awe—
Or first Prospective—Or the Gold
In using, wear away,

It lay unmentioned—as the Sea
Develop Pearl, and Weed,
But only to Himself—be known
The Fathoms they abide—
J732 (1863) / F857 (1864)

In Gilbert and Gubar's interpretation, the metaphor of husband and wife is explicatory of Dickinson's "psychic split" between the "strong, assertively masculine part of the woman that must be called *Himself* in the patriarchal culture," and the "social requirements, masquerading as cosmic laws, which obliged every woman in some sense to enact the role of Nobody" (588). Paula Bennett is categorical in interpreting the final stanza as a parodic version of Ariel's famous song in *The Tempest:*

Full fadom five thy father lies;
Of his bones are coral made;
Those are pearls that were his eyes:
Nothing of him that doth fade,
But doth suffer a sea-change
Into something rich and strange
Sea-nymphs hourly ring his knell:
Ding-dong
(I.ii.399)[14]

"Unlike the transformation which the lost father undergoes in Shakespeare's magic lyric," Bennett argues, "the 'sea-change' which the wife (mother) experiences in Dickinson's poem is only ironically a form of rebirth. It does not lead to an enhanced or more valuable being. . . . Instead, the wife's hopes and her hopes (her 'first Prospective') are drowned in the silence and obscurity of the marital sea. If anything comes of them, whether pearl or weed, only the husband knows. To the world, she might as well be dead."[15]

Finnerty, while endorsing Bennett's reading of this poem, makes another suggestion. He notices that Dickinson's wife does not drown and, tightening the links with the poem's putative source, *The Tempest,* he puts much emphasis on the secret powers of the "gifted woman": "The gifted woman will rise, revealing herself and her art to her chosen lover. Dickinson might be setting up an analogy between this 'wife' and Shakespeare's heroines who 'ideally' dwindle into wives; this Miranda-like figure drops the 'Play' things of her life, drowning her powers in order to return to Naples as Ferdinand's wife."[16] Also, Finnerty sets up the analogy between this woman, who renounces "her own riches and endowments, with Prospero's giving up of his magic powers,

'I'll break my staff, / Bury it certain fathoms in the earth, / And, deeper than did ever plummet sound / I'll drown my book' [vi, 54-57]."[17]

As one can discern, the interpretative possibilities are many. If it is incontestable that the requirements have a masculine connotation of intimacy, the metaphorical scope of the marriage image and of the transition from a girlish life to the more "honorable work" of Woman and Wife is not necessarily reducible to biographical correspondences, which in any case are only hypothesized. Dickinson's intense focus on her poetic endeavors and the persistent personification and gendering of abstract nouns allow for parallel interpretative possibilities. The condition of the woman in her new situation (and not the husband's, up to whose requirements she rose), might be comparable to the Sea (personified as male), who in producing pearls and weeds knows the toll these have to pay, namely, of "abiding" the profundity of the abyss. Such is the condition of the bride of poetry. Only she knows the cost of producing pearls, of doing the "honorable work." The time of "awe" and "amplitude" is now processed into a mature reflection, which propels her poetry on the cusp of signification. The contrasting metaphors, used in many poems, of night and day, sun and darkness, apart from their contextual and arguable meaning indicate that in the fathoms of the abyss "abide" the possibilities of transformation:

> The Daisy follows soft the Sun—
> And when his golden walk is done—
> Sits shyly at his feet—
> He—waking—finds the flower there—
> Wherefore—Marauder—art thou here?
> Because, Sir, love is sweet!
>
> We are the Flower—Thou the Sun!
> Forgive us, if as days decline—
> We nearer steal to Thee!
> Enamored of the parting West—
> The peace—the flight—the amethyst—
> Night's possibility!
> *J106 (1859) / F161 (1860)*

As Gilbert and Gubar remark, "If night is the interval when the repressive solar Nobodaddy relaxes his constraints, its possibility for a poet may be self-assertion" (*Madwoman*, 601). While in the final analysis they interpret this possibility as "abandonment" (602), that is, suspension of meaning and loss of control over the material, it may be argued that in the peace of the Night, the poetess discovers that the woman poet's longing for self-assertion is inscribed, as a possibility, in words' tainted history. Then a new configuration emerges, a "double bind" made up of loss and exclusion, which connects intimately the woman poet to her poetic word. Paradoxically, then, the poems where the comprehension of meaning seems denied are the ones in which "the wound" is finally registered, thematically and formally:

A great Hope fell
You heard no noise
The Ruin was within
Oh cunning Wreck
That told no Tale
And let no Witness in

The mind was built for mighty Freight
For dread occasion planned
How often foundering at Sea
Ostensibly, on Land

A not admitting of the wound
Until it grew so wide
That all my Life had entered it
And there were troughs beside—

A closing of the simple lid
That opened to the sun
Until the tender Carpenter
Perpetual nail it down—
J1123 (1868) / F1187-88 (1870)[18]

For Gilbert and Gubar, this poem is indicative of Dickinson's ontological "powerlessness" and imprisonment "not in a night's ambiguous possibility of fulfillment but in midnight's certainty of abandonment" (*Madwoman,* 604). However, the "ambiguous possibility" is willfully maintained by Dickinson and its possibilities are pushed beyond the limits permitted to women poets of the time. In her article "The Ample Word: Immanence and Authority in Dickinson's Poetry," Joanne Feit Diehl rightly argues that "the immanence and authority manifested in Dickinson's poetry bespeak of a will to power second to none in the history of Romanticism. Hers is an audacious poetics that pushes language to the very edge of meaning and at times, beyond."[19] Thus the "tender Carpenter" who "nails down" the "simple lid that opened to the sun" is in another poem identified with the poetess herself:

Myself was formed—a Carpenter—
An unpretending time

My Plane, and I, together wrought
Before a Builder came—

To measure our attainments—
Had we the Art of Boards
Sufficiently developed—He'd hire us
At Halves—

My Tools took Human—Faces—
The Bench, where we had toiled—
Against the Man, persuaded—
We—Temples build—I said—
J488 (1862) / F475 (1862)

In this poem, the woman poet is identified with a maker of things, who uncompromisingly rejects the alluring economic rewards of building "boards" and assertively defends the value of her less remunerative and most daunting work: "We—Temples build—I said."

Postscript: In the Sibyl's Words

In the crucial chapter of *The Madwoman in the Attic* called "The Parables of the Cave," Gilbert and Gubar analyze feminine interpretations of Plato's parable of the cave and of other narratives where the cave appears to be central. Interpreting the cave as "a female place, a womb-shaped enclosure" (*Madwoman,* 93), they develop an archetypal theory of matrilineal artistic heritage that can be traced back to the "mother-goddess myth" of the Cumæan Sibyl. In their reading of Mary Shelley's account of the story of the Cumæan Sibyl, as it is described in the author's fictional introduction to *The Last Man,* the cave is the repository of "female memory," the place where "the woman artist redefines and recovers the lost Atlantis of her literary heritage" (99). In Gilbert and Gubar's words, therefore, woman's art is the result of a painstaking process of re-membering what has been forgotten and of giving form to what has been dis-membered, of assembling the pieces of a shattered tradition that the woman artist finally recognizes as her own.

It is undeniable that, as with most archetypal theories, the myth of the mother-goddess is forceful and seductive. Above all, it provides a narrative that alleviates the anxiety of authorship that haunted the first generation of women writers. However, a fresh reading of this chapter might elicit interesting questions on how convincing (and convenient) it is to define women's creativity in terms of a nostalgic look backward. To begin with, one might speculate if by "the cratered night of female memory" (*Madwoman,* 99) one should necessarily intend a symbolic place where memories of a feminine subjectivity are preserved and ready to be given relief in women's artistic production. There are aspects of Mary Shelley's appropriation of the Cumæan Sibyl's story that are worth pointing out and that Gilbert and Gubar undervalue for the purposes of their theoretical configuration. Thus, in order to bring them to the surface, it might be interesting to begin with the Sibyl's story and then to consider Gilbert and Gubar's reading of Shelley's story.

Unlike Virgil in the *Aeneid,* Ovid in the *Metamorphoses* lets the Cumæan Sibyl tell her story. Noticing that Aeneas reveres her like a goddess, the Sibyl promptly reminds him that she is mortal and that revering mortals like gods generates errors. Thus, she tells Aeneas her story, "Lest you should err in ignorance,"

> when I was still an innocent young girl, I was offered endless eternal life, if I would yield myself to Phoebus, who was in love with me. While the god hoped for my consent, he was eager to bribe me with gifts, and said: "Maiden of Cumae, choose what you wish and you will have your desire!" I pointed to a heap of dust which had been swept together, and foolishly asked that I might have as many birthdays as there were grains of dust: but I forgot to ask for perpetual youth as well. Yet Phoebus offered me all those years, and eternal youth too, if I would suffer his love. I scorned his gift, and remained unwed. Now the happier time of life is fled, and with shaky steps comes sick old age, which I must long endure. For, as you see me now, I have lived through seven generations: in order to equal the number of grains of dust, it remains for me to see three harvests, three hundred vintages. A time will come when I shall shrink from present fine stature into a tiny creature, thanks to my length of days, and my limbs, shrivelled with age, will be reduced to a mere handful. No one will think that I was ever loved, or that I pleased a god, and perhaps even Phoebus himself will fail to recognize me, or else deny that he ever had any affection for me. So changed shall I be, and invisible to anyone. But still, the fates will leave me my voice, and by my voice I shall be known.[20]

Thus from Ovid we learn that the story of the Sibyl, more than of a mother-goddess myth, is the story of a woman's rebellion against the gods and of her subsequent punishment. As a result of her refusal to marry Phoebus, the Sibyl is doomed to carry out the task the gods have assigned to her, namely the task of mediatrix, of speaker on their behalf. She is allowed to speak, but never in her own voice. When Phoebus speaks through her, she turns and twists almost as if pulled by strings, like a marionette. However, she does not just *speak.* Her prophetic voice is also *inscribed* in leaves, which are then scattered by the wind, so that only the meticulous work of deciphering will make some sense of them. Peculiarly, it is in writing only that the Sibyl transgresses her designated role, in that she creates the condition for new meaning to be extracted out of the leaves. In the leaves, it is not so much the voice of the gods that speaks as it is her poietic skill which she consigns to posterity, namely her ability to generate a surplus of meaning awaiting to be deciphered. This is why in the *Aeneid,* Aeneas is concerned that the Sibyl should *speak* to him, rather than inscribing her prophecies in the leaves:

> But now commit no verses to the leaves
> Or they may be confused, shuffled and whirled
> By playing winds: chant them aloud, I pray.[21]

In her fictional introduction to *The Last Man,* Mary Shelley and her friend approach the cave together. As Gilbert and Gubar point out, it is "sad" indeed that "not Mary Shelley but her male companion is able to recognize the Sibyl's cave and readily to decipher some of the difficult languages in which the sibylline leaves are written" (*Madwoman,* 96). In the same passage, however, the fictional Mary Shelley also states that she is capable of understanding some of the languages in which the leaves are written, and that the "hasty selection" of leaves is made with the contribution and understanding of both:

> This was certainly the Sibyl's Cave; not indeed exactly as Virgil describes it; but the whole of this land had been so convulsed by earthquake and volcano, that the change was not wonderful, though the traces of ruin were effaced by time; and we probably owed the preservation of these leaves, to the accident which had closed the mouth of the cavern, and the swift-growing vegetation which had rendered its sole opening impervious to the storm. We made a hasty selection of such of the leaves, *whose writing one at least of us could understand;* and then, laden with our treasure, we bade adieu to the dim hypaethric cavern, and after much difficulty succeeded in rejoining our guides.[22]

While the solution of the enigma, which the sibylline leaves are, has traditionally been a male activity, in this version of the story the woman writer finally finds her way to the cave and laboriously embarks upon this difficult task. Shelley's fictional author, who keeps and finally deciphers all the leaves, gives them "a consistent form," although, she admits, the "main substance" "rests on the divine intuitions which the Cumaean damsel obtained from heaven."[23] In the resulting work (supposedly *The Last Man*) are therefore inscribed the Sibyl's intuitions (inscribed in the leaves), the author's friend's knowledge (the patriarchal tradition), and her own artistic talent (the feminine poietic). It is this poietic activity that frees the Sibyl from the spell of having to speak in someone else's voice and inaugurates the tradition of the woman artist. In this reading, then, the cave is the symbol of the female *imprisoned* in the role of prophetess and the "divine intuition," which Mary Shelley mentions, is the Sibyl's final transgression: by writing on the leaves, she transgresses her role as the oracle and turns the prophecies into fragments of poetic possibility. Only in writing can the Sibyl avoid being turned into the instrument of the gods; in writing she can express her own intuitions, although in an enigmatic and necessarily incomprehensible way. By giving poetic form to the sibylline leaves, the woman artist constructs "herself as a woman of art," as Gilbert and Gubar suggest. However, in this construction, she does not take upon herself the role of prophetess but of witness. The story of the Sibyl is the story of women giving voice to memories that do not belong to them and reframing them in a context in which their absence is finally registered. Thus, speaking in the Sibyl's own words means to bear witness to her sacrifice. In this sense, woman's lost Atlantis is not the cave but the realization of the fact that the leaves belong just as much to her as to her male counterpart. What belongs entirely to her is not the mimetic enactment of the role that once was the Sibyl, but the poietic conception of a new form of art, and therefore of a new time where the novel Sibyls can speak in their own voices.

Notes

1. Recent scholarship has offered radically alternative models of interpretation that pay less attention to the psychological implications of Dickinson's poetry and focus on its formal aspects. Particularly relevant for this essay are Cristanne Miller, *Emily Dickinson: A Poet's Grammar* (Cambridge: Harvard University Press, 1987); Joanne Feit Diehl, *Dickinson and the Romantic Imagination* (Princeton: Princeton University Press, 1981), and "The Ample Word: Immanence and Authority in Dickinson's Poetry," *Emily Dickinson Journal* 14, no. 2 (2005): 1–11; Jed Deppman, "Trying to Think with Emily Dickinson," *Emily Dickinson Journal* 14, no. 1 (2004): 84–103; Christine Ross, "Uncommon Measures: Emily Dickinson's Subversive Prosody," *Emily Dickinson Journal* 10, no. 1 (2001): 70–98.

2. Sandra M. Gilbert and Susan Gubar, *The Madwoman in the Attic: The Woman Writer and the Nineteenth-Century Literary Imagination* (New Haven: Yale University Press, 1979), xiii, xii. Subsequent references will be given parenthetically.

3. "To be sure, male writers also 'swerve' from their predecessors, and they too produce literary texts whose revolutionary messages are concealed behind stylized facades. The most original male writers, moreover, sometimes seem 'not quite right' to those readers we have recently come to call 'establishment' critics" (Gilbert and Gubar, *Madwoman*, 74). On the other hand, however, their labeling of Gerard Manley Hopkins as "the apostle of aesthetic virility" seems to cancel out the previous statement. For more recent interpretation of Hopkins's ambiguous poetics, see David Miller, *With Poetry and Philosophy: Four Dialogic Studies, Wordsworth, Browning, Hopkins, and Hardy* (Newcastle: Cambridge Scholars Publishing, 2007), chapter 3.

4. Hans Robert Jauss and Michael Shaw, "Poiesis," *Critical Inquiry* 8, no. 3 (1982): 595.

5. The following abbreviations are used for reference to the writings of Emily Dickinson: J—Emily Dickinson, *The Poems of Emily Dickinson,* ed. Thomas H. Johnson, 3 vols. (Cambridge: Harvard University Press, 1955). Fr—Emily Dickinson, *The Poems of Emily Dickinson,* ed. R. W. Franklin, 3 vols. (Cambridge: Harvard University Press, 1998). Citation in the text is by poem number.

6. Elizabeth A. Petrino, *Emily Dickinson and Her Contemporaries: Women's Verse in America 1820–1885* (Hanover, N.H.: University Press of New England, 1998), 4, 9.

7. Petrino, *Emily Dickinson,* 8. Elsewhere, I argue that Hölderlin's use of abstractions resembles Dickinson's treatment of abstract words such as Death, Immortality, Life, etc. See Lucia Aiello, "'Of Death I try to think like this': Emily Dickinson's Play with Death," in *Layers of Dying and Death,* ed. Kate Woodthorpe (Oxford: Interdisciplinary Press, 2007), 139–47. On Paul Celan as translator of Dickinson, see Kerstin Behnke, "Dickinson's Poetry in Translation: The Example of Paul Celan," in *The Emily Dickinson Handbook,* ed. Gudrun Grabher, Roland Hegenbüchle, and Cristanne Miller (Amherst: University of Massachusetts Press, 1998), 385–407.

8. Roland Hagenbüchle is quoted in Gudrun Grabher, "Dickinson's Lyrical Self," in Grabher, Hegenbüchle, and Miller, eds., *Emily Dickinson Handbook,* 230.

9. The definition of the "double bind" is from Suzanne Juhasz, *Naked and Fiery Forms: Modern American Poetry by Women, A New Tradition* (New York: Octagon Books, 1976).

10. Robert Langbaum, *The Poetry of Experience: The Dramatic Monologue in Modern Literary Tradition* (New York: W. W. Norton, 1957), 226, 227.

11. "Emily Dickinson, a poet whose work one hopes (but cannot be sure) Woolf read" (Gilbert and Gubar, *Madwoman,* 541).

12. Páraic Finnerty, *Emily Dickinson's Shakespeare* (Amherst: University of Massachusetts Press, 2006), 93.

13. Deppman, "Trying to Think," 84. Deppman rightly points out that this aspect of Emily Dickinson's poetry has not been adequately explored.

14. William Shakespeare, *The Tempest,* ed. Frank Kermode, *The Arden Edition of the Works of William Shakespeare* (London: Methuen, 1971).

15. Paula Bennett, *Emily Dickinson, Woman Poet* (Iowa City: University of Iowa Press, 1990), 12.

16. Finnerty, *Emily Dickinson's Shakespeare,* 116.

17. Ibid.

18. In the Franklin edition, the poems are two: Fr 1187 includes the first two stanzas, and Fr 1188 includes the other two. In the Johnson edition, there is only one poem.

19. Joanne Feit Diehl, "The Ample Word," 8.

20. Ovid, *Metamorphoses,* trans. Mary M. Innes (Harmondsworth, U.K.: Penguin Classics, 1955), 314–15.

21. Virgil, *The Aeneid,* trans. Robert Fitzgerald (Harmondsworth, U.K.: Penguin Classics, 1983), 6: 117–19.

22. Mary Shelley, *The Last Man* (Lincoln: University of Nebraska Press, 1965), 3; the italics are mine.

23. Ibid., 4.

Contributors

Lucia Aiello teaches in the modern languages department at the University of Strathclyde, Scotland (UK) and is honorary research fellow of the Bakhtin Centre, University of Sheffield, where she gained her Ph.D. in 2001. She has previously published in the *Modern Language Review,* and for the last three years she has researched and published on women writers, especially nineteenth- and twentieth-century Italian, British, and American women writers. Her latest article, "'Of Death I try to think like this': Emily Dickinson's Play with Death," appeared in *Layers of Dying and Death,* edited by Kate Woodthorpe (2007). She is currently working on a monograph on Emily Dickinson and the European lyric tradition.

Carol Blessing is professor of literature, member of the women's studies faculty, and department chair in Literature, Journalism, and Modern Languages at Point Loma Nazarene University in San Diego, where she teaches literatures from the Middle Ages through the seventeenth century. Her interests are feminist theory, women writers, and women in religion from many periods and cultures. She has published book chapters on Queen Elizabeth I, Mary Stuart, and women in early Methodism; her most recent work, on Aemilia Lanyer, appeared in the *Ben Jonson Journal.*

Katey Castellano is an assistant professor of English at James Madison University where she teaches Romantic literature, critical theory, and environmental literature. She has published articles on Edmund Burke and William Blake, and she is currently writing a monograph on the connections between Romantic conservatism and environmental conservation.

Carol Margaret Davison is associate professor of English literature at the University of Windsor. A specialist in Gothic and Victorian literature, African American literature, women's writing, and cultural teratology, she is the author of *Anti-Semitism and British Gothic Literature* (2004) and *History of the Gothic: Gothic Literature, 1764–1824* (2009), and the editor of *Bram Stoker's Dracula: Sucking through the Century, 1897–1997* (1997). She is currently at work on *Gothic Scotland/Scottish Gothic*, a theoretical examination of the Scottish Gothic tradition.

Thomas P. Fair is an adjunct professor of English for Adams State College and teaches graduate courses in nineteenth-century studies. His areas of specialization include nineteenth-century English women novelists and Victorian children's adventure literature, particularly the "Robinsonades." He is currently working on an alternative reading of Mary Crawford's role in *Mansfield Park.*

Annette R. Federico is professor of English at James Madison University. She is the author of *Masculine Identity in Hardy and Gissing* (1991) and *Idol of Suburbia: Marie Corelli and Late-Victorian Literary Culture* (2000). Her articles on Victorian fiction have appeared in journals such as *Victorian Studies, ELT,* and *Dickens Studies Annual.*

Keren Fite holds a Ph.D. from Haifa University and specializes in nineteenth-century women's fiction. Her fields of research are images of artist heroines and narratives of creativity. She is the author of "From Savage Passion to the Sweetness of Self-Control: Female Anger in *Little Women* and 'Pauline's Passion and Punishment,'" in *Women's Writing* (2007) and "Wrestling with the Angel in the House, Slaying the Monster in the Attic: The Artist Heroines in Louisa May Alcott's 'Psyche's Art' and *Little Women*" in *Autopoetica: Representations of the Creative Process in Nineteenth-century British and American Fiction,* edited by Darby Lewes (2006).

Susan Fraiman is professor of English at the University of Virginia. She is the author of *Unbecoming Women: British Women Writers and the Novel of Development* (1993) and *Cool Men and the Second Sex* (2003), and editor of the *Norton Critical "Northanger Abbey"* (2004). Her work on the gender politics of novels, popular culture, Left intellectuals, and the contemporary academy has appeared in such journals as *Critical Inquiry, Feminist Studies, Minnesota Review,* and *PMLA.* Her current project is on "shelter writing": writing that clings to domestic spaces, objects, and practices in the aftermath of traumatic dislocation.

Narin Hassan is an assistant professor at the School of Literature, Communication, and Culture (LCC) at the Georgia Institute of Technology. Her work includes Victorian literature and culture, postcolonial studies, literature and medicine, feminist theory and gender studies. She is coeditor (with Tamara Silvia Wagner) of *Consuming Culture in the Long Nineteenth Century: Narratives of Consumption, 1700–1900* (2007) and has written articles on women writers including sensation fiction authors Mary Elizabeth Braddon and Rhoda Broughton and travel writers Lady Mary Wortley Montagu, Lucie Duff Gordon, and Isabel Burton. She is completing a book manuscript titled *Foreign Bodies: Women, Travel, and the Culture of Colonial Medicine.*

Danielle Russell is an instructor in the English department at Glendon College. She has taught in both the English and humanities departments at York University. Her areas of specialization are women and literature, Victorian literature, and twentieth-century American literature. Recent publications include *Between the Angle and the Curve: Mapping Gender, Race, Space, and Identity in Cather and Morrison* (2006); "Familiarity Breeds a Following: Transcending the Formulaic in the Snicket Series," in *Telling Children's Stories: Narrative Theory and Children's Literature* (forthcoming); and "Homeward Bound: Transformative Spaces in Alice Walker's *The Color Purple,*" in the *Dialogue Literary Studies* Series (2009). She is currently working on "Immeasurable Yearnings: The Legacy of the Landscape in Cather's *The Song of the Lark.*"

Hila Shachar is a doctoral candidate in English and cultural studies at the University of Western Australia. She has recently submitted her doctoral thesis, *Wuthering Heights: Screen Adaptations and Cultural Afterlives*, which explores the cultural "afterlife" of Emily Brontë's *Wuthering Heights* and is particularly concerned with screen adaptations of the novel. Her research and teaching areas include film studies, screen adaptation, gender studies, and Romantic and Victorian literature and culture.

Marlene Tromp is John and Christine Warner Professor of English and Women's Studies at Denison University. She is author of *Altered States: Sex, Drugs, National Identity, and Self-Transformation in Victorian Spiritualism* (2006) and *The Private Rod: Marital Violence, Sensation, and the Law in Victorian Britain* (2000). She is also editor of *Victorian Freaks: The Social Context of Freakery in Victorian Britain* (2008) and coeditor of *Beyond Sensation: Mary Elizabeth Braddon in Context* (2000). Her essays have appeared in *Current Legal Problems* and *Victorian Literature and Culture.*

Tamara Silvia Wagner obtained her Ph.D. from Cambridge University and is assistant professor at Nanyang Technological University. Her books include *Longing: Narratives of Nostalgia in the British Novel, 1740–1890* (2004), *Occidentalism in Novels of Malaysia and Singapore, 1819–2004* (2005), and *Consuming Culture in the Long Nineteenth Century: Narratives of Consumption, 1700–1900* (2007, coedited with Narin Hassan). An edited collection on *Antifeminism and the Victorian Novel: Rereading Nineteenth-Century Women Writers* is forthcoming. Wagner's current projects include a study of financial speculation in Victorian literature, entitled *Speculation in Victorian Fiction: Plotting Money and the Novel Genre, 1815–1901,* and a special issue on silver-fork fiction and its legacies for *Women's Writing* (forthcoming, 2010).

Madeleine Wood has recently passed her Ph.D. at the University of Warwick with a thesis titled "Victorian Familial Enigmas: Inheritance and Influence," and also works as a tutor in the Department of English and Comparative Literary Studies at Warwick. Her research interests include eighteenth- and nineteenth-century novels, psychoanalysis and gender, and group psychologies.

Index

Abel, Elizabeth, 205
Abella, Olga, 44
Aeneid (Virgil), 252, 253
Aers, David, 71
African American feminism, 9, 132
Aiello, Lucia, 21, 237–55, 257
Ain't I a Woman: Black Women and Feminism (hooks), 132
Alcott, Bronson, 177
Alcott, Louisa May, 5, 7, 11, 20, 28, 170–81, 182*n*25
"The Angel in the House" (Patmore), 222
Anxiety of authorship, 2, 32, 43, 237
Anxiety of influence, 2, 43, 49, 61, 74, 204
Areopagitica (Milton), 65
Aristotle, 238–39
Armstrong, Nancy, 220
Art and Anger (Marcus), 8
Atwood, Margaret, 204
Auerbach, Nina, 1, 8, 25*n*24, 26*n*45, 37, 44, 46, 217
Aurora Leigh (Browning), 22
Austen, Jane: compared with Yonge, 192; Fraiman on, 32; Gilbert and Gubar on, xi, 1, 5, 10–12, 21, 29, 32, 119, 217; *Northanger Abbey* by, 21; as precursor of popular women novelists, 10–11; *Pride and Prejudice* by, 32; teaching of, 30, 32
Austen, Zelda, 43
Autokeonony, 47
Banks, Iain, 213*n*7
Baumgardner, Jennifer, 46, 47, 51
Baym, Nina, 44
Bearing the Word (Homans), 227
Béart, Emmanuelle, 152
Beaty, Jerome, 206
Beauvoir, Simone de, x, 15, 48, 148*n*16
Becker, Susanne, 189, 204
Behind a Mask (Alcott), 171, 172–74, 181*n*9
La Belle Noiseuse, 152
Beloved (Morrison), 19, 136–47, 148*n*22
Bennett, Paula, 248
Benson, Mrs. R. S., 123
Berman, Carolyn Vellenga, 148*n*23
Between Women (Marcus), 104
Bewell, Alan, 81
Bildungsroman, 3, 53, 205, 206, 214*n*12
Billington, Mary, 115
Binoche, Juliette, 158
Bitch magazine, 47
Blackstone, William, 208
Blake, William, 242
Blessing, Carol, 17–18, 60–75, 257
Bloom, Harold, 2, 28, 43, 48, 49, 52, 61, 74, 204, 237
Bonaparte, Felicia, 218–19
Book of Martyrs (Foxe), 63
Boos, Florence, 22
Booth, Wayne, 53
Braddon, Mary Elizabeth, 11, 186–90, 199*n*7, 201*n*24

Bradford, Richard, 71–72
Brain, Josephine, 9
Breuer, Josef, 95, 96
Brody, Jennifer Devere, 136
Brontë, Charlotte: anger in writings by, 7, 18; Fraiman on, 30–32; Gaskell's biography of, 100; Gilbert and Gubar on generally, xi, 1, 5, 8–9, 15, 18, 21, 217; postcolonial reading of, 18–19, 111–25, 129–31, 145–46, 147*n*6; *Shirley* by, 219–20, 222–25; teaching of, 30; as underappreciated novelist, 27. *See also Jane Eyre* (C. Brontë)
Brontë, Emily: anger in writings by, 7, 18; film adaptations of *Wuthering Heights*, 19–20, 149–67; Gilbert and Gubar on, xi, 1, 5, 8–9, 15, 19–20, 61. *See also Wuthering Heights* (E. Brontë)
Brontë Transformations (Stoneman), 151, 168*n*12
Brooks, Cleanth, xi
Brooks, Peter, 96
Broughton, Rhoda, 10, 189
Brown, Connie, 54
Brown, Lucy, 180
Browne, Sir Thomas, 73
Brownell, David, 192
Browning, Elizabeth Barrett, ix–xi, xiii, 5, 11, 13, 22
Browning, Robert, 242
Buell, Lawrence, 15–16
Butler, Judith, 26*n*37, 148*n*16
Butler, Octavia, 30
Byron, George Gordon Lord, 90

Cafarelli, Annette, 210
Cain, William E., 42, 46, 47, 70–71, 128
Cambridge Companion to Feminist Literary Theory, 47
Carrson, James P., 206
Carson, Dale, 4
Carson, Rachel, 91
Castellano, Katey, 18, 26*n*43, 76–93, 257
The Castle-Builders (Yonge), 184, 193–94
The Castle of Otranto (Walpole), 216*n*33
Cave parable, 251
Celan, Paul, 240
Céline et Julie vont en bateau, 152
Chapman, Edward, 220–21
Chase, Karen, 186
Chodorow, Nancy, 48
Chrisman, Laura, 124
Civil War metaphor, 171–72
Cixous, Hélène, 50
Clery, E. J., 208, 215*n*26
The Clever Woman of the Family (Yonge), 193
Clinton, Chelsea, 6–7
Clinton, Hillary, 6
Cohen, Michael, 236*n*23
Colasterion (Milton), 73
Colby, Vineta, 192
Coleridge, Mary Elizabeth, 11
Coleridge, S. T., 92*n*16, 238–39
Collaboration, ix–xiii, 6, 29, 51–52
Collings, David, 50, 52
Collins, Wilkie, 11, 186, 187, 189, 199*n*7, 213*n*7
Communities of Women (Auerbach), 37
The Complete Critical Guide to John Milton (Bradford), 71–72
Confinement metaphor, 20–21, 185–86, 206–9, 217
Constructionism, 148*n*16
Craik, Mrs., 11
Critical Inquiry, 64
Critical Middle Eastern Studies, 55
Cultural (or difference) feminism, 29–30
Curry, Gwen, 48
Cvetkovich, Ann, 28

The Daisy Chain (Yonge), 194, 201*n*23
"The Daisy follows soft the Sun—" (Dickinson), 249–50
D'Albertis, Deirdre, 218, 234
Daly, Mary, 30
Dangarembga, Tsitsi, 126*n*15
"Darkness" (Byron), 90
David Copperfield (Dickens), 187
Davison, Carol Margaret, 20, 203–16, 258
Dean, Margaret, 40
D'Eaubonne, Francoise, 91*n*4
Deconstruction, 10, 32, 33, 77
De Doctrina Christiana (Milton), 65
Defense of Poetry (Shelley), 162
Defoe, Daniel, 4
De Gruchy, Amy, 201*n*26
DeLamotte, Eugenia C., 206, 207

Demoor, Marysa, 45
Deppman, Jed, 245, 255*n*13
De Quincey, Thomas, 213*n*2
Derrida, Jacques, 10, 32, 50, 204, 212
Desire and Domestic Fiction (Armstrong), 220
Dickens, Charles, 95, 187, 214*n*12
Dickinson, Emily: Aiello on, 21; on Elizabeth Barrett Browning, ix–x, xiii; on "bursting all the doors," 23; experiments in poiesis by, 241–51; Gilbert and Gubar on, 1, 5, 12, 21, 29, 175, 239–51; on life "shaven and fitted to a frame," 1; poetry by, ix–x, xiii, 239–51; Ransom on, xi ; Rich on, xi ; self-effacement and isolation of, 175, 239–41; violent imagery in, 7
Diehl, Joanne Feit, 250
Difference (or cultural) feminism, 29–30
Dinnage, Rosemary, 9, 25*n*24
Disability studies, 55, 201*n*19
DiSalvo, Jackie, 66
Dissembling Fictions: Elizabeth Gaskell and the Victorian Social Text (d'Albertis), 218
Dissent, 22
Douglass, Ann, 1
"Drama's Vitallest Expression" (Dickinson), 244–45
DuPlessis, Rachel Blau, 44
Dutt, Toru, 115

Eagleton, Terry, 26*n*36
Ecofeminism, 18, 26*n*43, 76–91, 91*n*4, 93*n*21
Ecofeminist Literary Criticism (Gaard and Murphy), 77
Edgeworth, Maria, 12
Egan, Ken, 50
Eliot, George: compared with Gaskell, 226; Gilbert and Gubar on, xi, 1, 12, 15, 21, 205, 217, 226; *The Lifted Veil* by, 190; *Middlemarch* by, 73, 226, 236*n*23; *Mill on the Floss* by, 113, 119; and Milton, 73; and Satthianadhan, 118, 119; sensational elements in, 189
Eliot, T. S., 242
Elliott, Dorice Williams, 235–36*n*19
Elliott, Jane, 54
Ellis, Kate, 207
Ellmann, Mary, 64
Emerson, Ralph Waldo, 177
Emily Brontë's Wuthering Heights (1992 film directed by Kosminsky), 151, 158–63, 166
Emily Dickinson and Her Contemporaries (Petrino), 240
Emily Dickinson's Shakespeare (Finnerty), 244–45
English Journal, 50
Enlightenment, 82, 85, 90, 207
Environmental ethics. *See* Ecofeminism
Equal Pay Act, 40
Essay on the Principle of Population (Malthus), 90
Essentialism, 9, 18, 25*n*31, 33, 44–46, 77, 93*n*21, 124, 128, 148*n*16
Estes, Angela M., 172
Ezell, Margaret J. M., 174

Fair, Thomas P., 20–21, 217–36, 258
Fairy tales, 2, 13, 29, 76, 102, 121, 156–57, 168*n*15
The Fatal Three (Braddon), 187, 199*n*7
Faulkner, William, 213*n*7
Federico, Annette R., 1–26, 258
Felski, Rita, 7–8, 15, 170, 175–76
Female Gothic novels. *See* Gothic novels
Feminism: activism and strategies of second-wave of, 35–39, 42; African American feminism, 9, 132; and collaboration, 51–52; and constructionism, 148*n*16; and crossing boundaries, 49–51; dangers of ideological feminism, 43; difference or cultural feminism, 29; ecofeminism, 18, 26*n*43, 76–91, 91*n*4, 93*n*21; and Federico, 4; future of, 52–55; goals of second-wave feminism, 40; influence of, on *The Madwoman in the Attic*, x, 9; and mental "click" in recognition of sexism, 8, 24*n*20; and New York Radical Women, 37, 38, 44; and personal as political, 14, 37–41, 57–58*n*27; postfeminism, 6, 20, 47–48, 68, 163; postmodern feminism, 9, 10, 45; and race, 131–36; radical feminism, 37–42, 44–49; and Redstockings, 38–39, 40, 41, 44, 45, 47, 54, 56*n*2; relevance of

The Madwoman in the Attic for today's feminism, 17, 22, 30–33, 37, 52–55; and separatism, 30, 42; Shullenberger on, as neurotic, 66; and sisterhood as powerful, 29, 45–49; third wave of, 6–7, 34, 35, 37, 47–48, 51–55, 68; in universities, 40–45, 51–54; and Women's Liberation Front, 38, 44. *See also* Feminist literary criticism; Patriarchy
Feminism or Death (d'Eaubonne), 91*n*4
Feminist literary criticism: academic courses on, x–xiii, 5, 22–23, 30–33, 48–50, 128; academic institutionalization of, 14; Booth on, 53; Bradford's critique of, 71–72; and collaborative writing of *The Madwoman in the Attic*, ix–xiii, 6, 29, 51–52; and crossing boundaries, 49–51; differences and infighting within, 46–48; ecofeminist literary criticism, 77–91; and essentialism and universalism, 9, 15, 18, 19, 25*n*31, 33, 44–46, 77, 124, 128, 136–37, 139, 146; and feminist community, 45–49; on feminist literary criticism, 57*n*18; and gender specificity of works of literature, 29, 42–45; Gubar on, 10, 26*n*37, 47, 53–54; influence of *The Madwoman in the Attic* on, 8–17, 21–23, 28–30, 38, 40–55, 77, 127–29, 170, 203–4, 212; of Latin American women writers, 53; and New Criticism, 10, 38; objections to, 42–45; passionate innocence of Gilbert and Gubar, 8–11; and postmodern feminism, 9, 10, 45; and poststructuralism, 10, 32, 33; and pro-woman line, 42–45; questions on future of feminist literary theory, 13–14; and race, 131–36; reviews and criticisms of *The Madwoman in the Attic*, xii, 2, 8–9, 17, 25*n*24, 34–55, 127–30, 147*n*7, 204, 217; Showalter on, 15, 57*n*18; underlying assumptions of, 28–30. *See also The Madwoman in the Attic* (Gilbert and Gubar); and specific feminist critics
Feminist Milton (Wittreich), 62, 67–68
Feminist Revolution, 34, 39
Ferry, Luc, 79
Fetterley, Judith, 171–73, 181*n*9
Fiennes, Ralph, 158
Figes, Eva, 207
Film adaptations of *Wuthering Heights*, 19–20, 149–67
Finnerty, Páraic, 244–45, 248–49
Fite, Keren, 20, 170–82, 258
Fleenor, Juliann E., 205, 214*n*10
Flemming, Leslie, 114
Flower, Dean, 43
Foucault, Michel, 10, 32, 200*n*16, 209, 220
Foxe, John, 63
Fraiman, Susan, 17, 27–33, 258–59
Frank, Katherine, 8–9
Frankenstein (Shelley): angel/monster image in, 76, 86–88; anger in, 7; compared with *Paradise Lost*, 19, 61, 76, 79; critique of masculine logic of domination by, 81–84; ecofeminist reading of, 18, 76–84, 86–91; as female Gothic novel, 214*n*11; feminist readings of, 76–77, 79; feminist scholarship on, 50; Gilbert and Gubar on, 28, 61, 76–77; prophetic mode of, 78–81; vivisection allusion in, 82–83
Freud, Sigmund, 13, 95–96, 98, 109, 109*n*5, 213*n*2
Friedan, Betty, x
Froula, Christine, 64, 66, 71
Frye, Northrop, 63
Fuller, Margaret, 11, 177

Gaard, Greta, 77, 93*n*21
Gaia hypothesis, 91
Gainesville Women's Liberation, 56*n*2
Gallagher, Philip, 62–63, 65
Gaskell, Elizabeth, 21, 100, 218–35
Gender studies, 72
Gezari, Janet, 15, 38, 52, 189
Gilbert, Pamela, 186
Gilbert, Sandra M.: academic courses taught by, x–xiii, 5, 22–23, 48–50, 128; on academic institutionalization of feminist criticism, 14; and collaborative writing of *The Madwoman in the Attic*, ix–xiii, 6, 29, 51–52; on criticisms of *The Madwoman in the Attic*, 25–26*n*35, 45, 77, 128; on feminist device of mental "click," 24*n*20; and funding of *The Madwoman in the Attic*, xi–xii, 6; husband and children of, 37–38; on influ-

ence of *The Madwoman in the Attic*, 11, 77; on Life Study, 35; as mentor to feminist scholars, 36; on Milton's *Paradise Lost*, 62–63, 65, 72; and publication of *The Madwoman in the Attic*, xii, 6, 32, 36. *See also The Madwoman in the Attic* (Gilbert and Gubar)
Gilman, Charlotte Perkins, 11, 25*n*34, 190, 209
Girls Are Equal Too! (Carson), 4
The Gnostic Gospels (Pagels), 64
Goblin Market (Rossetti), 22
Goddu, Teresa A., 173–74
Gothic America (Goddu), 173–74
Gothic Forms of Feminine Fictions (Becker), 189
Gothic novels: by Alcott, 171–74, 181*n*9; anti-Gothic commentary on, 213*n*4; and bildungsroman, 205, 206, 214*n*12; as distinct literary type, 215*n*26; domestic Gothic, 186; female Gothic novel, 20, 173, 203–12, 213*n*7; Gilbert and Gubar on, 173, 203–6, 208–12
Graham, Ellen, xii
Great Expectations (Dickens), 214*n*12
"A great Hope fell" (Dickinson), 250
Griffin, Farah Jasmine, 46
Griffin, Susan, 91*n*4
Grigg, Elizabeth, 119
Grimberg, Eiko, 55
Gubar, Susan: academic courses taught by, 5, 6, 22–23, 26*n*38, 48–50, 128; on academic institutionalization of feminist criticism, 14; on Butler's style, 26*n*37; and collaborative writing of *The Madwoman in the Attic*, ix–xiii, 6, 29, 51–52; on female creativity, 64; on feminist literary criticism, 10, 26*n*37, 47, 53–54; husband and children of, 37–38, 48; on influence of feminist seventies on *The Madwoman in the Attic*, 9; on influence of *The Madwoman in the Attic*, 11; on literary criticism and critic's own story of development, 3; as mentor to feminist scholars, 36, 48, 50; and publication of *The Madwoman in the Attic*, xii, 6, 32, 36; on race and feminist criticism, 131–32. *See also The Madwoman in the Attic* (Gilbert and Gubar)
The Gypsy-Bachelor of Manchester (Bonaparte), 218–19

Hagenbüchle, Roland, 241
Haire-Sargeant, Lin, 151
Hall, Radclyffe, 30
Halley, Janet E., 69–70
Hanisch, Carol, 38, 47, 53
Haraway, Donna, 83, 86
Hard Cash (Reade), 186–87
Harper's magazine, 8, 10
Harris-Williams, Ann, 148*n*14
Hartman, Geoffrey, 81, 92*n*19
Haskin, Dayton, 73
Hassan, Narin, 18–19, 111–26, 259
Heene, Katrien, 45
Heilbrun, Carolyn, 2, 41–42, 46, 146
The Heir of Redclyffe (Yonge), 201*n*21
Heller, Scott, 52
Heller, Tamar, 208, 213*n*7
Hemmings, Clare, 9
Hidden Depths (Skene), 190–91
Hirsch, Marianne, 205
Hoagland, Sarah Lucia, 47
Hodge, Bob, 71
Hölderlin, Friedrich, 240, 255*n*7
Holmes, Martha Stoddard, 192, 198, 201*n*19
Holstein, Anthony, 213*n*7
Homans, Margaret, 227
Hooks, bell, 132
Hopes and Fears (Yonge), 192
Hopkins, Gerard Manley, 254*n*3
Household Words, 222, 225
Howe, Florence, 23
Hudson Review, 43
Hughes, Winifred, 185, 189
Hurlevent (1985 film by Rivette), 151–59, 162, 168*n*6
Hutchings, Kevin, 80, 81, 92*n*15

I Am Legend (Matheson), 78
Identity politics, 33
"I dwell in Possibility" (Dickinson), 247
"I'm Nobody" (Dickinson), 239–41
Imperialism. *See* Postcolonialism
"I'm 'wife'—I've finished that" (Dickinson), 245–46
Incidents in the Life of a Slave Girl (Jacobs), 30

India, 112–25
The Interpretation of Dreams (Freud), 95, 213*n*2
Intersectionality, 26*n*43, 133
Israeli Studies, 55
The Italian (Radcliffe), 210
"I think I was enchanted" (Dickinson), ix–x

Jacobs, Harriet, 30
Jacobus, Mary, 9, 44, 91*n*2
Jane Eyre (C. Brontë): academic focus on, 27; Adèle in, 106, 108; angry subtext of, 7, 18, 30–31; Bertha/Jane double in, 18, 19, 29, 30–32, 95, 97, 102, 105–6, 108–9, 111, 113, 129, 130, 143–46, 185, 188, 189, 208; Bertha's insanity in, 187; compared with *Beloved* by Morrison, 19, 136–47; compared with *Saguna* by Satthianadhan, 112–25; father figures in, 101, 109; as female Gothic novel, 20, 205–6; Ferndean in, 18, 107–9; first-person narrator of, 96; Fraiman on, 30–32; Gilbert and Gubar on, 19, 27–28, 30–31, 94–97, 101–3, 105, 108–9, 111–12, 121, 130, 136–47, 205–6, 212; Grace Poole in, 32; Jane's inheritance in, 99, 107, 138, 139; love in, 98–99, 102–9; Moor House in, 98, 106–8; patriarchal enclosures in, 94–109; and pilgrimage, 18, 95, 140, 145; postcolonial reading of, 18–19, 111–25, 129–31, 145–46, 147*n*6; preternatural hearing by Jane in, 190; psychoanalytic reading of, 18, 30, 32, 95–96, 98, 109; red room episode in, 18, 94–101, 140, 188; Reed family in, 96–100, 105, 106, 109, 139–40; Rochester's first appearance in, 101–2; Rochester's marriage to Bertha Mason in, 187; Rochester's relationship with Jane in, 95, 99–108, 141, 143, 145; significance of title of, and Jane's name, 138; St. John Rivers in, 106–7, 131, 138, 145; teaching of, 30–32; Teale's play of, 18; Thornfield in, 94, 98, 100–102, 107, 130, 140–42; and trauma theory, 18, 95–101, 109; Wood on, 94–109
Jauss, Hans Robert, 239
Jehlen, Myra, 44–45
John Marchmont's Legacy (Braddon), 201*n*24
Johnson, Claudia, 32
Johnson, Samuel, 72
Jonas, Hans, 79
Joshi, Priya, 114–15
Juhasz, Suzanne, 46

Kamala (Satthianadhan), 114, 126*n*18
Kaplan, Carla, 108
Keats, John, 162
Kelly, Gary, 210, 213*n*7
Kibbie, Ann, 55
Kipling, Rudyard, 119
Kizer, Carolyn, 15
Kolodny, Annette, 2, 43–44, 48, 49, 52
Kosminsky, Peter, 151, 158–63, 166
Krishnamma, Suri, 163–67

Lacan, Jacques, 10, 32
Lady Audley's Secret (Braddon), 11, 186–88, 190
LaGreca, Nancy, 53
Lalita, K., 114, 116
Landy, Marcia, 62, 66, 69, 71
Langbaum, Robert, 242
Langland, Elizabeth, 36, 53, 56*n*5, 205, 226
Lant, Kathleen Margaret, 172
The Last Man (Martin), 90
The Last Man (Shelley), 18, 78, 80–81, 84–91, 93*n*37, 251, 253–54
The Law and the Lady (Collins), 187
Le Comte, Edward, 71
Lee, Home, 11
Lentricchia, Frank, 25*n*35, 44, 147*n*7
Leon, Barbara, 42
Lerner, Laurence, 111
Levenson, Michael, 186
Lewalski, Barbara Keifer, 62, 67–72
Lewis, Matthew "Monk," 206, 209
Life Study, 35–37
The Lifted Veil (Eliot), 190
Liggins, Emma, 191
Linton, Eliza Lynn, 20, 183
Literary Women (Moers), 37, 204
A Literature of Their Own (Showalter), 1, 37, 189, 200*n*12
Little Women (Alcott), 7, 171–72, 177–81
Livingston, Jennie, 30

Lokuge, Chandana, 114
Lovelock, James, 91
Lurie, Susan, 132, 133

The Madwoman in the Attic (Gilbert and Gubar): academia's initial reaction to, xi–xii; on angel/monster image, 12, 13–14, 18, 76, 189; on anxiety of authorship, 2, 32; attic and confinement image in generally, 20–21, 208–9, 217; and class, 147*n*7; collaborative writing of, ix–xiii, 6, 29, 51–52; compared with *Playing in the Dark* by Morrison, 133–36; and crossing boundaries, 49–51; on doubles as monster characters, 189; and essentialism and universalism of "Everywoman," 9, 15, 18, 19, 25*n*31, 33, 44–46, 77, 124, 128, 136–37, 139, 146; and female gothic novel, 173, 203–6, 208–12; and feminist activism and strategies, 35–37; and feminist literary criticism, 8–17, 21–23, 28–30, 38, 40–42; first sentence of, on pen as metaphorical penis, 9, 27, 44, 134; funding for, 5–6; and future of feminism, 52–55; and Gaskell, 218, 234–35; and gender specificity of works of literature, 29, 42–45; and genre theory, 205–6; honors and awards for, 2, 37; and Life Study, 35–37; madwoman image in, 7, 20–21, 23, 23–24*n*4, 29, 170, 171, 174–75, 183, 205, 212; on metaphor of literary paternity, 9, 27, 44, 134, 237–39; on metaphors of sexuality, power, and embodiment, 9–10, 13, 27, 44, 128–29, 134; and Milton studies, 17–18, 40, 50, 60–74; on mother-goddess myth, 251–52; on patriarchy, 2, 8, 9, 13–14, 19, 38, 42, 44–45, 60, 76, 91, 128, 139, 146, 153, 206, 217, 237; pedagogical value of, 30–33, 49–50; preface of, 35, 37–38, 128; and pro-woman line, 42–45; publication of, xii, 6, 32, 36, 41; and race and ethnicity, 19, 31, 77, 129–36; and radical feminism, 37–42, 44–49; readers' responses to, xii–xiii; relevance of, for today's feminism, 17, 22, 30–33, 37, 52–55; reviews and criticisms of, xii, 2, 8–9, 17, 25*n*24, 25–26*n*35, 34–55, 77, 127–30, 147*n*7, 204, 218; on rise of English novel, 215*n*23; and Romanticism, 17, 18, 171, 174–75; sales of, 41; second edition of, 3, 5, 127–28, 130; significance and influence of, 1–3, 6–8, 11, 16, 21–23, 27–55, 77, 127–29, 170, 203, 212; and sisterhood as powerful, 29, 45–49; and teaching experiences of authors of, x, xi, 5, 22–23, 48–50, 128; underhistoricized readings in, 26*n*35, 44; on woman writer compared to Romantic poet, 171, 174–75; writing style of, 12–13. *See also* Feminist literary criticism; Gilbert, Sandra M.; Gubar, Susan; and specific authors and titles
Making Feminist History (Cain), 41–42, 70
Malthus, Thomas, 90
The Maniac in the Cellar (Hughes), 185
Manifesta: Young Women, Feminism, and the Future, 34, 46, 47, 51, 53
Marcus, Jane, 8, 46–47
Marcus, Sharon, 104
Mare, Margaret, 201*n*18
Marriage: in *Beloved*, 138–39; companionate marriage, 68, 208; and coverture doctrine, 208; in Gaskell's novels, 220, 222–34; in *Jane Eyre*, 95, 103, 105, 108, 121, 187; and Milton, 62, 65, 68, 70, 72–73; in *Saguna*, 116, 117, 121–22; in *Shirley*, 220
Marryat, Florence, 189
Martin, Carol, 40
Martin, Catherine Gimelli, 72–73
Martin, John, 90
Martineau, Harriet, 11
Marxist criticism, 16
Mary Barton (Gaskell), 219–22
Matheson, Richard, 78
Mathews, Freya, 90
Maude (Rossetti), 11
Maunder, Andrew, 186, 191
McClintock, Anne, 31
McColley, Diane Kelsey, 64–65, 68–71
McDowell, Deborah, 29
Mellor, Anne K., 78, 79, 82, 84, 162, 182*n*19
Merchant, Carolyn, 85, 91*n*4
Metamorphoses (Ovid), 252–53
Meyer, Susan, 31, 112, 131, 147*n*6, 148*n*19
Michie, Elsie B., 130–31

Middlemarch (Eliot), 73, 226, 236*n*23
Mikalachki, Jodi, 70–71
Milbank, Alison, 204, 212, 213*n*7
Miles, Robert, 213*n*4
Millard, Elaine, 51, 53
Miller, D. A., 28, 207
Miller, David, 50
Miller, Nancy, 29
Millett, Kate, x, 64, 217
Mill on the Floss (Eliot), 113, 119
Mills, Sara, 51, 53
Milton, John: Blessing on, 17–18, 60–74; Dean's scholarship on, 40; divorce tracts by, 68, 72; and George Eliot, 73; feminist critiques of, 60–62, 64–65, 66, 68–74; first marriage of, 68, 70; Gilbert and Gubar on, 17–18, 40, 50, 60–62; Samuel Johnson on, 72; liberal-humanist tradition on, 68–71; and misogyny, 17, 60–63, 65, 66, 68, 69, 72; *Paradise Regained* by, 63, 64; prose by, 63, 65, 72; rebuttals to *The Madwoman in the Attic* on, 62–68; *Samson Agonistes* by, 68, 72; teaching of, 50; universal appeal of, 62; Woolf on, 17, 60–62, 64, 65, 68, 72, 73, 149. *See also Paradise Lost* (Milton)
Milton and Gender (Martin), 72–73
Milton and the Idea of Women (Walker), 69–70
Milton Quarterly, 66–67
Milton's Eve (McColley), 64–65, 71–72
Milton Studies, 62, 63, 71
Miscellaneous Writings (Satthianadhan), 114, 122–23
Modern Age, 43
Moers, Ellen, 1, 22, 37, 204, 205, 214*n*11, 217
Moglen, Helene, 9, 52
Mohanty, Chandra Talpade, 53, 59*n*45
Moi, Toril, 45
Moll Flanders (Defoe), 4
Monk, Claire, 161
Montaigne, Michel de, 73
More, Thomas, 95
Morgan, Robin, 6
Morrison, Lucy, 36
Morrison, Toni, 19, 133–47, 148*n*14
Morton, Timothy, 84
Ms. magazine, x, 4, 8
"Much madness is divinest sense" (Dickinson), xiii
Mudge, Bradford K., 213*n*4
Mukerjhee, Meenakshi, 114
Murphy, Patrick D., 77
"Myself was formed—a Carpenter—" (Dickinson), 250–51
The Mysteries of Udolpho (Radcliffe), 204, 210, 211
Myths of Power (Eagleton), 26*n*36

Naess, Arne, 89
Nature. *See* Ecofeminism
Nayder, Lillian, 190–91
Nervous Conditions (Dangarembga), 126*n*15
New Criticism, xi, 6, 10, 38
New Historicism, 16
The New Magdalen (Collins), 187
New Woman, 115–24, 191
New York Radical Women, 37, 38, 44
New York Review of Books, 9, 204
New York Times, 6, 41, 47
Nineteenth-Century Women Poets, 22
No Man's Land (Gilbert and Gubar), xii
North and South (Gaskell), 219, 220, 222–25
Northanger Abbey (Austen), 21
Norton Anthology of Literature by Women (Gilbert and Gubar), xii, 24*n*8, 28, 199*n*4
Norton *Major Authors*, 5, 24*n*8
Nussbaum, Martha, 53
Nyquist, Mary, 68–69, 71

Oates, Joyce Carol, 3
O'Connor, Erin, 129
"Ode to the West Wind" (Shelley), 80
Oliphant, Margaret, 20, 183, 190, 226
Oppenheim, Janet, 185, 198
Orlando, Emily, 39
Ortner, Sherry, 87, 91*n*4
Other, 9, 111–12, 134, 148*n*14
Ouida, 189
Our Bodies, Ourselves, 4
Outbreak narratives, 78

Outram, Dorinda, 207
Ovid, 252–53

Pagels, Elaine, 64
Parable of the Sower (Butler), 30
Paradise Lost (Milton): Adam in, 61–66, 68; Blessing on, 17–18, 60–74; compared with *Frankenstein* and *Wuthering Heights*, 19, 61, 76, 79, 149, 150, 162, 164; Eve in, 17, 60–66, 68–71; feminist critiques of, 60–62, 64–65, 66, 68–74; Gilbert and Gubar on, 17–18, 60–62; God in, 66; liberal-humanist tradition on, 68–71; and misogyny, 17, 60–63, 65, 66, 68, 69, 72; rebuttals to *The Madwoman in the Attic* on, 62–68; as regenerative work, 65; Satan in, 61, 63, 66, 68; Woolf on, 17, 60–62, 64, 65, 68, 72, 73, 149. *See also* Milton, John
Paradise Regained (Milton), 63, 64
Paris Is Burning (Livingston), 30
Patmore, Coventry, 222
Patriarchy: and African women writers, 137; Auerbach on, 44, 217; in *Beloved*, 141, 142; and black women, 132; Dickinson on, 12; in fairy tales, 157; in female Gothic novel, 206–10; feminist debates on generally, 44; in Gaskell's works, 218–19, 226–27, 233–35; Gilbert and Gubar on, 2, 8, 9, 13–14, 19, 38, 42, 44–45, 60, 76, 91, 128, 139, 146, 153, 206, 217, 237; impact of, on all women, 146–47; in *Jane Eyre*, 95–101, 104, 106–9, 131, 136–37, 139–40, 142; and Milton, 60–64, 66, 68–71, 73, 149; and postfeminism, 161; in *Saguna*, 119–22; in sensation fiction, 190, 198; in Shelley's works, 78–80, 82, 83; in *Shirley*, 220; in *Wuthering Heights*, 156–58, 163. *See also* Feminism
Pearce, Lynne, 51, 53
Percival, Alicia, 201*n*18
Perera, Suvendrini, 31, 112
Perils of the Night: A Feminist Study of Nineteenth-Century Gothic (DeLamotte), 206
Perkins, David, 83
Petrino, Elizabeth, 240
Pettingell, Phoebe, 9
The Pillars of the House (Yonge), 201*n*23
Plato, 251
Playing in the Dark (Morrison), 19, 133–36, 148*n*14
PMLA, 53–54, 62–63, 65, 70, 73
The Poetry of Experience (Langbaum), 242
Polyvocality, 45
Poovey, Mary, 31, 225
Postcolonialism, 9, 18, 29, 77, 81, 111–25, 129–31, 145–46, 147*n*6
Postfeminism, 6, 20, 47–48, 68, 163
Postmodern feminism, 9, 10, 45
Poststructuralism, 10, 32, 33
Pride and Prejudice (Austen), 32
The Princess (Tennyson), 119
The Professor (Brontë), 28
"Psyche's Art" (Alcott), 182*n*25
Psychoanalysis, 18, 30, 32, 95–96, 98, 109, 109*n*5
Punter, David, 204, 212
Pykett, Lyn, 189

Queer theory, 29, 32, 33
Quilligan, Maureen, 66

Race: and *Beloved* by Morrison, 19, 136–47; and feminism, 131–33; hooks on, 132; and *The Madwoman in the Attic*, 19, 31, 77, 129–33; and *Playing in the Dark* by Morrison, 133–36
Radcliffe, Ann, 20, 204, 206, 209–11, 215*n*23
Radcliffe, William, 209
Ramabai, Pandita, 115
Ransom, John Crowe, xi
Reade, Charles, 186–87
Reconstructing Desire (Wyatt), 100
Reddy, Helen, 45
Redstockings, 38–39, 40, 41, 44, 45, 47, 54, 56*n*2
Reed, John, 187
Re-Membering Milton (Nyquist), 68–69
Rich, Adrienne, xi, 91*n*4
Richards, Amy, 46, 47, 51
Richardson, Samuel, 206
Rivette, Jacques, 151–59, 162, 168*n*6
Robinson, Solveig C., 203

Romanticism: and Coleridge, 238–39; and Female Romantic, 176; and nature, 90, 92*n*8; and prophetic mode, 81; and social ethics, 79; woman writers compared with Romantic poets, 171, 174–75; and Wordsworth, 78, 86–87, 92*n*19, 242; and *Wuthering Heights*, 19, 162
A Room of One's Own (Woolf), 17, 61, 148*n*14, 211
Rooms of Our Own (Gubar), 3
Rooney, Ellen, 47
Rosenman, Ellen Bayuk, 41, 54
Rosin, Hanna, 6–7
Rossetti, Christina, 11, 12, 22
Ruether, Rosemary Radford, 91*n*4
Ruskin, John, 238
Russ, Joanna, 205
Russell, Danielle, 18, 19, 127–48, 259
Rust, Marion, 40, 55
Rylance, Rick, 187

Saguna (Satthianadhan), 19, 112–25, 125–26*n*6, 126*n*8
Salem's Chapel (Oliphant), 190
Samson Agonistes (Milton), 68, 72
Sandbach-Dahlström, Catherine, 191–92, 201*n*18
Sanders, Valerie, 194, 201*n*23
Sarachild, Kathie, 40, 42, 45, 53, 54, 56*n*2
Satthianadhan, Krupabai, 19, 112–25, 125–26*n*6, 126*n*8
Satthianadhan, Samuel, 114
Schaffer, Talia, 191, 200*n*16
Scheherezade in the Marketplace (Schor), 220
Scholes, Robert, xii
Schor, Hilary, 220
Seitz, Jane, 54
Sellier, Geneviève, 168*n*9
Sensation fiction: by Braddon, 11, 186–90, 199*n*7; by Collins, 11, 186, 187, 189; confinement metaphor in, 185–86; emergence of, from domestic realism, 186; Gilbert and Gubar on, 183, 185, 189–90, 199*n*4; and insanity generally, 187–88; and literary canon, 185–91; by Yonge, 10–11, 20, 28, 184–85, 190–99
Separatism, 30, 42
Sexism. *See* Feminism
Sexual Politics (Millett), 217
Sexual/Textual Politics, 45
Shachar, Hila, 19–20, 149–69, 259
Shakespeare, William, 244–45, 248–49
Sharpe, Jenny, 112
Shelley, Mary: anger in writings by, 7; Castellano on, 18, 26*n*43; ecofeminist reading of, 18, 26*n*43, 76–91; Gilbert and Gubar on, 1, 12, 15, 28, 61, 76–77; mother of, 92*n*10; and Sibylline leaves in *The Last Man*, 80–81, 92*n*14, 251–54. *See also Frankenstein* (Shelley); *The Last Man* (Shelley)
Shelley, Percy, 80, 92*n*14, 162
"She rose to His Requirements—dropt" (Dickinson), 247–49
Shirley (C. Brontë), 21, 219–20, 222–25
Shiva, Vandana, 83, 84
Showalter, Elaine: on Braddon's *Lady Audley's Secret*, 188; on feminist literary criticism, 15, 43, 57*n*18; influence of, 1–2, 22, 29, 64, 217; *A Literature of Their Own* by, 1, 37, 189, 200*n*12; on separatism, 42
Shullenberger, William, 65–67
Sibyl and Sibylline leaves, 80–81, 92*n*14, 92*n*16, 92–93*n*19, 251–54
Signs, 9, 44–45
Silent Spring (Carson), 91
Sisterhood Is Powerful, 4, 54
Skene, Felicia, 190–91
Slate, 6
Smith, Gail K., 181*n*9
"Snow White," 13
Somerville, Siobhan B., 132
Song of Solomon, 65
Sorabji, Cornelia, 115
Spacks, Patricia Meyer, 1, 22, 217
Spaull, Sue, 51, 53
Spectres of Marx (Derrida), 204, 212
Spitzer, Eliot, 6
Spivak, Gayatri, 31, 45, 57–58*n*27, 91*n*2, 111, 113, 129–31, 147*n*6
Stanton, Elizabeth Cady, 11
Steadman, Carolyn, 96
Stein, Gertrude, 12
Steinem, Gloria, x

Stetz, Margaret, 52
Stone, Lucy, 11
Stoneman, Patsy, 151, 153–54, 168*n*12
Stratton, Florence, 137
Sturrock, June, 190, 200*n*14, 201*n*20
Swyt, Wendy, 157
Sypher, Wylie, 210

Taliaferro, Frances, 8
Teale, Polly, 18
The Tempest (Shakespeare), 248–49
Tennyson, Alfred Lord, 119, 194, 201*n*24
Tetrachordon (Milton), 72
Tharu, Susie, 114, 116
Thompson, Nicola Diane, 183, 191
Thoreau, Henry David, 171, 177–81
Through the Arc of the Rainforest (Yamashita), 30
Tractarian doctrine, 185, 190–92
The Trail of the Serpent (Braddon), 186
Transcendentalism, 172, 176–81, 182*n*20
The Trial (Yonge), 190, 193, 198
The Trials and Tribulations of Little Red Riding Hood (Zipes), 157
Trollope, Anthony, 189
Tromp, Marlene, xii, 14, 17, 34–59, 190, 260
Turner, James Grantham, 72
The Two Guardians (Yonge), 193

Understanding Poetry (Brooks and Warren), xi
Uneven Developments (Poovey), 225

Vicinus, Martha, 1
Victorian Psychology and British Culture (Rylance), 187
Victorian sensation fiction. *See* Sensation fiction
Victorian Women Poets, 22
Victorian Women Writers and the Woman Question (Thompson), 191
Victorian Working-Class Women Poets: An Anthology (Boos), 22
Villette (Brontë), 21, 108
Vincent, Sybil Korff, 206
Virgil, 252, 253
The Voyage In: Fictions of Female Development (Abel, Hirsch, and Langland), 205

Wagner, Tamara Silvia, 20, 183–202, 260
Wald, Priscilla, 78
Walden (Thoreau), 171, 177–81
Walker, Julia M., 69–70
Walpole, Horace, 216*n*33
Walzer, Judith, 22
Warner, Marina, 92*n*16, 92–93*n*19
Warren, Robert Penn, xi
Waters, Karen, 39
Webber, Joan Malory, 63–64, 66, 68–72
The Well of Loneliness (Hall), 30
Wheeler, Michael, 96
Whitman, Walt, 239
Wilder, Lina, 55
Winston, Elizabeth, 50–51
Wittreich, Joseph, 62, 67–68, 71
Wives and Daughters (Gaskell), 219, 225–34
Wollstonecraft, Mary, 92*n*10
The Woman in White (Collins), 186
Women's Liberation Front, 38, 44
Women's movement. *See* Feminism
Women's studies programs, 24*n*7, 72
Women's Writing, 191
Women Writing in India (Tharu and Lalita), 114
Wood, Ellen, 189
Wood, Madeleine, 18, 94–110, 260
Woodhull, Victoria, 11
Woods, Susanne, 69
Woolf, Virginia: and Dickinson, 255*n*11; Gilbert and Gubar on generally, 13; on Judith Shakespeare, 243; Marcus on, 8; on Milton, 17, 60–62, 64, 65, 68, 72, 73, 149; Modernist predispositions of, 72; in Norton *Major Authors*, 5; *A Room of One's Own* by, 17, 61, 148*n*14, 211; Rosenman's dissertation on, 41
Wordsworth, William, 78, 86–87, 92*n*19, 242
Writing Women's History (Ezell), 174
Wuthering Heights (1939 film directed by Wyler), 152–54, 157–60, 168*n*12
Wuthering Heights (2003 MTV version directed by Krishnamma), 151, 164–67
Wuthering Heights (E. Brontë): compared with *Paradise Lost*, 19, 61, 149, 150, 162, 164; film adaptations of, 19–20, 149–67; Gilbert and Gubar on, 18, 19–20, 61,

149–51, 153, 156–59, 161–64, 166, 167; and Romanticism, 19, 162
Wyatt, Jean, 100
Wyler, William, 152–54, 157–60, 168*n*12

Yale University Press, xii, 32, 41
Yamashita, Karen, 30
Yeats, W. B., 242
"The Yellow Wallpaper" (Gilman), 11, 25*n*34, 190, 209
Yonge, Charlotte Mary: *The Castle-Builders* by, 184, 193–94; sensation fiction by, 10–11, 20, 28, 184–85, 190–99, 201*nn*20–21, 201*n*18, 201*n*23; and Tractarian doctrine, 185, 190–92, 200*n*14; *The Young Step-Mother* by, 184–85, 195–99, 201*n*26, 202*n*28
Young, Robert J. C., 213*n*2
The Young Step-Mother (Yonge), 184–85, 195–99, 201*n*26, 202*n*28

Zagarel, Sandra, 25*n*24
Zernike, Kate, 6
Zipes, Jack, 157, 168*n*15